IN THE GARDEN
BEHIND THE MOON

To Abby,
Live magically!
Alexandra Chan

IN THE GARDEN
BEHIND THE MOON

A
MEMOIR
OF LOSS,
MYTH, AND
MAGIC

ALEXANDRA A. CHAN, PHD

FLASH
POINT

Published by Flashpoint™ Books, Seattle
www.flashpointbooks.com

Produced by Girl Friday Productions
Cover design: David Fassett
Interior design: Paul Barrett
Development & editorial: Ingrid Emerick
Production editorial: Katherine Richards
Project management: Sara Addicott

ISBN (paperback): 978-1-959411-54-3
ISBN (ebook): 978-1-959411-55-0

Library of Congress Control Number: 2023923533

First edition

Wendell Berry, "The Peace of Wild Things" from *New Collected Poems*. Copyright © 2012 by Wendell Berry. Reprinted with the permission of The Permissions Company, LLC on behalf of Counterpoint Press, counterpointpress.com.

The poem "Laundryman" by Gerald Chan Sieg, used by permission of Jerry Dillon and Daphne Murphy.

"No, I'd Never Been to This Country" by Mary Oliver. Reprinted by the permission of the Charlotte Sheedy Literary Agency as agent for the author. Copyright © 2015 by Mary Oliver with permission of Bill Reichblum.

"What's madness but nobility of soul/ At odds with circumstance?" from *Collected Poems of Theodore Roethke* reprinted by the permission of Faber and Faber Ltd as the publisher.

Excerpt from "Sometimes a Wild God" on page 364 used by permission of Tom Hirons.

To the ancestors—
our own, and the ones we hope to become.

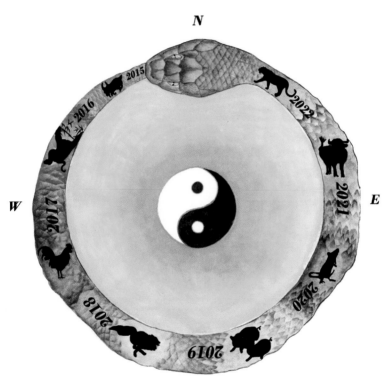

The Carp Leaps
Through the
Dragon's Gate.
*The characters in
the painting have
the same meaning
as the title.*

ABOUT THE STRUCTURE
OF THIS BOOK

We are a storytelling animal, for better or for worse, and the most important story we will ever tell is the story of our own lives. Are we telling the "right" story? Are we telling it well? That's important because it is the best storytellers among us who have the future in our hands. A good story isn't just entertainment. It has the power to heal us in the present and prepare a better future for all. It can awaken us to the truth of who we really are, what we want, what we came here to do— things we have perhaps spent a lifetime not permitting ourselves to know. It involves learning from the ancestors, yes, but also becoming better ancestors ourselves in the process.

This book follows the arc of the Chinese zodiac from Year of the Ram (2015) to Year of the Tiger (2022). For those not familiar, Chinese astrology is an ancient classification system composed of the twelve animals (Rat, Ox, Tiger, Rabbit, Dragon, Snake, Horse, Ram, Monkey, Rooster, Dog, and Pig) and five elements (metal, water, wood, fire, earth). Each animal has its own characteristics, and depending on the year, each element has its own features and associations with each animal (e.g., the Wood Ram or the Water Tiger). Thus the zodiac cycle is actually sixty years and not the twelve we often think of.

Each section of this book represents not only a year in my journey, but new developments in spiritual growth and understanding. The stories I tell in each explore different facets of that animal year's gifts and challenges. Come with me on a journey of ever-increasing enchantment. Enjoy discovering the magic of the ancients' wisdom and knowledge as you watch each year unfold, often as foretold. Take heart as you discover that there are no "unprecedented" times. The labyrinth of earthly life is known, for people and creatures of all times and places have walked it before you.

The Ouroboros, pictured on the dedication page, is an ancient emblem found in numerous cultures, depicting a snake, or sometimes a dragon, eating its own tail. The earliest depiction of the Ouroboros in China appears on pottery from the Neolithic Yang Shao culture, which flourished in the Yellow River basin from five thousand to three thousand years ago. It symbolizes wholeness, completion, and the eternal, cyclical renewal of life, death, and rebirth. It is this book in a single image.

A NOTE ON NAMES AND PRONUNCIATIONS

T'ai Peng, my grandfather, the Great Phoenix: dah BUNG
Alexka, a diminutive for Alexandra: a-LESH-ka
Seu, my younger son: SEH-oo

Throughout this book, names shown with an asterisk are unknown and/or have been fictionalized.

The Chan Family

Only the great-grandchildren (and beyond) of T'ai Peng
and Annie who are mentioned are shown

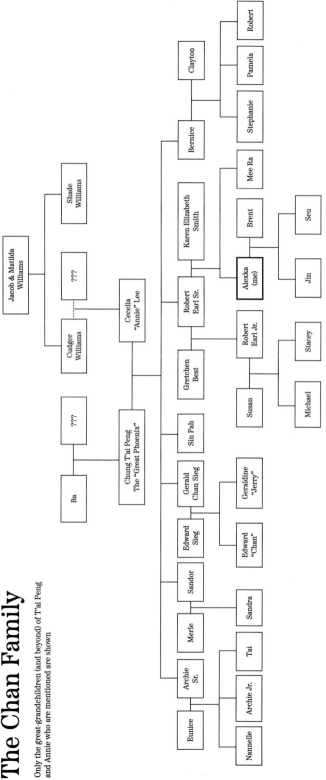

T'ai Peng, young revolutionary with Western hair, ca. 1889

T'ai Peng, laundryman, 1930s

1889
GUANGDONG PROVINCE, CHINA

THE GREAT PHOENIX

Grandpa Chan was eighteen years old in 1889, the year he escaped beheading and flew off across the horizon, stepping into the mantle of his own name, T'ai Peng, the Great Phoenix.

It is said of the mythical T'ai Peng that its back covers thousands of *li* (which measures about a third of a mile) and its wings are like clouds that hang from the sky. When it flaps its wings, the air thunders and the waters churn for three thousand li in all directions. The T'ai Peng starts its life, however, as a giant Kun fish in the North Sea, where it circles through the black waters, unknowing, unseeing, and restless. In time, it is written, the Kun fish sheds the dark, cold ocean of its youth, metamorphosing into the mighty T'ai Peng. As it rises from the deep, it grows wings and beats them ninety thousand li into the sky, where it enters a state of complete transformation and heads on its destined journey to the Celestial Pond.

What were my great-grandparents thinking, in a country village outside the capital city of Guangzhou, naming their youngest son and last-born child after the most powerful character in Chinese mythology? It was as if they knew he was never theirs to keep, and blessed him with a powerful spell of protection, spoken daily for eighteen years. "T'ai Peng." Great Phoenix. Each time their child's name crossed their lips, it summoned the otherworldly power and extraordinary destiny of the magical beast. Attached to each utterance of his name was a silent addendum: *You are enormous of spirit and powerful beyond measure. You will journey ten thousand li beyond the realm of what is recognizable. You will embrace transformation and soar to meet your destiny.*

And, too, *You cannot stay.*

As a boy, T'ai Peng received a classical education and was intent on going to university to become a Confucian bureaucrat and work in the imperial civil service, which was what all the best and brightest young men of his generation aspired to. The year of his exile, he had won a poetry competition in the capital, taking the prize not only for subject matter but also for the elegance of his brushwork. Recalling the moment decades later for his six American children, he described how, with notice in hand, he had been carried, swaying and triumphant, on the villagers' shoulders to see his father.

He stumbled to the ground and grinned at his friends, then straightened and composed his face to approach his father, who was schoolmaster for all the surrounding villages. Thus it was as the schoolmaster that his father took the notice and scanned it, gave a terse nod of approval, and handed it back. Only T'ai Peng, who stood close, could see the glint in his eye that bespoke a father's pride. It was one of the last times T'ai Peng would see his father, so his children heard the tale often. And so, eventually, did I.

T'ai Peng's academic work was in world studies at the university at Guangzhou, where he began to conceive of many modern ideas—from technology to day-to-day practices and observances to governance—that he wanted to see brought home to China, a backward and exploited country whose people suffered at the hands of the Empress Dowager Cixi and the Manchus. Within months of his arrival in the capital, he had taken up with a group of similarly minded young intellectuals in the Revolutionary Party. They held secret midnight meetings in the back room of an herb shop, fantasized about a free and modern China, and plotted the overthrow of Empress Cixi and the Manchu government.

In early 1889, the plot was discovered. T'ai Peng, born in the Year of the Horse, might almost have expected it. Soothsayers and old women gathered at the village well had reminded him that General Fu Youde—one of sixty heavenly generals, or Tai Sui, of Chinese mythology—had it out for the Horse. The happiness, health, and good fortune of all mortals were the Tai Sui's alone to rule for the year. It was bound to be an unlucky one for the Horse.

The young revolutionaries had time for one last meeting to alert their members that the empress had dispatched soldiers to destroy their plans and that the soldiers were now moving through the city with orders to round up and execute those named in the conspiracy. They should all assume their names were on that list. The group leader's final instructions were "Go now. And try to stay alive. China needs you."

As T'ai Peng fled the herb shop, he heard the quick-trot tread of soldiers' boots two streets over. His eyes strained in the dark, unable to see an escape route. But as the drumbeat of doom moved ever closer, the clouds suddenly parted and the moonlight illuminated a garden wall belonging to the neighboring monastery. In a flash, T'ai Peng was up and over it, crouching beneath large bushes at its base. The clouds then slid back over the moon and plunged the streets into darkness. From where he hid, T'ai Peng heard one of his comrades being dragged into the street, his wild screams cut short by the crisp, wet smack of sword cutting flesh and cracking bone and the sickening thud of something hitting the ground. An image came to T'ai Peng, unbidden, of his older brother chopping melons in the courtyard for a feast, smiling broadly, sleeves of his best shirt rolled to the elbows, cleaver in hand. *Chunk.* Juice spurted and glinted through the sunshine. T'ai Peng's small niece and nephew toddled after the geese. Home. He had to get there.

"Bag the head," said the captain. "Leave the body for the people to see."

A monk from the monastery discovered T'ai Peng in the bushes and gave him cover for the night, disclosing that he, too, belonged to the revolution. The monk arranged for food, clothing, money, and secret passage on a ship departing for America the following morning. He also promised to get word to T'ai Peng's parents. Home? No, he could never go home, the monk told the frightened young man.

Soldiers would be sweeping towns and villages throughout the province, looking for the conspirators. He must leave.

"Maybe you'll come back one day," he said to the boy, in reassurance. "And then you must come pay me a visit and tell me about the world."

And so T'ai Peng set out from the monastery and met a sampan driver on the banks of the Pearl River in the dark before morning. In silence, the sampan slipped toward the ship, where T'ai Peng climbed a rope ladder to its decks and stowed himself away, sleepless, terrified, and heavy with sorrow. The ship had been underway for less than a day when it mysteriously came to a halt. An imperial ship was checking departing vessels for stowaways and had sent a small band of sailors over to search the decks and cabins.

They found T'ai Peng and took him into custody, forcing him onto a dinghy with two of the sailors, who started rowing him back to the mainland to his execution. T'ai Peng, gripped by terror, thought of his mother and father, his sisters who doted on him, the terrible grief they would experience at news of his demise, and his terror settled into despair.

But unbeknownst to him, circling far below, the giant Kun fish had heard the call. The great beast began to rumble in the deep. Glimpsing for the first time another world above, it began its journey upward, flexing its powerful body side to side, churning the waters in all directions. Bursting through the surface of the sea in total metamorphosis, the T'ai Peng began to rise to the firmament. The clouds grew thick, the sky grew dark, and the air became dense with pressure. A peal of thunder rumbled across the sky as the great beast beat its wings, their awful power whipping up mighty winds and turning choppy waters into raging seas. Gigantic waves tossed the dinghy from peak to trough, throwing the three men about like rag dolls. The T'ai Peng ruffled its feathers, shedding the ocean waters of its youth as torrential rain. Futile attempts to row the little boat soon gave way to frantic bailing of the water that threatened to swamp it with every swell. The T'ai Peng beat its wings harder and the rain fell in sheets.

For many hours and all through the night, the men fought heroically to stay afloat. And when the great T'ai Peng eventually set off for the Celestial Pond and the storm passed, young T'ai Peng and the two sailors found they had drifted irrevocably off course and could no longer see land. The water was dead calm, and a blazing midday sun shone punishingly upon the scene below. The men were exhausted and weakened by their ordeal. Worse, the dinghy had not been equipped with provisions, as it had been meant to be only a couple of hours' row back to shore. Soon all three men lay inert and at odd angles on the bottom of the boat, using their shirts to protect themselves from the glare of the sun. They drifted for days. Their lips turned white and cracked. And as they continued to weaken, T'ai Peng took sips of seawater under cover of night, remembering from his school days that salt caused water retention. Enough to slow his dehydration? His own initiation had begun, and as he watched his captors grow ever weaker, he continued to sip and spit seawater at night. The wheels of destiny ground into motion.

On the third morning, young T'ai Peng struggled to his feet, wobbling the boat violently. He froze, afraid to rouse his captors, but incapacitated as they were, they barely seemed to notice. He carefully bent down, never taking his eyes from their faces, and wrapped his long fingers around the shaft of one of the oars at his feet. *The T'ai Peng must meet its destiny.* He raised the oar high into the air, like the Kun fish breaching the surface of the sea, and brought it crashing down onto the heads of his captors. Once, twice, three times. He dropped the oar, breathless in his weakened state, gagged, and let out a single, strangled sob. The dinghy rocked back to equilibrium while blood trickled and pooled in the boat's bottom. T'ai Peng wiped his mouth and brow and felt a blank calm overtake him. He rolled the two bodies overboard, checked the position of the sun, and began to row in the direction he thought land to be.

Of course the Great Phoenix found land; how could it be otherwise? He sheltered again with the monks until he had physically recovered from his ordeal. And then he caught another ship to America, this time without incident. When he set foot on the shore of San Francisco Bay, the first thing he did was grab the hated queue over his shoulder, a symbol of the tyranny that had robbed him of his family and his future (*one hairstyle to rule them all*) and cut the hair off at the nape of his neck. He threw the braid in a nearby dustbin and touched the brush of new growth above his forehead, for he had not shaved his head in forty-five days. *The T'ai Peng travels ten thousand li beyond the realm of what is recognizable. It embraces transformation and soars to meet its destiny.*

In time, he found his way across the country to an old student of his father's, Li Chin, who owned a laundry on Broughton Street in the port city of Savannah, Georgia. Chung T'ai Peng (who would live and die in the United States as Robert Chan) would eventually take over the Willie Chin & Co. Laundry, and there he lived out his days starching collars, raising children, writing poetry, and dreaming of China and a better world.

Years later, my aunt G.G. captured her father's longing in a poem.

LAUNDRYMAN

If I could hear once more
The call of dark winged birds across the fields
Of rice and slim young bamboo,

If I could see once more
A crane with yellow legs so straight
Among cool water grasses,

If I could touch again
Her hands whose fingers in their sleeve of scarlet
Are softly curled and gentle,

My soul would be content,
O gods,
To iron away eternity.

—Gerald Chan Sieg, *The Far Journey*

BOOK ONE

2015
YEAR OF THE RAM

Dawn breaks on Year of the Yin Wood Ram. The new Tai Sui, General Yáng Xiān, steps onto the dais. The Ram is a soft, gentle, and lucky animal, thought to bring health, wealth, and happiness. But not to the Ox. The General first scans the horizon for the animal, which is offensive to him. So determined and reliable, the Ox, so earnest. But the Ox is binary, stuck in its ways. The Tai Sui sucks his teeth and grins. *This should be fun.*

Such a hard worker can always be found in the fields or cooling off in the river after a day's honest labor. The General cuts his gaze to the unsuspecting animal and drops into a wrestling stance. He cracks his knuckles and sways on his feet, eyes snapping. For sixty years he has planned it. At long last, the Ox is his. What should he start with? Injury? Bankruptcy? Relationship breakdown? Death? The Ox will rue the day.

So say the Chinese.

Is it misfortune or destiny that I am an Ox—same as Dad? I never meant to offend a celestial being, but unbeknownst to either of us, Dad and I are on a collision course with 2015's Tai Sui.

The Chinese say the Ox should expect once-in-a-lifetime misfortune in 2015. The conjunction of the Ox with General Yáng Xiān comes around only once every sixty years. A wise Ox will lean into its inborn traits of honesty, diligence, strength, and determination. It must flex these preemptively and often, or it will wither under the unrelenting trials of the Tai Sui. Learn patience and hope. Look for personal areas in need of improvement. If the Ox cannot effect these changes willingly, change will be forced upon it.

I know nothing yet of the Tai Sui in 2015, but I shiver at the light whisper of a mustache as it brushes past my ear, and a voice purrs from the corners of my mind. *Burn to ash or forge yourself anew. The choice is yours.*

The Ox will be brought to its knees in 2015, Year of the Yin Wood Ram. It is written.

山風念佛聽

Mountain Wind Listening to Buddhist Prayer. *The characters in the painting have the same meaning as the title.*

CHAPTER 1

ALIEN LANDS

No, I'd never been to this country
before. No, I didn't know where the roads
would lead me. No, I didn't intend to turn back.

—Mary Oliver

Three and a half years after Mom died, in 2015, I went outside to the deck, fell to my knees, and let out a bloodcurdling, primal, and completely silent scream. *Don't leave me, Dad.* I called it a soul scream, for it took place wholly within my head, exploding mental shrapnel into the void, shattering my energy field to pieces. For a period of several seconds, it also had physical control over my body. I buckled under the weight of it, paralyzed, until it had passed. An observer might have seen my cramped figure on my knees, motionless in the sunshine, and feared I was having a stroke. It was the first of many such episodes over the next few years—in the shower, at stoplights, checking the ripeness of melons.

I had no answer or remedy for these screams. I didn't even know how to describe what was happening to me. Not that I told anyone about them; I feared their worried looks. I had made an identity for myself around the pursuit of knowledge and the ethos that you can solve any problem if you know enough about it. After all, I am the great-granddaughter of a village schoolmaster in China, the grand-daughter of a dean of continuing education at NYU, the niece of two award-winning poets, the daughter of an erstwhile librarian turned one of the first women programmers, and the daughter of a man who defied Jim Crow to go to high school and college and then rise to the upper echelons of the US military, work in top-secret missions that helped end the Cold War, and die with thirteen patents to his name. Because of his own meteoric rise "above his station," Dad put so much faith in the idea of going to school that I thought education must, indeed, be an elixir of the gods.

So, by this time I had accumulated my own bona fides as though they were the Golden Ticket to Everything, because as far as I knew, they were. At the pinnacle of my archaeology career, I was invited to be the keynote speaker at the inauguration of a research center in Germany—a center that was inspired, in part, by my own work. It was validation that I was doing everything right.

Dad glowed when I told him about the murmur that rippled through the crowd when I began my presentation in perfect German. He asked how I had overcome my fears to accept the invitation.

I said, "Oh, you know, I just asked myself what Bob Chan would have done."

"And? What *would* I have done?" His eyes twinkled.

"You would have said yes and then found a way."

Dad's laugh sounded like a shot. "You're damn right I would." He warmed himself for a moment at the fires of over a century of saying yes and finding a way. My dad, Robert Earl Chan, turned 102 that year. "Oh, yeah," he said. "You're *my* girl."

At the time, I had two interesting jobs—as a professional archaeologist and a photographer. I also had two boys at home who brought me a whole other kind of self-expression and fulfillment. So if I hadn't yet "done it all," I had done a fair bit and done it well. Though I had seen my share of heartache too. This wasn't my first rodeo. I was a capable person, even in confusion, disappointment, and loss, and as long as I remained ensconced in my fortress of knowledge, surrounded by beautiful facts and certainties, I was Bob Chan's girl. I would find a way.

But then came the prospect of losing him, my last parent, a man of such vitality it had seemed he would just always be there, like air. Or gravity. His presence in my life was planetary; I was but one of his moons. Or was he a star, the light of his life making my own feel twinkly and charmed? That light had been a homing beacon for me on every kind of sea. The thought of it now being extinguished made my fortress crumble. And the soul screams began.

What lesson could there be in this relentless landing of blows— broken bones, hematomas, infections, family fractures, long-distance parental care. There is no purpose here, only pain.

I recalled Mary Oliver's words in her book *Winter Hours*: "Knowledge has entertained me and it has shaped me and it has failed me." I understood for the first time, and with a searing sense of disillusionment, that knowledge had somehow failed me as well. "Something in me still starves."

FIRE AND ICE—SPRING 2016

I rarely took the wheel on a family road trip, especially when we were traveling in unfamiliar territory, but Brent had jet lag. And in the last few days I had been heartened to see that Iceland had only one road to speak of. All I needed to do was get in the driver's seat and . . . go.

The sun was lowering in the sky, but the candy-pink hue of an Icelandic dusk can be enjoyed for hours. The silence around me was textured by the sound of sleeping people—Brent in the passenger seat and our boys, Jin and Seu, in the back—and the hum of the highway beneath my tires. I zoned out until a stray thought of Dad caught me unawares and threw me into the jagged rhythm of the refrain that had haunted me for the last six weeks. *Hurt for life, I'm hurt for life.*

My throat closed over a soul-rending sob just as I saw, in my headlights, a sign that said VÍK Í MÝRDAL, and an arrow. For reasons I could not explain, I jerked the steering wheel left. Vik, whatever that was, was not on our itinerary. We were supposed to be making up lost time. And while I am an adventurous person, I also like to know where I am going, driving at dusk in a foreign country.

BECKONED TO THE NORTH

Over the past year I had learned by trial and error to follow the small voice in my head that always seemed to be saying, *Go there, Let's try this,* and *Why not?* It was often an invitation to something off the beaten path, and it had never led me astray. It was this voice that beckoned me to Iceland in the first place. After Dad's death the month before, a deep yearning came over me to gather my family and flee to the cool austerity of the North.

Why north? I asked myself. *To distill and to shed,* said the voice. *You come here to rest.*

I knew Iceland to be a strange and beautiful place but hadn't thought of visiting. The voice let me know, however, there was no time to lose.

Vík í Mýrdal, we discovered, is a sleepy seaside town on the southeast coast of Iceland, nestled at the bottom of the mountain Reynisfjall, an igneous rock formation that rears up 340 meters into the air. The town is perhaps most famous for its black-sand beach, Reynisfjara, and the hexagonal basalt columns that rise sheer from the shore, then ripple down the base of Reynisfjall like the scales of a dragon that has just settled in for a nap and turned to stone. This image came naturally, for in Iceland, the line blurs between reality and magic. It is no accident that many Icelanders are said to believe in elves. The land vibrates with mystery, and I am inclined to believe in them there myself.

Icelanders say that the columns and sea stacks at Reynisfjara are the remains of trolls who dragged their ship masts ashore and got caught out in the rising sun. I knew something about being caught out and turned to stone. The image of myself on the deck some months before, cramped and on my knees in the brilliant sunshine, came to mind. I hadn't imagined finding such a beautiful reflection of it in nature. My memory of the traumatic event softened. *That's curious,* I thought.

Considered one of the most beautiful nontropical beaches in the world, and long an attraction to geology geeks, it was a serendipitous discovery for us. The sand is truly black and displays appealing contrast against the white surf. More, each surging crush of wave receded gently, dragging behind it a delicate train of sea-foam, the push and pull of which was hypnotic.

Seabirds nestled in the grass-tufted nooks of the basalt mountain behind us, and we shouted with glee when puffins, so much smaller and cuter than we had expected, started to bumble in for their crash landings. Success! We had tried all week to see puffins. Jin had decided to hang the success of the trip on whether we found any. So we built several puffin stops into our itinerary but had been thwarted at every turn. Locations touted in guidebooks as puffin havens were devoid of them—at least at this time of year. One required driving through a mountain pass that took us from cerulean skies and balmy breezes at the base, up a harrowing switchback ledge of a road without guard-rails, and right into the heart of a menacing storm.

Puffins were supposed to be just ahead if we could only get there. Jin's mounting disappointment was a palpable miasma emanating from the back seat that pressed us forward, even as my inner voice countered with ever-greater urgency, *Don't go any farther. Turn around. Stop. Stop!* By the time I listened to it, there was no turning around. We were forced to drive backward down the ledge with almost zero visibility until we found a slight widening at a bend that allowed for a tight three-point turn. The sunny valley . . . and dashed dreams . . . waited below.

In the wake of that near disaster, Brent and I laughed nervously about the article we had read in a local newspaper a few days prior. Called "How Not to Die in Iceland," it was an irreverent guide for tourists, outlining the country's greatest dangers. The changeable weather and lack of barriers at sheer drop-offs were two of them. The article's final admonishment? Don't be stupid.

And so, we had largely given up on finding puffins (we weren't stupid), but here they were. Jin had a beatific look that made me chuckle. Surely this was a boy who had achieved enlightenment, not merely seen a bunch of gangly little goofballs wobble and pitch into the cliff above his head. Meanwhile, Seu, who at the first mention of a trip to Iceland had been most taken by the idea of black sand, had found his own Valhalla.

On our first day in the country, we did find a patch of the storied sand at a harbor, and he had grabbed a small fistful and stuffed it in his pocket, where he fingered the grains for the duration of our trip. Here, though, were fistfuls as far as the eye could see. He ran pell-mell at the waves, sounding his "barbaric yawp" before the waves chased him back up the beach, nipping at his heels as his legs bicycled him to safety.

After several such rounds of chase, in his exhausted and ebullient haste he fell face-first into the sand, with crashing waves roaring up behind him. *Well,* I thought, *here comes our magical detour to an early end.*

But lo, he went into a commando roll once, twice, three times up the beach, never more than a splash out of the sea's reach. He rolled with such force that it propelled his body back upright as he landed on his feet and bounced and jogged the rest of the way clear with a grin that cracked my heart open wide. We all saw it. I hadn't felt thrilled or joyful about anything in months, but even I gave an involuntary *whoop* at the sight—a spontaneous, almost painful, eruption of simple joy.

BEAUTIFYING THE GAZE

How often we hear that beauty is in the eye of the beholder. How quick we are to wave a dull assent, as if to say yes, yes, there is no accounting for one's personal sense of beauty, *blah, blah, blah.* But what about a subtler meaning, proposed by Irish poet, philosopher, and priest John O'Donohue, that when "our style of looking becomes beautiful," we "discover beauty in unexpected places where the ungraceful eye would never linger"?[1] By this definition, beauty isn't subjective, or even rare or fleeting. It is an autonomous force that abides inherently and secretly in everything—even pain. At stake, then, is only this: If beauty is in everything, can we beautify our gaze enough to find it?

Turning back up the beach toward the car, I felt a quickening within me, a leavening of my spirit and my grief. A nascent healing was undeniable. How rare that I should have been driving, and rarer still that I followed a whim to this precious place full of dragon scales and troll masts, puffins, and black sand. I looked down, shaking my head with a grateful smile, and saw at my feet that someone before

An invitation to see differently

us had scoured the black beach and found a collection of white stones. They were arranged into large letters that stopped me in my tracks. *I love u,* it said, with the word *love* represented by a heart shape. A message made for someone else, yes—but surely, I felt, *surely,* left for me.

"Thank you for leading us here, Dad," I said aloud. "I love you too."

Mine was a declaration not just of love, but of intent. I intended to accept this message openly as something meant for me. It was a conscious break from my rationalist past, which had brought me success in society, perhaps, but scorched my earth privately and run my well dry. I pondered the possibility (necessity?) of recognizing the natural world around me as perhaps the benevolent face of something altogether deeper—the visible shoreline of a mysterious, barely seen but bright other world, the uppermost layer of many more subtle layers of being. As an archaeologist, the idea of peeling back the layers and finding meaning beneath made sense to me. In effect, I was making a promise to myself to live more magically. Anything less didn't feel much like living at all.

Stykkishólmur, Iceland, at dusk

LOGOS AND MYTHOS

The ancient Greeks knew there are two ways of accounting for and thinking about what happens to us. There is *logos*—the realm of reason, logic, and rational thought. It involves a linear timeline and is preoccupied with the organization of facts into what we call knowledge. I had plenty of experience with logos. It is the dominant paradigm in the West today. "But facts," says mythologist Michael Meade, "never tell the whole story."[2]

Then there is *mythos*, which is the opposite of logos. Its organizing principle is story, not facts. In mythos, the archetypal myth that is trying to come into the world through you is more important and has more explanatory power than anything that has happened to you (illness, bereavement, betrayal), any details of you (birth date, education, income, or marital status). It is the difference between "knowing" something and "making sense" of it. Myths don't need facts per se, because their purpose is to reveal an *underlying* truth. Mythos is where we explore deep, subjective feelings *about* the facts, which in turn reveals elemental truths about ourselves. With mythos we use imagination to organize the world into a story of how we, as individual souls, are threaded into the tapestry of The Great Story of all that is.

OPPOSITE, TOP:
Snaefellsnes Peninsula, Iceland
BOTTOM: *Reconnected to myth and story*

If logos means thinking in powerful ways, mythos means transcending that earthly logic in equally powerful ways. The point is not to replace logos with mythos, but to recognize that today there is plenty of the former and not enough of the latter. True wisdom, according to the ancient Greeks, lies in seeing both logically *and* mythologically, enabling deeper perceptions of reality and new and better stories for how to proceed. Our world has lost that balance, and therefore also much of its wisdom and its life-sustaining capacity to transform itself in the face of radical change or collapse.

WHAT'S YOUR STORY?

Beside me on the black beach, a question hovered on the mountain wind. *Are you ready to come home?* My eyes welled. Nothing felt more

necessary. I just didn't know where home was anymore, or how to get
there. My parents were dead, my family through them dissolved or
dispersed. I had no hometown. But I looked at the black sand at my
feet and thought I might have just stumbled onto a trailhead, and that,

perhaps, in the words of Marcel Proust, "My destination is no longer a place, rather a new way of seeing."

As alien a land as you can find on this earth, Iceland's landscape reflected my own—wild and unknown. A world without Bob and Karen Chan was not a place I had ever been, not a place I cared to be, and the broken shards of it snagged painfully in my ordinary reality. I bumped into its edges and stumbled on its broken floor. The view from where I stood in my own landscape yawned ahead, colorless and tasting of ash. I breathed in the serrated edge of loss and felt myself at the base of a Mount Everest looking up. Worse, I was Sisyphus, condemned to push the boulder before me up the mountain forever. This was not a load that could be put down or tucked away. No one else could carry it for me. I was, simply put, hurt for life.

But then here in Iceland, the land and sky were so vast, wide, deep, and magic that they contained the whole of my broken heart and made it no more frightening or alien than the landscape itself. My grief became part and parcel of the ragged beauty before me, no longer a disruptor nor a cruel and indifferent master, but a partner and cocreator in a seemingly endless array of beautiful moments.

Every loss feels manageable when you go somewhere that makes you feel like you are on a quest. Your loss becomes, momentarily, part of your personal legend and the compelling seed to a story that is only now beginning to unfold. And for that moment, you cannot help but be in breathless anticipation of . . . whatever comes next. Thus, Iceland reconnected me to mythos—a sense of myth and story, the timelessness of human experience, and where my personal pain fit in the order of things.

THE WASTELAND

In 2021, Iceland experienced a volcanic eruption from a fissure near Mount Fagradalsfjall, which continued for six dramatic months. One of the most remarkable things about Iceland's landscape is how ancient and wizened it all seems, a mythic landscape from time immemorial. And yet, this is far from the truth. Iceland is geologically highly active and continually forged anew by fire. When I was there, I saw lava fields in what appeared to be ancient formations from before the dawn of humankind, but which dated to no earlier than the late eighteenth century. In my disoriented and enfeebled state, I took comfort in the idea that seismic shifts can create new and raw landscapes with unimaginable beauty. And that sometimes the fires of destruction are crucibles of creation.

My soaring feeling at the beauty before me and my keening for what I had lost were a swirling, almost musical, flourish of opposites, a dance of light and shadow, no more or less than that of an Icelandic twilight. Each evening, I beheld a physical manifestation, beautiful enough to make you weep, of my own inner state, hovering between light and dark, searingly aware of both but belonging to neither. It awakened a feeling of such grandeur, such immensity of spirit, that it bordered on the transcendent. Literally. I could feel myself expanding beyond the rigid confines of my grief. Iceland had restored in me a sense of awe and possibility.

Winds swept from craggy peaks, puffins reeled above, the sun traveled down the sky, and far below, I wandered the black beach while white stones jostled each other and giggled at the delight of having been seen.

In this magical place of elves and trolls, something had shifted. I watched the kids skipping to the car and heard another question on the wind: *What is your story?*

Frank Rose, in *The Art of Immersion*, says that story is "the signal within the noise."[3] We use story to make sense of our world and ourselves, and to share that understanding with others. Story gives our lives meaning, possibility, and purpose; it gives the storyteller and her listeners a sense of connection, belonging, and place. A person with a story has of necessity come from somewhere, and therefore has places yet to go.

Similarly, cultivating what psychologist Stephen Larsen calls the "the mythic imagination," in service to that story, is an ancestral birthright. As children we come by it naturally—the idea that life is a great mystery of wonder and magic, continuously unfolding.

Most adults dismiss the elevating power of mythos as childish illusion. But in that dismissal, we've lost something vital to our growth and our healing. A mythic perspective grants wisdom about our circumstances, rekindles the imagination about solutions, and revitalizes the soul to go on. Myth points us to an exhilarating sense of a sacred, animate universe absent from most of modern life.

In times of trouble, myth and story reintegrate the splinters of a fractured self, mending them into patterns of meaning. In the inexhaustible well of universal mythic symbols, there is also a "perennial field of inner validation," as Stephen Larsen suggests, that is life-affirming, for it "creates a sense of connectedness to people and creatures who have been through it before you."[4] Myth and story reveal that we are not alone in our brokenness. There is a place for us in The Great Story, of which we are all equal coauthors. "Whenever any of us becomes a hero, a dragon, a princess, or any of the other dramatis personae of the mythological world," Larsen says, "we are dissolved in an archetype—an identity *larger than ourselves*."[5]

This is how personal mythmaking wields its healing power. To see myself reflected in the columns and sea stacks at Reynisfjara, trolls caught by the sun and turned to stone, was not just interesting, it was alleviating. The trolls picked up some of the burden that I had thought I alone must carry, and for a moment they carried it with me. We were together. I understood them, and only they could really understand me. The mythic symbols I had just stumbled upon presented a still point through which I was connected to creatures and people of all times and places, at a time when I didn't feel connected to much of anything. This is what mythologist Joseph Campbell meant when he said, "We have not even to risk the adventure alone. For the heroes of all time have gone before us, the labyrinth is thoroughly known, we have only to follow the thread of the hero-path. And where we had thought to find an abomination, we shall find a god, where we had thought to slay another, we shall slay ourselves, where we had thought to travel outward, we shall come to the center of our own existence, where we had thought to be alone, we shall be with all the world."[6]

We are hardwired for pattern and meaning, and our life experiences lend themselves naturally to mythologizing in this way. We already weave personal myths day by day, consciously and unconsciously. If we do it consciously, we become aware of the timelessness of human experience. "We tread the same earth on which the ancient shamans danced and sang their spirit songs," says Larsen, and "King

Arthur's men rode in quest of the Holy Grail. Can it be that our journey through life is to be no less wonder-filled than theirs?"[7] The answer, for the successful mythmakers and storytellers among us, is *Yes, of course it can.*

However, in *The Enchanted Life*, Sharon Blackie writes of people who, by contrast, have become "unstoried" or have "fallen out of myth"—succumbed to logos at the expense of mythos. These unfortunate souls have either become disconnected from story altogether or mired in false stories and unconscious mythmaking, which imprisons rather than liberates. They are ungrounded and suffer great restlessness, loneliness, and a sense of being cast out. There is no feeling of connection other than to their own pain. While an individual who has a healthy relationship to myth and story expands and connects, finding ever-deeper layers of self and a sense of belonging that is sovereign and unassailable, the individual who becomes unstoried contracts and isolates, losing the sense of self and home.

In this desiccated half-life, in which most people, at least in the West, find themselves sooner or later, attachment supersedes connection, consumption gags creation, and we fall victim to addictions of all sorts, from social media to substances, to fill a hollowness that grows. Yet this wasteland is not only a hollow place but a rootless one, for where there is no connection there can be no rootedness. With no rootedness, there is no belonging. Without roots to nourish and hold us in place, the ground also grows infertile and erodes beneath our feet, making it even more inhospitable. The wasteland is made for soul screams.

It is also a place largely devoid of body and nature. A prison of the mind, for better or for worse. For better because if we create our own suffering, we can also end it. For worse because most of us suffer unnecessarily by telling ourselves untrue stories or forgetting to tell any at all. When we, a storytelling animal, become unstoried, we grow harrowingly distant from our own animal nature.

Some of us even forget that we have bodies—shut away from the earth, from the seasons and cycles of things, replacing sunrises and sunsets or the nourishing warmth of campfire and candle flame with the cold light of a screen. Spending our lives in houses, office buildings, and high-rises. Traveling in cars and buses and on shoe-shod feet.

How many of us have any actual contact with Earth, or meaningful access to the consolations of Nature or of growing things? How many of us live almost exclusively within the confines of our own heads and the blue light of our phones?

Sharon Blackie believes that having a sense of home is not a state of being, but a skill that can be learned. The heart flutters to think of it. One can learn to belong anywhere, she says. It starts with remembering your animal nature and continues by getting to know the land—whatever land you inhabit and walk upon.

Get out of your head and into your body. Go visit the land like the animal you are. Iceland will do it, but so too will your own backyard garden, a city park, a favorite tree, the mountains, or the sea. Visit it at all times of day, all seasons of the year. Learn to identify the plant and animal wildlife you find there, learn the mythic tales that belong to not only your own ancestors but also the region you inhabit. Sense the subtle, stolid presence of earth, tree, and stone. Observe the cycles of change. Find a spot or travel a route, make it yours, and feel the way you begin to belong to it as well. Thus you start the process of rooting and begin your journey home. Home to Mother Earth, home to self.

When the body is engaged as it is in Nature, the mind's chatter and torments quiet. This is enjoyable on its own, but it is also in this mental quiet that story can start to insinuate itself again. For story often arrives on soft feet and suggests itself through the physical senses. Easily missed, it can start with a breeze here, a scent there, a longed-for bird landing on a cliff above your head. Perhaps it comes in an arrangement of stones at your feet that a busier mind would fail to notice.

I believe that once we are in the wasteland, we are imprisoned there until and unless we can find a way, through myth and good, healthy story, to reanimate our weary, wounded hearts and make our way back to the world. Logos can tell us where we are. But only mythos can tell us why, what it's all for, and how to get back home. Successfully tending one's story in this way is serious business, for what's at stake is nothing less than life itself—the ability to let go of what must be let go of, to have a meaningful existence, and to die content without seeping wounds or bruising regrets. Blow story on a frozen heart and watch that heart begin to thaw. Story connects us to what is innocent and alive within us, stirs curiosity and courage, and instills the will to live and live well. Story is good rain and bountiful harvest. It inherently beautifies the gaze and lessens the load.

YOU KNOW THE WAY

About six months before Dad died, he didn't know who I was. We'd had a date to meet on FaceTime using an iPad station we'd set up in his bedroom. It had a Bose speaker surround-sound system that made our voices boom from the top of the stairs and all through the house. As a World War II veteran, scuba diver, and spear fisherman who had broken his eardrums, Dad had significant hearing loss. At age 102, he was practically deaf. His caregiver sent me a text shortly before our scheduled time.

Can you call in? Bob is very agitated, doesn't want to come upstairs, says he doesn't have a daughter. Maybe if he hears your voice, I can get him on the stair lift.

My stomach dropped, but the plan worked. I coaxed him to me, and by the time he was seated at his iPad some minutes later and saw my stricken face, the episode was past. Tears came to his eyes but didn't fall, and I could see that he not only remembered me but also remembered *not* having remembered me a few minutes before. A shadow swept across his face . . . *So it's come to this.*

He sat a little straighter in his chair, preparing for serious business. "Don't cry," he said, leaning forward as if to take my hand through the screen. "I'm okay now, honey. I'm okay."

I continued to stifle sobs.

He seemed to scan a range of tactics, then his eyes brightened and he settled more comfortably in his seat, back in command. "I'm still the guy who taught you how to walk, remember? I'm still the guy who took your training wheels off. I'm still here." He turned in his chair, motioning to his face and body as if to prove his presence. "Hey. Do you remember when I used to walk you to kindergarten? And then one day you turned and said, 'It's okay, Daddy. You can go home now. I know the way.'"

"Yeah," I said.

"And you never knew," said Dad, smiling at the memory, "but I stayed behind a tree and watched you walk all the way to school by yourself. I did that every day."

I nodded, wiping tears, and tried to meet him in his present state of warm reminiscence.

"Well, that's kind of the way it is now, isn't it?" he said, seeking eye contact. "It's getting time for me to go on home. But I'll be watching you for as long as I can on this earth. And when I can't do that anymore, I'll be watching from . . . oh, from wherever it is I am. And you'll be okay. Hmm? You'll be okay because you know the way."

FINDING THE WAY

I had fallen out of myth in the years surrounding my parents' deaths and the breakdown of my family of origin. By the time I landed on Iceland's shores, I had become unstoried. I felt cast out, abandoned, without home or family, and hurt for life.

My personal tragedy was compounded at the world level by cascading political, social, economic, and ecological crises, which gathered darkly at the horizon. Assumptions and expectations shattered, assurances evaporated, not just on one front but seemingly on all of them. Here at home the rise of Trumpism, White nationalism, and domestic terror left many people of color—me included—feeling cast out, abandoned, without home or family, and hurt for life by their own country. The rolling, traumatic betrayals under Trump of federal and local governments, agencies, and officials, community members, business leaders, colleagues, friends, and family would have left me flailing even without the loss of my parents. Coinciding as they did, my fear and grief became immobilizing and catastrophic.

In 2016, I entered a personal Dark Night of the Soul. And although I maintained a functional facade, privately I was in total breakdown and felt close to madness.

Then came historic wildfires, hurricanes, and flooding, mass shootings, and a crescendo of violence and murder against unarmed Black people. In 2020, Covid-19 began its rampage, economies collapsed, and there were epidemics of fear, racism, anger, and conspiracy theories for which there could be no vaccine. Then the storm of autocracy, nihilism, and fear stoked by the president himself, 147 members of Congress, and the spouse of a Supreme Court justice made landfall on January 6, 2021, when an armed mob tried to overthrow a secure, constitutional election, and thereby rob America of her greatest inheritance of all—democracy itself. The slow-rolling coup attempt continues even as I write this, with a fascist authoritarian assault on voting rights and processes, women's rights, and the rights of the LGBTQ+ community. Add to that a rogue Supreme Court hostile to women, minorities, and the environment, and it leaves the future uncertain and, for many of us, deeply terrifying.

Where and how to find refuge? We are facing problems that are mythic in scope, and yet we live in a society that has turned away from mythos. This is a sure way to land ourselves and our country in the wasteland. When a cultural paradigm is dying, there comes a quiet point—after the collapse but before a new paradigm has taken shape—where it is left to individuals to find and pick up the threads of renewal. People stuck in logos, or the wasteland, will see only apocalypse or a dead end and may freeze or give up in response—or worse, cling to reactionary ideas to return to the past and a perceived safety that never really was. People who have restored or retained a balance with mythos will see, instead of a death rattle, a birth pang, instead of an ending, a threshold of change. You must be able to see the threshold if you are going to step over it. You must be able to imagine a different world, even when it hurts, if you are going to build it.

Iceland jump-started something new for me. In the rubble of my life back in 2016, I picked up a strand of renewal, and had already begun a process of following it. I stumbled into a practice of personal mythmaking and story-tending that would change my way of being in the world vastly for the better.

I did this in a variety of ways. I began a personal practice of shamanic journeying, which involves traveling beyond ordinary reality and awareness, often with the help of a drumbeat, to go deep within oneself for the purposes of consultation and healing. It's a more active form of meditation. I found an imaginal world there full of wisdom, humor, and compassion. I plumbed the rollicking, soulful, and inspired stories of my family and my ancestors. I read classic literature from Homer to Cervantes to Tolkien and tended my wounds with their timelessness and relevance for anyone muddling through their own humanity. I began to write with abandon—stories from my family and memories of my own experiences, as seen through my now dynamically evolving worldview. I picked up a new hobby in Chinese brush painting, and stories began to pour forth that way as well—denizens, both animal and human, of my growing mythic imagination found expression through my brush, each coming with unique pearls of wisdom for living more beautifully in the world.

I had yet to fully understand the powers of integration and healing that myth and story contain, but I did have a sense that I was doing something right. And what I learned, ever so slowly, was that, just as Dad had suspected, I did know the way. And yes, there is still beauty and magic left in the world, and love and wonder left in me. I learned that in telling my own stories—the right ones in the right way—I freed myself from imprisoning narratives that had brought me to a precipice.

From a mythic perspective, I was not without a home—I was a selkie who had lost her skin, trapped in a world she did not know how to belong to. I was not hurt for life—I was the Little Match Girl, learning to warm *herself* in the cold by striking matches from memory and imagination. I was not without family—I was Telemachus in search of his father Odysseus's path, ultimately being asked to step out from the shadow of his hero father to embrace the mantle of his own worthiness. I was also Circe, a woman isolated on an island, not abandoned but spared, discovering her own sorcery, becoming feral and powerful there, and ultimately choosing a mortal life with its heartbreaks and limitations because she has learned that weeds are flowers too and make excellent potherbs and tonics.

This book is my pilgrimage off Circe's island, out of the wasteland, and a record of my return to the beautiful weeds of a mortal life. It is about answering the call of Beauty to transfigure my own wounds, finding my skin again in the healing dark, embracing my worthiness, and exploring the true source of my own belonging in a life and world gone wrong.

It is also a journey of enchantment, a word fittingly from the Latin *cantare*, "to sing," because it explores the unique power of story to re-enchant a life and make it sparkle, restoring the balance between logos and mythos. I found in telling my stories, which are a kind of soul song, that remembrance is good medicine, and that a strong mythic imagination can cultivate not just another way of seeing but a whole other way of being in the world. It allows us to carry our burdens more lightly and to intuit the possibilities for change that enable us to go on.

My purpose in turning back to story was not to write a book, but to rediscover for myself the signal within the noise.

It began with simple journaling. I wanted a more inwardly sustainable life—not just bearable, but purpose-driven and worthy and, yes, if it could be glittering and magical from time to time, that too. I wanted to tell the stories that helped me live more beautifully in a world I had come to see as ugly, and to rekindle a sense of amazement, which is the only real defense against despair. Gradually, in learning to beautify the gaze, I stumbled upon the most wondrous thing of all, that this new way of seeing had transmuted the ravaged landscape of my pain into something rich and fertile again.

Some years into this journey, spared but still stranded on Circe's island, I heard an interview with John O'Donohue. He was speaking about a threshold in life as being a line that separates two territories of spirit. "How we cross is the key thing," he said. "If we cross worthily, what we do is we heal the patterns of repetition in us that have us caught somewhere, and in crossing them we cross onto new ground." What he was talking about, in a much more beautiful way than I had ever heard, was ego death, a fearsome but often necessary rite of passage, whereby we are compelled to lose or let go of many of the things we have used to define ourselves. Structures we once used to build ourselves up and give ourselves a sense of reality and importance now threaten to drag us down and keep us from growing into that new "territory of spirit." That part of us must be allowed "to die" so that a newer and more healed version of ourselves can come forth.

I recognized myself, and our society, as being at such a threshold between two territories of spirit—logos and mythos—caught to varying degrees somewhere in the in-between, the wasteland, where egos go to die. Emerging triumphant in this case seemed a gaudy if not impossible task. I was no conquering hero, and I sought neither accolades nor glory. I wanted only truth. And peace. I didn't want to save the world—who but the greatest of charlatans could claim in a world such as this, "I alone can fix it"? I wanted only to move more gracefully through the world and to be able to acknowledge and accept the fullness of the human experience. I became fixated on the simplicity and dignity of a worthy crossing through brutal times. *There was something I could aspire to.* But it would require a more mindful, disciplined tending of my stories.

IN THE BEGINNING WAS STORY

The playwright Catherine Anne Jones wrote that "every story has a sacred dimension, not because of gods, but because a man or woman's sense of self and her world is created through [it]."[8] Stories link people to their past, orient them, establish their reality, give meaning and purpose, and influence direction. Stories also reveal and clarify something essential within us and are a vehicle for sharing that hard-won wisdom with others, providing a mirror. *Here is what is possible. What would you have done? And? Then what?*

To feel another's pain, joy, regret, shame, love, or grief awakens empathy. It also validates our own experiences and makes us feel the simple connection of being human. Stories are a source of belonging, however fleeting, for both storyteller and listener.

The science of storytelling shows stories that resonate raise the level of oxytocin, the "love drug," in our brains. Neuroscientists at Princeton examined the neural coupling that occurs between speaker and listener during effective communication, such as a good story. They found that the speakers' and listeners' brains exhibited joint, temporarily coupled response patterns to each event. Brains that undergo a joint experience are, by definition, not alone.

What they also found was that while facts light up the data-processing areas of our brains, stories light up our sensory centers. In other words, when we hear stories, *we are there.* So while it may seem obvious to say that stories evoke emotion and create connection, science tells us that this is literally what is happening.

Stories have been shared in every known culture, back to the cave at Lascaux and beyond. It is the essential human trait, along with universal facial expressions and contagious yawns. I used to tell my archaeology students that with the first evidence of the controlled use of fire, some one million years ago, we might really be seeing the first evidence of story.

Fire extended natural daylight into night for the first time, freeing our ancestors from the tyranny of sunset. It warmed them, expanding their geographical range. It protected them from predators, because most animals, including the big ones, knew enough to fear fire. But one couldn't stray far from the fire after dark. What did one do with other members of one's troupe, huddled around the burning wood? I imagine they communicated about the day—the things they had done and seen, the animals they had observed, the water and tubers they had found, the narrow escape they had made, the successful hunt they'd had and what had made it so.

Story is one way to weave facts together and communicate them to others, but it also happens to be the most effective way to do this because the evocation of emotion makes facts more likely to be retained. You were much more likely to remember how to get out of a scrape with a cave bear if you knew the story of how Uncle Droog got his bear claw necklace.

PAST, PRESENT, AND FUTURE

There is another aspect of story to consider. While stories link us to our past and give us a moral compass, they also allow us to project ourselves into possible futures. How can we know where we are headed, or where else we might want or need to go, if we don't know who we are or where we have been? Stories fulfill that purpose. And our memories are so wrapped in stories that it is impossible to extricate one from the other. Nor would we want to, because memories that don't take a narrative form are easily forgotten. Indeed, studies have shown that amnesiacs don't just forget the past but also lose the ability to imagine the future, a topic explored to great effect in a documentary called *Tell Me Who I Am*. It follows the story of one man who suffers from amnesia and, for his sense of self, has become dependent on his twin brother's stories about their lives and childhood together. The tension arises when he discovers that the stories were all fabricated to hide dark family secrets. The amnesiac loses his past for a second time and as a result finds he cannot move forward. Memory allows us to exist and to imagine a future. With it, we can feel that our lives have meant something, and if we are lucky, that we still have important work to do. Without it, we are lost at sea. If I found myself living in the past a lot in the years after my parents died, I make no apologies. I was looking for my future.

A STORYTELLING ANIMAL

Biology research in recent decades has demonstrated that consciousness is found in many of the nonhuman species with whom we share the earth—elephants, whales, crows, the great apes, dolphins, octopuses, and more—so I cannot say that we are the only animal to have a storied experience of the world. Dolphins call each other by name, elephants mourn their dead, whales sing in dialects that are regional and collectively change their tune every few years. Chimpanzees get involved in alliance making, political intrigue, border patrolling, and wars that can curdle the blood. So it may be that we are not the only storytelling animal. But we are certainly *a* storytelling animal. Amitav Ghosh, in a 2022 article in *Orion* magazine, even suggests that storytelling may be the most animal thing about us. Thus, becoming chronically unstoried has separated us from our very nature and resulted in the loss of our sense of home, belonging, and being a fully human animal. It has put our families, businesses, species, and very planet at risk. We have, as a collective and as individuals, lost our context. Thinking we have nothing essential to learn, we end up having nothing meaningful to give, and the emptiness consumes us all.

Story is the path back home. It lights the way. Healing starts with individual stories, but the idealist in me can't help but think that a critical mass of individuals able to awaken to their own inner myth and heal themselves through story, while enlarging their humanity to meet the moment as they do so, can lead to a complete paradigm shift in the collective. Good stories are rooted in love—for self, for others, for pain, for ugliness, for beauty—and "love," said Maya Angelou, "love liberates."

Good stories also rightsize our pain and make us less unique in our brokenness, a brokenness that only serves to keep us isolated and alone. The (lifetime) work of cultivating our personal stories and mythology is what reintegrates our shattered parts and gives meaning and purpose to our path and our pain.

What if we are sometimes asked to give up everything we hold dear, everything we thought we knew, so that we may experience the deep connection we all have to The Great Story and to each other? In this way we become like the centaur Chiron, half beast and half divine, who is known as the wounded healer. Having discovered that within the poison is the cure, we become able, and often called, to teach others the same. We all contain within us the essence of the centaur. Who among us isn't at least half beast, half divine? Who has no wound that has planted the seed of a healer? Where can you identify part of yourself or your story with Chiron?

Once you get the hang of it, there will be other myths, other ways of beholding the circumstances of your life. It is never too late, and indeed never too soon, to get started tending your personal stories.

Whenever we are faced with mythological levels of collapse and renewal, personally or societally, it becomes urgent for each of us to find a certain mythological element within ourselves with which to respond and carry on. Logic alone can't fix such collapse, because so much of it has no logic. For example, we might look to awaken the wise inner sage within our hearts, or to unleash our inner genius—not in the meaning of extraordinary intelligence, but in the old sense of the inner purpose hidden within each life, the unique calling of every individual.

In 2017, I started a series of paintings I called *The Little Monks.* I recognize them now as early inhabitants of my awakening mythic imagination, and my own wise inner sage made manifest. They did not come all at once, but at critical junctures over the course of years.

For example, the first was *Poet on a Horse,* who arrived in 2017 in a wild isolation that mirrored my own, and whose advice, "One time, one meeting," gave me courage to just *be* with my aloneness, recognizing that all of life's moments are fleeting and irretrievable, and all have their gifts to bestow. I mustn't miss the gift for fear of the meeting. I could look at *Poet on a Horse* and always find some way to endure the austerity of meeting myself in the wasteland.

Next came *Monk with a Brush,* who said, "Self-knowledge brings happiness." I looked at him and saw the ease and contentment that such wisdom can bring once the lessons have been integrated. He also reminded me of Dad and all my aunts and uncles, who had worn their old age with simplicity and a well-burnished joy. I didn't think any of them was in the wasteland by the time I knew them. They had made it out. *Monk with a Brush* restored a sense of purpose to my painful lessons—future comfort in my own skin and a peaceful old age, as my elders had had. Then along came the *Journey of 1,000 Li,* alluding to the Chinese proverb that the journey of a thousand li begins with a single step. This character made his way through a snowstorm and brought the wisdom that "Every day is a beautiful day." I looked at him and knew that I too could go the distance one step at a time, and that I too was learning to beautify the gaze.

And so it went, new monks, poets, musicians, and scholars arriving as was necessary or helpful.

In 2019, I was delighted by a baby monk who seemed to make meaningful eye contact with me as he emerged on the page beneath my brush. "Learn. Heal. Teach," he said, as if to tell me that many of my lessons had been integrated and it was time to share them with others coming behind me. That is how I have tried to live my life ever

Poet on a Horse—*"One time one meeting"*   Monk with a Brush—*"Self-knowledge brings happiness."*

Journey of 1,000 Li—*"Every day is a*   Learn. Heal. Teach.
beautiful day."

since, to learn from the ancestors and become a better ancestor myself as a result. It is the reason for writing this memoir.

I dedicate this book to the storyteller inside each of us. May they awaken, and soon. May all our geniuses learn, heal, and teach another. And to everyone standing at a threshold between two territories of spirit, may you remember that the stories you tell become the life that you live.

I intend to live more magically.

And you?

CHAPTER 2

SMALL WONDERS

Dear Family (What a lovely word, and how blest are they who have one!)

—G.G., letter to Robert Earl Chan, November 19, 1995

Magic happens.

Magic happens!

Mag-ic! Hap-pens!

The phrase reverberated and repeated, punchy and insistent, staccato and relentless, like rain on a tin roof, as if to carry it through the powerful amnesia that can obliterate even the bare moments between waking and opening one's eyes.

I reached clumsily to my nightstand and created a clatter of ceramic, plastic, and shuffling paper, sending my eyeglasses to the floor before remembering that what I was looking for was already on the floor. I grabbed my writer's journal and pen and fumbled to push the light switch and find the next clean sheet of paper.

I wrote at the top "Magic Happens," and then began to scribble full sentences, partial phrases, single words, which I hoped would be

enough to jog my memory later. The truth is, if I had never once believed in magic, this memoir would never have been started. It took
the Tai Sui's trials for me to remember to look for it again. And although I had not heard of the Tai Sui at this point, my ancestors had. I
like to think it was they who started sending me insistent and disrup-
tive dreams to shake me awake and meet the Tai Sui's challenge to "do
better or die."

Call off the dogs, General, I imagined them calling out to him.
We're working on her.

OLD CHAN MAGIC

To be a Chan is to be raised between worlds—somewhere between
Chinese ghost stories and ballpark franks.[9] It is to invite in Old World
mystery and wonder, even as you masterfully navigate the realms of
science, logic, and ordinary reality. Among us Chans you will find sci-
entists, philosophers, teachers, warriors, musicians, computer geeks,
artists, chefs, showmen, designers, and poets. Where ordinary reality ends and art and mystery begin within these endeavors depends
on who is doing the work, but most of us know that there is little to
separate them. True, I had become disillusioned, but I was not a born
cynic. I spent years before my exile in the wasteland hoping the world
was as magical as the Chans made it out to be.

It started early in my life. One day Dad grabbed the nose from
my face, which sent my hand flying up to make sure it was still there.
Luckily it was . . . but then *how could it be there in his hand?* I wondered about it for weeks. He could also wrap his pointer finger around
his thumb and lift it to take the top joint with it. "Did it hurt?" I once
asked, and he let me feel the joint, which was smooth and flat. *Hmm,
no blood or shards of bone,* I noticed. *Curious, very curious.* I looked up
and checked his face for clues. There were none. Only a twinkle. One
summer morning Dad brought me outside before breakfast, barefoot
and in my nightie, and leaned down in a hushed whisper to point out
a fairy circle of toadstools that had sprung up overnight after a wet
period.

"Where are the fairies?" I asked, breathless, squatting to peer under the bush to make sure I hadn't missed anything. The wet hem of my nightgown stuck to my calves when I stood up. An irrelevant nuisance. The world had just winked at me!

"They only dance in the moonlight and when they know no one is watching," said Dad. "But you know," he added, catching my disappointment, "sometimes they get drunk on dew and fall asleep, and you can catch them out in the morning if you're lucky. Looks like we just missed them."

I played with the toadstool ring for the rest of the day.

When Dad died, a woman at his memorial stood up and said, "Bob always seemed a little bit . . . magic to me." She paused, tentative, but rows of heads nodded in agreement. Of course I knew just what she was talking about. What they all didn't know was that Old Chan Magic ran wide and deep, and Dad had been but a gateway drug to the real Source.

Dad had moved to New York State after World War II, and so every summer he, Mom, and I hopped in the car and made the two-to-three-day drive down to Savannah to visit with the Chan family—the Source—all the uncles and aunts and cousins. Grandma and Grandpa were long gone, but there was still a large family down there in the

1970s and 1980s. Savannah, to me, was *steeped* in magic that had only little to do with the twisted limbs of the live oaks and the hanging strands of Spanish moss. At night, steamy cobblestone streets released a fog that swirled around antique lampposts in the squares and turned them into soft glowing orbs. It felt to me as if a glamour had been cast on this place. Things were not always what they seemed, for better or for worse. But that wasn't just a bit of moss and fog talking. That was Old Chan Magic, which seeped into every crevice.

"Do you hear them talking?" asked Uncle Sandor as he turned around in the front seat of the car, making the vinyl creak. We were sitting in a parking lot, waiting for someone to come out of the Piggly Wiggly after one of those big southern rainstorms. He wore his signature short-sleeved striped polo shirt, not quite buttoned to the collar, and in a shade of blue that accentuated his skin—brown, beautiful, and impossibly smooth for his age. His eyes gleamed at me expectantly, the same way Dad's had when he swiped my nose. I was the Chan family's own small wonder. No one had expected me to come along at this stage in the game, when most of my aunts and uncles were settling into retirement and my cousins were parents or even grandparents themselves.

OPPOSITE: *G.G., Archie, Dad, and Sandor—Old Chan Magic at its Source*

Sandor was waiting to see how long it would take for me to discern who "they" were that were talking, but I knew immediately. The windshield wipers, squeaking on the glass, had clearly been saying "sleepy Sally" since the moment we pulled away from the curb at his house on Sickle Drive. Sandor said they had something different to say every day if you were willing to listen.

Yesterday they had been going on about potato salad.

Another time I sat sullenly on an orange-and-green-flowered sofa in G.G.'s eat-in kitchen. I had slid all the way down so that only my head was propped against the back cushion, and my feet, in little brown T-strap Mary Jane shoes, dangled an inch or so above the wood floor. I stared straight ahead with my eyebrows knit into a frown. Mom was nowhere to be seen, and Dad had probably thrown up his hands and stalked from the room long before, muttering about my being a pill. He had no patience for pouting children, perhaps because he knew no remedy if the child was unwilling to take it, and Dad, you must understand, liked to fix things.

"Do you think Alexka will talk to her aunt Gerald?" asked G.G. of no one in particular.

I shook my head vehemently and clenched my jaw tighter. She tried drawing me out about her cats, Frodo and Miranda. Miranda (whose name meant "to be wondered at") was the smallest, and Frodo (Baggins) was easily the biggest cat I had ever seen, and since Miranda was Frodo's mother, they made a comical pair. G.G. was not wrong to try the cats first, but I was immovable.

G.G. with her cat Ptah—"Egyptian Creator God, Lord of Truth, Beautiful Face"

"Well, you're doing it wrong," interjected the lamp on the side table next to me, seeming to address itself to G.G.

My eyes jerked to the left where the lamp was, then quickly over to G.G., who was sitting there quite still and with a knowing twinkle. I looked straight ahead again, determined not to be tricked out of a mood.

"Oh really?" G.G. asked the lamp.

"Yes," said the lamp imperiously. "Any fool can see she's had it with *people.*"

And then, more solicitously to me, "Haven't you, girl?"

The voice was gravelly and small, and sounded like a gnome on his third horn of mead. I slid my eyes back to the lamp and considered. And then, because the lamp had got it just about right, I nodded.

"But you would talk to me, wouldn't you?" said the lamp. "Because *I'm* not a dirty, rotten human being. I'm just a lamp."

I sat a little higher on the couch and nodded again. I looked to

G.G., who kept smiling at me, eyes sparkling, legs crossed, not moving a finger.

"What seems to be the trouble, little girl?" said the lamp.

I turned straight to the lamp and leaned in on the armrest and said to it in a stage whisper, "Daddy's a liar. He said we were going to go to the beach and catch clams today, and now we're just going grocery shopping."

"I hate when that happens," said the lamp, with gratifying emphasis on the word *hate*. "Why are you going grocery shopping?"

"A family party," I said, rolling my eyes and flinging myself again into an aggrieved slump.

"I hate family parties," said the lamp. "They're the pits."

I giggled because I *loved* family parties.

"What do they need groceries for?" the lamp pressed on. "Let's just feed them cat food."

I laughed out loud and that was that. Add perfect ventriloquism to the list of small wonders one was likely to find if you hung around the Chans for very long.

It wasn't that everything was a bowl of cherries. Dad had stopped vis-

Me in the age of fairies, climbing trees, and talking lamps, 1978. You've brought your wand, haven't you?

iting family sometime around 1953. That was the year both his father, T'ai Peng, and his baby sister, Bernice, a diabetic, died within weeks of each other—Bernice at just thirty-eight, leaving three children under the age of ten behind her. That would put any family under strain, regardless of other underlying troubles that might have existed. But things picked up again when Mom (and I) came into his life in the early 1970s.

G.G. was a poet and the Keeper of Dreams in our family, and she would brook no bad blood or ill will among the lot in her presence. She allowed for the best in everyone. She knew your heart and sussed out your greatest yearnings without your even having to speak them.

What's more, she caught them for you and kept them safe, filing them into the family lore as if they were a done deal, even if you yourself fell *spectacularly* short of what you had intended. All you had to do was *want* to be something, and you were already it in her eyes. Everybody was their best self in her calculation—a writer, a filmmaker, a showman, an artist, a hero. Isn't that the most magical thing of all? Dad called it poetic license, but I knew it was more complicated than that.

After Dad, it was G.G. who showed me that the best way to find magic was to look for it, and she set about doing it at the slightest prov-

ocation. Even in the giant slugs—the width of my hand—that invaded the cat bowls on humid mornings, on the back-door stoop, two flights up. She presented these beings to me as closer to fairies than goblins. To her they were tiny nighttime revelers riding on mysterious moonbeams to her door. "Wingless, footless, boneless, blind," she'd almost chant. One day she wrote a poem about them, "Snail Without a Shell," and she called them fondly a "Lethe for old pain."[10] I wanted to live in the world she saw.

To call a slug beautiful and make another see it too is Old Chan Magic in action. It also rightsizes your humanity and your pain because it implicitly acknowledges your place within a wide, wondrous web of creation that has nothing, and yet somehow everything, to do with you. If slugs are beautiful and can do hard things, then, by god, so is everything and so can you.

Old Chan Magic is not just magical thinking. It fully expects you to have your feet planted and to get your hands dirty and your feelings hurt in the real world. But it simultaneously inspires you to relate to life with a sense of mystery and wonder. John O'Donohue writes that functionalism without reverence or wonder is lethal—the old ideas of logos and mythos again. He says the hardening of our modern minds in this way has deadened our ability to sense the sacred presence in the world as our ancestors did, so simple and available, with magic under every rock. We have, in essence, "killed the gods" and paid a terrible price, losing the inner divinity of Nature and ourselves along the way.[11] Old Chan Magic helps restore the balance and reveals the gods to have been sleeping, not dead.

G.G. taught hushed reverence before ugly things, but because she cussed, wore one earring like a pirate so she could answer the phone comfortably, and had a crush on Magnum, P.I., she breathed witty *irreverence*. Nothing is to be taken too seriously, she seemed to say, nor was it meant to be. Least of all ourselves.

To believe in magic, cultivate this combination: an expectation that beauty and mystery can be found anywhere, a willingness to search for and see it, and an unabashedly held belief that oneself is not to be taken too seriously.

OPPOSITE: *G.G. shows me some small wonder out her back door.*

In October 1995, G.G. wrote Dad a letter shortly after our latest visit. In it she showed perhaps her most practical form of magic: how to embody the Tai Sui's tasks of honesty, patience, and hope—how to see and tell truth without falling into bitterness or harm. No one had to tell *her* to do better or die. "Doing better" was her natural state.

Now back to our quarter century of annual visits. Our members (all the generations) lacked none of the faults that other families display: pettiness, gossip, criticism, coldness, misunderstandings, downright lies. But somehow this group has had that streak of nobility that kept us together—since there have [also] been mutual admiration, sympathy, generosity, union in sorrows, happiness in attainments, pride in achievements. I like to think that our father and mother could come in and join us smiling, because they had brought up "good" children. As I go over the second, third, and fourth generations, I thank the mates we have had to produce such excellence.

The Sinnie problem [second-oldest sister, Sin Fah] has meant a silent telephone. However, I wrote her to explain how you had to get going on a day's notice, just as you told me to do. Her birthday is celebrated from the actual day 11/6 to 11/11, formerly Armistice Day. If possible, I hope you will send her a note or card. "Be ye kind one to another."

Robert Earl, you have stayed young, strong, with legs good-looking enough to go bare down Bull Street! I am sorry you don't ever want to meet any of our old friends so that they could see how you look and talk. I thank your wife for some of that! (The physical, not the indifference to the "friends.")

Love to all

And then three weeks later:

Sinnie called the Sunday night after you had gone. She was most amiable. She felt that you had come down because of Eunice's death to see the family and especially Nannelle. So she did not regret missing your visit, as she said she hated death and burial events and never went near them. Said you, Robert Earl, had "matured into a good person" and that the two of you could talk for hours, both so well educated and traveled.

I didn't meekly say, "Well, I ain't never been to no collitch or been much farther than Pooler 'cept wunst or twicet."

Your visit was a pleasure to all of us. But nothing erases the years when this place had cots and suitcases all over, and midnight lemon pie (homemade) and trips to the night spots with SANDOR AND AT LEAST ONE PLAY. These caps are volunteers, not of my making.

We have much to be thankful for, all of us. Muchas gracias, Padre Dios. Pardon errors. The light is terrible in "before dark of morning."

Karen, I was so happy to see you walking [after hip replacement], calm, and your nice, diplomatic self. You need it among the mad Chan Clan.

—Gerald

I grew up steeped and rooted in everyday magic. Lamps and windshield wipers could talk. Fairies were real. Slugs were old friends. Disappointments and failures were just steps along the way. And serious family rifts were distilled down to a hilarious essence that, if it didn't always heal, at least did a lot less harm. It was a magic that temporarily inoculated you against the bitterness and cynicism of the world.

Much later, when I had fallen into the wasteland, I suppose at the very least all this left me still aware that there are other ways of being. What good role models I'd had, open to seeing things from a variety of angles, able to seek and find beauty in hardship as well as in ease, and ultimately understanding that some things just need to be felt rather than known.

I had gotten away from a lot of that in recent decades. I'd been busy differentiating myself, being serious, and making my own way, as children do. But in my newfound state of catastrophic grief over Dad's death, memories like these flared and flickered before me, often in waking moments before I grabbed clumsily for my journal, like matches struck in a snowstorm—bright, warm, reassuring, and, of course, gone all too quickly. But what they seemed to suggest was a better way. Better for me.

Dad had special reverence for the Hans Christian Andersen fairy tale "The Little Match Girl." I remember him telling us the story at the dinner table with exquisite sensitivity in his voice. He gloried in the tragic ending, while sending shivers of fear and loathing down my spine. Because of course she dies in the end—cast out, unloved, and all alone. What could be worse? But then there is the light, warmth, and allure of flame, the way it forces a storm to the background. And the fact she dies with a smile on her face, having been for herself all the comfort and love she needed. Maybe Dad was on to something.

I began to play with the idea of lighting memories instead of matches, and the possibility that, just as with the Little Match Girl, everything I lacked in the outside world right now might be found somewhere within myself.

I lit a memory and watched its fire flower into the darkness, the petals flickering and reaching wildly before settling back into the quiet, steady, reassuring shape of hands in prayer. I took what warmth

I could find and challenged myself to step forward in the fleeting light this little prayer emitted.

I lit another memory—*strike!*—and took another step. Sometimes I lay curled and motionless, unable to move, but still saw the light from afar as a place I'd like to get to. I didn't know where this exercise would take me, but it seemed clear it was leading me away from *here*, and anywhere was better than where I was. So I began lighting matches like my life depended on it . . . because it did.

Let's light a match together, right now.

Strike!

Now watch it flower.

Hands in prayer.

CHAPTER 3

THE MOST INTERESTING
MAN IN THE WORLD

"Mommy," said Seu one day at age four, while watching a nature show on big cats. "Grandpa could never ride a cheetah, right?" His voice conveyed he wasn't sure if this was true. "Because cheetahs are *really* fast, and Grandpa is *thuper* old!"

I chuckled. There went Dad, at a hundred years of age, achieving hero status for his four-year-old grandson and obtaining for himself a seat in the pantheon of preschool idols. For Seu, this included the usual suspects of big cats, superheroes, and ninjas, but in there among them, perhaps somewhere between ninja and cheetah, was Grandpa Bob. And according to Seu, the only reason his grandpa *couldn't* ride a cheetah was because he was too old.

"Well, honey," I said, "you're right. Grandpa Bob can't ride cheetahs because he *is* too old. But if there was ever a man who rode cheetahs in his youth, it would have been your grandpa."

Except it wasn't cheetahs. It was giant sea turtles off the Georgia coast. He told us if you can grab one, you can keep it from diving by holding it by the collar of its shell. To turn, you hold one flipper and let the other one do the work.

PIPE SMOKE AND MAGIC

Such stories of whimsical and/or improbable deeds were one of the best parts of growing up Chan. There were escapades like capering with giant sea turtles, jumping from rooftops with an open umbrella, planting whoopee cushions on the seats of the church ladies, or electrifying the scoutmaster's toilet seat. There were also swashbuckling and cautionary tales of escaped beheadings, relieving three assailants of a knife in a street fight in Manhattan, passing oneself off as Japanese to walk up and shoot a Japanese sniper between the eyes, and being taken prisoner only to hijack a plane and fly oneself to freedom. And finally, there were ghost stories and weird-but-true tales that brought you face-to-face with the Great Mysteries.

Dad seemed to delight in pipe smoke and magic, casting the earthly folly and muddling of human beings into the realm of poetry and the gods. His eyes twinkled a lot, as he was in a steady state of curiosity and amazement, and he peppered his conversations with allusions to Greek mythology and literature. He could find an archetype or literary familiar to elevate any old sorry sap, himself included. The magic lay in how it always seemed to take some of the sting out of any kind of setback or give purpose to any sort of pain.

The old Chan family—the original six children born to T'ai Peng and his wife, Annie—never ceased to walk with wonder in this way. It made ordinary lives seem extraordinary, and extraordinary lives seem downright mythic. The modern world leaves little room for such wonderment. In this modern digital age, we have collectively suffered such a profound split from Spirit that we are awash in information while starved of wisdom and succor. My family was, in many ways, an antidote to this. Not because they led otherworldly lives—they didn't—but because through it all, many of them retained a connection to both real life and real wonder, and that was an early lesson to me in beautifying the gaze. It was all danger and humorous hijinks with them, impossible exploits, monstrous evils, miracles, triumphs, and true love. It was marching to one's own drum and getting lucky.

Although Dad was always quick to say, "Chans make their own luck."

YOU SHOULD WRITE A BOOK ABOUT YOUR DAD

"The only person gonna write a book about me is *me*," said Dad.

I nodded and gave an amused chuff in agreement, but my smile didn't quite reach my eyes, which I'd already lowered just slightly. Ever since I began to show an aptitude for storytelling—probably sometime late in high school—people had been telling me, "You should write a book about your dad." I dismissed the idea at first, and yet with the constant and unvarying repetition, it did begin to take hold and continued to issue a distant siren call for decades.

OPPOSITE: *Greetings at the diner, age 102, in 2015, Year of the Ram*

I had just finished floating the idea past him, not directly but as a curious anecdote to see what he thought of it. "Hey, Dad, you'll never guess what so-and-so said to me today."

I didn't know what to expect, exactly, but his casual dismissal of the subject pulled me sharply back to earth. I reddened at my own presumption.

I had a strong sense of being Bob Chan's Daughter long before I had a sense of who I was on my own. Even as an adult with degrees, honors, and accolades, I could come home and know that anywhere we went people would still point and say, "There go Bob Chan and his daughter." People grabbed his hand and beamed when they encountered him on the street. The waitresses at the diner called him Mr. C. and openly flirted with him about his killer legs and short shorts. *Legs good-looking enough to go bare down Bull Street!*

When you were with Robert Earl Chan, greetings were open arms and hearty laughs, strong and meaningful handshakes, or teary clutches to the breast. When he was in his dotage, often slurping on a cup of chicken noodle soup at the local diner, women I didn't know pushed back tears as they kissed him on the forehead or grabbed his hand in both of theirs. "Such a special man," they would warble. There were no words in reply. One simply had to accept that emotions ran deep wherever he went, and you could try to analyze, ask what the story was behind this one or that one, or you could just sit back and bear witness.

It also didn't seem to matter where we went in the world, there was always someone simply overjoyed to see him again. I remember

hustling through an airport in Switzerland on a family ski trip to Davos in 1985. We were simultaneously trying to locate the restrooms and the next gate when a voice rang out above the throng, "Bob? *Hey, Bob! Bob Chan?!*" As a teen I hated the hoopla that surrounded these ribald surprise encounters. That day I ducked into the bathroom to avoid the initial greetings, and later learned that it was a man Dad hadn't seen in decades. Reunited with his old comrade in an airport in Europe. Well, doesn't that just take the cake?

When he was a younger man, Dad's habit of knowing everybody and being personally unforgettable got dangerous. He was in California on a mission for his employer, which was officially Kodak. But Kodak didn't particularly want its presence known in Southern California at the time of a top-secret launch of a new rocket. This was part of the Corona program, the nation's first photoreconnaissance spy satellite initiative. It was an interdisciplinary project with contributions from numerous industries, government agencies, and private companies, Kodak included. The project was declassified in 1992, but at the time it was so top secret that even the people doing the work didn't know for whom they were doing it or why, but the answer to the former was the CIA, and to the latter was to spy on Russia. Billed simply as the Discoverer program, the people involved, like Dad, imagined themselves to be part of a push for space technology development, for the sake of discovery alone.

A chemical engineer who learned optical engineering on the fly, Dad would eventually not only master it, but obtain thirteen patents in his work for Kodak and the Corona program. Dad's job was to create a panoramic camera lens that could take pictures of Earth from space and withstand the heat and forces of a rocket launch, leaving and reentering Earth's atmosphere without melting. It also had to be powerful enough to distinguish between two solid yellow lines on a road, as well as read the headline of a newspaper . . . all from space.

What did the CIA learn from these missions? For one, that the Russians were weaker, less equipped, and less prepared than they had touted themselves to be. Some have credited the Corona program with helping to deescalate and ultimately end the Cold War.

OPPOSITE, TOP: *Spearfishing with Aqua-Lung and rubber underwater camera housing, 1957* BOTTOM: *Scuba diving in 1957 with a homemade Aqua-Lung, and an underwater self-portrait before the invention of underwater cameras*

Ground control for these satellites was based in California, and Dad had to make trips out there throughout the 1950s and 1960s, presumably to advise on the launches. These trips were classified top secret, and Kodak, on behalf of the US government, pushed Dad to absurd lengths to keep them under wraps.

On one trip, an old acquaintance saw him from afar in the airport. "Bob! *Hey! Bob Chan!*" the man yelled over the milling passengers in the terminal. "So good to see you, old friend," he said, striding toward Dad with outstretched hand. "It's been years! What brings you to California?"

Dad was in a fix. There was no escape, and no getting around the fact that he could not be known to be there. He made a quick calculation, pulled back, and shook his head.

"I'm sorry," he said. "You must be mistaken. I'm not Bob Chan." He walked away, leaving the man befuddled and never the wiser about what had just happened or why. The idea of someone who looked like Dad successfully going undercover or being unnoticed was pure farce, but there it was.

In 1957, inspired by the explorations of the famous aquanaut Jacques Cousteau, Dad built his own Aqua-Lung and invented both metal and rubber underwater housing for his camera—some six years

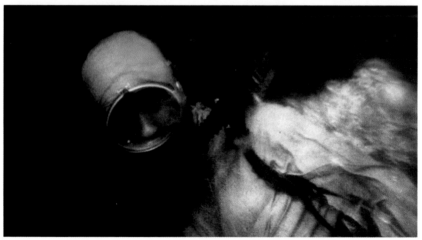

before the release of the Nikonos, which was the first commercially available underwater camera and codesigned by Cousteau himself.

Dad's efforts, as well as some of his dives, were profiled in *Kodakery*, Kodak's weekly newspaper for all its US employees that was published from 1943 to 1985.

One day, I was straightening some things on my desk when an underwater self-portrait of Dad in his full, homemade scuba equipment fell to the floor. I had been preoccupied that morning with the

gap between my vision—if you could even call it that yet—of writing a book about the family and how to get there.

Dad always thrived in the gap, whatever and wherever it was, bending the world to his vision. Don't have an Aqua-Lung? Build one. Need a lens to take pictures from space? Make one. I looked at Dad emerging from the murky gloom of his scuba picture in exactly the way my book idea was coming to me—as through a glass, darkly. *Do not mind the gap,* he seemed to say. *The gap doesn't spoil the fun; it* is *the fun.* I framed the scuba portrait and set it prominently in the house so I could be reminded daily to embrace the adventure of not knowing but embarking anyway.

In 2006, Dos Equis, the Mexican beer brand, launched its "Most Interesting Man in the World" campaign, which has been heralded as one of the most successful and ingenious ad campaigns of the twenty-first century. Each commercial ends with the tagline "Stay thirsty, my friends." It is about grabbing life by the lapel and swinging it around a few times before kicking it in the tail.

OPPOSITE: The Most Interesting Man in the World, *1970s*

I thought from the very first airing of that campaign that Dad could be the real-life counterpart to this fictional character. Part MacGyver, part Jean-Claude Van Damme, part James Bond, and, yes, part Ward Cleaver—the man was, on top of everything else, the most popular Sunday school teacher at our church. He really did seem to do it all.

Partway through 2015, when he was 102 and his life was coming to an end, I began a social media experiment, sharing stories and pictures of Dad's life in the spirit of the Dos Equis ad campaign. "I don't always get mugged in Manhattan, but when I do, I lay them all out and keep their knife on my desk." That sort of thing. "Stay thirsty, my friends." It was a way to start collecting the stories in one place and to see the threads that connect them through time. It was also a reconnaissance mission. Did people like these stories? Should I do more with them? The consensus seemed, overwhelmingly, to be yes.

And finally, its most important purpose of all was the simplest one, to bear witness. Bob Chan led an extraordinary, courageous, colorful, and authentic life that, on paper, seems almost mythic in scope. And yet he was but the youngest son of the Great Phoenix himself, only one in a large family of extraordinary characters. In my effort to save myself by turning back to their lives and deeds, I found that in them there might just be a blueprint for others. The ancestors were feeding me stories, building blocks for something new, and the Tai Sui hovered near to see what I would make of them.

Here. Let's light another match together, right now.

Strike!

Now watch it flower.

Hands in prayer.

CHAPTER 4

BA COMES TO VISIT

Twenty-nine years had passed since the giant Kun fish underwent its metamorphosis in the South China Sea and young T'ai Peng made his way to Savannah, Georgia, and took over the Willie Chin & Co. Laundry on Broughton Street. He was often heard commenting that the heat, greenery, and location on the banks of the Savannah River reminded him of his home on the banks of the Pearl.

"It quiet," he said, "and it have park everywhere, green tree, not-too-tall house. It warm and soft like Guangzhou. Big river and island, ships anchored. Smell low earth, just like Guangzhou smell. Sometime I say to me inside, 'Am I at home in Guangzhou?' That why I make up my mind stay in Savannah when not travel in work for overthrow Manchus. I go to Havana, Tampa, New Orleans, Mexico, all about, tell Chinese of need for money at home."

At the word *home*, he pulled out a pencil and sheet of paper from the buffet drawer and began to draw. "See? Straight little house, one moon window here, roof turned up on corners, flower tree in front. Inside house you look out moon window can see river, tree, boat like pretty picture in round frame. You know, Chinese people always like have circle. Means whole, bountiful, complete. Represent family, too, like on Moon Festival. Circle not supposed ever can break. Always children take care parents, parents take care ancestors, ancestors take care more children. See? Circle." T'ai Peng shook his head and sighed, caught in a reverie. "When I leave my home, I break circle."

Then he continued. "All around have big fields. You know, I always like have farm myself. I like smell earth, make things grow. But here farming not pay. Once I have farm and restaurant. I not can work for nobody else, no man can order me what I must do. But earth too poor, not can work both, so both bust up. That time I almost go back to China."

"Ah Ma and Ah Yeh must miss you, Papa!" said the children, referring to his parents and their grandparents, whom they would never know.

"Oh yes, they want me to come home," said T'ai Peng, thinking especially of his father. "Ba said I very smart, ought to be teacher like he do. When I small boy, I go his school. We stay in Guangzhou and go home to rice farm once a week, sleep all night. Ride on muddy road in slow oxcart, leave city wall behind, see green country with mulberry tree, peach tree, billy goat, man walking barefoot in field. Then Ba and me be very happy and sing together."

"What was school like with Ah Yeh?" asked the children.

"Oh," said T'ai Peng, smiling. "In school we have to learn many poem, and I still remember maybe hundred poem by heart. You know, if a man study poem, his spirit not can ever be evil."

The children wondered how poems could protect from evil, but they knew Papa would never tell a lie, so they stashed it away as an important true thing.

"My father have us make up poem too, and my poem always one of three best in school. I ever tell you I win big poetry prize in Guangzhou before I flee home?"

The children nodded vigorously. They knew the story well.

"If I stay in China, maybe I make plenty poem, but I come here, marry, *have six children*." He widened his eyes at the children, who giggled. "Work hard, got no time. Ba too mad, but say more better for me to be in America alive than have old empress cut off my head."

He checked the effect and noticed how the children shuddered and thrilled.

"My brain too hot in China," he said. "Get plenty mad, same as firecracker going off."

The children laughed, for they loved the strings of firecrackers Papa ordered every year from China for Christmas. They threw them down in the walled courtyard behind the laundry and danced on tiptoes amid the writhing strings, the shooting sparks, and the snap, crackle, and pop, which filled the air with the hot, acrid smell of gunpowder.

"Smells like China!" they would cry.

Yes, T'ai Peng had made a good home on the banks of the Savannah River *and* was quite sure he hadn't had anything good to eat in thirty years either.

"No dried beetle, no devilfish, no nothing what I like," he complained. "American cabbage taste like hay. Chinese cabbage sweet!"

"Mama cooks Chinese sometimes," cried Gerald.

"Yes," said Papa. "Okay, we make American food Chinese-style. But, you know, not same thing as Chinese food Chinese-style." He patted Gerald on the head; she nodded in concession.

Like many refugees, T'ai Peng had lost not only his favorite foods, but also his identity, his language, his religion, the future he had been led to believe was his, the privilege of cultural competency, his family of birth, and the interdependence of a Chinese family and community structure that ensured everybody got by, everybody had help when needed.

Here he was all on his own, except for Pong and Li Chin, who had taken him under their wing when he arrived. Here, he was also no longer the Great Phoenix, but had become Robert Chan, or worse, Robbie, a child's name. He'd even lost the surname of his ancestors, which was Chung.

On the night he arrived in Savannah, the steeple at the Independent Presbyterian Church had toppled in a portentous conflagration, the Great Savannah Fire of 1889, which also consumed a large chunk of the city. T'ai Peng had joined the bucket line to help put it out, still dressed in his odd, quilted clothing, slippers, and black pillbox hat with the button on top. He felt certain the burning of the steeple against the black sky on the very night of his arrival was a sign—perhaps that his old life had just gone up in flames. Perhaps that he, the Great Phoenix, must rise again from the ashes and make a new life, find new dreams. He was too young at the time to let himself believe it, but twenty-nine years later, that night loomed large in his own mythic imagination. *Burn to ash or forge yourself anew.*

In time, after the church was rebuilt, he became a member of that congregation. Americans had by now taken to calling him Robert, which was respectable and easier to say than T'ai Peng, a name that his Savannah Sunday school teacher, who had been giving him both language and religious instruction, had called "outlandish." But when he joined the church, the minister misstated his family name as well, introducing him to the congregation as Robbie Chan. To protest it now would cause the minister to lose face, and so T'ai Peng accepted his new name and carried it for the rest of his days. It wasn't so very unusual among the Chinese to adopt a temporary sojourner's name while wandering far from home. Sojourners kept their real names close and secret, like a protective talisman.

What else had been lost? In China, he had been politically engaged, a hothead filled with the fire of hope for change and the belief that he had a part to play in bringing it about, which gave him a sense of purpose, destiny. This is what had landed him in exile in the first place. But here, because of the federal Chinese Exclusion Act (1882–1943), he was

barred from becoming a citizen or even working for wages. He had a keen sense of civic duty and engagement, but here in America he found he could not even vote—ever. Further, a classically trained scholar, he had landed unwittingly in the Jim Crow South, where not only did his own knowledge and talents have no value but his children were not allowed to go to school at all. He was forced to hire private tutors to teach them in the family home above the laundry.

He counted himself lucky that he had a smart, kind, and beautiful wife. Her name was Annie, and she was barely bigger than their children. He liked to tease her with the story of the fair in Atlanta where he first glimpsed her.

"She walk like little grass," he would say, ever the poet, to the children. They had heard the story often and never tired of it. Their favorite part was when their father would then bounce and sway across the room on his tiptoes, looking remarkably like their mother, and just the way you would imagine a blade of grass might if it ever decided to go for a walk.

He and Annie had three girls and three boys, the last born in 1915, of whom they were immensely proud, so not all was lost. The children remembered him as a strict but loving father, and their parents as having a long, loving marriage. But they felt his longing, especially when he was down by the river and saw the great egrets standing among the grasses, or when he received letters from Honorable Father, the grandfather they would never know. These letters brought T'ai Peng news about his mother and grandmother, who grew old without him, his little nephews and niece who were growing up without Youngest Uncle, and always with the same sad admonishment from his father. *Don't come home. It is not safe for you here.*

Thus the children came to see Cathay, the beloved home of his youth, as he did: a lost fairy country fading in the mists, held just beyond reach. A mythical, bright world of dragons and moon goddesses, ghosts, temples, drums, and firecrackers. Of colorful silks, magical fish, and intelligent animals of all kinds. Of a wicked empress, then emperor (the last emperor), and resourceful countryfolk who knew how to navigate a world every bit as ensouled and animate as themselves.

OPPOSITE: *Cecelia "Annie" Lee, 1881–1959*

One humid morning, in 1918, twenty-nine years since his banishment, T'ai Peng came to breakfast with his eyes downcast and slid out the chair at the head of the table. He sat down to the sound of sausage sizzling beside him and, to the consternation of the whole family, raised a tear-stained face. His father was dead, he said.

Annie dropped the iron frying pan, making a great clatter on the stovetop. *"What?!"* she cried.

Archie, the oldest child, stopped midchew, his biscuit hanging limply from his fingers, dripping egg yolk to the plate below. He felt a stabbing tightness in the pit of his stomach. Any significant changes in family fortune fell heavily on his shoulders. Sandor was goofing off as usual, until Sinnie slapped him. Gerald had one hand over her mouth, and Robert Earl sat still as a mouse, taking in the scene. Bernice, the littlest, looked with wide eyes from face to face and began to whimper.

"What do you mean?" said Annie.

Questions tumbled over each other from around the table.

"How can you know? When did the mail come?"

T'ai Peng said there was no mail. He had awoken the night before and seen his father sitting at the end of the bed, weeping, one hand on T'ai Peng's leg. His face frozen in disbelief and alarm, T'ai Peng had scrambled upright in the bedclothes. He screwed his eyes shut and opened them again, wider, to make sure he wasn't dreaming. "Ba?" he said, clutching a fold in the sheet. But there was no answer. His father only hung his head in his palm and wept. So many years gone. So many miles of farewell.

Six weeks later, a letter arrived from China. Ba had left this world on the very night in question. But not before crossing the globe to visit his son in exile for a final farewell.

CHAPTER 5

THE GIFT

The universe is full of magical things patiently waiting for our wits to grow sharper.

—Eden Phillpotts

In the 1970s, my parents were stylish and social. They both drove Corvettes, his maroon and hers white. They were on the local bowling team and were serious enough to have their own balls, taking care in polishing and maintaining them and keeping them stored in striped, pungent vinyl cases that opened from the top like old doctors' bags. His ball sparkled in mesmerizing swirls of deep burgundy red, while hers was a cool, silvery blue. There is no mistaking the personalities behind these color choices.

It wasn't just fast cars and fondue for those two, though. They may have seemed an odd couple at first glance—the twenty-seven-year age difference; he, brash and hotheaded, she quiet and unflappable. But they were a true meeting of the minds.

My parents were not each other's first loves but were certainly each other's last and deepest loves. And both loved parties. Not the wild and hedonistic kind, but smaller gatherings of intimate friends with whom they could sing, talk, dance, laugh, and discuss in equal measure. Together they read Edgar Cayce and threw meditation parties. They made Swedish meatballs and threw bridge parties. They frequently hosted Christmas and Halloween parties, and sometimes they threw just-because parties. It was as though they were so happy to have found each other and gotten another chance at love that it all spilled out over everything else. Fondue and dancing could be had in the basement of our midcentury split-level ranch house. They held each other close and danced cheek to cheek. Mom in silver strappy sandals and Dad in a turtleneck and blazer. I loved Mom's sparkle, glamour, and quiet knowing, and Dad's quickness to laugh and command of brilliant conversation. The happy din of their soirees lulled me to sleep, a pillowy cocoon of safety, love, and belonging.

Sometimes, a sudden silence awakened me. Creeping up the stairs from my bedroom and peering through the balustrade toward the living room, I might see that everyone had gone home or to bed. But other times I saw the partygoers still there, sitting in a circle on floor cushions of primary colors, lights dimmed, palms up, eyes closed, and faces soft.

And yet despite this early and rather glamorous introduction to the practice of meditation, in 2015, when I was forty-one, and around the time of my first soul scream, I had never meditated. I couldn't sit still, couldn't clear my mind, and got easily distracted or bored. But by the spring of that year, it was more painful not to do it than to sit and try harder. I remembered Mom and Dad's old parties and the looks on their faces while they sat in low light with their eyes closed. I remembered the feeling I got watching them. There was salvation there, I knew.

I struck a match of memory in my mind, watched it flower, and came back to prayer.

It is many years ago, and I am lying on my back with my head in Mom's lap. She has cradled it with one hand and is touching my temple and pulling the tips of her fingers through the long strands of my hair with the other. Her voice is low and soft. Upon first meeting, you might think she didn't have much to say, but that was far from true.

Mom and Dad met in Rochester, New York, where Dad was

employed at Kodak as an optical engineer and served in the army re-
serve as a colonel. He had been living there since shortly after World
War II, with his wife, Gretchen, and their son, Robert Earl Jr. That
marriage ended in 1965, when Dad came home from work, and my
brother from school, to find Gretchen gone, and the furniture with
her. The divorce was finalized two years later, the result of irreconcil-
able differences.

Mom, Karen Elizabeth Smith, was married at the time to a man
named John. Although she was still in her midtwenties, John was
her second husband, and it seemed that key patterns were repeating
themselves. Both Mom's first husband and John were alcoholics—the
kind that drink themselves to death. When John and Mom came to
Rochester in 1964, however, this was not yet apparent.

In an autobiography that Dad wrote around 1980 for the adoption
application he and Mom were filling out for my sister, Mee Ra, he described their early relationship.

> *John was a second lieutenant in my Army Reserve unit.*
> *He found out that I was taking my dinner at a restaurant*
> *on meeting night and invited me to have dinner with*
> *him and Karen on those nights. Karen, very hospitable,*
> *encouraged it, and we became fast friends. The atmo-*
> *sphere of their apartment and the conversations were*
> *without equal in any group, and not for many months*
> *did I discern John's problem with alcohol. For two years*
> *I tried in vain to help—joyous when John checked in*
> *to the hospital, saddened when he checked himself out*
> *again. I don't know when Karen and I discovered that*
> *marriage was in the works for us. I do know that three*
> *years after my divorce [in 1968] we were married in*
> *Rochester, NY.*

She was twenty-nine and he was fifty-six.

He once told me that the first time he saw John and Mom at the
restaurant, John was holding up a newspaper. Mom, facing a wall of
newsprint, ate her meal in a silence that cut through the dinnertime
pandemonium of the diner and drew the attention of the colonel across

the room. Dad wondered that night in passing, *What kind of man has a woman like that and lets her eat alone?*

My parents tempered each other in all the most important ways. *Ours is not an ordinary marriage*, Dad wrote in the adoption application. *But then, we are not ordinary people.* She helped to tame the dragon in him—a creature both magical and fearsome. He gave her the confidence to clear her throat and speak, in ways both big and small.

In time, Mom became someone with great personal, if soft, power in her life, with quick and brilliant mind machinations that, I am sorry to say, our society still typically attributes to men. They allowed her to succeed in a man's world of business as a Kodak executive in the 1970s, '80s, and '90s. After Dad retired, she stepped with aplomb into the role of primary breadwinner, and none of us ever wanted for anything. Meanwhile her capacity for love—spreading it freely, finding the ones who needed it most, and giving it there in immeasurable abundance— made her something like a walking Guanyin, the goddess of compassion and mercy.

At this moment, in the light of the memory flame in my mind, with her fingers running through my hair, her voice is even softer than usual as she tells me to imagine a safe, beautiful place, going so far as to suggest a moss-carpeted stream bank, maybe with some tall trees, butterflies, the sound of running water, and a breeze. Having gotten me started, she invites me to fill in the rest with whatever makes me feel good inside.

Once I am there, she tells me to tighten and then release the tension in my body, one muscle at a time. From the tip of my toes to the top of my head, she takes me on a journey of ultimate relaxation. I don't know that what we are doing is called meditation, but I know it feels good.

I had a lot of anxiety as a child and adolescent. Almost anything could throw me into a negative spiral of impending doom, and I paid for it in debilitating stomachaches, nausea, and sometimes in extreme cases, vomiting. Uncontrollable crying was another symptom of my crippling fears of failure in anything, or rejection, or judgment from anyone.

She had no master plan in this exercise. Mom was a healer by nature. Her daughter was working herself into a state and needed help self-regulating. A seed was planted.

How thankful I am that Mom showed me when the world is falling apart around you, you can find peace within. Even more remarkable was my discovery as an adult that direction and guidance can be found there too.

CHAPTER 6

THE CHINESE TEAHOUSE

Though I do not believe that a plant will spring up where no seed has been, I have great faith in a seed. Convince me that you have a seed there, and I am prepared to expect wonders.

—Henry David Thoreau

There is a teahouse at the edge of a cliff overlooking the jagged, misty blue peaks and sandstone pillars of the Wulingyuan District in China. The air there is rarefied. Each inhale cleanses the lungs, while stagnant thoughts, stuck energy, and untruths leave the body with each exhale.

The teahouse is a low building hunkered down among the cypress, weeping willows, and crooked red pines that partially disguise its artifice, making it seem almost a natural part of the landscape. But then there is the circular entrance in the rose-colored garden wall, carved to contain dragon heads at your feet, and there is the yellow clay-tiled roof that rises just above the trees, with its flying eaves at the corners. These do seem to betray at least a modest assertion of joyful vanity that cannot be suppressed or fully hidden.

Half the building is supported by cleverly hidden pylons that make it appear to hover over a large koi pond edged with white pea-gravel pathways and chartreuse tufts of Japanese forest grass tumbling like water down to the pond's surface. Orange and red daylilies pop up at strategic points.

If I sit, as I often do, on the wooden breezeway that cantilevers out over the pond, with the double shoji-screen doors behind me slid wide open, my feet dangle just a few inches over the water. From there I can see, off to my left and in the middle distance, an arched bridge spanning a narrowing of the koi pond and a series of stone steps leading up to a pagoda on a hill, whose higher perspectives I have not yet meandered over to enjoy. The fish swim in an eternal loop, there and back again, as far as the water will allow them, as if to encourage me to follow.

Next to me are rounded stepping stones that allow me to jump right from the ledge of the teahouse and cross the water with barefooted ease, either to climb up the far bank and wander the garden or to visit with and feed the large koi that follow me from stone to stone. Lanterns bedecked with moss and shield lichens light the scene at dusk.

To the right of the pond and garden is a large, flat gravel surface that leads all the way to the cliff's edge. There, a lone cherry tree clings, sculpted by the wind into ripples and swirls that appear to wave and flap like a banner over the precipice. I can climb this tree—my toes have found all the right footholds—and lean out over the gorge, feeling the space stretch vast above and below me. There, I can also feel the wind that buffets the tree day and night. I realized the first time I stood there that the wind is not violent, and so the tree, whatever it may appear to be on the surface, is not twisted or bent so much as it is burnished and shaped.

Just to the left of the tree is a small frog pond ringed with fieldstones. In the summer you can see the frog eggs clinging in jellied masses with centers like small black pupils under the surface, while freshly hatched tadpoles whip their tails around in the joy of new life. Sudden movement on my part will also send little frogs, cool and green as spring grass, darting back into their watery realm. *Bloop! Plunk!*

Although you, as an honored guest, would approach the teahouse through the rose-stucco garden wall with the round dragon entryway, I do not come in this way. I always enter the teahouse . . . from my mind. It exists only there. Influenced by places I have been and things I have seen, yes, but purely imaginary in its unique totality. It is the grown-up version of what Mom told me to find all those many years ago—a safe and beautiful place inside myself where peace and clarity reign.

JOURNEY TO THE SOUTH

All my meditative journeys anchor at my teahouse and garden. I can leap off the cherry tree and fly upward, exploring realms above the clouds. I can slip into the frog pond and dive deep, finding worlds upon worlds. I can simply stay in the teahouse and sit at a stone basin of clear, sweet water overlooking the koi pond and garden, and wait for "them" to come to me. Who are they? Well, it depends. They can be animal or human, friend, loved one, ancestor, guide, or shadow-part of myself. But they all come with love or challenges, and wisdom that helps me dispense with illusions and tap into creative insight.

I usually have a question, or at least an intention, before I "go in." I also try to keep it simple, one question or issue at a time. "What can I do to carry this grief more lightly?" for example. Too many, or even just two, and things can get garbled. From the teahouse I can see to the heart of most any matter and feel unconditionally loved, guided, and supported through it all. Some might call these visitors and guides figments of my imagination, or at best my subconscious, but I have questions.

Very early on in my meditations, in the spring of 2015, I had read that a popular thing to do among those who journey is to visit the Four Directions—East, South, West, and North—because in many traditional societies across the globe, each of the Four Directions holds unique insights and wisdom. I was way outside my ken, but my first soul scream was evidence enough that I had just collided with the limitations of logos. I had also come to know there was much I didn't know.

I slipped silently beneath the surface of my frog pond and dove to the bottom, where I emerged through a hole into a moist, subterranean tunnel that appeared to lead out to a streambed in the middle of a jungle. I noticed that I was surrounded by ancestors down there, males to the right (Grandpa! Uncle Sandor! The two Archies!) and females to the left (Grandma Wiltrude! G.G.! Oh my god, *Mom*!). They were so real my eyes pricked with emotion. They seemed to guard the entrance to this world, and they sent me joyously on my way.

Exiting the tunnel whose opening faces East, I turned hard right and headed South, soon finding myself leaving the jungle and entering the desert. A herd of mustangs galloped before me in a circle of tossing heads and shaking manes. The sun was going down, turning the sky candied hues of purple, pink, and melon. Buttes and mesas silhouetted by the sinking sun stood like inky flourishes on the horizon. I took it all in, then turned away from the canyon before me and walked into the desert, the light turning flat and gray, until I came upon an unattended campfire. I sat by the fire and waited as the sun went down. Something told me *the South will come.*

I heard footsteps and looked up to see soft-shod feet enter the circle of firelight across from me. My eyes traveled upward and fell upon the countenance of an unnervingly handsome, barely clad man, the picture of youth and vitality, with skin the color of chestnuts and hair that fell in a sable sheet down his back. His ethnicity was ambiguous, like my own, but I discerned more than one kind of East Asian.

This man had an impish grin on his face, then he laughed outright with a flash of teeth and my heart stopped. He thought it *amusing* that I found him so beautiful. *How embarrassing.* I felt real-world sheepishness to be caught out like this with zero chill. But to be chill in the presence of such a man could only betray the dullest and primmest of tendencies.

He took a seat near the fire, where light flickered across tattoos distinctive enough that later, when the meditation was over, I felt compelled to draw them. They covered his chest and shoulders in a yoke or boatneck fashion and were done in distinct parallel lines with visibly bare space between them, almost like lines of text. Tiny triangles or points formed one line, and then what appeared to be squiggles formed a second line and maybe a third.

He left the fire and, after a time, came back a little out of breath, carrying a desert hare by the ears. He skinned it and roasted it on a spit over the fire. He cut a piece and jerked his hand upward toward my face, encouraging me to try it. He laughed in agreement at my expression when I got the taste. After we ate, he pulled out a long clay pipe, leaned against a tree trunk behind him, and looked up at the stars.

I tried asking for a name, which I had read one should do if one encounters any characters on these journeys, but he simply smiled at me. I also asked if he had a gift for me, which was another suggested tactic. At this he put the pipe aside, sat up, spread his fingers wide and scooped them through the sandy soil beside him, then raised his hands again, watching the dirt slide back through his fingers. He picked up a handful of the soil, reached over, and let it shift and slide in a thin stream onto my own outstretched palm.

Without speaking, he let me know that I was to ground myself and not get lost in ruminations about Dad, or to take my physicality for granted, for I was a spiritual being having a human experience—not the other way around. He told me to build a garden to remind myself of these things.

"Well, it's not like I haven't been trying," I said. My attempts at gardening for the last several years had been ruled by trial and error . . . with emphasis on the error. One of my main obstacles was that I didn't accept things for what they were. A few years ago, a day might have found me planting irises and tulips against their nature in the shade, because that was where I could see and enjoy them. They would cling to life for a season and not return. Growing grass was also a problem. I tilled the yard by hand with a lawn-aerator roller, then spread seed, fertilized, limed, and watered the land to have a little patch of grass to call our own. Every year, shoots would grow and fill in, only to die off the first time we left town for a long weekend. I tried all the different seeds on the market, including the ones "as seen on TV" that claim to allow you to grow turf anywhere, even on a concrete block. Apparently, my yard was less arable than concrete.

But the soil the man in my meditation had given me was not quality loam either. It was much like the soil in my own backyard. He seemed to be urging me to not only reconnect to the earth in a general sense but also to know my small patch of it for what it was, to see its potential and act accordingly.

Now, all of this was happening in a grocery store parking lot. Having gotten what we needed for dinner, I was resting my eyes in the driver's seat, waiting for the time to pass until I had to go pick up the boys at tae kwon do. This entire scene had played out in my mind with just a ten-minute recording of drumbeats meant to facilitate journeys into the active imagination.

As I pulled out of the parking lot and drove to the *dojang*, I began to feel a strange pressure in the space above and to the left of my forehead. It was not a physical pressure. It felt like something pressing on the outside of my energy field, like a finger poking a block of Jell-O without penetrating it. Springy. I felt it press in, then bounce away—*boing!*—then press in harder and bounce away again. Then I heard myself say aloud as I was turning the car into the dojang lot, "Oh my god, he's going to tell me his name."

Next came a hollow popping sound, or more of a popping *feeling* because I didn't hear anything. It felt like a thick, viscous bubble bursting, and I spoke out loud again, this time involuntarily. My tongue felt thick and heavy as it struggled to wrap itself around an unfamiliar sound. "Nam Toc."

I shook myself from the experience and repeated, "Nam Toc? Is that a name? What does that mean?"

Later that evening, I googled "Nam Toc" on my phone and found that *nam toc* is a Thai word for a savory, well-seasoned piece of meat. I felt a prickle in my spine, remembering the rabbit. And a new idea seized me. If the name Nam Toc indicated Thai origin, maybe I should look up indigenous Thai tattoos. *Are* there any indigenous Thai tattoos? I had no idea.

I typed it in the search box, screamed, and threw the phone as if it were hot to the touch. It hit the couch and lay there face up, compelling me to keep looking. Not that I could have looked away. For there were the tattoos I had drawn in my journal, tattoos I had never seen before. They are called a *sak yant* collar. Sak yant tattoos have an ancient history in Indian and Thai Buddhism and depict sacred geometry. The little triangles I had drawn are known as *gao yord*, or Buddha peaks, and distinct parallel lines of writing and prayers are often tattooed beneath them.

I was so overwhelmed by what had happened to me, I confided everything breathlessly to my friend, Sung, texting furiously.

And do you know what happened? Nam Toc is a Thai word meaning a juicy, well-seasoned piece of meat. Then I looked up Thai tattoos and they were the tattoos from my drawing!!! The only thing is, he didn't really look Thai. He looked more mixed, like me.

I stared at the phone for a minute, willing Sung to read the text and get back to me. And then, three little dots began to ripple and shimmer on the screen. Hurrah! Sung had read my message and was typing.

Well, I literally do not know what is going on right now but it seems like you're having a pretty weird experience. I should probably tell you that Nam Toc—and actually, I would probably spell it Nam Tuck or even Nam Duck—is also a Korean name.

A prickle rose in my spine again, this time reaching further. Almost afraid to hear the answer, I texted back.

What does it mean?

Silence. Then rippling dots . . .

Mean? Well, Nam means south, like the direction, and Duck is like . . . a virtue or a benevolent force. But more than that, it's one that actually helps you, so like, I would translate it as Helpful Virtue.

WHAT?!

Yes, I typed at the top of my lungs.

Yeah. Sounds like your guy, Nam Duck, is actually Helpful Virtue from the South.

The South will come.

I burst into tears and didn't stop crying for two hours. Something profound and mysterious had just happened, and logos simply had no answer for me. Clearly, some of my long-accepted theories about how the universe works needed to be revisited. My dataset was changing. Mythos had come knocking.

So I built the garden as Nam Duck had suggested. I billed it on social media as the Great Gardening Rampage of 2015, and none but my closest friends knew its origins or what it meant to me.

THE GREAT GARDENING RAMPAGE OF 2015

When the dump truck filled with beige-colored pea gravel backed into our side yard, I walked out to the second-floor deck and held my iPad over the railing with the camera flipped forward so Dad could watch the hydraulic rams lift the truck bed to a vertical position. Tons of gravel slid down the metal bed in a great cacophonous *whoosh* and rumble, forming an enormous heap just outside the access to the back of our lot.

"Oooh boy, look it, look it," cried Dad. "Wow!"

I flipped the camera back and smiled.

"What are you going to do with all that gravel?" he asked.

I flipped the camera around again and made my way down the spiral stairs to the garden level, panning the scene for him while I talked.

I said, "Remember how I was telling you that I've been trying to grow grass for years? Well, I suddenly realized, *Who needs grass anyway?* I started thinking about the rock and gravel gardens you see in the desert and in Europe and Asia, and thought, *Why not here?* Why not accept the fact that grass doesn't want to grow here, and make the most of it? So, as you can see, I've removed all the sod and laid out three garden beds ringed in stone where I think something can grow. And I've just finished laying down landscaping fabric on the rest, so now I just need to spread this gravel everywhere."

"You did that all by yourself?" Dad asked with admiration, and I thought maybe some nostalgia too. Dad was a project guy himself, or at least he had been.

"Yep. Completely. I'm an archaeologist, you know. I do know how to use a shovel. And also," I added, carrying on a little joke of his, "I got musk-els."

Dad laughed, repeating the word under his breath to savor the humor. "Musk-els" had been delighting him for seventy-five years. I found him using it in letters as far back as the 1940s.

Ever since, anytime we talked, which was most days, he wanted a report and sometimes a tour of the garden to see how it was coming along. He was unfailingly enthusiastic about it. My garden was the best thing he had going that summer. I did not tell him I considered it my Grief Garden.

After my visit with Nam Duck, in accordance with his advice I had taken every ounce of fear, dread, and anticipatory grief that I felt about Dad's slipping away from me and deposited it into this garden. I had only recently been brought to my knees with my first soul scream. I was at a breaking point and looking for a grand intervention. It was not that he was at death's door, or that he couldn't still be amiable, curious, and cheerful, for indeed he was. The slippage could be felt in his little forgetfulnesses, his flagging ability to keep up rigorous conversation, his fears and paranoias that no amount of reassurance or logic could dispel. Somehow, though he was still quite lively, I simply came to know that he was not much longer for this world . . . and it felt like the end of my own.

But here I was, feeling better as the summer progressed. This garden project was no poking around with gloved hands and a miniature spade. This was serious earthmoving. I wore steel-toed boots and a sleeveless undershirt to do it. I sweated profusely, my breath came hard, and my back and shoulders ached at night. I made involuntary grunting noises as I pried up rocks the size of my head and heaved them out of the way. They landed with great, earthen *thud*s. I used loppers along with all my body weight and torque capacity to cut through tree roots as thick as my wrists, just to clear the way for more digging.

Then there were the dozen or so trips to Lowe's to get paving stones to line the garden beds. I loaded the back of the CR-V and drove home riding low in the rear, only to unload and head straight back for more stone, more soil, mulch, landscaping fabric, and pins.

Endorphins flooded my bloodstream and helped keep me fit. The planning part consumed my waking mind. My skin bathed in the fresh, clean air and soaked up vitamin D from the sun. I tan quickly and soon had a vital glow about me that made my outside more closely resemble my new and improved inside.

This wasn't a placebo effect. A study published in the *Journal of Health Psychology* reported that gardening was more effective at reducing stress and restoring mood than reading a book. As an avid lifelong reader, that one really made me sit up and take notice. Another study, in the *Journal of Public Health*, found that working in a garden for just thirty minutes increased not only mood but also self-esteem. People who garden feel more worthy and purposeful than those who do not.

My stress levels were undeniably lower as I turned my private little stretch of nature into a restful haven. I was able to do this because I was no longer fighting upstream. For the first time I was going with the flow, even if flow in this case meant backbreaking labor. I had accepted that we were not meant to have grass back there. I spent time at the nursery finding plants that were pleasing to me but also had a chance of surviving the soil and light conditions they would be inhabiting. I learned to love hostas, those plain Janes of the gardening world. Who knew there were so many varieties if you cared to look? There are the Patriots and the Blue Angels, the Pathfinder and the Striptease, the Wolverine and Paradigm, and who can forget the darling little Blue Mouse Ears? Who wouldn't want such a cast of characters in their garden?

I planted hardy desert grasses. I placed my sun-loving silver mound, bachelor's button, sea pinks, purple coneflowers, daisies, black-eyed Susans, irises, and a Korean lilac, not so I could see them where I wanted to see them, but so they could thrive. I filled spaces with sedum and other succulents and put creeping thyme in the walkway for the bees.

I also bought a large container and made my own little fishpond. I filled it with water lilies that bloomed a peachy pink, and purple iris, and kept a shubunkin fish I named Rocket. I could sit by the pond, listen to the water-spitter frog trickling, and watch Rocket flick and dart between lily pads before coming to the surface in search of the food he had learned to expect from me. I breathed deeply and invited expansion, released fear.

It occurred to me that every patch of ground has its own version of perfection, and it cannot be imposed upon. So does every life. You cannot force artificial rules upon it or demand specific outcomes. You must make the best of where you find yourself. If you show patience and perseverance, a willingness to accept what is, a trust in the growth process, and an understanding that whatever you nurture will grow for better or for worse, you will find that no ground is truly infertile.

REVENANT

And what do you suppose happened next? The birds came. Sparrows, yellow warblers, house finches, blue jays, cardinals, chickadees, dark-eyed juncos, tufted titmice, crows, mourning doves, and ones I couldn't identify, in all colors of the rainbow. The squirrels and chipmunks defied my attempts to keep the bird feeders full, but I was feeling flush, and I did not begrudge them their prewinter fattening. By the end of the summer I could sit at the dining table I had set up under the deck, where I was less noticeable to wildlife, and watch the birds swoop and dive, in and out, warbling, chirping, and whistling, shimmying in the birdbath, grabbing a quick bite, and then flying back up into the branches of the hemlocks, rhododendron, and hydrangeas to tell their friends. The constant twittering sounded lush, like water dripping.

Much to my delight and surprise, my obstreperous little plot of land was bursting with life. Perhaps it was really I who had been barren and obstreperous. Fighting the flow of things, making unreasonable demands. *Irises should grow here! Parents should never die!*

I had lacked the imagination to see things in a different way, to find or create beauty, and had robbed myself of the light of hope as a result. And so I had festered in darkness. I looked out now and saw a promise of healing and joy to come—one day, in time. But more immediately, that even in a storm there is still brightness and beauty to be found.

Out of my fear of death, I had brought something wildly, beautifully, and movingly to life. *My grief did that,* I marveled. Grief for Mom, anticipatory grief for Dad. And where was my grief now, anyway? I found it had become significantly smaller, more manageable, confirming my suspicions once and for all that grief is just the pain of love that has nowhere to go.

If that's true, I thought, *then it wasn't grief that built this. It was love.* This was not a Grief Garden, but a Monument to Love.

My garden had taken my grief within itself and cleaned it, giving it back to me as something beautiful. Now I could look out at the garden and simply feel the love. My own that had built it, as well as the love of a compassionate universe that reflected it back to me tenfold. I got to thinking about transformation as opposed to apocalyptic loss—a neutral concept of change, neither good nor bad, just existing.

One day, as the weather began to turn crisp, I noticed something new growing in one of my garden beds. I had not planted it, and my first instinct was to pull it out as a weed, but something stayed my hand. *Wait. Wait and see what it is first.*

Days, then weeks passed as the mystery plant grew larger—a single stalk with leaves somewhat like maple, only bigger. The suspense was great when a large bulb formed at the tip; it looked like a Chinese lantern plant, only green, with a papery shell in an acorn shape that concealed something growing plump within. *What on earth could it be?* And then one morning, toward the end of September, I left the house with Seu and stopped dead in my tracks. The pod had opened, and from it had emerged a large white flower the size of a dinner plate, with a fuchsia center. I was beside myself. I took a picture with Seu, who was five, for scale, and posted it on Facebook.

YOU GUYS!!! LOOK WHAT JUST HAPPENED TO MEEEEE! I did NOT plant this in my garden. Today's small win.

And what if I told you it turned out to be a hardy hibiscus, the national flower of South Korea, symbolizing resilience and indomitable spirit? *The South will come.*

Somewhere far above, the Tai Sui sat back. In life, the General had shunned fame and material comforts. Living like a hermit, he would go to the mountains and commune with nature and wild things. Brooding now on the efforts of the Ox below him, his hackles lowered without his even noticing. Something new and unfamiliar was coming upon him. Was it curiosity? Approbation even? *The little Ox that could,* he thought, stroking his beard and chuckling. *Intriguing.*

BOOK TWO

2016
YEAR OF THE MONKEY

The Red Fire Monkey has fast-paced energy, ingenious ideas, and a lot of cheek, which puts everything into flux. Just about anything can happen, for better *and* for worse. Collective action will devolve into chaos, but individual efforts are rewarded this year. Focus on what you can control, for there will be much that you cannot. Year of the Monkey is about breaking free of stale patterns and overthrowing old conventions and accepted wisdoms about oneself and the world.

The Monkey embodies creativity, innovation, and developing one's unique gifts. It is a good time to be rebellious, follow a heart's desire, and dare to think outside the box you have put around yourself. Opportunities will come fast and hard, but only the most agile, inventive minds will notice them and be able to act swiftly. Have the courage to leave your own beaten path. Doing so leads to unplanned-for success.

CHAPTER 7

MOTHERS DON'T DIE

Let's light another match together, right now.
Strike!
Now watch it flower.
Hands in prayer.
"I know I'm not the only one who thought, when you first moved here and for years after, that you didn't have a mom," a friend said. "Because you only spoke about your dad."
I flinched.
His words reverberated for days. I shook them off, physically, like a horse twitching flies away. But flies don't go away, they just circle and look for a better place to land. If you want to get rid of the flies, you must first clean up the mess. It was 2016, Year of the Monkey, and I had some stale thought patterns to get rid of, messes to clean up. Monkey brought good energy for such endeavors, and I decided to write about Mom for the first time, five years after her death. I had begun a writer's blog, which was really just a more beautiful and formal way for me to journal. It encouraged me to take my rambling and work it into more structured essays and stories, which deepened the healing for me.

A RECKONING

Is it true? Do I never talk about Mom?
Images flipped through my mind like a Rolodex, spinning faster and faster. Doing puzzles on my bedroom floor; riding the *Maid of the Mist* beneath thundering Niagara Falls; gazing out from an overlook on the Danube; Mom teaching me to knit my first baby hat; the warm softness of her hugs; the low, hesitant cadence of her voice; the chuckle that lay just

Mom passed on her love of books, games, and puzzles to me.

Mom and Dad on their honeymoon in Austria, March 1971

beneath the surface, making her speech slightly melodic. I remembered the way she never gave full voice to her negative feelings, either
banging out the front door to go for a walk or slamming pots and pans
in the kitchen when she was angry. And I remembered the way she
never told us she was dying, but preferred to say cheerfully, "This too
shall pass," even about terminal cancer. And now people think I didn't
even have a mother. *She doesn't deserve that.*

  Shame flooded my chest. Regret stabbed me in the left palm. I
came home, chest burning and palm throbbing, and started scrubbing
the kitchen floor on hands and knees like a scullery maid, harder than
necessary, getting all the corners the mop can't reach. Only when my
breathing came swift and heavy did I toss the brush in the sink and
the filthy paper towels in the trash. The floor looked good. I felt better.

  I never thought Mom would be the first to go. Not even her

terminal diagnosis could pierce the Great Lie I had been telling myself. Once, early in her diagnosis, I found a magazine article about multiple myeloma. I put on my dutiful daughter / curious scholar cap and began to read. It was about a woman who had gotten the disease in her early thirties and soon became a massive, record-breaking fundraiser for its research. I was ready to look the symptoms dead in the eye and figure out how I could be of most help to Mom.

But when I got several paragraphs in to the part about prognosis—at five years mortality was around 50 percent, and nobody made it past nine years—I slammed the magazine shut. Right up until I was saying goodbye to her on the phone on a Tuesday night while dinner burned on the stove and Seu whimpered in the background, I did not think she was going to die.

OPPOSITE: New parents but still dancing cheek to cheek

It was impossible. Who would spend the next couple of decades remembering and missing Dad with me? I had thought of all the ways she might fall apart after losing him, all the ways I might have to stretch myself to meet her needs as well as my own. I had thought of mother-daughter trips abroad, a tearful spreading of ashes, quiet holiday times with laughter over the man who had been our North Star. When I was younger, I imagined her walking me down the aisle to give me away, holding her grandchildren alone, maybe getting a small apartment near me so we could be closer. I took cues from her and how she interacted with *her* mother, my grandma Wiltrude, who had been widowed ever since my grandpa Russell, at the age of sixty, had gone for a walk in the woods in Vermont and fallen to his knees on the forest floor. Their poodle, Jacques, who was a clever dog, fetched help, and Grandpa made it to the hospital but never home again, and Grandma went on without him for another thirty years.

I had anticipated things going similarly for Mom and me. I had *seen* it for so long that it had taken on the heavy weight of prophecy. It's not that I wanted it that way. A life without Dad was the most painful thing I could imagine, but imagine it I did. I invited the thought, sat with it, needled it, pressed it, shivered with it, but was unable to stop it. I wanted to be prepared. My folly was to take for granted that Mom would be doing it with me.

Of course, this is what my parents also expected. They dithered at

first about the wisdom of having a child at all, with Dad entering his seventh decade. But with Mom now on her third marriage and with no children, this was her last chance. They both thought the rewards were worth the risk. It's better to have loved and lost, and all that. Perhaps their happiness at getting another chance in life after painful disappointments made them feel invincible.

And so I was born on March 9, 1973, when Mom was thirty-two and Dad was fifty-nine, almost the same age his father-in-law would be when he went leaf-peeping and never came home.

WORRYWART

One of my earliest memories is of fretting about Daddy dying soon. Mom called me a worrywart. On that day, around age four, I lay on my back in bed with my legs perpendicular against the yellow wall, sliding them self-soothingly side to side, my Sniffy (once white with a smooth satin trim, now in grayish tatters) shoved to my face. A fat tear worked its way down one temple to the bedsheets. I could feel a question lingering in the air between us. Mom sat on the edge of the bed, patted me on the stomach, and told me not to be silly. But as far as I could see, the last thing I was being was silly. Everyone at the playground thought Dad was my grandpa, and I knew grandpas die.

Years later, in fifth grade, I sat in the cafeteria choking back tears of regret while my classmates chucked napkins at each other, banged the tables, and scarfed Ding Dongs. *What if Dad dies and never knows how much I love him?* My throat was thick with emotion. An apple rolled with purpose past my feet.

When I was twenty-five, Brent and I had a practical conversation over burgers in Boston about getting married. Under consideration was how many of our loved ones were getting up in years. Brent's grandparents and great-aunt Dee, G.G. and Grandma Wiltrude, Da—

I didn't let myself think it, let alone say it.

Later, we went about having babies the same way. Mom had her diagnosis by this time, but I felt sure she was going to be one of those people who was mysteriously able to live with terminal illness for decades. Look at Magic Johnson! Five years in, she looked remarkably well and was active and vibrant as ever. She talked about the approaching Thanksgiving, long-term repairs to the family cabin, and future get-togethers, as if she knew she was going to be part of them. She never let her illness limit or define her. Most people didn't even know she was sick. From what I could tell, the only thing that had changed was that she had lost weight and become diabetic due to the steroids she was on. Whenever she came to visit us in New Hampshire, she kept her insulin in a fanny pack and discreetly checked her blood sugar throughout the day, and that was that.

To me, the realest thing about her illness was her hair thinning. She never went bald, but at some point her nearly waist-length hair got so thin she had to relent and cut it short. I had always thought her long hair a bit dowdy, but the first time I saw her after her haircut I sensed how the wind had left her sails. I felt her fear and sadness keenly. She had never had short hair and didn't know how to style it. She had never had a part, and so even when it was short, she simply brushed it flat back off her forehead, where it ended bluntly behind her ears. Dad tried to cheer her up with humor, saying she looked like Al Sharpton. That went over about as well as you'd expect, and was ironic, since if there was anyone in the house who looked like Al Sharpton, it was Dad.

I sought to cheer her up by taking her to the drugstore beauty aisle and helping her pick out some of my favorite hair products, including a good hair dryer and a round brush. We came home and I washed her hair in the same sink where she had bathed me as an infant. I put in the volumizing mousse and dried her hair in the mirror, showing her how to lift each section of hair, use the dryer hot on the roots, followed by a cold shot to set it. Then there was hair fudge and hair spray to keep the volume. I gave her a part and tucked the sides behind her ears to create an attractive shape.

Mom was self-conscious about her ears and wanted to pull the hair from behind them, which was, I thought, a terrible idea. I convinced her to live with this new do for the day and see how she felt. The truth was, I couldn't tell how she felt. I was enthusiastic about the result, and she agreed to let me take a picture. She smiled wanly for the camera. *Her ears, of all things! What on earth could be wrong with her ears?* They were lovely ears, shapely and flat against her head. I felt helpless in ways I couldn't articulate.

Today, looking at this picture, I think maybe tucking her hair behind her ears made her feel girlish and young. Perhaps the whole exercise of going to the drugstore and playing with beauty products with her daughter was a lively and optimistic thing to do. But maybe when death is in the room, girlish and lively things hurt.

Mom, after I helped her style her newly short hair

This was the last occasion for a very long time that I saw any hint of vulnerability in Mom. I chastise myself for pretending for nine years that she wasn't going to die, but she also encouraged me in this fantasy. She didn't want me to be her crutch or confidante. As a mother now myself, I know and empathize with the primal urge to protect your children. Mom decided early on that she would not let her illness affect me in any negative way if she could help it. The possibility that this might one day leave me with regrets or guilt about how it all unfolded was, I am sure, an acknowledged and accepted outcome. She had faith that I would, with age and experience, see the wisdom in it.

I sometimes saw her lying on the couch, staring out the window, or with a forearm flung across her eyes while Dad sat on the edge of the cushions and held her hand in both of his, murmuring things to her I couldn't hear. They were no doubt talking about love, death, hope, and carrying on. But I let myself imagine that she'd had some trite disappointment that day, like a silk-painting project that hadn't turned out the way she'd hoped.

In time, Mom seemed to settle into things. Multiple myeloma is free of severe symptoms at the outset, and one can live a reasonably normal life if one chooses to. I continued the old pattern, then, of assuming Mom was fine and fretting over Dad. As I entered my early thirties and he entered his nineties, the urgency I felt about having children revolved around him.

I knew him as a deeply generous, funny, and fun-loving man, but he had a volcanic temper and was prone to fits of moroseness. A dark cloud would descend on his features, and you knew nothing you said at that point was going to be right. He frequently got the last word in arguments with an unceremonious "It doesn't matter. I'll be dead soon anyway." So some of my earliest memories are of me trying to commit him to memory. He became the singular focus of my gaze from earliest childhood until the day he died. When he spoke, I listened, trying to remember every story, deed, opinion, facial expression, bit of body language. I had to collect memories to sustain me for a lifetime.

On moving-in day at the beginning of my sophomore year in college, I discovered I had lost some hardware for the dorm room bookshelves Dad had made me. I felt sick. "Oh no!" I groaned as I started shoving objects around in the box in front of me. "No. No. No-no-no-no-no-no. Oh my god."

I sat on my heels, hand over my mouth, then my forehead, trying to think. My brain had gone to mush. I dove back into the box.

"Please, god, no." And then, with a loud *"Fuck!"* I batted the box away in resignation.

Brent watched from the bed.

"Calm down. What's the big deal?" he said.

"You don't know my dad," I said, and went on to make a lengthy prediction some six or seven deeds deep of *exactly* what Dad would do and say when he found out, which would be any minute because he was coming back up the stairs with another load from the car as we spoke.

First, I predicted an incredulous *"What?!"* followed by a very loud, very long sigh. Next, he would tuck his lips against his teeth, half roll his eyes, and shake his head in long-suffering disgust. Then he would raise his eyebrows high and, in a great show of self-restraint, start but not finish a question, "I thought I told y— . . . Why didn't y—" which would dissolve into another loud exhale through the nose, nostrils flared to maximum width. "Oh boy," he would say in the least oh-boy voice you can imagine. Next would come the sound of him sucking on his front teeth. And finally, in a voice of ultimate resignation, "Oo-kaay. All right. Welp. That's that, then. Can't do anything about it. We'll just have to get some more."

When Dad clumped down the hall carrying my Apple computer in front of him, I sneaked a sideways glance at Brent to make sure he was watching.

Dad put the computer down and let out a throaty exhale of satisfaction. "Ahh," he said through his teeth, which were clamped around a pipe, as usual. He grinned from behind his flip-up sunglasses and stood with arms akimbo, surveying our progress. *The Jolly Green Giant goes to college.* I was loath to speak.

"Dad, I . . . I'm really sorry," I said as brightly as I could. "It looks like I lost the hardware you got for my bookshelves . . ."

My voice trailed off as the smiling face fell and the whole pageantry unfolded exactly, and I do mean *exactly*, as I had foretold.

Brent was yelping on the bed. He had to wipe his face repeatedly

after that incident. He still talks about it to this day. "I was crying," he says. "*Crying!* And your dad couldn't figure out why!"

The point is, I knew my dad.

Dad was in many ways the center of my universe, and not just because I had spent a lifetime thinking he was about to die. He had charisma for miles, he was seductive in all senses of the word, and he was uniquely gifted with children. Within these pages you'll find him compared to Greek gods and to beer commercials. How many people can you say that about? He was also my primary caregiver from preschool on as Mom forged ahead, being among the first generation of truly professional career women in this country. While she was a computer systems analyst at Kodak, Dad became a stay-at-home dad at age sixty-five, about the time I entered kindergarten.

So it was he who taught me to tie my shoes and the difference between *who* and *whom*, and *I* and *me*, and why I should care. It was he who took me out fairy hunting on dew-covered mornings and brought me to the Rochester Museum & Science Center on Friday afternoons. My black patent leather Mary Janes clicked satisfyingly on the marble floors as we strode hand in hand to the ticket counter, ready to see dinosaur bones and First Nations dioramas, every week as exciting as if it were the first.

Come snack time, my eyes crinkled at him over my special treat in the red-and-white-checkered café—a Twinkie for me, coffee-and-cream-no-sugar and a plain donut for him. It was also he who woke me up early on certain mornings to watch *Captain Kangaroo*, and he who spun elaborate tales for me at night when Mom had fallen into an exhausted stupor after dinner.

My favorite tales were what he called "The Thirty-Nine Kids." They were all about me, shrunk to about six inches in height, sneaking into the science museum after dark and getting into all kinds of hijinks. The thirty-nine kids referred to all the friends I added to the stories as we went along. Before every telling, we had to spout off the list of thirty-nine who were going to be joining me on that night. It started with my niece and best friend, Stacey—the granddaughter of Dad and his first wife, Gretchen, who was the same age as me—then grew to include a bunch of kids from school, and finally even Bugs Bunny and Daffy Duck, the Chipmunks, Chip 'n' Dale, Porky Pig, and Yosemite Sam. Dad did all the voices.

OPPOSITE: *Dad, my primary caregiver and colossus*

I remember one story in which he had me tease the night watchman from inside the jaws of the T. rex skeleton over his head. The watchman spun around with his utility flashlight and yelled, "Huh? What was that? Who's there? Who said that?"

"Nobody!" Dad had me call down from behind a dinosaur tooth before sending me sliding down the skeleton's spine to make a fast getaway off the tip of its tail. I screeched and rolled with laughter. Yes, Dad had invented the story of *Night at the Museum* thirty years before the movie was ever made. Can anyone who knew him be surprised?

But now here I was, my thought-train about Mom being hijacked once again by memories of Dad, leaving me violently scrubbing the kitchen floor and asking myself, *Why don't I talk about Mom more? Have I erased her in the eyes of others?* And more shamefully, *Have I overlooked her to an extent myself? Why couldn't I have been for her the daughter I was for Dad?*

DENIAL

Most people think of being in denial in pejorative terms. Denial seems cowardly, childish. But my friend Christine, a prominent psychologist, said one day, "You know, denial can also be necessary in times of upheaval. It's a protective strategy and eases people's painful passage through traumatic change."

This was news to me, and welcome.

I had been in denial about Mom's condition for nearly a decade, since I read that article on multiple myeloma. In the interim, I had thrown myself into establishing a life and career. I finished my PhD in historical archaeology at Boston University. I took a prestigious visiting position in the Vassar College Anthropology Department. I wrote my first book. I presented at national conferences and published peer-reviewed articles. I also eventually left academia to become an archaeological consultant. In all this time, I did not call Mom more than usual or make any effort to visit her more often. When I did go home, I regressed, as I always did, into adolescence.

"What's for dinner, Mom?" I asked one night, even noticing that there was now a stool in the kitchen where she could sit when she got too tired to stand.

As the illness progressed, the suspension of disbelief became harder to maintain. Dad spoke freely and humorously about Mom's "fancy pants," which were for her newfound incontinence. She would just chuckle back at him. "Oh, you!"

Watching my parents *flirt* over adult diapers is about the most loving thing I've ever witnessed, but it scared me and made me head to the kitchen for a snack.

When Jin was born, I was so overwhelmed by new parenthood that I found visits home exasperating. The house had no childproofing, and Mom was careening toward a hoarding problem. Once, when Jin was in the cruising stage, I put him down in the house and went out to the car to collect the luggage. By the time I returned moments later, my child was teetering wildly through the dining room with two un-sheathed hypodermic needles in one hand and a sword-shaped letter opener in the other, heading straight for a vacuum cleaner cord uncoiled across the floor in loops just looking for a foot to grab. The bathrooms were filthy and dishes filled the sink. There were only two places to sit, and the whole house smelled like cat pee. I bleached the bath-room in a frenzy with my mouth turned sharply down at the corners and my chin tucked against my throat. I checked the late hour, thought of the eight-hour drive behind us and the sleepless night with an infant ahead of us, and judged Mom for being a terrible housekeeper.

OPPOSITE: *Dad declares Mom "the Champ" at a Gilda's Club Gala.*

THE UNRAVELING

When Jin turned one, Mom and Dad made what would be their last trip to New Hampshire, for his birthday party and to see our new house. Here in my own new space, I felt free to enjoy my parents' com-pany. Mom plopped on the couch next to me one morning, the cush-ions warm from the sunshine. She stretched her legs and arms out and purred, "Mmm, this place feels so good, sweetie," then reached out a hand to pat my thigh.

Jin stood on the other couch with arms clamped at his side and waited for Dad to say, "Tim-*berr!*" before falling backward into the cushions. He gave bubbling belly laughs and scrambled back into a standing position to do it all over again.

"Again, Bop-Bop," Jin said. Bop-Bop was Grandpa Bob. Grandma Karen he called Bop-Bop Kayn.

I was proud of the life we were building and so happy to have them there. Despite my lifetime of worry, *both* my parents were able to know and love my kids, and to see me inhabit the role of mom.

Dad dissected a hundred-year-old doorknob on that visit and

figured out how to fix it. He also stewed and plotted for days over how to jerry-rig a perennially running toilet, which became his Moby-Dick that week. I found him there morning, noon, and midnight trying out new ideas. He gave daily reports over breakfast. Engineering problems to be solved were his specialty. They were dragons to be slain, and they made him come alive.

Jin's birthday party was large and lively, and Mom and Dad were popular guests. I went to sleep on a cloud of well-being.

The next morning I awoke to muffled shouting from the guest room downstairs.

"Hold on to me, Karen! I can't lift you!" Dad was saying.

"I told you, *I can't*, Bob!" Mom cried.

Brent and I bumbled down the stairs. He knocked and entered without waiting. Mom was in bed and needed to use the bathroom, but couldn't move her legs. Dad was in a fuzzy robe pulled open to the waist, revealing his emaciated frame. Spending time with him, you could forget that Dad was ninety-five years old, but seeing him half-naked made you remember.

Brent slid one arm under Mom and got her to the bathroom, helped situate her on the toilet, and left her in privacy. We three—Dad, Brent, and I—stood outside the door and took turns leaning in to listen.

"Are you done, Mom?" I asked.

"Yes," came a small voice.

"Do you need help?"

"No!" she cried.

"I'm calling 911," I said.

"*No!*" she yelled. "Don't!"

By the time the ambulance arrived, she still had not come out. Nor would she let the EMTs in.

"You have to go to the hospital, Mom," I called through the door, using my new-parent voice. "This is nonnegotiable. The ambulance is here. We need to find out what's going on."

Silence.

I looked at Brent and began to cry.

"I can't go in there, Brent," I said in a choked whisper. "I can't go in there."

Brent, stalwart in crisis, knocked on the door and said, "Karen? It's Brent. I'm coming in to help you, okay?"

After a short silence came her weepy voice again. "Okay."

He went in with the professionalism of a nurse. Mom was stuck on the toilet and couldn't move. And that is the day my husband wiped my mother's behind without hesitation, comment, or complaint.

So, this is what "for better or for worse" means, I thought.

When he brought her out, she was clean, clothed, and had her dignity intact. The EMTs took over from there and brought her to Wentworth-Douglass Hospital. While Dad and I talked to the doctors, Brent took Jin, who was getting whiny, to the family room and spread some puzzles and blocks on the floor for him. At some point that evening, Dad and I found ourselves in the hall, looking through the window at Brent on the floor with Jin.

"My god, honey," Dad said in a quavering voice. "He's completely selfless, you know?"

I leaned my head on Dad's shoulder and nodded silently.

"I mean, *completely* . . . ," he said, the words trailing off, his voice thick with emotion.

Mom had several tumors growing on her spinal cord, which were causing the partial paralysis. With treatment and years of PT, she did regain some mobility, but she couldn't drive anymore and never walked unassisted again. Her hands were also clumsy, so she could no longer paint silk, which was one of the artistic pursuits she had picked up in midlife and turned into a successful little side business she called Chance Designs. It was a deeply fulfilling counterpoint to her career in computer programming, and a cruel blow for her to give up.

That first night in the hospital, I sat on the edge of her bed, held one of her hands in mine, rested the other on her stomach, as she had so often done with me, and said what years of denial had never let me say. "I'm sorry, Mom." I hoped she knew how much bigger the feeling was than the words I was able to get out. *Sorry* just didn't even come close.

She nodded and her eyes welled. "I know. I'm sorry too, sweetie."

She stayed in the hospital in New Hampshire for a month until taking an eight-hour, $11,000 ambulance ride back to New York. With this episode behind us, Mom lived for another three years of her new normal.

MOTHERS DON'T DIE

Let me tell you about the last weekend we spent together, which also happened to be the last weekend of her life.

Mom went out on a high note, on the most beautiful, breezy, sun-drenched summer's day of the year, which then yielded to a clear night unusually full of stars. By some graceful turn of fate, Brent and I and the boys, now ages four and eighteen months, were able to spend five of Mom's last seven days on earth with her, unburdened by any knowledge of what was to come and doing the things that she loved best—talking about love, life, art, and politics; going to the Main Street festival in my hometown; enjoying pancake breakfasts with the boys; and going out for good Chinese on Saturday night.

After dinner Mom stood outside the China Garden, leaning against her walker in the parking lot while Brent and I, along with my brother, Rob, scurried in circles around the car trying to figure out how to get the door open. Rob had locked the keys in the car. As the seconds turned to minutes, I seemed to feel the weakness in Mom's legs behind me and began to fear she might fall over. I looked back and saw Dad, too, leaning heavily on his cane. My mind whirled through possibilities—get them back inside, find a seat, call AAA . . .

Just then, the proprietor of a small liquor store stepped outside and rattled the door handle to his shop to make sure it was secure. He turned around, noticed the commotion, and came over to find out what was happening. Seeing the pickle we were in, and the odd angles at which my parents were standing, he ran to his car, ransacked the trunk, and came jogging back with a wire coat hanger in one hand. "I've had this thing in my car for twenty years," he said, triumphant. "Never had to use it till now. My kids think I'm crazy."

Why was *this* the guy we encountered in an empty parking lot just when we were in exactly the kind of sticky spot that he was equipped to handle? I felt the buzz of what writer Elizabeth Gilbert calls Big Magic going on.

The man quickly untwisted the hanger, leaving a hook on one end, and slid the wire between the passenger-side window and the weather strip at its base. It only took a couple of tries to get the door open. Rob hopped into the driver's seat and zipped the car around in a wide curve, almost screeching to a stop in front of Mom and Dad.

We were rescued, and the liquor store owner had a twenty-year quirk vindicated. "Who's laughing now?" he might be saying somewhere to a skeptic of coat hangers in car trunks.

Mom was full of vim on this visit, something I didn't question because it felt good, and I wanted to enjoy it. In hindsight, though, it does seem this was the great burst that signals a dying star. As if something deep inside was motivating her to make this time count.

When we first walked into the house that Tuesday night, she'd straightened herself on the couch, eyes bright and sparkling. I noticed her cheeks were plump, pink, and pretty as could be as she took us all, one by one, into her arms from her seated position.

"Wow, you look so great, Mom," I said. My heart fluttered with optimism.

I could feel her body humming in my arms. All week she was up, dressed, and downstairs ready to go by eight o'clock every morning, delighting in the boys' antics, which were many and played out at her feet. The visit was rich and full, the best I can remember.

On Sunday afternoon we hugged goodbye on the couch, and she told me she'd see me at Thanksgiving. We made the long drive back to New Hampshire with stormy skies overhead, and at one point we drove right into a full double rainbow that arched across the sky, straddling the whole of I-90. It was my first double rainbow, and it was big and bright. Mom had rainbow stickers on her kitchen windows, she'd sew rainbow patches on my childhood clothes wherever I wore holes in them, and she bought rainbow sheets for my sister's and my beds. When the kids were born, she sent rainbow makers to hang in their nursery window—faceted crystals suspended from a small motor that cast tiny rainbows all over the room. She was, you could say, a rainbow *enthusiast*.

I tried to take a photo of the phenomenon but couldn't get it into the frame. I would have to tell her about it next time we talked.

And then . . . two days later she died. Brent had to fly to California the day before, so I was alone. I had picked up Jin and Seu at preschool and put them on the floor outside the kitchen while I began to cook. Seu whimpered about wanting his after-school snack, but before I could get it the phone rang. It was my sister-in-law, Susie. She said Mom had gone to the hospital with a fever and was having trouble breathing. I took that in for a moment, trying to reconcile it with what I had seen just thirty-six hours before.

"She's lost consciousness, Alexka," Susie continued, "and her organs are shutting down. Your dad is here, and Rob and I are here. She's peaceful. She's quiet. She's not in any pain." Susie hesitated a moment and said, "She probably won't make it through the night."

"Tonight?" I pushed an exhale through pursed lips the way I had learned to do in childbirth classes. "Okay . . . wow. Um . . ." My mind was both screaming and empty at the same time.

Seu whimpered more loudly, *"Snack!"*

"I thought you might like to say something to her," said Susie.

"Can she hear me?" I asked, stalling.

"I don't know. They say hearing is the last sense to go. I'll hold the phone up to her ear now, okay?"

And so I started talking into a silent telephone. My heart found the words for me, and when I could think of nothing else, I said, "I'm going to miss you so much, Mom. I love you. Goodbye."

Afterward, on the phone with other family members and pacing wildly from room to room, I heard Jin, who was only four, get a stool from the bathroom and go into the kitchen and open the fridge. Whereas this was normally the time of day I could count on him to bedevil and frustrate his baby brother, today he got out the jug of milk by himself, which he had never done before, and a sippy cup, then filled the cup, screwed the top back on, and brought it to Seu, along with a small bowl of Cheerios, no less.

Seu took the cup and Cheerios and quieted down, but then started worrying. "Why Mommy kwy?"

While I listened to my uncle losing his composure on the other end of the line in my right ear, I heard Jin with my left. "Seu. It's okay. It's okay. Mommy is just sad because she's losing her mommy tonight. Grandma Karen is dying."

I couldn't believe what I was hearing.

He went on, his voice getting more animated as he spoke. "But Seu, it's going to be okay because guess what? Grandma Karen is going to go live up in the sky and become a big, bright, shiny star, and then *we can all make a wish!*"

"I ahna mekka ish," said Seu, intrigued.

I looked at them over my shoulder. Jin sat on his heels, shaking his head at the ceiling. "I can't wait to see that star."

We had never talked about death in these, or any other, terms. What made Jin think she would go into the sky and become a star to wish upon? When I tucked him in that night, I told him I thought he had saved me that day, because now I could look for that star too. He had given me a different story to tell, a better story.

"Yeah," he said, squirming. "I saved you."

I didn't sleep that night until the wee hours. I searched through my phone's deleted messages on a hunch. There, buried deep within, was a message from Mom. Left several months earlier, it had happened to be *another* Tuesday night, and another eight o'clock hour, and the words seemed like something she would have said to me on this night too, if she could have. And so, in a way, I felt they really were her final words to me. She gave me a health update on a recent downturn, encouragement not to worry, a joyful focus on the boys and newly posted pictures of their latest silliness, and a farewell befitting far more than a Tuesday night voicemail: "Love you. And love to all the rest of . . . your . . . *marvelous* family. Bye-bye, hon. And much love."

At the memorial, which took place three weeks later, I learned many things about Mom that I had had no idea about. How did I not know that she had qualified for the 1976 Olympics in fencing, but didn't go because it was too expensive and, presumably, because she had three-year-old me at home to take care of? Why didn't she ever say anything about it? And why had I never asked? I knew she had fenced in college, and I remember going to the gym with her and watching her swordfights, as I called them—but Olympic qualifiers? Another woman told the story of how she and Mom went on a cross-country road trip and got to laughing so hard in Texas that they had to pull to the side of the road until they could see through their tears again. *Mom went on road trips?* Other people stood and talked of her almost as their personal Angel of Mercy. Even her physical therapists were there, wanting to talk about her gumption and attitude and good humor since she had fallen ill again in New Hampshire. People like her were the reason they did what they did. Mom's reach was broad, I realized. Her touch, loving and light.

I also reflected on her resilience that day. I had learned so much from Mom's quiet grace in the face of relentless adversity, about how to deal with my own hardship in losing her. This was her gift to me. I resolved to face forward and outward. As Mom always had.

Even so, I couldn't speak her name or hear her voice for a year after she died. I listened to that voicemail one time, then carefully put it away. In truth, I couldn't let myself think about her, which became its own source of pain for me. Shutting my grief up in a box and stashing it in the deepest, darkest corners of my heart had unwittingly shut me *away* from her. *She doesn't deserve that,* I thought to myself. But what I did not yet understand was that *neither did I.*

POT OF GOLD

The following August, my nephew, Michael, and his family flew in from Oregon; my niece, Stacey, and her family came up from Connecticut; Rob and Susie drove Dad up from New York; and we all met at a lake house in Vermont to celebrate Dad's ninety-ninth birthday and to remember Mom on the first anniversary of her death. It was a healing time for me, but a bittersweet one. Mom lived for family, and I felt keenly what she was missing. It was also hard to see Dad so old and alone. On the other hand, I couldn't remember the last time all the families were together in one place, and it was a great opportunity for the grandchildren and great-grandchildren to get to know each other again, and for Dad to survey his legacy. There was a lot of laughter.

On the twenty-third, which was the day Mom died the previous year, I stood out in the front yard, which served as a promontory overlooking the lake, and watched Brent and Jin sitting on a floating platform out toward the middle of the water. Seu, who was still too small to paddle-kick the inner tube out there with the others, came trundling behind me with a pair of binoculars, wanting to see Jin. I was filled with a sense of well-being.

For the first time in a year, I let my thoughts fall and rest on Mom, and I spoke to her in my mind. *Was there ever a person who deserved a peaceful send-off more than you?* I asked. *I think you won that prize fair and square, Mom, and deserved it more than anyone I can think of. Dad turned ninety-nine, you know, and we've had a beautiful week. I'm so sorry you aren't here to see it. It's the first time I can feel we are all going to be okay. I know we'll continue to lead rich, rewarding, and productive lives—living, loving, laughing, doing . . . It just won't be the same without you.*

Jin's voice yanked me from my reverie.

"Mom-my!" echoed across the surface of the lake. My gaze snapped to where he was standing in bare feet and an oversized life jacket, with one arm pointing out in front of him.

"Looook! A rainbow!"

A chill ran down my spine and out to all my extremities. Indeed, there was not just one rainbow, but two—*another* full double rainbow, this one brighter, more vivid, and closer than I had ever seen or imagined possible. It had appeared out of nowhere in the blink of an eye, and it looked almost close enough to touch.

Even more remarkable, both arcs landed *in the water* a few yards from the platform where Jin was hopping around, screaming in wonder. Brent and Jin were sitting at the end of a rainbow. I, for one, hadn't known that a rainbow's end was a real thing. I thought the physics of rainbows probably just made that an imaginary exercise. But here we were—the lake, the lake house, our family, and I—we were all literally at the end of a rainbow. I was standing in my own pot of gold.

Again I tried to take a photo, but I needed my wide-angle lens. I weighed the costs and benefits of sprinting to get it or staying rooted to the spot to soak in the wonder. I chose the latter.

CEREMONY

The lake house trip, and the appearance of the double rainbow, felt like the beginning of an integration ceremony for me—demonstrating for the Universe my commitment and budding ability to fold Mom's loss into a life that had new and unexpected outlines. I felt I was crossing a threshold. When I got home, I continued the ceremony by facing my yearlong avoidance of her memory head-on. I made a memorial video for Mom using the voicemail I had found the night she died. I also took out the plastic grocery bag bulging with pictures of her that I had gathered the year before but had never been able to look at until now. I spent the next several nights curating a photo album, where she now resides in her multifaceted glory—big sister, affectionate daughter and granddaughter, brilliant scholar, career woman, textile weaver, music lover, silk painter, Olympic-class fencer, world traveler, personal-boundary pusher, loving wife, doting mother, enthusiastic grandmother, and cheerful sojourner of life in sickness and in health.

While I worked on that photo album, I ended up answering some of my own questions. Why couldn't I have been the daughter for her that I was for Dad? *Well, that's easy,* I thought. Because I wasn't that person yet. Losing Mom was the fire that tempered my soul for that job. It toughened and strengthened me to step into the much more challenging role I would have to inhabit to see Dad to the end of *his* life. I could never have ensured that Dad had the end-of-life he deserved if I'd still been the girl who couldn't go into the bathroom to help my own mom.

In a way, then, for Dad's final years, my newfound ability to intervene on his behalf, to advocate for his needs and see them through, and the relationship that blossomed between us during that time were Mom's final gifts to us both.

"Thank you, Mom," I whispered to one of the album pages open before me. "I could never have faced this alone without you."

When I finished the album, I poured myself a glass of wine and flipped the book to the beginning to go through it page by page. Somewhere in the middle, I stumbled upon a pearl of wisdom for myself. *Mothers don't die.*

Jeez, I thought, looking at the pictures and recalling the old memories, *I don't feel like she's gone when I'm looking at these. She feels alive.*

This triggered a whole new set of questions, answers, and revelations. A small voice piped up in my head. *She feels alive in these pictures. Okaay . . . ,* it said, trying to draw me toward further logical conclusions. *Where is she still alive?*

"In my mind," I answered aloud.

And before she died? the voice continued. *Where was she alive for you then?*

"In my mind," I answered, my heart beginning to open.

Did anything change between then and now? the voice asked. *At all? Besides you telling yourself two different stories—"my mother is alive," and then, "my mother is dead"?*

"No, nothing has changed," I said.

Good, said the voice. *And doesn't that really mean that Mom lives in the place she has always lived? And you access her now in the day-to-day the same way you have always? And she hasn't gone anywhere?*

Many years later, in 2016, Year of the Monkey, I stumbled upon a video on The Work, by Byron Katie. It was called, almost unbelievably, *Fathers Don't Die.* In it, she takes an audience member, almost verbatim, through the conversation I'd had with myself over Mom's photo album in 2012. How is it possible that two such similar conversations happened independently, years and miles apart? My heart continued to open.

The Monkey hooted its delight above me.

Once again, I felt the buzz of Big Magic going on.

Can you feel it too?

CHAPTER 8

THE ROOM WHERE LOVE LIVES

Why am I here?

I am standing outside the wrought-iron gates of an eighteenth-century French château. The stone gateposts are covered in ivy—not the delicate green tendrils one imagines from fairy tales, but effusive foliage that almost completely disguises the true size and shape of the pillars it obscures.

Am I worthy of writing this book?

I have lost faith, and somehow have found myself at the gates of a French château.

In my mind's eye, I push the gate open and walk barefoot down the earthen drive leading to the front patio and entry door in the distance. The earth is hard-packed, with only small pebbles rolling free, easy for bare feet to walk on. The center line of grass pricks one foot, then another as I meander down the path. I remember that the Monkey says it's time to leave the beaten path.

Outside, in real life, it's a blustery March day, but here in my mind the air is warm and thick with the late-summer scent of baking meadow grass. I inhale deeply and feel my spirits rise. The saw-and-chirp of crickets fills the spaces between. My pace quickens as I break into a tiptoeing little trot, and soon I am passing a pear tree on my left, where I grab one of the fruits, take a bite, and begin to spin in circles, arms flung wide, smiling skyward. To my surprise, my spinning picks me up off the ground, *leaving the beaten path*, and sends me shooting into the air, where I explode like fireworks into a shower of sparkles, feeling one with everything.

From there I rush hither, thither, and yon like a joyful wind, wrapping ribbons of air in my wake—around the pear tree right to its crown, down the driveway, up above the château, and back again. In my bodiless state, I look down and see my own sparkles falling to earth, where they rearrange themselves in the form of my body again, reconstituting me from the toes up, pausing at the heart to reinforce it, making it pulse and glow like a gem catching the light—first red for life, and then white for healing.

I am now at the front steps, which feel warm from the day's sun, and I enter the front door, which stands ajar. Large flagstones pave the floor, and the château windows are flung wide, allowing breezes and beneficent smells to billow and brush by. Although the château is practically a ruin, there are floral arrangements everywhere. I look to my left, down a hallway to another entrance, and see an old man with a wheelbarrow silhouetted against the light from the open door. I sense other people about as well. Not servants, but caretakers perhaps, and they are part of what makes this place feel like home.

I turn to my right and skip up a wide, winding stone staircase with curved wrought-iron handrails. Windows and a skylight let in bright sunshine, a column of white light that illuminates the stairwell from above, making it look enchanted from ground level. I take the stairs to the second floor and slow my pace to stroll down the hallway to my left. The corridor is naturally lit by the tall window at the far end and similar windows running at regular intervals down the right side, throwing grid patterns across the passage floor. On the left there are tall, wooden double doors, each set leading to a different room.

I come to a stop partway down the hall and take a moment to look at the doors' intricate carvings. They are vaguely floral in nature, with a large heart carved in the middle of each door. Hearts are also on the brass doorknob, which is more of a lever, with one larger heart on the lever's central knob and a smaller one on the curlicue at the end. *This must be the room where love lives.*

I push the handle down and walk into a room that is a combination of ruin and romance. The walls and floors are largely bare, but with numerous plaster patches. A luxurious Turkish carpet has been flung across the floor at an angle beneath an open window that overlooks meadows of goldenrod and asters, bluish mountain peaks in the distance.

An eighteenth-century bed frame with a mattress covered in colorful layers of textiles and pillows sits at a diagonal to the window, on top of the carpet. A delicate antique writing desk is against the wall between two windows, with its drawers and cubbies begging to be gone through. A tufted stool upholstered in the palest blush silk is pulled out to just the right spot for sitting.

I notice several sheets of gorgeous paper on the desk, and resting on them is my current favorite pen. In the last year, with my growing reliance on journaling to soothe and regulate my nervous system, my lifelong enthusiasm for flashy pens has begun to take an obsessive hold over me.

As if a pen could save a person.

Mightn't it, though?

A wooden cup holding several others is off to the right. Upon closer inspection, I recognize all the writing implements as being pens I have owned over my lifetime. As I push them around in the cup, I see two that Dad had presented to me with some amount of ceremony, as if to say he had been waiting for the right time to do so, and after long observation had concluded the time was now. It felt like I had earned something special when he gave them to me, although what, I was not quite sure.

He gave me the first one when I was about ten. It was a silver Cross ballpoint pen, the kind you can get for a few bucks at a Hallmark shop, but it came in a box bedded in blue velvet that felt very special to open. It shone in the light, and he demonstrated how you had to twist it to reveal the tip. The second one he gave me in high school, a Waterman fountain pen that was sleek and black with straight sides and gold accents.

I look at these pens and *know* why I am here. I came to this meditation wondering if I had the ability, the right, to write this book and tell stories about Dad and the family, and in my vision, Dad reminded me that it was he who gave me my first pen. It was a gift that said he knew I had something to say, that it was worth writing down, and worth reading.

I sit at the desk and begin to write, and the ink flows easily from the nib.

Dear Dad, I love you.

And it writes back.

I love you too, kid.

I sit back and thrill in the magic of it. The year's Monkey softly hoots its wonder and curiosity with me. I begin to write in earnest. Although I cannot read any of the words, I pull back and can see myself at the desk. I watch the words flow in through the top of my head, across my newly fortified heart, down my arm, out the tip of the pen, and onto the page. The words flow in abundance and with ease, and as each new page fills, it slides to the ground, a cascading waterfall of paper rising around my feet on the stone floor.

CHAPTER 9

GHOSTWRITER

It was a few days after Christmas, and I was helping Dad in the upstairs bathroom with his dentures. The room was unbearably hot. Between that and the anxiety of experiencing role reversal with a parent, I had begun to feel a prickling sensation in my underarms and at my hairline. I was overcome with an urge to flee.

Dad was seated on a stool in front of the sink, his robe falling open on his emaciated frame. His hair, which had been perfectly coiffed for over a century, was now as mussed as a newborn kitten's, the remains of a nasty hematoma from earlier that year still visible at his temple. When at long last his teeth were in and I was trying to help him stand, he couldn't get good purchase on the counter and could neither shift his weight forward enough nor bring his legs back enough to stand.

He collapsed in a heap on the stool, exhaled sharply, and shook his head in disgust. "I might as well be dead," he muttered.

My heart constricted. I had never heard him talk like that. Even after Mom died, his true love and wife of forty-five years, he had almost immediately taken to saying of the kids, "Golly! I hope I can stick around long enough to see these boys grow, you know?"

I sank down to his level to hug him and told him I hated the stupid indignities of old age too. "But Dad," I said, steadying my voice and wrapping my arms around his torso, encouraging him to grab my neck while I lifted him to his feet, just as he had done with me on those *Captain Kangaroo* mornings so many years ago, "just remember, where there is love, there is life."

"Where'd you hear that?" he said.

"I don't know," I said. "I just made it up."

"Where there is love, there is life . . . ," he murmured under his breath. "Okay." And about a minute later, "Gee, honey, you make this old age thing livable, you know?"

Rattled, that evening I seized on a new mission. I snapped on a light, a naked bulb screwed into a ceramic wall socket at the base of the stairs, and started down to the basement of my childhood home, intending the impossible. But the Monkey knows nothing is impossible. Its curiosity and cheek led me into the musty depths. *This way.*

A BASKET OF WAR LETTERS

I wanted to find a letter I had last seen some thirty years before, that Dad had written to Gretchen from the Indian or Burmese jungle during World War II. He had signed it *Earl and Gus*, and next to Gus's name was a tiny, human-looking handprint no bigger than my thumb. It belonged to a small *monkey*, perhaps a young macaque, who'd been separated from his mother and had accompanied Dad in his tent and around camp in the China-Burma-India (CBI) theater. He liked to eat bits of banana from Dad's hand and ride on his shoulder.

The letter came from a basket filled with the many letters he'd written on thin, crinkly paper—now yellow and brittle, often water-stained, and some still in envelopes with red stripes on the edges and official-looking government stamps emblazoned on the front. At ten, when I had found the basket, I was only mildly interested in the other letters. I noted them, but wanted principally to find out more about who this Gus character was. Now, at forty-two, I decided I needed to find that letter and share it with Dad to lift his spirits. But by god, I knew enough of what lay ahead that I now needed to find all those other letters too. For me.

The erstwhile fondue palace of my parents' basement was now a

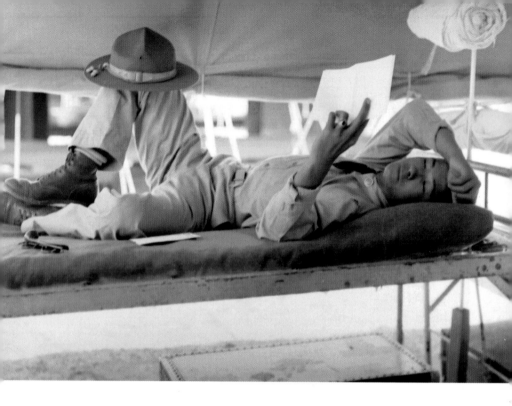

dark and musty catchall for half a lifetime of junk. I stepped gingerly on piles of scrap wood from forgotten projects and around toppled piles of books and magazines. Dad had the complete set of some fifty years of *Playboy* he thought might be worth something someday, and Mom had the same for *National Geographic*. Bolts of silk from Mom's silk-painting business, Chance Designs (as in a *Chan* who has left the beaten path and *chanced* on something new), spilled dustily from plastic shelving erected helter-skelter, the ruins of several failed attempts to stem the rising tide of mayhem. Meanwhile, her sewing station had just space enough for a chair and a machine, sitting in the eye of a hurricane of paisley, calico, and checkered gingham dating to the last time she used it.

Next to this were Dad's old hip waders and fishing baskets draped on a jerry-rigged coatrack that leaned to one side. Having discovered his impressive tackle box when I was about eight, I was most taken with the artificial lures, gummy worms that stuck moistly to my fingers, and the colorful and iridescent crank and spinner baits made to mimic minnows. They looked like toys and smelled wonderfully industrial.

I did not recognize the real treasure inside, however, which was

OPPOSITE: *Letter from home, Burma, 1942–1945* ABOVE: *His and hers Corvettes in the 1970s, the heyday of my parents' social lives*

Dad's delicate handiwork in fly tying. He tied fur, feathers, threads, and other materials onto hooks to mimic the look of a fish's natural prey, which could be anything from insects to crustaceans, worms, or minnows, or even amphibians or vegetation. Because each fly was tied for a target species, this activity required that he know a fair bit about his quarry, its behaviors and quirks, and how it went about being in the world. It required imagination and getting inside the head of an elusive creature. There was strategy and creative problem-solving involved. In short, fly-fishing was made for Dad. And although the war turned him off guns and hunting forever, he never lost his taste for standing in a cold stream and casting a line out into the current.

Dad used to say, "When I go fishing, the fish just crawl up on the bank and open their gills for my string. They know it's no use to resist."

A collection of the most popular home exercise equipment re-called more optimistic days too. There was a rowing machine under a good two millimeters of dust, a NordicTrack with slack lines and skis askew, and a five-spring chest expander that no one in the family could expand, and somewhere I knew there was a ThighMaster.

This was not the first time I had tried to find the letter from Gus. Over the years I had searched for the basket several times. Dad seemed

ABOVE: *Fishing with sister-in-law Merle in halcyon prewar days, ca. 1935* OPPOSITE, LEFT: *Dad and Gretchen after the war, 1945* RIGHT: *They were married for 26 years.*

to neither know nor care where it could be. He was never one to dwell on the past, and had a most infuriating way, I thought, of looking and moving forward, until the very end when his early memories were his most vivid. Which was why my current intention to find these letters seemed doomed from the start. I cannot explain it, though. I simply knew that for the first time in fifteen years I was going to look for Gus again, and I had a hunch that here in the Year of the Monkey, I was going to find him.

And sure enough, there in the fondue-palace-turned-domestic-landfill I found the basket of letters exactly as I remembered it— inexplicably, indeed unbelievably, sitting out in the open on the edge of a waggle-legged side table that should have been thrown out in 1979. The lights were blown in the back party room, so my flashlight fell on the basket like a spotlight. I was struck with the amusing image of the singing frog from Looney Tunes tap dancing and kicking his way across the stage, shouting, "Hello, my baby, hello, my honey, hello, my ragtime gaaalll," and then falling into a mute lump as soon as anyone looked at him. The basket was like that—mum, but heavy with song. An invitation. A prince in frog's clothing.

I did not find the Gus letter, which had been separated from the basket . . . by ten-year-old me? . . . until over a year later. It was not as magical as I remembered it to be. *Never mind, he got me what I needed. Thanks, Gus.*

As with the tackle box, the real treasure lay hiding in plain sight. There were three hundred or so letters, starting on November 25, 1941, with a young man bursting at the seams to legally marry his

girlfriend, who was White, and to find a church willing to do it. Dad and Gretchen would have to marry in Washington, DC, because their home state of Georgia was one of many that still had punishing anti-miscegenation laws. His letters proceed to the bombing of Pearl

Harbor two weeks before the wedding; document his call into active duty, throwing everything into question; and then go on to follow his entire career in the China-Burma-India theater, tracking his rise from Second Louie, as he called lieutenant, to major in the US Army. At each advancement he promoted Gretchen to the rank above himself in hilarious and tender fashion. When arguing, she would sometimes either fire him or demote herself to Private Gretchen or Buck Private Gretchen, and tension would ease.

Who knew all the wonderful ways there are to begin a letter?

Dearest Girl

Beloved

Dearest Sweetheart

Dear Little Bluebell with Oak Roots

Dear Wife in Whom I Am Well Pleased

Dear Synthesis of Sugar and Spice and All Things Nice

Hello, Beetle Brow

Dear Little and Also Other Woman

Dear Rag, Bone, and Hank o' Hair (1942–1945)

Or to end one?

I'm tired tonight so I'll tell you I love you in geometry.

Yesterday < I love you < tomorrow. 4-13-1944

Over time, I digitized and organized the letters by theme. Alternately humorous, erudite, philosophical, petulant, and lyrical, they speak in remarkable detail about his experiences in the war. They include shipboard life on the way to India, and the quirky and inimitable Chan family as experienced by Gretchen, who went to visit them after he deployed. She described, in one letter to Dad, the way T'ai Peng "nearly pops a button off his vest every time your name is mentioned," and shook her head at what she called Dad's "terroristic antics as a child."

Darling, you must have been the neighborhood brat! Yes, I know I would have loved you anyway, and I always shall.

Dad warned Gretchen of his father's "unsound Chinese ideas," and about the laundry.

You must not pay any attention to the confidentials of Merle, Eunice, or any of the rest of the family. Like the six blind men of Hindustan who went to see an elephant, each is partly right in his biased and extremely narrow viewpoint, but all are wrong. I, alone, of all the tribe have a clear picture of the situation. 3-15-1943

There are exquisite descriptions of the local wildlife and scenery in India and Burma, where Dad slept to the nightly serenade of jackals and hyenas, shot a bear, saw an orchid and a pangolin for the first time, and was proud to be the only one of the company able to identify them. He described native peoples, customs, cultures, and religions. The officers also had numerous civilian personal servants, each for a specific job. Dad's bearer, or valet, was especially keen to serve, which sometimes annoyed Dad.

I have to fight him off when I dress. He wants to dress me!

The valet was also a very great pilferer.

My bearer steals like hell and there's no way I can catch him. Every time I discover something missing, he protests, "Nay, sahib, nay!" to my accusing finger. 5-12-1943

He described remarkable examples of ingenuity and resourcefulness. He once made a photographic enlarger from downed airplane parts and a headlight from an abandoned Japanese vehicle, and built

an outboard motor for a small boat they had acquired out of engine parts scattered about the jungle. He discussed questions of race and interracial marriage in American society, and where there might be a place for him and Gretchen within it, and the Chinese soldiers he was charged with training in methods and weapons of the West, but who personally amused, frustrated, and offended him, making it clear that whatever he might be seen as at home, he was not Chinese. He found his Chinese machinist hiding up a tree one day, avoiding a welding job he didn't feel like doing, leading Dad to take an axe and start chopping down the tree, pretending not to hear the man as

TOP: *Doodle of a bathing station he set up in July of 1944* ABOVE: *On their scavenged boat on the Irrawaddy River* OPPOSITE: *Dad carries a "bullet with his name on it" as a protective talisman.*

he yelled for him to stop because he was on his way.

Ever a jokester, his teasing could be both funny and off-color.

See if you can list all the things adorable you gave to me to wear. Ring, knife, locket, Chiquita [a pipe], wallet,

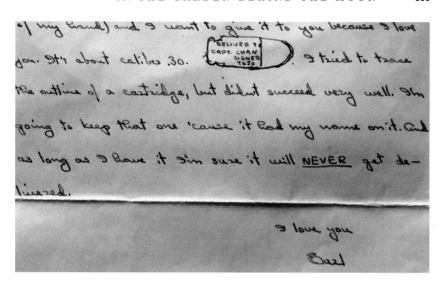

pen, cigarette lighter. What a rich prize I'd make if killed or captured! 3-24-1944

Base is a madhouse, full of rules, red tape, and alternately dust and mud. I'm glad that my work has carried me far ahead of all that. I know that scene by heart, and if you could look around the bend, you'd probably see a disgruntled me in my Jeep hoping to get started before that tottering tree on one side could be cut through and felled right smack on top of me. I still contend that the Japs are only 3rd on the list of dangerous people. First are the Chinese engineers who fell trees with unnerving accuracy across the road. . . . It's none of their affair if you happen to be in the path of the falling tree. And they never yell, "Tim-bu-u-uh!" Second on the list is the Air Corps trying to hit people with food. 4-28-1944

The letters are full of doodles and hilarious, philosophical, and gut-churning anecdotes about freeing Korean Comfort Women from an abandoned Japanese post, burying Japanese dead only to have them wash right out again in the monsoons and choke the air with rot, and Chinese execution methods, to name just a few. He describes a giddy couple of weeks on leave in Darjeeling, where one day, to the surprise of no one, a long-lost someone from home—a nurse and bosom pal of his sister's—recognized him and dragged him by the ear away from some shenanigans he was into in the hotel lobby and took him to the hotel bar, where they drank and reminisced the night away. And then, as his time to go home drew near, there was an increasing sense of dread about what he had to lose.

> *Be sure of one thing, Beloved. I'm through setting up too close to the fighting. It's too close to time for me to go home, and I don't want to be eliminated at the last moment. You see, I love you. And I want to see you again.* 8-31-1944

The letters end with his final discharge in February 1945. After the war, based on a review of his wartime activities, he was promoted

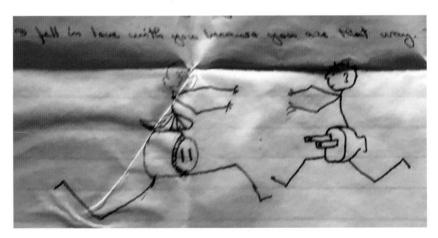

to colonel, and in 2021, along with other Chinese Americans, he was awarded a posthumous Congressional Gold Medal for extraordinary service despite the racism and discrimination they faced at home.

A BOX OF NEGATIVES

The letters were the icing on a cake that had been baking for almost a year. Brent had gone into the basement following a whim of his own and came back up with a box of four-by-five-inch negatives. No one knew what they could be—not even Dad, who, predictably, didn't figure they were much. He had been an amateur photographer all his life, and also dabbled in professional work, doing some weddings and family portraits here and there as well as commercial food photography.

I had seen the eight-by-ten-inch color negatives of Shelly Brand sausage and smoked meats, and Mother Goose first-prize meat food products, which surfed the wave of America's post-war love affair with processed foods. There were candied-looking bone-in pork chops decorated with maraschino cherries and cored apple slices, liverwurst finger sandwiches with olives and grim-looking parsley sprigs, bologna slices, deviled eggs, and cut radishes stacked in strange tiers and towers thought to be appetizing in the day. Breakfasts were especially amusing. Hearty *OPPOSITE: Dad imagines a happy homecoming at the war's end. May 12, 1944* sausage-and-egg platters were pictured with canned pineapple slices and cherries arranged into alien faces with bug eyes that made it look like your breakfast might be coming to eat you.

But this box contained much smaller black-and-white negatives, many curled at the edges, some stuck together, with visible water damage and mold spots throughout. I took the box from Brent's arms. How could anything important have escaped our family's collective consciousness until now? How could Mom, at the very least, have not known about everything important in this house, or gone to the grave without telling me about it? *More junk to sort through.*

I peered and strained at the negatives all that holiday week, holding them up to the light, but I couldn't make out much. I saw figures, and some hints at good-natured chicanery underway. Enough to pique my interest, but only in passing.

By the time I was in kindergarten, Dad was a sharply dressed older gentleman who often looked fifteen to twenty years younger than he was, but a senior citizen nevertheless. I had never seen a picture of him as a young man, except for his 1940s army portrait, the wooden stoicism of which evoked neither an individual nor a life.

In fact, I believed Dad had no early pictures of himself or the family. It was the Deep South in the early twentieth century, after all, and the family was large and often poor—six kids and a dozen or so employees living off the income from one Chinese laundry. And if my

ABOVE: *The first three Chinese children born in Georgia (L to R, youngest to oldest: Gladys Geraldine (a.k.a. Gerald, or G.G.), Sandor, and Archie* OPPOSITE: The Smiling Man. *The first negative pulled from the box.*

grandparents did take a picture here or there of the older children in Chinese robes with tasseled headgear, by the time the fifth and then sixth came along, who had time for costumes and keepsakes? Dad— Robert Earl Chan, fifth child—did not even get a Chinese middle name like all his older siblings. It was as though my grandparents had just

thrown up their hands in defeat . . . and with still one more child to come!

The first negative I pulled from the box was of a smiling man. Who could it be? A friend of the family? Some local townsman? I didn't even have a good sense of the time period I was looking at. Nevertheless I took the box with me when we left from our Christmas visit to see Dad, and when we got home, I pulled out my photo equipment—a macro lens, light box, and Photoshop—and went to work on the smiling man first.

When I had the file in the photo viewer and inverted the negative to a positive, the air left my lungs in a great *whoosh*. Champagne bubbles rose in my chest and tickled my spine.

I would know that smile anywhere. It was the one that had beamed down on me since my birth. No longer just an attractive, well-groomed older gentleman, this radiant being smiling at me from across the century was Dad. The smile reassured me because, while the man sitting upstairs was tenuously tethered to a life that was waning, this was a person fully immersed in and saturated with life force.

And it was just the first negative of over five hundred more waiting in that box. Brent had found it at the peak of my dread, around the time that the Tai Sui had first clapped eyes on me. I knew by this time, without being able to speak it aloud, that Dad had about a year left. I was only off by eight weeks.

And then that box appeared, revealing decades of a life lived out loud—boldly, beautifully, imaginatively, and with great good humor. Pictures ranged from his early childhood in the 1910s, being homeschooled in the segregated South of Savannah, Georgia, to the

CLOCKWISE FROM TOP LEFT: *College capers in "dentistry" with a co-ed. Sandor, second oldest, and his wife, Merle. Sin Fah, fourth oldest. G.G., third oldest, in Forsyth Park.*

bombastic capers of his college years, to a young soldier in love, to the sobering and hardening effects of war, to the work of reentering civilian society with the pluck and resilience needed to either pick up again on abandoned dreams . . . or find new ones.

I worked feverishly, consumed for months digitizing and converting the box of negatives. Fifty years' worth of stories and memories. Looking at the pictures as they came to life on my screen, stories I had heard since childhood began to tumble through my mind. I saw the personalities I knew so well, writ young. Uncle Sandor, the funny and gentle one, with his wife on his lap and holding a bottle of Coke, surreptitiously flipping Dad the finger. G.G., saucy and pensive even then. What lyrical language, what stories, poems, and visions might have been spooling through her head, sitting there in Forsyth Park?

And this must be Sin Fah, known to all as Sinnie. Selfish, vain, and a reported kleptomaniac in later years. Relations between her and Dad, her younger brother by just over a year, were irreparably strained. It had probably started in infancy, with the younger siblings all jockeying in a kind of zero-sum game for the family's love and attention. It only got worse when Sinnie stole one of Dad's high school essays and submitted it to a writing competition with her own name attached, winning first prize with it. When Dad learned what she had done and went to his parents, demanding they rectify the situation and set the record straight, they refused. Why? I imagine they were as appalled as Dad was. But there was no security for people of color in Georgia at that time. Maybe they calculated that the brouhaha of a public retraction of such a prize would not only bring shame on the family but also put an unwelcome target on their home. Dad, being fourteen years old, had no such insight. He could only perceive the injustice, not the danger. Things escalated with his father about it until T'ai Peng hauled back and slapped the indignant teen clean across the face. Dad ran away that night, sleeping rough in the parks around the city for three nights until a policeman rounded him up in the rain and brought him home. His parents opened the door to see their son hanging by the shirt collar in the policeman's hand and drenched to the bone. He entered the house sullenly and no one spoke of the incident again. But Dad never forgot what Sinnie did.

Sin Fah told you I was the pampered pet of the lot. She lied (as usual), he wrote to Gretchen in December 1941. *For it wasn't until I showed determination to remain at* [Georgia] *Tech that I got any support, and that was moral, not financial.*

Aunt Sinnie—I didn't expect her to be quite so lovely. Or to look so much like me.

Most moving was a little girl I couldn't place at first, always standing alone or to the side, with dimples and a close-lipped smile I could relate to. It was the smile of a girl wanting to please and to belong, but not necessarily knowing how to. And maybe, too, of a girl with a rich inner life barely guessed at by outsiders.

By a quick mental process of elimination, I determined it must have been my aunt Bernice, the littlest of the bunch, who had died tragically of diabetes as a young woman and whose picture I had never seen.

So this was the dear little girl who had put mosquito netting over her head and walked into the living room one night announcing that a *boo*-tiful lady had walked into the room.

At this, Sandor had remarked, "Where's the beautiful lady?" and Bernice had torn the mosquito netting from her head in a fury and stomped out. Dad still stewed and frowned over this moment as an old man, for he had a tender spot for children and liked to help them shine.

Sandor also liked to tease Bernice by zapping at her food with his long musician's fingers. *"Zap!"* he would cry, flicking at her meal with all ten digits, which he had told her magically rendered it inedible.

Grandma Annie berated him for putting the baby off her food when so many in this world go hungry, then turned back to the stove, only for Sandor to zap the food again, this time with silent, exaggerated enunciation, eyes wide and brows arching to his hairline.

Bernice, sixth and last child

Bernice wailed, Grandma Annie

spun around, and Sandor found out once again that the jig was up. At least until dinner.

So this was Bernice. Poor sweetie. No easy thing to be the youngest of six, and shy in a family of showmen. *I see you, Aunt Bernice. I know.*

Dad was a rapscallion. When he got sick of the church ladies stopping by and taking up his mama's time, he planted whoopee cushions to scare them off in a cloud of humiliation. The thicker-skinned ones who returned might have been treated to the theatrics of his throwing a little chair down the back stairs and pretending to cry as if it had been he who'd taken a tumble. Annie and the church ladies would come running. Looking now at a picture of him sitting on a chair too small for him, with his dog, Tricky, in his arms, I couldn't help but wonder, *Was this the chair?*

And here was Uncle Archie, the steady, responsible firstborn, standing alone by the laundry's new car. All the family was dressed in their Sunday best. It was no small thing for the laundry to move from horse-and-cart delivery to automobile.

TOP: *Dad, fifth oldest, with his dog, Tricky, possibly in the Chair of Ill Repute*
BOTTOM: *Archie, oldest child, with the first family car, ca. 1923*

This must have been the car that Dad, at the age of ten, drove away in while Archie smoothed his clothes and walked up to a customer's front porch to deliver a pile of pressed shirts wrapped in brown paper and tied neatly with string. As Dad told it, when he came around the block and saw the customer standing agape in the doorway and Archie running from the house with raised fist, he decided to just *hit the gas and keep going.* When he came around the block a second time, Archie

ABOVE: *Boy Scouts. Dad eventually made Eagle Scout.* OPPOSITE: *Dad, ca. age 15, outside the laundry*

had switched tactics. He waved, tamped his hands in the air in a "slow down" motion, and smiled. Dad, figuring it was safe, brought the car to a halt and watched his big brother stride round to the driver's seat, open the door, and offer him a hand down.

"Are you okay?" Archie asked.

"Never better!" said Dad, beaming, whereupon Archie gave him two slaps, forehand and backhand, right across the face.

"*Whap! Whap!*" Dad would say, mimicking the sound, and laughing loudly at each retelling.

Another picture showed him with his Boy Scout troop, his bandanna tied jauntily over one shoulder. To me, he looked like a chocolate chip in a bowl of vanilla ice cream, someone you might expect in 1920s Savannah, Georgia, to be an outsider in the group, or not allowed in the group at all. But this was the kid who had enough charisma to get a gang of those boys together to electrify the scoutmaster's toilet seat. *He looks like a nice enough man,* I thought. *What must he have made of little Robert Earl?*

This would have been around the age Dad started his paper route. He came in as a boy of twelve or thirteen and ended up replacing the adult who had held the position before, mainly because he knew how to rake the money in. He soon had a legion of newspaper boys working for him, from whom he collected his own share of their earnings

in return for his managerial skills. So, this was the wee Newspaper Don of Savannah. One advantage he had was that he was not afraid to deliver to minority communities. He had grown up around the Black people in the laundry, and because they were mostly lifetime employees, he came to know some of them quite well. The laundry foreman, a man named Charlie, even bought Dad his first BB gun.

Dad said the Black and Jewish folks on his paper route, located mostly on either side of West Broad Street, took a shine to him. Had anyone at that time ever seen a Chinese boy before? Likely not. The Chan kids were the first Chinese American children born in the whole state of Georgia. And he was cute, charming, and best of all, fearless. The Black and Jewish residents were great customers, he said. They always paid on time, gave tips, and were grateful for the service. He laughed and said you never could get the White people to pay up.

More negatives came out of the box and leapt to life on my screen. Here was the mischievous teenager—just look at the rakish twinkle!— who flouted Miss Cubage's Latin homework assignment and composed a poem on the fly instead.

Darkibus nightibus,
lightibus norem,
raggibus gatepost
britchibus torem.

Not the kind of poetry, perhaps, his father and grandfather had been feted for. But he was so brilliant and charming about not doing the work, all he got was a giggle and an extension. Charm sometimes worked at home too, when he swept his mama off her feet to distract her from chastising him. He danced her around the room, her feet dangling off the floor, and waited for her anger to turn to mortification

and then peals of helpless laughter.

"Whatchya gonna do, Mama?" *Step, slide, step, twirl.* "How you gonna stay mad now?"

"Robert Earl!" she'd cry. "Put me *down*! Do you hear? *Stop this!*"

He always had his arm around her in these pictures. Here was a boy who loved his mom.

Soon enough, I was elbow deep in the college years. Here he was in a dorm room, lying in bed and clutching a pillow to his chest with a smile of dreams fulfilled, on what appears to be his first day on campus at Georgia Tech. WELCOME! reads a banner on the wall above his bed. Who could know, looking at this cheerful picture, all that he'd had to do to get there? He had worked for two years after high school graduation to earn money so he could be the first in the family to go to college, and periodically he had to take semesters off to work and earn more to continue.

He'd had his paper route, but that alone wouldn't cover tuition and lodging, and not every job was open to him in the segregated South. He was a lifeguard at Savannah Beach during the summers, scanning the waves for riptides and silent flailing. He waited tables for a day, but that ended when a slick customer trying to impress a girl snapped his fingers at Dad and gave him a nickel tip, winking at his date as he did so. Dad flicked the nickel back at the man and said, "Keep it. Get yourself a haircut and a shoeshine with it." The date laughed, and in the eruption that ensued, Dad untied his apron, bundled it in one hand, and threw it on the floor of the establishment as he strode out the front door.

ABOVE: Dad and his mother, Annie OPPOSITE: Freshman at Georgia Tech (colorized by the author), ca. 1933

He had picked up boxing as an adolescent. When he was in fifth or sixth grade, he would pass the fire station every day walking home from school. That was always where a gang of bullies caught up to him. They liked to kick him in the seat, hit him in the back of the head, or knock his books from his arms. One day, they pushed him to the

ground. An Irish fireman had been watching the scene unfold day after day from the stoop where he sat, smoking his stub-stemmed clay pipe.

"Why don't you fight back, lad?" he finally asked.

Dad picked himself up and frowned, fixing his hair and rubbing a sore spot on his arm. "My mama says it's wrong to fight," he said, catching the Irishman's eye.

"Jesus, Mary, and Joseph," said the Irishman, grabbing the pipe from between his teeth. "Sometimes it's wrong *not* to fight, boy. Come by the station tomorrow and I'll show you how to pan 'em out. Those lads won't trouble you again."

Dad showed an aptitude with the Irishman, and sure enough, one day he panned the bullies out flat. Eventually he joined a gym and began fighting in the local pro circuit under his gym name, Chino Chan. Asked in old age how he had stayed so pretty, he'd just shrug and grin like the cat that ate the canary. "Well, gee, I guess nobody could hit me." He was undefeated 33–0 when he hung up his gloves.

But there still wasn't enough money for college.

That was when the brothel earnings came in. Not everyone knows that the family laundry also cleaned the sheets for the local brothel. They were not the only client, of course. Many people came through the doors of the Willie Chin & Co. Laundry. Dad met Henry Ford there, as well as Juliette Gordon Low, founder of the Girl Scouts, who was a Savannah native. But they also did laundry for the brothel. When Dad was old enough not to just tag along with his brother Archie, he did the deliveries himself. When he arrived at the brothel doors, the girls would come running, calling out in their little singsong voices, "*Robbie!* Hello, Robbie! Girls, Robbie is here, come and say hello!"

They'd touch his cheek, tickle his nose with a handkerchief, ruffle his oiled and groomed hair. One might even tug at his hand, until the madam arrived and bustled her way through the gaggle, shooing the girls in all directions. "Get back!" she'd snap. "Leave him alone. Can't you see that's a *nice boy*? Hello, Robbie, thank you so much. Here . . . for your trouble."

"She was a truly decent woman," Dad said to me once.

As the years passed and Dad found that he had finally saved up enough for his first semester's tuition at Georgia Tech, he made his last delivery to the brothel. The madam wished him well, gave him a hug, and handed him an enormous tip. (How much? "A lot," Dad said.)

"This town's too small for you, Robbie," she said. "The world awaits."

I noted in his college pictures that he was always surrounded by a group of friends, a gadfly engaging in every kind of socializing and tomfoolery, from head shavings and food contests to cow milkings and picnics, in heroic poses and in humorous scenarios. Ever the popular novelty, he was the only brown-skinned person there, but he was always front and center, frequently with young women in tow. I discovered that he was a founder of the college camera club, which would explain some of the experimental shots like artistic silhouettes and double exposures I found. He played piano well, and gigged campus dances and parties with a band he pulled together called Robbie Chan and the Georgia Five, which made the campus gossip column frequently.

There were also lots of photos of a serious student hard at work—the sleek-haired young chemist in coveralls standing at a Bunsen burner with his flasks, beakers, and ampoules, or at it all night in box-

OPPOSITE: *Dad majored in chemical engineering.* ABOVE: *Dad, sister-in-law Merle, and Sandor appearing to be up to no good.*

ers and dress shoes, a folding rule and pencil in hand. It was all so over-the-top and cinematic, and . . . moving. I was heartened to learn his college dreams had not simply come true, as I had always known, but had done so in such an effusive and joyful manner. That part of the equation I had had no knowledge of before finding the box of negatives. *Go, Dad. I'm so happy for you.*

But then came the war. Was I mistaken? Had the boyish twinkle hardened, just slightly?

After the war, I saw the dapper *Mad Men*–era Kodak engineer re-settling into civilian life in double-breasted suits and a brown trench coat, washing the car in shorts on the weekend, having a son (Robert Earl Jr.), and snapping photos of birthdays and card games, fishing, hiking, and diving.

In the late 1940s, Eastman Kodak gave him and his team the important task of creating a commercially viable competitor to the Xerox photocopying machine. Little did they know that Xerox had a secret sauce that nobody else could duplicate—no pun intended. Dad, who already had more than one chemical patent to his name at this point, struggled to find the correct chemical cocktail for document duplication and to control print quality. I found his notebooks from this period, *full* of calculations, drawings, tables, and gobbledygook. But Xerox was like the Apple or Google of its day, and no one could touch it.

Eventually Dad knew he was on a fool's errand, and what's more, he didn't even *like* chemical engineering. On the day of his big presentation, he fell asleep under a tree in the sunshine, his fedora tilted forward. He hadn't intended to miss the presentation, but when he awoke with a start and saw the time, he remained untroubled. He sauntered into the conference room as if he had not a care in the world, because for the first time in months, he didn't. He was one foot out the door, and if no one had figured it out yet, they were about to. He found the marketing team sharing the new name they had come up with for the product: the Verifax. The executives seemed to think it had a good ring to it. They nodded and mumbled to each other over the conference room table.

At which point Dad could have left it alone, but he didn't. "Yeah," he said. "They call it the Verifax because the quality *varies* so much. Good luck to you all. I quit."

When word spread that Bob Chan had quit in a blaze of glory, someone somewhere caught wind of it before he had even packed up his desk. *What was that? There was a job opening elsewhere at Kodak? Where did you say? You mean in those conspicuously inconspicuous buildings behind fences and alarms that nobody ever saw anyone they knew go into or come out of?*

OPPOSITE: Sharpshooter. *Dad wore a work hat around base and in his machine shop regardless of rank.*

Yes. There was a job there.

"Well," said Dad, his interest piqued. "It all de-pends. What would I be doing there?"

"I'm sorry," the man said, "but we really can't tell you that."

At this, they locked eyes across the desk. The clock in the corner ticked each silent second as it went by.

"So," said the man.

Tick, tick, tick, tick.

"Do you want the job?"

Tick, tick, tick, tick.

"Sure," said Dad, the twinkle returning. "I thought you'd never ask."

And so it was that the laundryman's son who became a scholar, the scholar who became a warrior, and the warrior who became an inventor, now turned to help spy for the empire, where he became, rather infamously, "Not Bob Chan."

I sat back from my computer after another day of digitization. My eyes hurt and my body was drained, but my spirit soared. For the first time I understood that I had nothing to regret on Dad's behalf. People always used to drop well-meaning platitudes about his having "lived such a long, wonderful life" whenever I voiced my fears that I was losing him. Such bromides did not encourage further sharing. Now, though, I did not have to just imagine what a long, wonderful life meant. I could see it all right before me.

Saying goodbye, I realized, is the hardest thing in the world, but I had a box of hellos here by my side. I received them like quenching rain.

One night, in the Year of the Rooster, a little over a year after my worst fear and greatest gift had come to pass and Dad died in my arms, I woke up at 3:00 a.m. with a burning desire to write a book about him. I started scribbling in a notebook—aspirations, limiting beliefs, and so forth, not least of which were Dad's own words echoing back to me. *The only person gonna write a book about me is me.*

BELOW: *The smiling man is Dad, with G.G.'s dog, Ho Tsui ("ho-choy"), ca. 1933. Portrait of my ghostwriter.* OPPOSITE: Crows Bringing Word

On this night, I got quiet and asked in my heart what he thought about me wanting to write a book, and then waited to hear what he might answer. His voice came fast and clear. *This is* your *story, honey, and I just get to be a part of it.*

Of course! How could I have missed that salient fact for so long? I wasn't trying to write a biography, but a memoir. The insurmountable problem of how to tell another man's story was now solved, because all I really had to do was tell my own.

You have a box of photos to see the world through my eyes, I heard his voice in my head say, *and a box of letters to read about it in my words, while you yourself are powerful and inspired. We're a great team, aren't we? Oh yeah. Only fear stands in your way of so many things. I'll be right there with you every step of the way if you do it. Are you going to do it? It ain't a bad story, you know.*

And then he got sly, which was his way. *You don't really think you've been doing all this writing by yourself, do you? I'm what you might call your . . . ghostwriter.*

"Is that true?" I asked, torn between rolling my eyes and widening them.

I could feel him shrug. Then he quoted a favorite jazz composer of his, Fats Waller. *One never knows, do one?*

CHAPTER 10

THE GOOD DEATH

PAGODA ON THE SEA

On the day I went out to the deck and fell to my knees, in 2015, the year of the Yin Wood Ram, a premonition thrummed in my core, vibrating like a bass string plucked by a divine hand. There was no misinterpreting it because I had received the same thrumming vibration the year Mom had died. At that time I had told myself it was nothing, because I didn't know any better, but within eight months my mom was gone. Feeling it again now, I recognized it immediately for what it was: not a threat, but a fair warning, and—I felt this too—offered with love. Dad would be gone within a year.

The terror of losing him was matched by the fear that I would not be up to the task of easing him out of this world in the way he deserved. Or worse, that I wouldn't be there at all, trapped eight hours away, unable to reach him in time.

One day in September, when the fear was especially sharp, I sank into the frog pond by the Chinese teahouse in my mind and dove to the bottom, emerging once again into a subterranean creek bed that led out into a jungle. From there I journeyed to the West, which is associated with completion and maturity. It is where one goes to face fears, limitations, and stale patterns. Your experience in the four directions will be very different from mine. Who you meet depends on who you are and what you need. My spirit of the West is a Chinese scholar and kung fu master who told me his name is Zhou Heping. He hosts me in a stone pagoda on a high cliff overlooking the sea. On this occasion, I spilled my questions to him over a bowl of oolong tea. How can I shed my fear? Does Dad need my help in letting go? Can he let me know when his time is near? Am I holding him back? What do I need to take from this situation?

Zhou Heping gazed at me, eyes twinkling. "That's a lot of questions," he said. His silence invited me to try again.

Embarrassed, I narrowed them down to the one essential, "Does Dad need my permission to let go?"

"Why don't you ask him yourself?" he replied, and in strode Dad. Not as he was in the present, but as he had been: able-bodied, strong, straight, and lithe, with uncurled fingers and a relaxed and dazzling smile.

"Fifteen-and-a-half collar, twenty-eight shorts," he said, appearing to read my thoughts. He was extraordinary to behold. When he smiled, radiant. "Hi, Sugar," he said, and took a seat.

"Dad, are you only hanging on for my sake, because you know how afraid I am?"

Dad looked at me, understanding all. "No," he said. "Believe it or not, I've still got a few lessons of my own to work out. And the truth is, I've kind of liked being Bob Chan. I'm not too keen to let him go."

I laughed out loud. *These journeys are a trip.* "Dad," I said, "can you visit me or send me a sign when your time is near?"

The image of Ba sitting at the end of Grandpa's bed and weeping is the principal image I have of my great-grandfather. I may not know much, not even his name, but I know he crossed the globe with an important message when it was necessary. As a little girl, when I asked Dad how that was possible, he said, "Well, I suppose people who love each other are connected."

"Really?" I asked, hopeful.

"Sure! You and I are connected. Can't you feel it?"

"I guess," I said, wanting to please.

"If anything ever happened to you, don't you think I'd know it? I think I would."

I wondered.

Back at Zhou Heping's stone pagoda, I said, "Dad, I don't want you to die alone. Mom had you. I want you to have me." I proceeded to make my case as if I were bargaining for a higher allowance. "This would also be an important milestone for me," I said. "Facing my greatest fear willingly? Spiritually, it would be a formative moment. I can do it, Dad. Please."

He smiled, nodded, and said, "Well, let's see if we can make that happen."

The drumbeat's rhythm changed, which is the "callback" to bring a person who is meditating in this way back to ordinary reality. I let myself become aware of the soft textures of the bed beneath me, the familiar paintings on the wall, the eclectic trinkets and curios I had collected from around the world and set up on surfaces all around. Who could say whether I had accomplished anything? I only knew that I felt better. At worst, I had just engaged in some powerful self-soothing, and where was the harm in that?

THE SUMMONING

It was February 2016, and Brent and I had taken the boys on a ski vacation, which would interrupt my daily conversations with Dad. I didn't enjoy the trip as much as I usually would have. The first three nights were plagued with anxiety dreams about death and dying. In one dream it was I who was dying, and I felt the fear of the unknown, sadness and worry plaguing me. *How will I be able to tell my children? What will they do without me?*

These dreams left a low-burning malaise threading through my days. I described it in my journal as a kind of soul sickness that I struggled to characterize. It was very uncomfortable. This all culminated in a mild anxiety attack in the pool toward the middle of the week. Although I'm a strong swimmer, I suddenly did *not* want to be in the water. Vivid images of drowning and other water-related tragedies flickered intrusively in my mind's eye like real flashbacks of things that had never happened. I lunged out of the pool and tried to shake it off, pacing to and fro with my face in a towel, Brent casting me a questioning look.

By Thursday, my fitful sleep was worse than ever. I was parched.

I kicked the covers and had to get up three times for water. Coming back to bed, I thrashed around to the same low-grade dread that had hounded me all week. I felt stifled, afraid, but of what? It was nonsense. Everything was fine.

Sometime early Friday morning, I fell into a peaceful sleep, and woke up cool and refreshed. *Man,* I thought as I swung my legs over the side of the bed. *It's like a fever just broke.* I took my first unencumbered breath of the week and stepped into the day, feeling only relief.

Later that morning, however, I got a call from Dad's caregiver. Dad had fallen ill on our first night of vacation and had declined until his fever was raging Thursday night. The fever had broken that morning, the caregiver said, but they were still opening a hospice case for him and thought we should come home.

On that long dreadful drive on Friday night, I realized Dad had, in effect, fulfilled his September promise to somehow send me a sign before he went so I could be with him when he died.

We *are* connected, just as he said we were. *Yes, Dad, at long last, I can feel it too.*

Dad was in a bad way when we got home, but he was awake and happy to see us. We spent three days together, talking, even laughing a little.

The boys had fun feeding him because he was weak. "Open wide, Grandpa! Here comes the airplane!"

Jin read aloud from *Adventures of Frog and Toad,* which Dad had read to me, and I had read to them. Seu showed him how fast his tae kwon do punches were, and Dad the undefeated boxer cringed and hid his face in mock fear and pain.

I showed the kids pictures of Dad feeding and reading to them. "What goes around comes around, you see?" I told them, flipping through the pictures, comparing them side by side. "You give love, and you get love, you get love, and you give love. This is how it works."

THE DEPARTURE

There was time for saying important things, and optimism that it might not have to be the last time. Dad spoke with family from across the country and around the globe thanks to the miraculous technology of Skype and FaceTime.

Tuesday morning, however, I awoke to the wild cawing of a murder of crows surrounding the house, and I sensed that something had shifted. I was not afraid, for these were not the crows of Western horror literature. I did not receive them as harbingers of doom, so much as of change. They are associated with my spirit of the North, an Inuit elder woman named Tulugaaq, meaning "raven," and I understood them to be her way of pinging me. On our long drive home, I had done a meditation with her. "It is time," she had said and embraced me. To me, the crows were her signal that the process had begun. *Fair warning. With love.*

Brent and the boys had to go home. Work and school beckoned. I would stay behind.

Dad was visibly struggling, but you could see him rally for those boys, to give them something meaningful to hang on to. "Oh, how I cherish my boys," he said, wrapped in my nine-year-old's arms.

"I love you, Grandpa!" said Jin, cuddled by his side in bed.

"I love you too," said Dad. "We make a great team, don't we?"

"Yeah," said Jin, smiling like he just got a gold sticker.

When it was time to leave, the boys and Brent stood at the foot of the bed, promised to come back at Easter, then saluted the colonel, the boys with childish glee. He saluted back and told them, "Do it with more snap!" It was by any measure a lovely goodbye.

The shift heralded by the crows did come to pass, for after the boys were gone I could see Dad begin to fold in on himself, as if to say, *My work here is done.* That evening, pain came upon him that made him weep, and I was forced to start him on morphine. Of course, I also knew this meant that Dad might never emerge again. What was such a fear, though, in the face of a loved one's pain? It was a duty, sacred, tender, and profound, which I undertook with determination and reverence.

Dad's first night on morphine, however, I awoke between alarms at 4:00 a.m. with an urge to go see him, even though it wasn't time for his next dose. What a surprise to find him awake. I reaffixed his oxygen tube and then I cupped his face in my hands, looked into his eyes, and told him all the many ways that I loved him.

He nodded and said, "Me, too, you." Then he turned his head to the left and said, "Huh? Who said that?" I glanced in the direction he was looking.

"Said what? I didn't say anything, Dad."

"I thought I heard a voice say something," he said, turning back to me.

"What did it say?"

He looked at me for a moment. "It said 'Don't worry.'"

I looked back at him, held his hand in both of mine and said, "I don't know who said that, Dad, but I think it's a good voice to listen to." I told him that I had received little signs and mementos from Mom, G.G., Uncle Sandor, Grandma Annie, Grandpa Robbie (T'ai Peng), and many others, and that I knew they were all here to lift him up and away if he needed it.

He perked up and asked, "What's Sandor up to? What's he feeling right now?"

I said, "Dad, I don't know, but I'm pretty sure it's anticipation. He can't wait to see you."

Dad nodded and closed his eyes, and indeed, never opened them again.

The next morning, Wednesday, I was awakened by crows again, this time only three. *Things are moving quickly.* That night I struggled with my own shortness of breath and the anxiety-inducing feeling of air hunger that Dad had. I took deep breaths, changed my body position, fluffed and rearranged pillows, even stood on my feet and touched my toes to clear the passage and breathe deeply. To no avail, for I felt the same inexplicable and frightening need for air.

Thursday morning, I awoke and heard but one crow. I lay motionless in bed for a while, letting acceptance creep over me. When I sat up, I checked my Facebook feed. There at the top, the very first post, was the poem "On the Day I Die," by John Pavlovitz.

So it is true. Today is the day.

I got up and went for a walk. It was much colder that day, and as I walked past Johnson Park, something told me to go in. I didn't want to because I had been going there each day all week. But I was learning to follow the little tug that tells me to *go there, turn here, do this,* the one that would, in the next few days, tell me to go to Iceland.

So again I trudged into the park and went to stand on a little bridge under a weeping willow that was still bare, its branches falling like strings blowing in the wind. The creek was running more slowly today. Yesterday's bright burbling had given way to a sluggish flow. *Winding down.*

I looked up at the iron sky just in time to see a small group of geese coming back north. As they honked overhead, it recalled a quote from Plato in a movie I love, *Lady Jane*, that accompanies the scene of geese flying overhead: "The soul takes flight to the world that is invisible."

I spoke the words aloud as I watched the geese fly over. In migration, geese remind us of the changing of the seasons, the passing of one state of being and the start of something new. For Dad? For me? For us both?

I went home. I didn't rush. I made myself a fortifying breakfast of eggs, bacon, and coffee. I dashed off an email update to family, then walked deliberately up to Dad's room and climbed into the bed with him, snuggling myself into his left side, one arm thrown over his torso, my face tucked into his neck. I whispered my heart into his ear all morning and christened his collar with tears.

Ron Steaves, a friend from the senior center, called midmorning and asked if he could come and see Dad. Ron is a deceptively imposing man. That morning he was carrying a little box with a dainty bow. In it was a silver bolo tie, Dad's preferred neckwear, depicting *The End of the Trail*, a well-known sculpture in which a warrior slumps on horseback at the end of a long campaign. Dad had seen Ron's at one of the senior center lunches and coveted it. Unable to find another one, Ron came to give Dad his own as a parting gift. He asked if Dad was awake and I told him no, but that he should go in anyway. *Hearing is the last sense to go.*

Ron entered the room and asked my permission to put the bolo tie around Dad's neck. Seeing it lying on his chest, Ron began to weep for this "dear, dear man." It was both startling and moving to see such a large man crying over Dad's bed, and although I had never met him before, seeing this I knew their friendship had been a good one.

About an hour later another friend from the senior center stopped by—my own second-grade teacher, Marilyn Randall—and we talked quietly about life and loss, and we laughed and cried together. At a few minutes after noon, I glanced at Dad and saw he wasn't breathing. He had waited until I looked away, leaving so quietly I didn't hear him go. And so a great tree fell. And as in the Maya Angelou poem "When Great Trees Fall," even powerful animals seemed to run in fear, seeking shelter. Even rocks and hills seemed to shudder. My reality crumbled, and my senses and very mind. I lay there and held him for two hours until the undertaker came, telling him my heart, kissing his cheek, trying to remember its smell and texture.

After a busy day and a kind invitation to dinner, I returned to a house whose silence was deep, but which did not yet, even now, feel empty. I hoped and felt that he was still near.

That first night in the house alone, as I wandered about, unable to be still, I pulled a card from Dad's desk. It was an anniversary card to Mom from 1997. Their forty-fifth wedding anniversary would have been on Sunday, just three days away. I also rediscovered a little chapbook of poetry called *Mother* that he gave her "just because" in the spring of that same year. Flipping through it despondently, I landed on a poem called "A Long Parting," by Charlotte Gray. It is narrated by a person who has lost someone dear and struggled to find normality. But then they are reunited, hand in hand (perhaps in life, perhaps in death), and the narrator has no more hidden pain, and is complete again.

Once, a few months earlier, I had told Dad, "Send me some signs when you are gone, Dad, so that I'll always know you are with me."

He laughed and went along with it. "Oh, you betcha I will! You probably won't even know I'm dead!"

I sat on the edge of his bed, now stripped, and wept because I wondered if these two things—the anniversary card so close to their anniversary and this poem, found together—were Dad's first message to me. Or maybe his second—the first being a preemptive one for us both, "Don't worry." The poem and card being a reassurance, *Everything is okay. We are together, and look at this, a sign! We are still here for you.*

Friday morning, I awoke and waited for the crows. As anticipated, they did not come.

My meditation in September did what I had hoped it would. My heart was broken, but the wonderment of it all kept me buoyant. Year of the Monkey had put a crack in everything I thought I knew and shown me that just maybe there was some magic under every rock after all. Nothing extraordinary, just there as it had always been, wondering if I'd ever allow myself to see it.

A friend marveled at my foresight to get into Dad's bed that day. I told her foresight had nothing to do with it. It wasn't even particularly mysterious. A Universe I had never really believed existed had handed me a road map. All I had done was follow it.

OPPOSITE: Monkey Swinging on Vines

CHAPTER 11

RISING PHOENIX

Let the beauty we love be what we do.
There are hundreds of ways to kneel and kiss the
ground.

—Rumi

I clicked the ferrule of the pencil against my teeth—*tick tick tick*—then squeezed the meaty eraser between them and stared at a blank spot above my head. Returning my attention to the small notebook in my lap emblazoned with I LOVE LISTS in red metallic letters, I made a quick calculation.

Wow, I thought, sitting back and raising my eyebrows. *I made $1,478 last month on painting sales. And that's just the sales I can remember.* I scribbled a few more figures and sat back again. *And around $966 the month before. Hmm. What do you know? This is turning into a nice little side business.*

I dropped the pencil to my lap and pressed my fingertips into my eyes to ease a momentary stab of grief, but it left as quickly as it came. "Do you even know, Dad?" I said aloud to the empty room.

It had only been three years since I picked up a Chinese brush for the first time. No, it's even more amazing than that. Three years before, I hadn't even known I could draw.

I met the man who would become my teacher, Bruce Iverson, at the local farmers' market years ago and was drawn to his beautiful Chinese artwork. There is no one else around here—deep in New England—who does that kind of art. From adolescence on, I've always had what I thought to be a far-fetched idea that I'd like to learn some Chinese calligraphy one day.

T'ai Peng had been a prizewinning poet and calligrapher in his pre-exile life. We have one of his poems, written in old age on whisper-

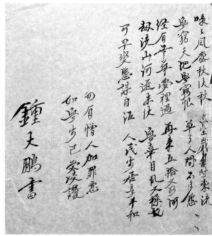

T'ai Peng writing poetry, late 1930s; One of T'ai Peng's poems, n.d.

thin and yellowing parchment. The spidery strokes and loops trickle down the page like water. Visually, you can appreciate his sense of balance and rhythm, his eye for composition on a page. I can't read it, but when Chinese people have seen it, their mouths fall open. This makes me warm with pride, but also makes me feel left out because I'll never be able to appreciate it on the level that they do.

"Your grandpa is *so profound*," said one grad school friend in the cubicle office we shared, a tear glistening in the outer corner of her eye. She was the first native Chinese-speaking person I had ever met, and I had shyly brought the poem into the office one day to see if she could help me understand it. She struggled to translate it, for her English was functional, not fluent. While I know now that it is a melancholic poem written by an old man whose life did not turn out the way he had imagined, or even hoped, I cannot *feel* the poem the way a native speaker can. It cannot make me cry.

When I brought it to a Chinese couple I knew who had a store at the mall, the husband dropped the poem on the glass display case by the cash register and said, "I think your grandpa is a very important person!" He told his wife to get her phone and google him.

"Oh," I said, "you mean, like, a *historically* important person?"

I waited, interested but skeptical, while they searched. They didn't turn up anything on him, and I relaxed back into daily life.

WELCOMING PINES

That day in 2014 when I first met Bruce, I had a deep-seated attraction to and curiosity about all things Chinese, but I'd spent a lifetime hovering on the margins, coming into fleeting contact with my family history and traditions. The internal pull of Asian art stumbled upon in a New England farmers' market overcame my natural introversion in the public square. I approached Bruce's stand like an entranced Teletubby and bought a framed picture of a sleeping cat that reminded me of G.G., Miranda, and Frodo. I also signed up for his mailing list.

A full year passed until one spring night I walked the three blocks to his home studio, Welcoming Pines, for my first workshop in Chinese calligraphy. A lifelong dream was finally coming true. When I stepped through the white metal screen door and into the converted garage for the first time, my senses were bombarded with the unfamiliar familiar. I knew and didn't know everything around me, and there was nowhere else on earth I wanted to be at that moment. My spirit soared for reasons I could not quite articulate.

An old pool table that had been covered to make a large painting surface that the class could gather around took up most of the space. Narrow tables and shelves lined the perimeter of the room. To my right were elegant paintbrushes, a small violet-colored orchid, some whimsical bits of driftwood, and a little CD player that was issuing low, evocative strains from an *erhu*.

To my left were shelves and cubbyholes stuffed with rice-paper rolls, and a desk wonderfully disheveled with stacks of books, cups of brushes fanning themselves in a circle, and white ceramic paint dishes stacked in a tower. Facing the large central table was an easel where Bruce would demonstrate techniques for us to copy. In the far right-hand corner was a utility sink with several slate ink stones on its edge, freshly rinsed and ready for use. Students already there were filling old plastic Chinese takeout containers with water to rinse their brushes. There was a slightly burnt smell in the air too, which I could not identify at the time, but would soon learn is the smell of Chinese ink.

At the end of that first two-hour class, I walked out into the balmy May evening feeling as relaxed as if I had just emerged from a natural hot spring on one of Japan's snow-covered hillsides. My limbs felt like rubber and a warm sense of well-being was bubbling up from my belly. The ceaseless chatter of my monkey mind alerting me to nonexistent dangers, reminding me of my to-do lists, shoving worries in my face— *You haven't forgotten these, have you?!*—was, amazingly, silent.

I had no expectations for myself in signing up with Bruce, no aspirations beyond the simplest and most heartfelt desire to feel . . . good. At that point in my life, it seemed to be the one thing I couldn't do. Mom was gone, Dad was failing, and I felt helpless. When I wasn't loving my little boys, I was wretched. I needed an active intervention, a great disruptor, something that would shock my system with such newness that, just to get my bearings, I would have no choice but to focus away from my now-habitual feelings of fear, grief, and exhaustion.

MYTHIC RARE

"I need to do something for myself," I told Brent one day. "Something that has no functional, earthly value except to delight me."

He enthusiastically supported my taking calligraphy lessons and said he'd take care of the little guys' dinner and bedtime on those nights.

Well, I went in wanting to feel good and came out feeling great.

I signed up to learn some calligraphy and went on to learn all kinds of Chinese brush-painting methods, techniques, and traditions. Every few months when Bruce's emails came around, I found another class I wanted to take—painting iris, bamboo, birds, bugs, and beasts. I learned wash and mounting techniques, uses of color, the effects of different media like wet brushes, dry brushes, practice paper, Xuan paper, and crinkled paper. We read poems from the ancients and talked about some of the philosophies and traditions behind different painting styles. Although I didn't feel that I showed any real talent for painting, that didn't matter to me at all. I was proud of what I was doing, and most important, I was having fun with other people—veterans, divorcees, widows, and retirees who, like me, were living proof that it's never the wrong time to try something new.

In between workshops, I practiced a lot. I watched YouTube videos and tried to paint along on fish, birds, pandas, amphibians, and insects. What I found was that in painting them, even poorly, I seemed to pick up elements of their energy in myself. This, it seemed, was the whole idea behind Chinese brush painting, that in the creation and contemplation of it, you can absorb and transmit certain universal energies.

Eventually I began to refer to it as "calling it in." Different paintings will invite very different energies into your space. Through painting, I tapped into my near-forgotten whimsy (panda), peaceful sure-footedness (heron), quiet power and equanimity in the face of danger (tiger), higher perspectives and clear-sighted seizure of goals (eagle), feelings of optimism and rebirth (frog), perseverance (turtle), and contentment (cat).

It was balm for my sad and weary heart. Sometimes I didn't paint anything for months and felt the sticky energies of fear and grief creep back in and take root, tainting everything. Then I went into a flurry of activity for weeks at a time and felt myself washed blessedly free of them . . . for a while.

I liked to challenge myself and try to surpass my previous best. I often chose subject matter that was way above my skill level, undeterred and unashamed. Grief clung to my energy field like a sticky goo. But the harder a composition was, the cleaner I felt when I was done. It was its own reward. And eventually my abilities did begin to rise to the task.

Once I shared with my Facebook friends a painting I was proud of, a monkey swinging on vines, and received a private message from an acquaintance I hadn't seen since high school. "Can I buy that monkey?" he asked.

Incredulous, I responded that it was just something I was playing with, it wasn't very refined, there was a little smudge on the paper, and it was irregular size and would be hard and/or expensive to frame. I asked if I could do another one, better maybe, and to his size specifications.

"No," he said. "I want that one." So I sold it to him.

Well, that just happened, I thought. *An old-world Asian saw my stuff and didn't snicker up his sleeve; he asked to buy it. How about them apples?*

As I got better control over the brush, I began to make little gifts, tucking a Chinese character—love, joy, or tranquility, for example—into my Christmas cards. For Dad's 101st Christmas, I painted a calligraphy message on a long sheet of gold-flecked Xuan paper and had it framed. *No matter the distance, we are under one sky.*

He hung it on his bedroom wall, where I could see it over his shoulder every time we FaceTimed. I also gave him some mangled-looking goldfish that were supposed to be swirling around each other in a bowl. He received them with equal admiration. Dad was always my biggest fan and found outsized ways to express it. "You should change your career," he said, turning the mangled goldfish from side to side to see them from all the angles.

I rolled my eyes. Preposterous! I only just started a year ago! And had he forgotten so soon that I had quite recently changed my career already, when I left twenty years of archaeology and academia to become a full-time photographer?

"You're probably the best photographer in the world," he had said about that.

I fumed in humiliation at the hyperbole.

"I'm serious," he had said. "You don't believe me? You don't trust my judgment?"

No, I thought, although I didn't say it. He was pulling rank on me as the first professional photographer in the family. To argue with him on this point would, in some way, come across as impugning his expertise, so I let it go. Dad regularly thought I was the best cook, the best writer, the best photographer, the best parent—*perfect* was the word he used, and without a hint of irony—and the most beautiful woman on earth. These were not opinions to him, but facts in his world. To be these things, not in the estimation of some hapless rube, but in the estimation of Colonel Robert Earl Chan, the Most Interesting Man in the World . . . If I weren't all these things to him, where might I be today? Probably nowhere nearly as special. Never underestimate what your faith in someone can empower them to do and be.

One day, after I had taken several workshops with Bruce, Jin and I ran into him on our walk into town. Bruce was wearing cargo shorts and sandals with a windbreaker and a faded cloth baseball cap. We chatted on the sidewalk for a bit, then waved and went our separate ways.

"Who was that?" asked Jin.

I pulled up with a jerk while Jin kept walking. My family had never met Bruce before. "I thought you knew!" I said, trotting to catch up. "That's my brush-painting teacher."

Now Jin stopped dead in his tracks. "That *White guy* is Bruce?!" he said with all the animation of an eight-year-old who'd just had his world rocked.

"Yeah." I chuckled. "I never told you he was White?"

"No," said Jin. "I imagined him looking like Grandpa, but maybe with a topknot on his head and one of those little mustaches and beards."

"A Fu Manchu," I filled in for him.

"Yeah! I thought he'd be an old Chinese guy with a Fu Manchu. Maybe some robes."

Not an unreasonable assumption, I suppose. I mean, his name *is* Bruce.

"Whoa," Jin continued, still integrating. "Bruce is, like, *mythic rare.*"

"Mythic rare." An ingenious use of language. I took it and tucked it away like a lucky charm, to bring out and remind myself at any time of things to be grateful for. To me, the entire experience of stumbling into Chinese brush painting the way I had, exactly when I needed it and without knowing what I needed, was itself mythic rare.

THE ALCHEMY OF THE BRUSH

About a year after this, I was topping forty miles per hour on skis at the resort in Sunday River, Maine, my lungs and thighs burning, when the phone in my breast pocket rang. This was the same trip that had been plagued with sleepless nights and an unshakable sense of dread throughout the week. The boys were in ski school, and so, thinking one of them could have had an accident, I grabbed my glove in my teeth and pulled my fingers free to unzip my coat and fetch the phone. "Hello?" I yelled over the wind.

It was not the ski school, but Dad's home-care case manager. I pulled in at the base of the slope and practically ran out of my skis, heading for the lodge where I would be able to hear better. I just made it through the door before needing to find a wall. I fell back against it and slid unselfconsciously to the floor while ski boots clumped all around me this way and that, in a whirl of red, yellow, white, silver, and blue. Dad's fever had broken that morning, but he had been put on home hospice.

Aware that I was sitting crumpled on the floor and crying into my phone in a high-traffic area, I felt a small voice try to assert itself for a moment. *You're a Chan, act like one!* But it was soon drowned out and swept away.

After Brent had taken the boys back to New Hampshire, I was clearing clutter by Dad's bed and trying to stay busy when he turned his head to me. The quiet hum of the oxygen machine whirred in the background.

"Hey, honey," he said, gasping a little. It took some effort to talk. "Why don't you change your career and start selling those paintings you make?"

"Oh, Dad," I said, shaking my head, speechless. *Not again. Not now.* I would have thrown gasoline on all my painting supplies and gladly seen them burn if I thought anything in the world could make me feel better about losing Dad. But the thought was laughable. I was certain I would not survive this—not in any recognizable form. I also knew this might be one of the last times I would ever be cheered on so faithfully in my life.

That was the last lucid thing he said to me. He died in my arms three days later, the greatest cataclysm I have ever experienced and the most sacred gift I have ever received. You don't forget a parent's final words to you. You put them in your pocket and rub them like a worry stone, this way and that, examining them from every angle. They take on depth, meaning, and symbolism that you perhaps missed in the moment, whether good or bad, and are also apt to sink in and become a personal mantra for you. You hear them day in and day out, repeatedly, incessantly, maybe for the rest of your life. Though gradually, I was sad to discover, I couldn't hear his voice saying them anymore. Just the words remained, echoing. *Start selling those paintings you make. Start selling those paintings.*

GRINDING THE INK

It wasn't a week before I was home and wandering in a daze back into my painting studio—unwashed, ungroomed, not caring about much but seeking relief of any kind. I swung my wooden drafting surface up to level and laid the felt on top. I drew a tall stool up behind me and rested on the edge of the seat. Then I reached for the glass eyedropper of water, the ink stick, and the slate grinding stone. The tinkling of the dropper against the glass bottle was a merry sound that I appreciated. *Tink, tink, tink.*

Chinese ink comes in the shape of a stick, a mysterious combination of charcoal and glue that, when mixed with water and ground in slow circles in a slate dish, turns first to a paste, then finally into a silky, viscous liquid. Some people want to rush the grinding of the ink because they want to get painting, but this is a mistake, and you'll pay for it one way or another if you do not attend to the preparation as you should. Your ink will be thin and weak, your painting or calligraphy sloppy-looking. Rather than thinking of it as something to get through, make it a time when you have permission to let go of all worries and frustrations, all to-do lists and deadlines. My sole purpose, at that moment, was simply to grind.

As the ink began to form, the faint but sharp smell of charred wood rose in a little ribbon. I inhaled the ancient smell and relaxed further into my task. I heard but paid no heed to outside sounds—the muffled thuds and flops of three cat bodies tumbling playfully outside the door, street sounds through the window, the occasional phone ringing. While in such a meditative state, I sometimes begin to contemplate the work I am about to create—the strokes and composition, the color. On this day, I contemplated nothing at all, just sank further into the blessed silence.

The concentration required for Chinese calligraphy and brush painting makes the grinding of the ink much more than a simple preparation of materials. It is a form of meditation, and in undertaking it, you are also preparing your mind and body for the task to come. The artist prepares herself as she prepares her ink. It is said that by engaging in this process, or even watching another do it, one can gain a glimpse of the Tao, often translated as "the Way." It is an ineffable concept in ancient Confucianism and Zen Buddhism, for the Tao can be known and experienced, but never really defined or expressed. It can be roughly conceived of, however, as the flow of the universe, the essence or pattern behind all things, transcending all differentiation. The Tao is Source Energy.

I quickly learned that there was no other thing that alleviated my pain as well as Chinese brush painting—losing myself in the Tao—so soon after Dad died, I began to paint with abandon. I bubbled with raw and ragged energy. But I learned that one's state of flow, one's level of immersion in a task, whatever it may be, is like a vessel. It is built to contain whatever you have to give it. It can receive the enormity of a broken heart, and even, through strange alchemy, create a joyful one. For me, grief flowed into the brush, and lightness and renewal flowed out.

One day, I walked into my studio defiant. I suppose I was in one of the stages of grief. I didn't want relief, or beauty, or peace. I was mad as hell and wanted my personal power back. I decided to paint a tiger.

To me, big-cat energy is about quiet power and intensity, supreme competence matched with utter equanimity. There is no hysterical judging of a situation or task as either good or bad, possible or impossible. A tiger simply sees what needs to be done and then does it. Imagine if I could see a life without Mom and Dad . . . and then live it? That's the kind of power I was talking about. I wanted that.

What came of that session is now one of my bestsellers, *Tiger Lapping at a Stream*. But when I painted the first one in the weeks after Dad's death, I made unintentional eye contact with the tiger and a peculiar thing happened. I felt his energy start to rise in me—the sinuous coil of his body, always at the ready, relaxed but never taking his eyes from the target. I added calligraphy from an old Asian proverb in the bottom corner: *Fall down seven times, get up eight.*

I walked out of the studio that day feeling like a totally different person from when I had walked in. It was so stark it could not be denied. *There is medicine in this,* I thought.

Over time, I found that Tiger energy (whether you are painting it or just looking at it) is good for low vibrations of fear, loss, grief, fatigue, or exhaustion. You don't need to have lost a loved one. The world today offers plenty of opportunity for these low vibrations to take root and make us feel we can't go on. But I also found I could call in Tiger energy when I was taking on new, exciting, but perhaps intimidating endeavors. Things like starting a new business, or reaching a life milestone such as marriage, parenthood, or a job change. I found that I could tap into Tiger energy and then the calm of total competence and supreme equanimity would descend upon me.

On one tiger I painted for a coffee shop downtown, I added calligraphy that read, *True victory is victory over oneself.*

It's about releasing limiting beliefs that keep us from getting what we want in this life. After that first tiger encounter, I began to pay close attention to how different animal energies made me feel, and I started treating their creation and contemplation as Big Medicine for myself.

Too serious? Being downtrodden by the estate settlement? Take two pandas and call me in the morning. Feeling lonely and disconnected from even your best friends and family? Nothing a little pig or some rabbits can't help with. Need to remind yourself of your own resourcefulness and abundance? Rat is on his way.

At times, life seemed too painful, the future yawning before me gray and ashen. So I made myself infinitesimally small and took a journey on a sampan through a clouded gorge. I wrote down the side of that one, *My path is mine to me. I treasure it and follow it to the end.*

OPPOSITE: Tiger Lapping at a Stream

Meaning no person can walk our path for us, nor can we walk any path but our own. To step into the mantle of your own journey, inhabiting it without squawking, judging, wishing, or sighing, is the highest calling we can answer and the greatest form of respect we can give ourselves and the people and forces that gave us life in the first place.

Some of my internal musings during this time reminded me of discussions one might hear between two ancient Chinese scholars. Thus

CLOCKWISE FROM TOP LEFT: Eagle on a Branch; Panda Swinging in Bamboo; Rat with Mushrooms—"*Abundance*"; Cat and Dish OPPOSITE: Sampans in a Clouded Gorge—"*My path is mine to me; I treasure it and follow it to the end.*"

my *Two Scholars* series was born, inspired by the Zen Buddhist philosophy that the obstacle *is* the path, and each painting explored some
unique aspect of that. *Scholars in a Clouded Gorge*, for example, was
about deep, radical acceptance of the path we are on. This painting
reminded me that no matter the steep cliffs I encounter, or the mist
that clouds my way, my path *is* my own and should be embraced for all
it brings me to, and that like minds will occasionally accompany me.

Scholars on a Bridge speaks to the importance of staying curious.
Maintaining a willingness to learn and integrate even the toughest
lessons will enable you to ford any obstacle. Curiosity is the bridge.
I see these scholars as being deep in discussion, talking about life's
mysteries and illusions, the shape of the world's wounds, or the language of trees. Deep acceptance and integration of all that life has to
offer, without loaded judgments, will get you pretty much anywhere
you want to go.

Then came *Scholars on Stepping Stones*, which speaks to a special
weakness of mine—the importance of connecting to a greater sense
of play as we travel on our life journeys. After all, obstacles are really
what we make of them. *Stay light on your feet*, these scholars seemed
to say to me. *Remind yourself to have fun. Sometimes the obstacle is the
path, a stepping stone, and you don't always have to do it alone.*

The idea of not doing it alone led quickly to *Two Scholars and the
Moon*, which speaks to friendships of the heart and the importance of
being truly seen and understood by at least one other person. Everyone
needs the person they can go out under a night sky with and whisper about things great and small, magic and mundane. No one can
walk our path for us, and no one may do so. That's one of life's brutal
awakenings when the going gets tough, but it doesn't mean we can't go
through it with good company.

OPPOSITE, CLOCKWISE FROM TOP LEFT: Scholars in a Clouded Gorge;
Scholars on a Bridge; Two Scholars and the Moon; Scholars on Stepping Stones

RISING PHOENIX

Another symbol I found myself rallying around in those early days was that of the phoenix. I am, after all, the granddaughter of the Great Phoenix. Within hours of Dad's death, I began to encounter phoenixes in every manner conceivable.

It started with a book that I noticed lying face down on the living room floor just after the men from the coroner's office had strapped Dad's body to the gurney and rolled it out the front door. What in the world was it doing there? I had not taken it from a shelf or left it in the middle of the floor, and yet I was the only one in the house other than Dad, who hadn't left his bed in a week.

The book was an old collection of fairy tales that I didn't recognize. It smelled musty and sweet. I turned it over and saw on the cover a great phoenix rising to the heavens. I clutched the book to my chest and called out to T'ai Peng, the grandpa I had never known. Here was the Great Phoenix, come to lift me from my knees just as my father's body had left the house. I felt the gentle reassurance of another presence by my side as well as a directive to rise from the ashes. *You are enormous of spirit and powerful beyond measure. You will journey ten thousand li beyond the realm of what is recognizable. Embrace the transformative power of pain and soar to meet your destiny.*

And just for that moment I knew I could do it, because the Great Phoenix had done it before me.

Where I live, the iconography of rustic cottages and boat-and-anchor themes reigns supreme. Go looking for a phoenix around here and you are unlikely to find one. And yet, once I got home, I began to encounter phoenixes and more phoenixes—in readings, on television, on textiles, in poetry and paintings, in a display case of porcelain at the local library. One day a friend sent a photo of her son in costume for a school show. And what was he dressed as? I knew before I even clicked on it. A phoenix. They were everywhere.

During all this, I also went to another of Bruce's brush-painting seminars. The first character we were to do as part of a larger piece was the character for Peng. A knowing went through me.

The saying we were to paint was *Pengcheng Wanli* (鵬程萬里)— literally *Peng carries you ten thousand li* or, more loosely, *Blessings for a bright/unlimited future.* It is an appropriate gift for graduations, a new job, or opening a new business, or for anyone who is experiencing a life transition, such as divorce or bereavement. *Peng* symbolizes greatness—great accomplishments as well as great promise. The phoenix symbolizes the power of self-transformation, the ability to lose oneself completely and rise again from the ashes of one's former self. You can hardly doubt that I also took it to mean that I was not alone, nor would I ever be. T'ai Peng, the Great Phoenix, my grandpa Robbie, would carry me ten thousand li. Embracing the transformative power of pain would carry me far. It was a message to me from him and all the ancestors, and an auspicious blessing for a new venture, a new life. *We've got you.*

For four months I did almost nothing but paint, and when I came up for air to look around, I was nearly buried by my own production—large, medium, and small works, the entire Chinese zodiac, scrolls and framed works, and calligraphy of all kinds.

"It's almost like the inventory of a small store," I said to Brent.

I began to see a new path, an unexpected way forward, laid out by the Monkey, leading to a future I had not imagined.

But Dad had.

With his simple but profound statement—*Start selling those paintings you make*—he was drawing my attention away from the present moment and casting it into the future. He did it *for me* because he knew that I could not. He knew that I looked ahead and saw nothing but darkness and pain. So he used his last strength to show me how it was done.

In July 2016, I pressed PUBLISH on my new Chinese brush-painting store, Rising Phoenix Arts, and burst into tears. I had no idea what I was doing. But the next morning, like magic, I had three orders waiting for me when I checked my email.

My path is mine to me.

The T'ai Peng carries me ten thousand li.

Magic happens.

Dad, do you even know?

BOOK THREE

2017
YEAR OF THE ROOSTER

This Year of the Rooster, 2017, is also a fire year, which compounds the fiery temperament of the Rooster. This will infuse enthusiasm and energy into our activities, but also usher in a destructive relationship with the status quo. Challenges may proliferate for everyone during a Fire Rooster year, and seismic change is inevitable. Rather than quail in fear, it is good to remember that Roosters are brave and chivalrous, unafraid to face opposition, adversity, or stress. What is more, Roosters are communal birds, and 2017 promises to be a lucky year for collective action. Suddenly you may find help where none has appeared to be. So lean on each other. Despite all the flap they may cause, Roosters know that rude awakenings can also be beneficial. Roosters do not back down from a fight or raise a ruckus when thwarted, but they know how to embrace change as transformation. In this way, they are like another beast from Chinese mythology—the Phoenix.

CHAPTER 12

JUNGLE SCOUT

By 2017, I was reading the annual predictions, invitations, and challenges offered by the Chinese zodiac. Just for fun. I used them as meditative prompts for my own life and thrilled a little at how accurately they seemed to foretell the year's unfolding, at societal as well as personal levels. They made me feel less alone, less left to the wolves. I also took inspiration from them in my writing and art. We were in the first year of the Trump administration, and Fire Rooster's energy of the righteous, pugnacious, but ultimately communal bird and defender was a perfect antidote for our divided times. I began painting roosters of all sorts and writing stories I thought of as embodying the spirit of the Fire Rooster. One war story I had grown up hearing stood out. It was about collective action (of the Allies) and righteous defense of life and freedom against terrible foes. It was also about the magic of finding help where none had appeared to be, and perhaps allowing ourselves, too, to have faith that unlikely help can be found. Rooster knows that it can.

JUNGLE AMBUSH

America entered World War II after the rest of the world had been on fire for more than two years. The fighting took place on multiple fronts, but America's Europe First strategy made it impera-

BELOW, TOP: *Dad on a Harley-Davidson, Ramgarh Training Center, India, ca. 1943* BOTTOM: *Bath time at APO628—Ramgarh, India* OPPOSITE: *Dad trains a Chinese soldier in weaponry captured from the Japanese, November 1943.*

tive that China stay in the war in the East to tie down the million-plus Japanese soldiers who might otherwise interfere with the Allied defense of the Pacific. The problem was that China was depleted from years of fighting, and it was questionable whether they'd be up to the task of mounting an effective defense against Japanese military might.

In September 1940, the Japanese invaded French Indochina and cut off all sea and rail supply routes to the Chinese mainland. Then, in April 1941, they signed a five-year Soviet-Japanese neutrality agreement, which further cut off land routes through Russia and Turkestan. Only the Burma Road remained as a link to China from the outside

world. But with the fall of the Burmese city of Rangoon and the airfield at Myitkyina, even this last lifeline was severed.

So, by early 1942, weeks after the bombing of Pearl Harbor, when American forces were just rumbling to life, our key ally in the Pacific was hobbled. It was the Allies' mission to use India as a staging point to eject the Japanese from Burma and build the Ledo Road there in order to restore a land connection to China from India via Burma.

To that end, in the summer of 1942 General Joseph "Vinegar Joe" Stilwell established the Ramgarh Training Center on a tea plantation in India. He believed Chinese soldiers could be as good as any, if trained. As survivors straggled over the Indian border, starving, wounded, and in defeat, he recruited Allied officers from around the world to come to Ramgarh to train these Chinese soldiers in weaponry and jungle warfare (i.e., guerilla tactics developed in the West). The aim was to raise vast polyglot armies to fight the Japanese. Dad was among those officers called up, and he arrived at Ramgarh around December 1942,

two months after the Americans took over operations there from the British. He was put in charge of the Chinese troops, and while at Ramgarh he taught hand-to-hand combat, weaponry, and other guerilla tactics. He wrote a letter home in 1943:

> *My gang pokes fun at me in a little poem which they*
> *chant first thing in the morning when I arrive at their*
> *area of work.*
> Ta sher choong gwan rin, may gwan ping,
> Ta boo doong choon gwan whah!
> *(He not understand Chinese language*
> *He is Chinese man, American soldier)*
> *Roars of laughter at my expense follow this ditty,*

*and they crowd around slapping my back to show there
is no malice in their joke, and some of the more loqua-
cious ones shout nee ding how (you very good)—in other
words, you're a damn nice feller.* 4-29-1943

American engineers arrived at the same time and started construction on the road. The problem was that Burma, besides being the
size of Texas, is also one of the most inhospitable places in the world,
with jungle so thick that whole armies could pass within a short distance of each other without being any the wiser.

To march through Burma was to hack through wilderness in a
perpetual, often deadly, struggle against nature. Climate extremes of
intense cold, smothering heat, and three months of monsoon rainfall,
more torrential than anywhere else in the world, met with dense jun-
gles and swamps. Cholera, malaria, scrub typhus, beriberi, dysentery,
tropical fevers, and sores claimed the lives and limbs of many Allied
soldiers, and the morale of most everyone.

Furthermore, the Himalayas presented a formidable barrier, with
no roads through them, only narrow tracks. Supplies were brought in
by mule. Imagine supplying an army with only what a single-file line
of pack animals can carry over treacherous mountain passes. Many
mules fell to their deaths in mudslides or by losing their footing, taking the supplies and sometimes their Sherpa guide with them.

Meanwhile, air supplies had to be flown in "over the Hump," the
highest part of the highest mountain range in the world, a flight path
fifteen thousand feet up through a cauldron of air currents containing
ghastly levels of turbulence. Pilots described great gusts that hurtled
planes toward earth like titans spiking a ball. Sometimes they were
flipped upside down, lifted to dangerous heights, then dropped into
free fall. Hail, sleet, and torrential rain were the norm, and roiling
thunderstorms appeared out of nowhere, blacking out all visibility and
turning the heavens into a bubbling mass of treachery where no man
could tell earth from sky. Finding a land route was critical.

Conditions on the ground for building a road, however, were
hardly better than the conditions for flying a plane. The Ledo Road
project dealt with impossible terrain and monsoon rains that washed
away progress, critical equipment, and supplies.

The dense jungle offered almost zero visibility, and the lurking dangers were legion, from Japanese ambush squads to pythons, insects, bears, leopards, and angry baboons that could rip a man limb from limb. Yes, American soldiers sometimes lost their lives to local wildlife. Dad wrote in 1943:

> *Tigers, of course, are plentiful, and this morning I ran across the spoor of elephants. What a curious land this is, where big cats are as plentiful as rabbits in America, and everything—including life—is cheap.*

Dad scouted the advance of the road, sent with his guerilla teams to conduct long-range penetration missions behind Japanese lines to gather intelligence, blow up bridges and rail lines, call in air strikes, rescue downed Allied fliers, pillage crashed Japanese planes, and engage in guerilla warfare tactics when necessary.

I asked him once over a sandwich why they needed hand-to-hand combat. "Why didn't you just use your guns? Did they jam in all the wetness of the jungle, or something?"

"No," he said, hesitating. It brought him no pleasure to dash my innocence. "No. It was because we had to kill silently."

I stopped midchew, swallowed, and recovered myself. "How long were you over there?" I asked.

"Long enough to come back a hard son of a bitch," he said.

As captain, one day Dad was moving his men through the jungle. He had received intelligence, however, of a Japanese ambush planned for somewhere along their route. The problem was, nobody knew where it would be.

Scouts who'd been sent ahead a few days earlier had not yet returned, but timing demanded that Dad's unit move, so he and his men embarked despite the danger, following a faint trail. The jungle is awash with sound—birds, crickets, monkeys, snakes, insects. Modern ecotourists and travel bloggers in Myanmar describe jungle treks as invigorating, and a not-to-be-missed experience that is well worth the fleeting discomforts. But for soldiers at war, it was more akin to being buried alive. The foliage closed in around you, hiding untold terrors from view and inviting your imagination to do its worst. The constant *chirp* and *whir* of crickets seemed to amplify the asphyxiating heat, and the lonely call of an Asian koel sounded like a slide whistle piercing through the din. As the call increased in pitch and frequency, like string instruments in a thriller, so too did the men's sense of suspense and dread.

And then in between all the sounds there was the silence, barely discernible but felt in the marrow of one's bones, falling like a choking blanket. It was the silence of nonexistence.

Eventually Dad came to a fork in the trail—a Morton's Fork—and stopped. Down one path lay certain death, down the other, only possible safety. Sweat stung his eyes. No one spoke or moved. The Asian koel sang its song.

Suddenly, *movement ahead!* Narrowing his gaze and homing in on the source, Dad saw that it was a friend of his, one of the scouts who had left three or four days before. He suppressed a great "Whoop!" of celebration. *Deliverance!* Far ahead at a bend in the dense foliage, the scout jerked his head and beckoned silently with his hand, *This way,* then disappeared. Dad followed.

Each time he came to another split in the path, he looked ahead and there was his friend, beckoning them on. This continued for several hours, and Dad anticipated handshakes and a slap on the back at day's end. There would be stories to tell.

As the day waned, the men reached the end of the trail, rattled but safe . . . and found the scout's lifeless body lying there. But at a level of decomposition indicating that he had been dead for several days.

CHAPTER 13

BY YOUR SIDE

There were mornings I couldn't get out of bed. Grief crouched on my chest and held me to the mattress, perched there like a bird of prey on a branch, indifferent to the frantic, earthly scuttling below.

On one such morning, I said to the empty room, "Dad, what am I going to do without you?"

He answered in my head. *You're going to live a life. That's what you're going to do. And a heck of a good one, too.*

"But I miss you, and it hurts so much I can't even get out of bed. I don't want to live a life without you."

I know. But we'll be together again. And until then, I'm right here by your side. Hmm? Always. I told you I would be, didn't I?

"Are you, though?" I asked.

Oh, c'mon! This in his shucks-gee-whiz voice. *You better believe it!*

"I want to," I said.

What would it do to you to believe it?

I lay with that for a minute, and thought about Ba coming to visit and the jungle scout who had saved Dad during the war. *Lean on each other. Help where none had appeared to be.* I was seized with a whim.

"Dad, can you send me a sign today?" I asked. "Can you send me the words *by your side* so I know I'm not just talking to myself like a loon?"

All right. Sure. I can do that.

"Okay," I said, not at all confident. "We'll see."

You will see.

I got up and trudged through life for six hours, then walked to the post office to mail some packages. On the way home I passed by a shop called Serendipity. In the window, a greeting card printed in big block letters was prominently displayed. It read: MAY THERE ALWAYS BE AN ANGEL BY YOUR SIDE. The three magic words were printed in double-the-size font for emphasis.

I bought the card and pasted it in my journal.

CHAPTER 14

THE SPIRIT OF PLACE

It had been a year since Dad died, and the Year of the Fire Rooster certainly seemed to be in conflagration. I felt "hot" in indescribable and deeply uncomfortable ways. Our nation's house was on fire, as was my own life. I felt myself burning to ash, but the Rooster's invitation was to ante up and kick in.

I opened Messenger and was greeted by a screenshot of what appeared to be the remnants of a barn, though it was hard to tell. A great mass of ivy and underbrush threatened to topple its silo and one remaining gable-end wall, and the roof sagged to the ground behind them. It stood on a flat stretch of grass with no identifying landmarks around it.

My childhood best friend, Stacey, who is actually my niece but of similar age, had attached a note to the barn photo, which she had snagged from Google Earth:

> *Because sometimes I torture myself and find places where I lived as a child on Google Maps, only to find this . . . Mary's barn isn't what it used to be, and for some reason that hits me hard.*

Mary was Mary Cinetti, a curly-haired dynamo and horse enthusiast who had boarded horses at a barn that belonged to a local farmer named Mr. Bean. Mary made it her own, though, not just boarding horses, but offering riding lessons, putting on shows, and hosting foxhunts.

Mr. Bean and Dad were friends because, among other things, they both liked to fly Piper Cub airplanes and sometimes did so together, cruising in bluebird skies over the pastoral patchwork of the hay, alfalfa, corn, and wheat fields of Upstate New York.

It was only natural that Dad and Mary would eventually meet and hit it off. As it turned out, he loved horses too, going way back, and both had charisma for miles.

Mary's barn was where Dad introduced Stacey and me to one of his old passions and one of our first—horseback riding. He drove us there once a week on Saturday mornings and stood gladly by, leaning on the fence or with hands in pockets, making conversation with Mary.

"Hey, Bob!" she called out on one visit, walking up to him, brushing her hands on her thighs, and picking a piece of straw out of the poof of hair over her eyes.

"Mary!" said Dad, placing a hand on each of her shoulders and holding her out to look at her. He looked her up and down, and moved her side to side, peering behind her in feigned puzzlement. "Hey, where's the rest of ya?" he joked, referring to her short stature. Mary was the definition of "small but mighty." Mary cackled and punched Dad in the arm.

Mary didn't just teach us how to ride. Stacey and I learned to feed and groom the horses, and we hauled hay bales, brushed the horses' coats to a gloss, and sometimes braided their manes or tails. We learned that when picking mud and stones from a horse's tender hoof, you should not stand behind the horse, but instead stand next to it and run your hands gently down the front of the leg to lift it. We learned to offer, with open palms and fingers flat, treats of carrots, apples, and the occasional sugar cube, and reveled in the feel of velvet noses snuffling on our skin. We learned how to put in the bit and fasten the harness, then to choose our own saddles and tighten the girth, adjust our stirrups to the correct hole for our growing legs, and eventually to mount and dismount without so much as a stool or a helping hand. We learned that horses, like people, are intelligent and have personalities that must be respected, and that we'd like some better than others. Of course, the latter seemed to be a two-way street.

I asked Stacey if she could remember details about our horse friends. She did.

Wheeler, she wrote. *Big, gorgeous, we rarely got to ride him, liked to drink Coca-Cola.*

Native—slightly Appaloosa perhaps, grayish. Skittish when it came to cars. I always loved to ride him when Mary passed him over.

Tea Biscuit—red, fat oaf, liked to eat instead of walk, stubborn. I remember him jumping over poles on the ground like they were real jumps. He also hated water and would avoid it at all costs, even if it meant sending the rider into the tree branches as he hurled himself over a creek.

Bailey—another stubborn boy who was fatter than he was tall, a bit goofy.

Ahh, it was all coming back to me. Tea Biscuit threw me in a meadow once too. The laziest horse in the barn suddenly decided he was scared and reared up on his hind legs, sending me sailing through the air. I landed flat on my back, which broke my collarbone, but I was unable to scream because when I opened my mouth to do so I found, in utter panic, that I couldn't take in breath. My lungs didn't work. I saw a circle of cloudy sky above my head, ringed by tall meadow grass, and heard my own grunts and pants as I gulped for air like a fish out of water. I also heard thumping footsteps and saw Mary's curly head come into view, silhouetted above me as she fell to her knees by my side. I looked at her with wide eyes and gasped and panted some more but could not speak.

"She's okay!" she yelled over her shoulder to my parents, who were making their way more gingerly across the uneven surface of the field. "She's just had the wind knocked out of her!"

Almost as if on cue, I drew my first breath and let out a bloodcurdling scream. Mom told me later that my scream was the most beautiful sound she had ever heard. Adjusting my arm in the sling, I raised my eyebrows at her.

"We saw you tossed into that tall grass like a sack of potatoes and thought, *Uh-oh.* Then you didn't get up or make any sound, and we got scared. When we heard you scream like that, though, we knew you were going to be okay."

"Yeah," quipped Dad with a chuckle. "A girl who can scream like that sure ain't dyin'!"

Mary taught us to walk, trot, and canter in the open-air ring in front of the barn, and eventually she set up jumps and put on informal shows, where all those who placed were awarded colorful satin ribbons with shiny buttons. The most coveted, of course, was the blue satin for First Place. But what Stacey and I loved best were the cross-country rides. We would cross the road and plunge into the corn and alfalfa fields, hugging the borders to get to streams and lightly wooded hills, and from there the big, wide world.

This was where I learned the word *fallow,* for it was through fallow fields that we could run the horses. I liked the idea that a place that looked barren was not dead, but only resting. I liked to imagine the fallow field in a few years' time, bursting with green growth again.

While I cantered across the fields, the wind whipped strands of hair from under my helmet into my mouth and out again, leaving moist trails across my cheek. My lavender satin windbreaker billowed like a sail, and my spirit soared. I loved the earthy roundedness of the hoofbeats, the gentle rocking beneath my saddle, and the rhythmic and airy exhalations of the horse, who tossed his head in exhilaration, for he too felt free.

A SACRED GIFT

Dad was not an equestrian by any means. Riding had simply been transformative for him, bringing him healing, pleasure, and even excitement while in the CBI theater of World War II, a time and place when these things were hard to come by. Perhaps he thought riding could be transformative for everyone in one way or another, and so he wanted us to experience it.

Back in Savannah, the family had owned two old nags to pull the laundry cart. One, named Charlie, was resentful and stubborn. The horses were kept in an urban stable nearby, and as eldest son, it was

Uncle Archie's job to clean the stalls every morning. Charlie was a workhorse and not for riding, although Dad figured out more than once a way to do exactly that.

Years later, serving in the war, with the Chinese cavalry stationed nearby, Dad found that when he was off duty, he had opportunities to borrow horses to ride. He spoke of the Mongolian breed as "ponies" because, unlike the horses at home, they were compact and sturdy, with strange coloring that made them look half-wild. But these ponies had been bred for war and conquest for thousands of years. It was not unusual for them to be in camp.

Dad wrote to Gretchen frequently about riding and encouraged her to get lessons while he was away so they could ride together when he returned, although he was quick to clarify: *P.S. Don't buy a horse.*

He had stumbled upon an escape for himself that he was eager to share.

This afternoon late my Mongolian pony and I (he's not really mine, but my Chinese friend lets me use him when I come out) went up into the hills again—farther than we've ever been before. The landscape there is beautiful, and the dense foliage contrasts sharply with the barren desert waste of the surrounding flat country. Naturally the trees are stunted because of lack of water, but there are enough to provide cool shade from the extremely hot sun. Eucalyptus seems to predominate, and there are a great many Indian-type flowers, which I do not recognize. I did see one flower, which I believe was an orchid, however it was the darkest I've ever seen, and in some parts of the petals the purple was so deep that it was almost black. I remember wishing that you were with me so I could pick it up and give it to you, but you weren't, and there's no one here worthy of it, so I let it grow. 9-4-1943

BLACK MAN IN DE WHITE MAN SUIT

When Dad was finally discharged in February 1945, at the age of thirty-two, and after nearly three years of deployment, he had a layover of a few weeks in North Africa while waiting for his transport back to the States. The war wasn't over yet, but his part in it was. He was alive and heading home, gripped by a euphoric sense of limbo. He was between worlds—death behind him, life ahead. But exactly what kind of life had yet to be imagined, built, and lived. The sky really was the limit. It was heady stuff, and for a short time it left Dad feeling invincible.

There, in the North African desert, he and some friends found a place to rent Arabian stallions by the day. His was a stunning white that shaded to gray around the muzzle and eyes. They galloped those horses through the desert day after day, whooping their exhilaration into the wind, calling jocular insults at each other over their shoulders as first one, then another, pulled his steed ahead and dusted the others behind him. They came back each afternoon with sand-chafed cheeks and merry hearts.

Once, when Dad was a very old man and he was reliving this story for the family, I asked him how he managed to stay on. Arabian stallions were not for beginners. He got a funny little smile on his face. Words sometimes failed him at this point, but his comprehension was good. He puffed his frail frame up into a Mr. Universe pose, flexing his stiff, withered arms over his head and looking up and to the left, shoving his lower lip and jaw out. "With my mus-kels," he said.

The kids hooted.

One day, at the end of one of these rides, Dad returned to camp, slowing the horse down to a calmer, more loafing gait. He came upon a basket weaver sitting by the road in many-layered textiles. She glanced up at him. He was dark as a Brazil nut after three years in the jungle and looked impressive in his uniform, sitting on a white horse. Their eyes met, and hers began to shine. Dad's shone back. Seeing his comprehension made her merriment grow, and it spread down to her cheeks. Dad's grew in equal measure. Was she going to say it? He knew just what she was thinking. He waited, the ball in her court. At this, her face broke wide open, showing two rows of impossibly white teeth.

A hearty, wheezing laugh rose deep from her diaphragm, and she said, "Well, now, look at de Black man in de White man suit!"

Dad flashed a dazzling smile, lifted two fingers to his forehead in a casual salute of camaraderie and mutual understanding, and urged the horse on to camp.

FREEDOM FROM AND FREEDOM TO

I have many fond memories of my riding lessons with Stacey and Mary, but I did not know much about what riding meant to Dad until I found his basket of war letters.

References to riding were many but buried deep in three hundred ramblings that spoke with equal depth and introspection about love, life on the front, natural surroundings, religion, philosophy, history, literature, native cultures, photography, science, and resourceful inventions he had made in the jungle. It took months to read and digitize them all, as well as to discern and label themes that threaded through the collection and connected disparate letters to each other.

Stacey's message about Mary's barn falling to ruin brought the theme of riding into acute focus. I looked at the picture of the ruined barn, and my mind telescoped both forward and backward in time, faster and faster—life since my childhood riding lessons speeding up in fast-forward to the current moment. Middle school, high school, a year abroad, college, grad school, marriage, family, Mom's death, career changes, Dad's death, riding lessons for my own kids. At the same time, I saw Dad's life before my childhood riding lessons speed backward in a rewind, faster and faster—him standing at the fence watching us ride, his new baby (me), his first grandchildren (Michael and Stacey), a divorce, life after war, Black man in de White man suit, Mongolian ponies, college, the Jim Crow South, sneaking Charlie the laundry horse out for a ride. Mary's barn was the culmination of one sequence, the starting point for the other. It was also my link to his past.

I could see it all now, in full color and context. For Dad, riding meant freedom—*freedom from* and *freedom to*. It freed him from the circumstances of war; freed him, temporarily, from racism; freed him *from* his own worst demons as a man, a person of color, and as a military commander. It also freed him *to* imagine a better world, to visualize the life he wanted, to step into the power of his own true potential. Riding made him feel at home in his own skin and able to be the soul he was born to be.

With one's feet planted firmly on the ground, it was hard not to see the world as it was. Flying over the desert on an animal of mystical power, stamina, speed, and beauty, it was hard not to see the world as it could be. And everyone knows you must see it to build it. That is the power of mythos.

Dad gave me and Stacey riding lessons because he wanted us to discover our own freedom from and freedom to, our own ingrown sense of home and self. I didn't understand the gift until I became an adult and began to better understand the man. This was one of his sacred gifts to me, one of several, which included piano, the writings of Rumi and Gibran, photography, and downhill skiing, to name just a few.

With a sacred gift, the intention is to plant a seed—not necessarily to become an expert or a professional in whatever it is, but to expose one to an embodied life. If suffering lives in the head, transcendence lives in the body. And while steeped in Dad's letters for long months, I became certain that a lot of what enabled him to smash barriers again and again and rise above everything, from personal hardships to a racist society that sought to limit him, was his learned ability to drop down into his body. When the body is engaged, the tortures of mental chatter go quiet and a new way of seeing or doing becomes visible. New and better stories suggest themselves. An embodied life restores the balance with mythos.

I knew why Stacey said the photo of the barn lying in ruins hit her hard. It was because it felt like the end of all that. Wherever Mary is today, I send a little rocket of gratitude her way.

GHOSTLANDS

The picture of the barn and the ruminations that it awakened in me soon found me searching Google Earth for the street I grew up on.

Once I was hovering above my neighborhood and had located the Presbyterian church around the corner and the elementary school at the end of the street, I descended from on high to Street View. I landed with a bounce and walked on Street View to the elementary school in the footsteps of my kindergarten self. Then I turned around and walked back home.

I stared at the house—a white stucco midcentury split-level ranch—and I knew Dad was alive somewhere inside. I could see the jewel-toned glass bottles Mom had lined up on the windowsill above the kitchen sink to catch the light and cast rainbows. Dad's extra-long hose was also there against the front of the house, a reminder of more ambitious and capable days. Those were the days when unruly grass and shrubbery, grungy window screens, hornet nests, sagging gutters, and popped slates from the breezeway consumed his waking, and often sleeping, hours. Many a morning he would complain of insomnia because some puzzle or conundrum dogged him. But just as often he leapt out of bed with the solution at the ready, as it had appeared in his dreams the night before.

I zoomed in on the windows. Could I see anything inside? The resolution wasn't great, but indeed there was some large pale thing sitting on the dining room table—a package, perhaps? My heart skipped a beat. What else could I make out? I searched for a shadowy shape, perhaps going through mail at the table, or shuffling to the kitchen for some cookies and milk. But nothing.

The satellite images were copyrighted 2015, the cursed Year of the Ram. Taken in spring or early summertime, judging by the profusion of small purple and white flowers in the garden, and the Korean lilac planted for my sister to mark her adoption, still green and unflowered. I would have just been embarking on the Great Gardening Rampage and putting in daily FaceTime calls to Dad. I guessed he was sitting in his TV chair in the living room, probably drifting in and out of a snooze.

At that time he would surely have been lonely. Mom had died four years earlier. He had not yet had his fall of late June 2015—a ramping up of the Tai Sui's trials—and the companion service we had hired for him was sending someone out to see him just once a week for three hours. Because he had, appropriately, lost his driver's license at age 101, and sadly also lost his mobility as the bone-on-bone arthritis in his knees continued its creep, the rest of the time he was almost entirely alone. To characterize it as solitary confinement in no way exaggerates the situation.

I smiled to see the house looking so neat and just as I remembered it. My eyes stung with the memory of what was, by this time, transpiring within its walls. I shook myself free and tied the laces on my sneakers. My reflections on the barn and my childhood home had taken more time than I expected, and I was now running late for my CrossFit class.

I hopped in the car, tuned the radio to the new Coffee House station, and put the pedal to the metal. Construction forced me to take a different route to the gym, and about halfway there I was overcome with the emotions of the morning. I was considering turning back and just calling it a day, when my ear picked up a song on the radio: "My Little Girl," by Jessica Allossery, a song from a parent to a daughter grown.

At the words *by your side*, I cocked my head, looked up to listen better, and saw a big triangular sign nailed to a telephone pole, bright yellow against the blue sky. It depicted a child on horseback, a caution for motorists. I glanced around and found I was driving by a horse farm advertising lessons for kids.

Could Dad have been watching over Stacey and me this morning, reminiscing about our riding lessons right along with us? Did I even believe in any of this stuff? I had to pull over to compose myself. My tires crunched to a halt in a small parking area next to a Baptist church. I took a deep breath, wiped the tears from my face, and got out of the car. I walked up the road to take a picture of the sign to send to Stacey. It was all so remarkable.

I breathed in the beautiful day and turned back to my car, feeling my heart fill with hope and gratitude. I had reached the car door and had my hand on the handle when I came to a sudden halt, my other hand flying to my mouth. There, behind my car, was the church's roadside sign, whose plastic letters could be switched out each week to leave a new message. Today it said, WHERE THERE IS LOVE THERE IS LIFE. The very words I had said to Dad that day in the bathroom, two years before, when he had been unable to stand.

THE SPIRIT OF PLACE

After Mom died the house was as empty as it had ever been, but it didn't feel empty. The parties were over, the kids were grown, the twenty exchange students had come and gone, the animals had grown old and passed on, and mountains upon mountains of junk had been cleared out. It was just Dad and the house now. But I felt every corner of the place burbling with memories. I could almost see everyday scenes playing out before me in empty rooms—an impromptu jam session with musical friends from the neighborhood playing bass, trumpet, and saxophone, and singing, crowded around the piano on a Halloween night; Mom with her laptop loom on the couch; the family playing Clue at the dining room table.

The house didn't feel empty after Dad died either. At least not at first. I had watched the coroner wheel his body out

Never happier than dressed for Halloween at one of my parents' impromptu jam sessions, ca. 1982

the front door that afternoon, feetfirst and in a burgundy corduroy body bag. There aren't many scenes more final than that. That evening, friends of my parents, Lee and Marci Loomis, had called me to check in, and upon learning that I was there alone, cried, "Alone! You're not *alone*, are you?"

And because I admitted I was, they swooped in and gathered me under their wings and clucked over me and took me to dinner and let me laugh and cry and reminisce with them over a delicious sesame-encrusted tuna steak drizzled in wasabi ginger sauce.

I remember fighting the urge to demur and ask, "Are you sure it's okay?" before ordering the most expensive thing on the menu. Something stopped me. Something told me that life isn't just about knowing how to give, but also about opening yourself to receive. The Loomises (or the Loomi, as I was tickled to discover they call themselves) were offering me a sacred gift of their own—companionship, presence, and parental love—just hours after my last parent had died. My only job at this point was to receive it. So I ordered a second glass of wine. If I couldn't gracefully accept a tuna steak and a couple of glasses of wine on the night my father died, how would I be able to receive the bigger stuff in life?

When I got home, I didn't bother to turn on the lights, and made my way mechanically to Dad's overstuffed TV chair in the living room. I fell into it and stared into the dark, not moving, barely breathing, and quite numb. My first night on earth without Dad yawned around me. Funny though, I did not feel alone. I examined the feeling, turning it this way and that. Was it true? Yes indeed. How odd. What's that about?

Then I jerked my head to the sound of Dad's voice in my right ear—loud, crisp, and clear as day. "You couldn't have done a better job, honey," he said.

I nodded my head. "Thanks, Dad," I said aloud.

The house felt full all the next day too, as well as when I locked it up to make the long drive back to New Hampshire and a post-parent life I still had trouble visualizing. But when I returned for the memorial a few weeks later, the house and the town felt decidedly empty. I wandered the rooms of the house the same way I strolled the streets of the neighborhood—listlessly, hoping to recapture some sense of belonging. I trailed my fingers along the walls behind me, listening, remembering, and plucking small leaves from the town's hedges, stopping before key landmarks, waiting to feel not alone again. But the house and town stayed remote, offering me no succor that week. Whatever it was that had filled them before and made them feel like home was gone. Amazing how a person can fill a whole town. I had felt an urgency in coming back for the memorial, for I had spent three weeks in a dark loneliness I could scarcely find words for, but now I felt let down and adrift. Home was gone as sure as Mom and Dad were. There was no getting it back. It got me to thinking about how we confuse the physical structure of place with the spirit that inhabits it. At that time, I felt that the spirit had left, and I was home no more, nor would ever really be again.

HOMECOMING

About a year after the memorial, I found myself in the south of Spain on assignment to photograph a yoga retreat. There, I mixed my parents' ashes and released them to the wind from a mountainside overlooking the jeweled waters of the Mediterranean. It seemed fitting. Spain had been their last big trip together, around 2006 or 2007. On my walk back down the mountain, I picked up a natural garnet and a large, pearly-white sea snail shell on a desert slope miles from the sea. I collected the unusual objects, and I've kept them ever since as a reminder of the small sacred ritual I did for myself. But it took me over a year before I was struck with the meaning behind them and why my intuition might have guided me to take them home with me.

Sometimes grief is so thunderous that you can't hear anything else. It takes time before the small whispers in your mind can break through again. One morning, when I opened the cupboard to make coffee, as I do every morning, and was greeted with the usual view of the garnet, the snail shell, and a picture of Dad and me dancing at my wedding, I was struck dumb. I suddenly knew why I had picked up those objects.

The garnet is a semiprecious stone, one that signifies the heart, connection, and love. In its raw state, you can see it peeking out from under a rough cortex of rock. My quiet inner voice spoke to me. *It means that love and connection are ever present and always inside you. That they are gone from you now is just an illusion. You need only break open the rock.*

I picked up the shell and ran the fleshy part of my thumb over its whorls and ridges. *Snails carry their homes with them wherever they go,* said the voice. I dropped my hand holding the coffee scoop to the counter and continued to stare at the shell in my other hand as comprehension began to set in. *Home is where the heart is,* the voice continued. *You do not need to mourn it. You do not need to search for it. You do not need to visit it. It is with you always, because it is a part of you, the way the shell is a part of the snail.*

"So . . . I've not lost anything at all," I answered back. "Mary's barn may be a ruin, and the house may have felt empty when I last saw it, but the memories that made them feel full and made me feel loved are with me still. Is that it?"

You got it, said the voice.

"Then home was not the structure, but the feeling it gave me inside," I went on, "and that feeling, that spirit of place, can be accessed anytime and anywhere. I need never again feel orphaned, homeless, or rootless. I *am* home. Home is inside of me."

And more, said my quiet inner voice with emphasis, *it always was.*

I remembered my last visit to Dad's house and the feeling that the spirit of place had left it, and by extension, left me. It was a feeling of crippling abandonment. But if, as I now suspected, the spirit never leaves because it resides within you, then at most you may only block it through grief, fear, anger, anxiety, or sadness, or by too narrowly defining it.

I thought parental love would never be mine again, because I thought parental love could only come from my parents. But then the Loomi showed up, and I opened myself to receive the parental gift that was being given. My lesson that night was that it is still possible to feel held up and taken care of. There is an archetypal parental love that always exists and can be received. You have only to be present enough to recognize and accept it when it appears. The same can be said of all other kinds of love.

To really come home, I realized, I only had to remember what home meant to me—love, connection, belonging, freedom from, and freedom to—and then open myself again to those feelings when, wherever, and in whatever form they are offered. I am worthy of that gift, and it does not have to, nor often does it, come from the usual suspects.

We are so demanding of the Universe, aren't we? We want our love and our connection and our belonging, and we want it now. We also only want it in certain forms, from specific people, and in predesignated places. But what happens then? When those people and places are gone, or show themselves incapable or lacking, we imagine that so, too, is love gone. What a terrible disservice we do ourselves, spending our whole lives meticulously setting ourselves up for failure in this regard. Because the Universe is *full* of love we are simply not prepared to receive.

See the love when it is being offered, even from unexpected places. Be the love you want to feel and see it mirrored back to you tenfold. Create the home you want to inhabit and watch your fears subside. Your authenticity in this is your greatest gift.

Since that morning contemplating the garnet and the snail over my coffee, I've had cause to reflect on my sense of home, which was built and nurtured with loving care by real people in a real place, the spirit of which continues in my life even as the people and place have disappeared. My sense of home, when I tap into it, gives me freedom from isolation and loneliness, freedom from despair about the state of the nation and the world, freedom from the worst forms of self-doubt and self-loathing. And it gives me freedom to be daring and bold, freedom to challenge myself and follow my whimsy, freedom to visualize a life I never thought possible for myself: my best creative life as archaeologist, photographer, painter, author, speaker, writer, raiser of amazing children, surrounded by animals. And all this without parents, without a "home."

Snail on a Mushroom

Somewhere high above me, the Rooster crowed in triumph. I had uncovered a gift in a fiery year. And accepted help where none had appeared to be when it was offered.

Everyone knows you must see it to build it. The spirit of place, which never leaves me, is my magic mirror, where I can see it all.

CHAPTER 15

SKETCHES OF SPAIN

A LETTER WRITTEN BUT NEVER SENT

Villa de Níjar—May 9, 2017

Dear Mom and Dad,
You would be delighted to know that I am currently on assignment in Spain, where I am both photographing and participating in a weeklong Kundalini yoga retreat. I am sitting outside my little white stucco cortijo at the estate. It is close to 9:00 p.m., but because it is the south of Spain, it is still nearly broad daylight.

I associate you both with late nights and laissez-faire, worldly attitudes. I can see you as a couple fitting right into a Spanish lifestyle. Late dinners and friendships of the heart.

Spain drips with life—layers of it that feel downright voluptuous to a New Englander like me. Life in New England seems more . . . strategically placed if that's the right phrase. In Spain, by contrast, it is effusively, riotously present. It cares nothing for borders, boundaries, or personal spaces. It is indifferent to there being twenty-five different life-forms already on a patch of earth. It will sprinkle several more liberally on top for good measure. I dare say it enhances the "flavor." Is this why Spanish cooking is so diverse, multilayered, and colorful?

We saw a Spanish wedding let out from the church in the local town square one afternoon, the women all brightly colored and groomed birds of paradise. I will say this: Spaniards know how to live.

Spain was also the last big trip you made together. So tonight, I am looking up the mountainside behind the yoga shala where I have been taking pictures, practicing yoga, and building community for the past week. There is a wind-scooped hollow about halfway up the mountain where I spread some of your mingled ashes today.

I spoke to each of your remains, fingered the ash and bone fragments through the plastic of the little bags I brought you in. I remembered what these bones once supported—the arms you hugged me with, the teeth you ate good food with and that showed freely when you laughed, the feet that led me on adventures, the hands that held mine. I thanked you for your unique gifts, and then I cried a good bit.

When I was through, I commingled your ashes into one bag—Dad, by some strange alchemy of the ovens, you were the light/white one and Mom, the dark. A funny little reversal, but I suppose in one way it makes sense. Dad, you were my sun, and Mom, you were my moon. You lit my days and my nights.

When I had finished reminiscing and offering up the most heartfelt thanks a daughter ever mustered, I gathered myself for what I had come to do, and then hesitated.

The air was still, and I fretted at what would happen if, after great ceremony, I let you go only to watch you fall immobile to my feet. I had come to set you free, not just to pour you out. But lo, when at last I was ready, a wind gusted up strongly out of nowhere and I watched you fly free over the mountain, over the valley, and over the little white stucco village clinging to the far slope like barnacles on a ship's hull looking out over the Mediterranean in the distance. It was magnificent.

I enjoy thinking that you were by my side and saw it all. That you've seen the lovely trip I have been having and connections I have been making at the shala below, and that you therefore also find this a beautiful and meaningful place to rest. Though of course you are never resting, but blowing and tumbling through brush, ricocheting off mountainsides, wafting across expanses of warm air, landing in ponds, streams, and the Mediterranean. Always and forever on the go now. Just as you were in life.

I invited all our family who have passed to join me on the mountainside to spread your ashes. I like thinking of all of you there, reflecting together on two lives lived so well, and all the things that continue to connect us.

I asked you for a heart rock today and you did not disappoint, even taking care to make it a rich, hearty red. I held it as a talisman as I climbed the mountain and trusted it would let me know when I had found the right spot. And because you knew that it was not my intention to keep it, but simply to find a heart rock to give to another yoga friend as part of an assigned kula-building exercise, you also let me find another auspicious thing, just for me, on the way back down the mountain, a pearly-white, quite large sea snail shell, miles from the ocean and sitting there for no obvious reason on the slope of a desert mountain.

Thank you for the heart. Anytime you deliver on one of my "asks," it makes me feel close to you. I hope I infused the heart with some of that energy so it will pass to Sebastian when I give it to him on Thursday. Thank you, too, for letting me find something else for

ABOVE, LEFT: *Found a place*
ABOVE, RIGHT: *Ready to
release* LEFT: *Forever on the
move now* BELOW: *An invitation to breathe again*

myself to still remember this remarkable day by. I love you. I miss you. Are these the new ways we must learn to communicate? Please don't ever stop—even, and perhaps especially, if you see me having a hard time seeing, hearing, or believing you. I live for such moments regardless. I live for the flicker of recognition and the hope they ignite.

This morning, Dad, I felt you near when I was by the beautiful eco pool on this stunning Spanish estate. Yellow jackets are out, and no matter where I went one always came and buzzed or crawled a few inches from me. All its friends were hanging out in a cloud far distant—barely even visible over the frog pond by the eco pool. This one, however, came to investigate my glasses on the ground, crawl by my arm, or buzz past an ear. Just one. I would have been a little anxious at his unremitting attentions but remembered the yellow jacket mascot on your Georgia Tech Ramblin' Wreck coat you so prized when you went to college ("I'm a ramblin' wreck from Georgia Tech, and a helluva engineer!"), and I knew that yellow jacket meant no harm, so I stretched more languorously in the sun, closed my eyes, and let him buzz as he would.

Love forever,
Alexka

On the breezeway outside my *cortijo*, I finished writing the letter to my parents in my journal. I sat back to watch the way a joyful breeze picked up and played with the pages. They flipped slowly first, and then accelerated into a cascade, flowing forward for a few moments, and then backward, ever playful and dancing this way and that. I sank into a deep calm, watching the movement fan back and forth, and listened to the rustle of pages. And then they fell open to the card I had pasted there months before. MAY THERE ALWAYS BE AN ANGEL BY YOUR SIDE.

And the breeze fell away and played no more.

It's okay. Help is on the way.

BOOK FOUR

2018
YEAR OF THE DOG

There is no rest for the weary in a Dog Year. Dogs are binary by nature, and so too is 2018 expected to be. Light and dark, good and evil, life-giving and life-draining. Which will it be for you?

The dual energy of the Dog has asked you a question, and yes, it is a test. Testing will take you to your limits on all planes of being or it wouldn't be a test, do you agree? The initiation of a Dog Year asks you to discover and demonstrate what you can do. To stop asking, *Why me?* Or, *When will it end?* And to start asking, *How can I do this better? Is there a wiser or more creative way of looking at it?*

The duality of the Dog can bring conflict and chaos, and it is said that Dog Years are ripe for revolution and rebellion. It is up to each of us to tap into the best qualities of the Dog. Stand for what is right and protect what is dear. Trust. Hope. Be creative. Believe in miracles.

Ground and connect with yourself and watch connection spread to all things.

Guard against a closed heart and the shadow side of the Dog. A healthy Dog has the instinct, altruism, and tenacity to find the golden door that offers passage through any trial. Justice, friendship, and optimism are on its side. And through the golden door? Triumph. A new level of consciousness.

CHAPTER 16

BE NOT AFRAID

A scene from a childhood photo of mine hovers behind my lids as I start to wake. Except it isn't the picture, but the scene itself, in explosive color and realism. A dream, hyperreal and what some people refer to as a "visitation."

Fuzzy red tights hug my calves, and I reexperience for a moment the expectant joy that anything red brought me as a child, as if red never just came by itself.

I am on a concrete pad overlooking a duck pond, hanging with both hands from a metal railing and leaning out over the water. Dad, squatting behind me in a blazer and with a pipe clenched between his teeth, holds the ties on my dress from behind.

My big toes wobble and roll as I swing my weight forward and back. A duck paddles in wide circles to my right, letting out a listless quack of greeting as it nears me. I hear the lap of small ripples against the concrete at my feet and smell the mineral, earthy aroma of pond water.

I am there leaning out over the water, testing my strength and courage. I feel brave because I know I am safe, and I swing myself out even farther. A giggle bubbles up in my chest. The sash pulls taut across my front, and I feel, though cannot see, the strong hand holding me from behind.

I lie in bed and let consciousness seep in, but I keep my eyes closed to savor the moment. I let myself inhabit the scene for as long as possible, and as a tear leaks out from behind one lid, Dad speaks to me. *This is our relationship now. You may not see me, but I'm right here behind you and I won't ever let you fall. This is how it will be.*

Be brave.

All is well.

This is how it will be.

CHAPTER 17

THE WIND SOCK

I didn't often have interesting or helpful dreams before Mom and Dad died. As a kid I had simple nightmares, no doubt helping me process various childhood anxieties about living life. As a young adult, I stopped remembering my dreams at all, except for one, especially fearsome, which I set aside as one of my old childhood anxiety dreams again. Mom and I were at the family cabin in Vermont. The sun was streaming through the window behind us as we leaned against the dining room table, wrapping us in a veil of golden light. She had poured us some orange juice and handed me a glass. All appeared normal on the surface, but it was not. For it was not Mom who was standing next to me, but her soul, who had come to comfort me and tell me that she had to go. While the "action" of the dream was quite serene, the emotional substrate was forbidding. I cried to the point of gagging and begged her not to leave. It shook me. I awoke with feelings of doom that never fully went away. It had been so real. It caused me to think on Mom's mortality in a way I simply never had before—a healthy woman in her fifties! Her mortality wasn't even a blip on the radar. It became one, though, after that dream. My consciousness had been pricked.

When she got her terminal diagnosis, some eight years later, I found out for the first time that she had known this was a possibility for years and decided to keep it from me. I was at such a critical time in my life that she didn't want me being distracted by fear, especially when the probability of its developing into something serious was so low—only 2 percent. But now that it had come to pass, I learned that they found her elevated protein levels at about the same time I had that dream. I shivered in recognition and remembrance.

After Mom died, I prayed for her to visit me in my dreams again, as she had with the orange juice, but she never did, not until six days before Dad died—the only time I have ever dreamed of her since her death, in fact. We were together in my kitchen while the boys scampered around our feet (aged four and eighteen months, as they had been when she died). She tiptoed this way and that to let their squirmy bodies run by, chuckled, and snapped pictures of them, repeatedly and from different angles, smiling at me as she did so, as if to assure me that she hadn't missed a thing. And when Dad died less than a week later, I began to think that what she had really meant for me to know was that he wouldn't miss anything either.

Nevertheless, Dad's death was a spiritual sonic boom that shattered me like a glass flute on a stone floor, reducing me to glittering, atomized powder. Nothing I recognized about myself remained. And so began the slow and painful process of figuring it out.

As an archaeologist, I have spent thousands of hours in the laboratory, mending glass and ceramic sherds into plates, glasses, tumblers, teacups, chocolate cups, milk pans, butter pots, and punch bowls, as well as bottles for gin, French wine, English beer, and port. Green glass is just green glass unless you can identify the form it once belonged to, to talk about date, function, use, and meaning. The thing about mending something that has been broken beyond all recognition is that it never goes back together quite the same as before. But in the mending, you discover the meaning.

I have found that in my own mending I have seams where before there were none, and there is a looseness and openness to me that I didn't have before my parents died. If the absolute worst can happen, so can everything else. So can *anything* else; my disbelief has been permanently disabled. It's freeing, empowering even, if you can let it be. There are times when I have found it to be downright magical.

For example, one thing that has changed dramatically for me in the mending is that my dream life has become rich and varied and not at all frightening. My dreams have emerged in my new state of openness as a mysterious but reliable source of kindness, care, and wisdom. When I dip my toe in the magic there, I reemerge heartened and amazed.

Thus it was that I was once again newly awake and fixated this time on a wind sock, in the shape of a koi fish, blowing in the breeze behind closed lids. I pulled the covers tighter around me and continued to watch as the fish slipped from one airstream to another—up, then down, side to side. Sometimes it spun in place, never getting tangled in its own string, while at others, it emptied and snapped like a flag before filling again with wind. It was a hypnotic kind of dance, peaceful, as was the knowledge that came with it: that I was meant to be more like a wind sock.

HEAT WAVE

The summer of the Year of the Dog, 2018, I experienced a heat wave of an unusual sort. Acute feelings of anxiety, fear, grief, and betrayal ran roughshod over my spirit, as the hellfire and nihilism of Trumpism raged across the country. Of course, it had been dark and terrible times since Election Day, but that summer, I think it is safe to say, was particularly painful for people of color. "Send her back," they screamed in their chilling rallies, reminiscent of Nuremburg. We had begun to live in a house of mirrors, where treason is confused with patriotism and patriotism with treason; where racists call their victims the "real racists," and real Americans "un-American." Black was white; down was up; three-year-olds were just future MS-13; foxes guarded the henhouse in every major government agency. We were under active attack from a foreign adversary while the administration told us there was nothing to see here. Orwell's *1984* was now reality: the dystopian future was present.

When Dad was a young man, he carried around a notebook—known in the old days as a "commonplace book"—in which to scribble deep thoughts, clever insults, and humorous observations. Finding it right before he died was an incredible gift to me and let me "spend time with him" in a special way. I was healed, invited into the inner workings of his unique and brilliant mind, scribbled and/or typed on these little yellow pages. And if ever I am really missing him, he leaps to life when I open his commonplace book. "Every man should have a wife, preferably his own" was one memorable entry. "Here's champagne for my real friends and real pain for my sham friends," he wrote another time. But there was pain and sorrow and introspection in there too—philosophy and poetry, his own and that of others. I am always reverent before these pages. They are the closest thing I'll ever have to a prayer book.

In summer of the Dog, the one I kept returning to was this:

> *Mankind was dancing—unmindful of the fiddler's recompense.*
>
> —Robert Earl Chan Sr., ca. 1936

I lost my balance that summer. I felt emotionally unsafe, distrusting of my fellow citizens, wondering particularly where the outrage, or even concern, was among certain White acquaintances and colleagues, who seemed to be skating breezily along, untroubled by what the people of color in their lives had been experiencing, and uncommitted to seeing an end to it. Silence is its own kind of betrayal. It was unnerving, and I could feel myself cramping up over it, clamping down around the feeling, contracting, and recoiling. The wall slamming down around my heart felt like an actual, physical thing. And as for the rest of me? It was all on fire—searing, scorching, melting fire. I felt *hot* in ways I couldn't quite articulate.

That was when I had the cooling dream about the wind sock.

COOLING IT DOWN

What I wordlessly understood, before I even opened my eyes, was that I had been holding myself apart from, or outside of, the real current of life for a good while after Mom and Dad died. That was a necessary part of my healing, but I was perhaps being invited to something more. No more clinging to the banks and splashing in the shallows like a spiritual invalid, where the water flows less forcefully but I also don't get anywhere.

Like the wind sock in a storm, life demands a return to whole immersion. The image I saw in my dream showed the wind filling the sock to maximum capacity, rushing over it and around it, but most importantly—through it. Ah, there was the rub, and the real insight of the dream.

I had been stepping more boldly back into life, true, but I was contracting over the painful feelings I encountered there, and in effect trapping them within me. A wind sock only works because it is open on both ends. The wind fills the sock, yes, but passes through it. So too can we work to let uncomfortable feelings pass through us instead of overidentifying with them, clamping down on them to "stop the bleed," so to speak, but creating a blockage in the process that prevents them from ever dissipating or healing. I remembered that the pain of childbirth was *infinitely* worse when I allowed my muscles to contract over the pain instead of consciously releasing the tension and remembering to breathe. In one scenario, the pain could pass through me; in the other, it filled and threatened to replace me.

Now here's a pro tip: if you convert the wisdom you receive from your intuition (be it in a waking, dreaming, or meditative state) into real-life action, you will soon find yourself living your best life, regardless of external circumstances. Have I not shown that it is so? Thus the first thing I did upon receiving the dream of the wind sock was go online and order some koi-shaped wind socks for my deck.

I chose them, in what felt like a random manner, in shades of blue, green, and red. They looked festive and summery, and I felt a spark of joy at each of the colors. However, when I checked, on a whim, the meaning associated with each of these colors, I was delighted, and somewhat amazed, to learn that blue—the color of the throat chakra— is associated with fresh air, openness, and liberation, the perfect antidote for my cramped spirit. Green—the color of the heart chakra—is associated with love, connection, integration, and compassion, the perfect antidote for my walled-off heart and suspicion of friends. And red—the color of the root chakra—is associated with feelings of security, safety, belonging, and pioneering, the perfect antidote for my feelings of fear, endangerment, and retreat.

In the weeks after the wind socks came and I hung them on my deck, I felt called outside to watch them on numerous occasions, often when the news cycle had delivered another killing blow and I felt the old spiritual cramp trying to take hold. I watched the wind socks spin and blow and dance; I breathed deeply and filled my own lungs with air and allowed myself to open to the cleansing power of the wind. I felt the cramp, it filled me whole, and then . . . I let it go.

CHAPTER 18

BINGO!

I was out to lunch one day with a lawyer friend of mine and a couple of her brilliant friends in a little riverside town near me. They were older and quite soulful women, so I shared with them that I associated wasps with Dad. For one, the yellow jacket was the mascot of Georgia Tech, and figures prominently on his college jacket in old photos. I see the wasp, too, as reflective of the intense duality (like the stripes) of the man himself—yin and yang. He was a peaceful warrior with a powerful sting.

Eventually talk turned to my photography. I had some business swag with me, and I pulled out a postcard to share with one of the women. It was a mosaic of twelve faces, mostly former clients of mine, representing a wide array of ages, races, and genders. Dad's face was among them.

I laid the postcard on the table, and out of nowhere a wasp appeared and started hovering over the thumbnail pictures of faces, eventually landing on Dad's picture. It crawled all over his tile, only an inch square, never leaving it, just circling back and forth and all around on Dad's face.

"Oh my god, you won't believe this!" I practically screamed to my lunch companions, *"That's my dad's picture!"*

There was a collective gasp, followed by laughter and some tears. And I heard Dad's voice in my right ear. *"Bingo!"* he said. It was an exclamation he made when he was engaged in a concentrated effort and had just nailed it.

Bingo.

I spent the rest of the afternoon walking and shopping before returning to the car, passing the place where we had been seated for lunch. I pulled up short when I saw a little antique 1968 Austin-Healey in robin's-egg blue parked right in front of our table. Dad, who fixed up an abandoned Austin in the jungle for wartime adventures and drove a 1967 Corvette Sting Ray at home, loved vintage cars—the smaller and sassier the better.

This one had a vanity plate. BINGO, it said.

CHAPTER 19

AMERICAN AS APPLE PIE

Let's light another match together, right now.
Strike!
Now watch it flower.
Hands in prayer.

What, my Darling, will you do with your holiday today? (It is Fourth of July evening for me, Fourth of July morning for you.) This used to be the day for every family in Savannah and for miles around to have a picnic at the beach, swimming in the morning and afternoon— fireworks at night—also a big dance on the pavilion, which was really nothing but a belly rub, since the floor was so crowded that the couples could not move. Once when I was seven years old, I carried in memory for a whole year the picture of a lovely girl of about twenty who smiled at me on the sideline every time she danced close by.

Today was in a way [like] the old days, except that we were not celebrating, nor did I know it was July 4 until someone told me this evening. The picnic and swimming—I took some men down to the front on a job. It was raining hard all day, and we got soaked. At one place we had to wade through a chest-deep stream, luckily K-ration is waterproof, so I did not miss my lunch or supper.

The fireworks—the Japs no longer throw artillery at us. Reason—we've captured both of the 150 mm howitzers (Big Nellie) and all but one of their 70 mm howitzers. That one, however, gives no trouble because they cannot get ammunition for it. So today all the artillery fireworks came from our own batteries. Not so with small arms, and at dusk on the trail leading home we ran into a five-man patrol, which sent a burst of light machine-gun fire in our direction before diving into the bushes. Their bullets were wild, however, and no one in my gang was hit. And, because everything happened so quickly, we did not have a chance to fire a single shot. We tossed three hand grenades into the bushes where they had disappeared and then made double time for about a quarter mile.

The girl—our way led through a village of refugee Kachins and Burmese. A pudgy little fat girl with TB and buck teeth smiled at me and I smiled back. Then she walked alongside of me and said, "Jig-jig two rupee." I pretended not to understand and walked on. 7-4-1944

Seventy-five years later to the day, I made a Facebook post that went semi-viral, and we calculated, just for fun, that as many as hundreds of thousands of people had read about and perhaps were speaking the name Chan at their barbecues and gatherings across the land on the nation's birthday.

Anti-immigration rhetoric was at a pitched frenzy in the spring and early summer of 2018. The "dog days" of summer had taken on a terrible new aspect. My wind socks spun wildly on the deck. I had spent most of 2017 trying to forget Dad's death and the election of Donald Trump to the presidency by stress-eating ice cream, rice, and dumplings. I also began drinking a lot and alone. The Chupacabra—a bitingly spicy margarita at a local farm-to-table Mexican joint, named for a mythical vampire-like beast that sucks its animal victims dry— felt to me like the Elixir of Life.

But living with your hair on fire, as I did in the Year of the Fire Rooster, is not sustainable. Eventually the fire that got you out of bed in the wake of a disaster burns up everything in its path and you are destroyed again, by your own hand. By the dawn of 2018, I was a pile of dispirited ash. And a bloated one at that, who didn't fit into any of its clothes.

On January 1, I poured a bottle of my favorite wine down the kitchen drain as a symbolic gesture and felt something picking itself up out of the dirt and getting to its feet again. I then managed my social media accounts. This went beyond hiding or deleting people and pages that annoyed me. I unsubscribed to news outlets and on-line groups, even ones I agreed with, that required sustained fear and outrage. I followed people and things that inspire me—Dan Rather, the Ocean Cleanup, Academy of American Poets, Lin-Manuel Miranda, and anything at all #Hamilton. I turned off the news sometimes to let other people carry the outrage for the day, because I needed respite and restoration. I stopped keeping wine in the house, recommitted to diet and exercise, and lost fifteen pounds.

I also planted a grove of trees in America's forests in celebration of my parents and their indefatigable growth mindset.

I felt back in the driver's seat—of my own life, at least—and I was achieving ever-longer periods of radical acceptance of the turmoil that swirled around us. I found you can still call your senators and con-gresspeople without letting the subject you are calling about control your emotional landscape.

Outrage is insidious. It makes you think you've been busy because it is exhausting. Paradoxically, it also soothes you in your inertia be-cause it makes you feel morally superior. What better recipe for apathy than perpetual exhaustion and a sense of moral superiority? *Get mad, sure, but then do the work. Even better,* I thought, *get less mad and still do the work.*

But then came the news of family separations at the southern border, the cages, the youth of the victims, and the administration of antipsychotics to get compliant (i.e., drugged, lobotomized) behaviors from traumatized children. Forced injections of antipsychotics into healthy children! Children who don't know where their parents are, who aren't even allowed to hug *each other*, let alone be held or comforted by their captors. Five months of work evaporated with a *pfffft*. I fell to my knees for a second time, and my soul screams returned.

But this was 2018, not 2016, a Dog Year. The Dog had asked me a question, and yes, it was a test: *How can you do this better?* And so, when I got up off the floor, I did what I do every time now. I called my own senators to tell them to keep at it. I called Republican senators and let them know that strong words were a day late and a dollar short, and I wanted to know what actions were being taken. I called Susan Collins and told her to stop catering and kowtowing to those malignant forces, or soon enough there'd be a Russian flag flying over the US post office. I called the Office of Refugee Resettlement and demanded they allow entry and oversight by senators and congresspeople. I donated money to the ACLU to protect civil and voting rights, to KIND to reunite children at the border with their families, to White Helmets to help with the refugee crises abroad, to the International Rescue Committee for the same. These organizations do the work that almost no one has the guts or the means to do themselves. We can support them and be engaged citizens. Disengaging is reckless and no longer permissible if we do care. I picked my battle(s) and got ready to fight them in whatever way I could. Our country and the world needed us, and still do. The ancestors had their eyes on me.

I have another weapon I can wield, and that is the power of the pen. And so, in my rage, despair, and isolation, and because I had taken real-world measures in response to the current crisis, I turned to an invitation-only Facebook group called Pantsuit Nation and dashed off a good old-fashioned rant like the days of yore, in search of connection and in hope of helping to galvanize our collective spirit in this brutal time.

My family and I were sitting in a darkened theater at the start of the movie *Black Panther* when I got the first notification of someone responding to the post. I got that first hit of dopamine—my rant had made the cut. And then the notifications started to accumulate and accelerate before my eyes. I could not finish looking at one without getting a dozen more as the feed started to self-scroll upward, the phone pinging anew every second. I turned to Brent and said, "I think the Chans are blowing up!"

I knew why. It's because we are as American as apple pie and people could feel it in their bones on the Fourth of July.

"What a post! Pure soul-nourishing poetry! This is a tale of America. Our America. The one we are taking back. The true narrative. Grateful you shared this."

—Harriet M., Facebook user, July 2018

I turned the phone off to watch the movie. Afterward, the notifications were in the many thousands, and over the next couple of weeks the number continued to grow.

I have two kids and three jobs, I had written, illustrating with a handful of evocative photographs. Not counting Mom in Chief. Do I want to be fighting mortal combat to preserve our democracy right now? No. I don't. I'm tired. I miss my parents. I am a joyful and loving person. I don't want to be the Firebrand. But here's a newsflash for everyone: I will do it. I will do it because my ancestors did it, and far worse. I'm from slaves and sharecroppers, a Chinese laundryman, revolutionaries, village schoolmasters, Unitarian ministers, educators, artists, and poets. Survivors and trailblazers nearly to a (wo)man. That is a heavy and humbling legacy. But I for DAMN sure ain't going to be the one to drop the baton.

My grandpa fled China at eighteen, condemned to beheading by the empress dowager, Cixi, for his leadership in the rebellion that would eventually depose the dynasty. He never laid eyes on his family or home again, though he died an old man. A poet, a scholar, and now revolutionary and refugee, he lived out his life in America as a laundryman in Savannah, Georgia. Together with his mixed-race wife, he raised six feisty, resilient, hilarious kids.

Many decades later he was interviewed by Roosevelt's Federal Writers' Project during the Great Depression. The interview is called simply "Laundryman." He was seventy at the time of the interview but was described as looking much younger.

"Yes, I look young," he said. "Always work hard, not eat too muchee, not worry too muchee. If you worry about trouble, you better go die."

He had escaped his own beheading and been forced to start again from nothing. This was the world as he saw it. When his son, my father, was a grown man in his own right, my grandpa told him, "I not worry about you. You got a stiff neck, like me."

My dad, the next generation, faced his own brand of tyranny abroad (in the China-Burma-India theater of WWII) and at home (as a person of color in the Deep South). Before WWII, Chinese Americans were mostly used as coolies in the US Army. My dad was the first generation to widely serve, and he made a meteoric rise to full colonel. He went on to become an optical engineer with Kodak and worked on the top-secret Corona Project, which was only declassified in the 1990s but is now credited with having helped to end the Cold War. His task? To create a camera lens that could take the first pictures of Earth from space, with resolution high enough to discern between two yellow lines on a highway or to read the headline of a newspaper. Of course, it must also withstand the forces of launch and reentry. He had thirteen patents in aerospace engineering and optics, many of which continue to be used today. He died in 2016 at the age of almost one hundred and three.

And now here I stand. Third in a line of tyrant crushers. Can I rise to the call? I'm tired and afraid, but my ancestors are my crucible and my guides in this terrible new challenge. I won't back down because they didn't. And if current political climates were different, I might memorialize these two men and their families in other ways—meditate on different aspects of their journeys and their characters, which were legion, but things today being as they are, what I find myself thinking most about is that they did it all in a time when our society was almost as unfree as it ever was for people like them. Neither man could marry freely, my dad couldn't serve the way he wanted (in the air force), although he was already a licensed pilot, because of race, nor could he work the same jobs as his classmates to help pay for college . . . My grandpa never got citizenship or the franchise.

But they did it all anyway. And they fought and stood for your rights as well as mine—not just in rebellion and war, but in their very being. Their mere existence was a bullhorn for equality and social justice. I can't, won't, and don't believe it was for naught.

Perhaps we all thought the Greatest Generation's job was to eradicate fascism and beat tyranny back to the gates. But we were wrong. Maybe their job was to do their time, and to inspire future generations to pick up the baton and continue the fight. Will we pick it up? Will there BE a baton to hand to future generations? Or are we simply unworthy inheritors?

I have compared my dad, Col. Robert Earl Chan, to a hickory, which is known as a "pushing" species. Strong and flexible, it can endure poor soil and harsh conditions better than other hardwoods. They persist. May they inspire us to, as well.

My grandpa's name was T'ai Peng, the Great Phoenix. That means rising from the ashes. Stiff neck, America! Don't bow your head to tyranny. I can hear my grandpa telling us, "Chop wood, carry water," and my dad, "There is no try, only do."

Who are your ancestors who have fought the fight, and now need you to carry it forward? Look to them as I look to mine. There is wisdom, assurance, and fortitude there; I can feel it. Can you?

I read and responded to every comment. Among all the thousands of them, there was not a single snipe, troll, or insult. A slow-rolling atomic love bomb was going off in my face, and I realized that what the world needs now—at least one small piece of it—is some of that Old Chan Magic. And what I needed now was affirmation that I was not alone. And I got it in spades. Connection had trumped tribalism.

Click. The golden door cracked open, and the Dog Year released me from its muzzle.

BOOK FIVE

2019
YEAR OF THE PIG

The Pig is the laughing Buddha of the zodiac. Legend says that the emperor hosted a race for all the animals of the realm, promising to award the first twelve with a place in the calendar. Pig came in last because it was so comfortable where it was. The Pig embraces openness, creativity, spontaneity, and a determination to nurture, not destroy. It is also the ultimate, contented homebody, and knows how to belong anywhere.

The Pig asks, *What is your relationship to the divine Yin? To creativity? To curiosity over certainty?*

The end of the zodiac cycle is akin to an exhale. It is wise to take time at the base of the breath to appreciate where you are and how far you have come. The storm is breaking up. What detritus will you let go with it? Analysis of the previous years will help you to project yourself more serenely into the next cycle. Have you focused too much on differences and disagreements? Will you allow for wonderment? Growth? Connection? It is a sacred moment. Pig's thoughtful, inspired action has the power to break you free from a dreary survival of circumstance and return you to your natural state of joy in discovery. Pay attention to dreams and visions, even daydreams, for this is where the Yin resides. Stay curious and creative about the world. It is bright with meaning. The sooner you accept it, the happier you will be.

CHAPTER 20

DREAM HOUSE

My deepening sense of there being magic all around us (the marvelous, unquantifiable, and inexplicable in all its forms, inviting our attention and our wonderment) was anchored by a few childhood stories that brought me face-to-face with the Great Mysteries. "Ba Comes to Visit" was one such story, when T'ai Peng awoke to the sight of his father's spirit sitting at the end of his bed; the dead jungle scout was another, when Dad was guided to safety by a comrade who turned out to have been killed days before. It continued with my own experiences, beginning in the Year of the Ram. Questions about whether these stories were "true" or "real" or happened the way the storyteller (or I) thought they did were far less important in their retelling than an examination of the way the stories made me feel. Did they get me to meet them halfway? Did they awaken hope or wonder? Crack me open, even just a little, to the possibility of something bigger, and the acceptance of something unknowable? And didn't that opening, for as long or as short as I was able to maintain it, make me feel better about a lot of things?

These stories were hard to believe, yes, but equally hard to dismiss. And now here we were in the Year of the Pig, being asked to lean into curiosity over certainty. *Why so rigid?* asked the Pig. *Why so certain about everything? What are you afraid of?* Trying to separate facts from magic is like trying to separate words from a poem. The Year of the Pig gave me permission to accept the stories as real because how can I be certain they are not? How can you? *How would it change you if you felt the truth rather than knew it?*

And so I turned to yet another story I had heard since childhood and let it work its magic on me.

It was during the long-range penetration missions ahead of the building of the Ledo Road that Dad began to have a recurring dream. It was of a well-appointed house somewhere in America that evoked feelings of safety and familiarity.

The dream was always the same. He walked to the front door, entered the house, and wandered from room to room, enjoying the sense of ease and belonging. The house was not anything from his life back home, nor did it seem to contain hidden meaning. He simply went there, explored it, and woke up in the morning. He chalked it up to battle fatigue. Who wouldn't want a lovely home to retire to in their dreams while their body rotted in the jungle—wet, shivering with malaria, or expiring from scrub typhus?

It's funny how we've learned to laugh at our misfortunes, wrote Dad in 1943. *Take dysentery, for instance.*

In Delhi, the men called it Delhi Belly. At Ramgarh, it was the Ramgarh Runs. And on the Ledo Road, it was the Ledo Leaks.

> *Dearest Sweetheart—*
> *If I stay here much longer, I'll go crazy. We die if we don't eat, and if we do eat, we get the [redacted by Army censors] -sentery. We get dhobi itch from the washing, and B.O. if the clothes are not washed. We studied language in one dialect, and the men speak another. The only two congruous things over here are that I love you and you love me.* 4-28-1943

Or take this beginning to a letter, the paper browned and rotted by rain, sweat, and mold, a rambling missive from the depths of a fever dream.

> *Beloved:*
> *Diss iss plenty no goot. Da chills, dey come, and da*
> *chills, dey go, but mostly dey come.* 8-8-1943

Scrub typhus, a mite-borne form of the illness, made him wish for death. It didn't kill him, but it left him nearly sterile.

The dream house was a welcome respite.

At war's end, when he was stationed in Washington, DC, he was out for a drive in the outskirts of the city when he started getting a powerful sense of déjà vu, though he had never traveled that route before. He was still sorting out this uncanny feeling when he came upon the house from his jungle dreams. He stopped the car, incredulous, and stared. His ears rang and his vision swam for a moment.

He made a snap decision, got out of the car, and strode to the front door. He took the brass knocker in his hand, hesitated, and let it fall. Footsteps approached on the other side, and a white-uniformed cook opened the door. She appeared to be in the middle of preparing a meal. She took one look at the man standing before her, let out a yelp as if she had seen a ghost, and slammed the door. Dad heard her hurried footsteps receding into the depths of the house. He stood on the porch for a moment and knocked again.

This time, the lady of the house appeared. She saw Dad in his army uniform, regarded him for a moment, apologized, and invited him inside. She asked the cook to bring lemonade and finger sandwiches. The other woman, still visibly shaken, curtsied and fled to the kitchen. The lady of the house invited Dad to sit in the parlor, where they exchanged introductions and engaged in a little small talk. Dad was exceedingly good at charming banter.

But while they talked and sipped lemonade, he scanned the space around him. He knew where every room in the house was. He asked if he could use the bathroom to wash his hands and found that he knew where that was too. He went there in a daze and splashed water on his face. Patting himself dry, he stared at himself in the mirror above the basin, but he found no answer there.

When he returned, the woman said, "Well, Major Chan, it has been so lovely to spend this time together, but what is it now that we can do for you?"

Dad decided that the simplest thing was to tell the truth. He thanked his hostess for her hospitality, apologized for the unusual intrusion, and said, "It was no whimsy that brought me here. I felt compelled to come to the door because, while I was in the jungle in Burma, I had a recurring dream . . . *about this house.* I never did know what it meant, but it felt like home. I was deep in a sense of déjà vu when I saw the house as I was driving by. I recognized it instantly. The uncanny thing is, once I walked inside, I knew where to find everything." He paused a moment. "Even the bathroom. I only asked you where it was to be polite."

Expecting to be laughed at, invited to leave, or worse, deemed a madman and threatened with police action, he awaited her response with trepidation. But who could have foreseen the truth?

"Well, Major Chan," she said, "what *might* surprise you is how little this all surprises me. You see . . . we've seen you here many times."

I reminded Dad of this story in his final months. He teared up and nodded, momentarily at a loss for words. Yes, he remembered.

"I don't know what it was," he mused, choking back emotion, "that told me I belonged there."

"This is one of the boys' favorite stories," I said.

"Oh?" he said, letting out a little chuckle. "And what do they say about it?"

"They think your life has been full of magic," I said.

He was silent, his gaze fixed in the middle distance, eyes glistening again.

"Yes," he said, and nodded, turning back to me. "That it has."

CHAPTER 21

MR. SAVANNAH BEACH

The ocean seems to try to tell you things.

—Commonplace book of Robert Earl Chan, 1930s

No summer trip to Savannah was complete without Dad driving us to Tybee Island to splash in the surf, build sandcastles, and my favorite, look for air bubbles in the sand left by baby clams tunneling away from me with impressive speed and agility.

I dug with all my might, and often came up empty-handed, but with perseverance I found I would eventually pull up a fistful of wet sand, and as it drained down my arm, there the treasure would be. A collection of baby clams in my palm, the size of my fingernail and in all fruity colors of the rainbow—pink, purple, blue, yellow. Every year I would put them in a glass jar with sand and seawater and bring them home to G.G.'s house. I'd set them on the kitchen table and watch them burrow, my nose pressed against the base of the jar. By morning they'd be dead, shells spread wide on the surface of the sand, beseeching the heavens.

One time Dad came up behind me and lowered his face over my

shoulder to look. "Aw, that's too bad. It's all right, honey. They need the sun and the movement of the tides," he said. "Nobody likes to stagnate, not even bivalves."

On the way home from the beach, Dad always said, "Let's stop at Chu's." Chu's was a warehouse-sized gift shop where you could find anything from sunglasses and candy bars to a whole spectrum of household goods made from seashells. Books about haunted Georgia sat next to blow-up rafts and flip-flops. It was a temple to American insouciance. Dad's favorite treat, and his main reason for stopping—or so I thought—was a Zero bar. It came in a wrapper of ocean-blue with white letters that cooled you off just to look at them. A Zero bar was a delicious combination of caramel, peanut, and almond nougat, with a layer of white fudge that made it distinctive in both flavor and look. I've never seen Zero bars anywhere else, before or since. Only at T.S. Chu's, only on Tybee Island. Dad said they tasted like summer.

Those were good times. How curious, then, that I spent much of my adult life shunning the beach. This came down to several pseudo-philosophical reasons and a few pragmatic ones. For one, I haven't always been near a beach. Also, my tan lines don't fade. In fact, the longest I've had an accidental tan line is three years. It's kind of a hassle.

However, I had also come to believe that there were two kinds of people in the world, curious and incurious, and that the world was dying for want of the former. I came up with a mental shorthand for the incurious—a person who stays put unless traveling the world to sit by the pool. The incurious don't move; they stagnate.

Curious people, by contrast, are restless; they move like the tides. They are visionary—striving, asking big questions, bending the world to their will. They elevate the conversation. This type of person travels the world the way others eat food and breathe air—because they have to. They do it to break the world (and themselves) wide open, to drink it in and spill themselves out, and to feel the expansion and connection that the blurring of boundaries can bring.

In short, the incurious are clams dying in a jar without even knowing it; the curious are free and in the wild. I considered myself part of the latter group and had frowned freely for decades on sun worshippers, those shallow, lazy beings who skimmed the surface of life, probably going on group vacations and lubricating with mai tais. Nothing could interest me less.

This contrarian view may have been no more or less complicated than a product of adolescence. Most people, as they move through that muddled period, first learn to define themselves *in opposition* to something. We often know what we're against before we know what we are for, and for a good stretch of time I was very much against sunseeking. I also idolized my father, who made curiosity an art form. He didn't just sit there and stagnate. He was the Most Interesting Man in the World. Sunseeking was the opposite of all that.

And so I embarked on a life of doing, saying yes to life's invitations, asking why about everything and, when appropriate, *Why not?* I pushed myself to the next level, the next accomplishment, the next mastered skill. I got plenty of positive reinforcement along the way. People began to see me as impressive, and maybe I got hooked on the feeling to the extent that I internalized the idea that my true worth lay in my deeds. I determined never to sleepwalk through life, and to do something even bigger next time.

And now here I am today, a doctor of archaeology, a multilingual former college professor, author of numerous peer-reviewed articles and a well-received book on a globally important topic. I am an international speaker, have a second-degree black belt in tae kwon do, and am a decent pianist. I was also named Best Photographer in my region in the Seacoast Community Choice Awards for five years running and have a Chinese brush-painting business. That may not sound like sleepwalking, but it was its own kind of trance. Conceive, reach, perform, achieve, master, rinse, and repeat. Stillness is stagnation, and stagnation is death. March. March. March. March.

When you are stuck in a trance, however, something will always happen that interrupts the flow and shakes you awake. You will realize that what you have done and who you have been thus far, no matter how much it has defined you, can carry you no further. You must invent yourself a second time or die. For me, that day came on March 3, 2016. Dad slipped away in my arms, and I said to myself, *I'm not going to survive this, not in any form recognizable to me.* And I was right.

LIFEGUARD

Dad was a lifeguard in his youth. He worked at the local Sheraton, and he also cruised the beach on Tybee Island, looking for riptides. He shared alternately harrowing and swashbuckling tales of that time. I shuddered to hear of the shark that ate a boy's heel for lunch but thrilled at the thought of riding giant sea turtles, controlling their flippers like rudders on a boat.

My cousin Jerry said to me once, "Alexka, your father was a *gorgeous athlete*." She let the words hang in the air for emphasis, then continued brightly, "He was just fun to look at, you know? I used to take my friends to the Sheraton pool down the street and watch the girls *fall* over him and the way he could do those dives, with all the twists and flips and things. I loved it. Everybody wanted to be close to him, but he was *mine*, you know. I was proud of him. That was *my* uncle Earl!"

When Brent discovered the box of old negatives in my parents' basement, these never-before-seen photos seemed to document a sweeping, audacious life, carried out with impossible good cheer. I plowed through the box, digitizing fifty years' worth of photos, deep in my trance of doing.

I was somewhat surprised at how many of the pictures were taken at the beach, where no one was really doing anything. The phrase *Dad went to the beach like it was his job* was no less true for the fact that his job was being a lifeguard. Look at the gaiety! These were some of the

OPPOSITE, LEFT: *Dad as a high school or college student in his lifeguard uniform* RIGHT: *Off duty and dreaming* THIS PAGE, TOP: *Mr. Savannah Beach* BOTTOM: *Stay thirsty, my friends.*

CLOCKWISE, FROM TOP LEFT: *Sin Fah; G.G. as a young mother; After the beach, dinner and dancing. Whether Sandor is enjoying or entertaining, with his band Blue Velvet, I don't know. Merle, G.G., and Sandor cutting up*

toughest times in American history to be non-White, but who would know it from these pictures?

Would you know that even after having graduated from high school (remarkable because there *were* no high schools for non-Whites in Chatham County, Georgia, at that time) and entered college, discrimination continued to limit his employment opportunities? Would you know from the interracial mingling seen in the photos between him, his siblings, and their partners, spouses, and friends that Georgia had some of the toughest anti-miscegenation laws in the country? Would you know that, while Dad was generally welcomed in White homes as part of a group of friends, that welcome only lasted as long as his anonymity? That as soon as he distinguished himself as something special—which was inevitable—he found his way barred by immovable fathers standing in doorways?

I began to perceive the beach not just as a respite from the blazing heat of a Georgia summer, but also from the infernal fires of a racist society. Social codes relaxed there. It brought relief and laughter. You could let your guard down—just be human and, unmolested, maybe get quiet for a moment or an hour. You can't imagine a better world or find your place in it if you can't get quiet for a minute to see it. Modern society is critically imbalanced toward the yang, logos, but the beach opens one to the Yin energy of the Pig. The beach invites mythos.

Throughout my childhood and adolescence, the big joke was that anytime we looked over at Dad in his living room chair, he'd be sitting with his legs crossed and his eyes closed. Someone would say, "Dad! Wake up!" and he would open his eyes and say, "I wasn't sleeping."

I like to say he was dreaming. While I rely on apps and spoken guidance, and sometimes drumbeats, to help quiet my mind, Dad was like a mythical shaman from the Asian steppes. He could close his eyes and he was *there*. Seeing things. Dreaming them into being. Making the Pig dance with joy.

Maybe the beach was the first place Dad learned to tap into that magic he would eventually be memorialized for. Maybe this was why, years later, when he had survived the moral injury of war, divorce, disappointment, failure, and the loss of parents, siblings, and friends, he was still dragging us out to Tybee Island and taking us to Chu's. The sun was always shining there, and he knew what kind of magic

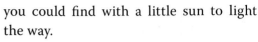

you could find with a little sun to light the way.

I started at the realization. Was Dad—athlete, scholar, warrior, inventor, spy (or perhaps more accurately, the spy's inventor-sidekick, Q)—a *sunseeker*?

A TALE OF TWO LEGENDS

Most of the faces found in the box of negatives were familiar to me, but there was one I didn't recognize. He was a young Chinese man, but not family, who seemed to spend a good deal of time capering about with Dad at the beach. There they were shaking hands, laughing, riding bikes, posing in both formal and silly attire . . . Who was he? I didn't know, and as Dad's needs got ever greater in his final months, I never got around to asking.

One day, as I was sitting alone by Dad's home-hospice bedside, the pump and whir of the oxygen machine murmuring in the background, he turned his head on the pillow, crinkled his eyes at me, and gasping a bit between words, said, "Tell me about your friends, honey."

Most of our conversation at this point consisted of easy prompts like this, followed by my talking and his listening with eyes closed, dreaming.

I stroked his hand, gnarled and soft, in mine and talked to him about people I knew who liked to ask the big questions and plumb the dark depths with me, the ones I could count on to celebrate my

OPPOSITE, TOP TO BOTTOM: *Dad and a new friend I didn't recognize; Dad in a silly cap and parasol; Who was this Chinese man with Dad in so many of his pictures? I had no idea, but I got a good feeling from him.* ABOVE: *Dad, resting but engaged, days before his death; Listening*

victories and weather my disappointments, the ones who knew when reverence or irreverence was called for and never confused the two. There weren't many.

"Well, you only need one or two," he said.

It was really a final act of love. Knowing that I could see no future without him, he was helping me remember how to make one, how to turn toward the light. Only, like Socrates or a Zen master, he didn't give me the answers. He just posed the important questions and trusted I would take it from there.

BIRDS OF A FEATHER FLOCK TOGETHER

Not long after Dad died, I was sitting on the floor by his stripped bed, rummaging listlessly through some of his files, when I came upon a newspaper clipping. The headline caught my attention.

Tybee Legend, Ting Shan Chu, Dies

Ting Shan Chu? Was this the T. S. Chu who sold flip-flops and Zero bars? Although aged by several decades, I couldn't mistake the face looking out from the newspaper column. It was the young man from Dad's old photos. *He* was T. S. Chu! We didn't go there to get Zero bars; Dad was going to visit his old buddy's place and whatever memories came up with it. The clipping was an obituary in the *Savannah Morning News.* G.G. had scrawled the date August 6, 1984, in her unique handwriting in the margin. She must have clipped the write-up and sent it to Dad. His old friend had died.

I read on.

OPPOSITE: *"Shall we strike up a friendship, Mr. Chu?" "Agreed, Mr. Chan." Chan and Chu, an original Optimist Club of two.*

Ting Shan Chu, 79, who came to America from China virtually penniless and built a business empire on Tybee Island, died Sunday morning in his home after a short illness.

He had come as a representative of Shanghai to the Chicago World's Fair in 1933, but afterward on a trip to Florida, he decided he wasn't going home.

Ting Shan Chu of Tybee Island was living proof of the American dream come true. . . . From a small beginning in business as a swimming pool concessionaire in Coral Gables he began to make his fortune. It is significant that an act of kindness to a visitor in Florida is what directed him to Tybee—the visitor was so appreciative that he gave Mr. Chu his small souvenir shop at Tybee if Mr.

Chu would pick up a business debt of a few
hundred dollars.

Hard work and thrift came into play,
Mr. Chu scrimping, saving, and expanding.
When he died Sunday at age 79, he was the
owner of the famed T.S. Chu's shop at Tybee,
in which a shopper can find just about anything. . . . He died a wealthy man.

He also served as head of Tybee's Cham-
ber of Commerce and its Optimist Club, and
over the years he had multiplied manifold the
initial act of kindness that propelled him to
Tybee. His many kindnesses and benevolenc-
es were well known.

Ting Shan Chu was a legend, and one of
our most beloved citizens.

I dropped the clipping to my lap and let out an audible guffaw.
President of the Optimist Club?! Of course Dad would be cavorting
with such a man, and within weeks or even days of his arrival at Tybee
Island. The pictures showed that Mr. Chu hadn't even changed the
name of the shop to Chu's yet. It must have been his first summer!

Birds of a feather really do flock together. Both lived the dream and died legends.

That's why Dad prompted me to think about who my friends were before he died. He knew you can weather every storm and reach any height if you have the right people around you. Make sure they are the kind that lift you up and help you learn, heal, and grow, the kind you yourself aspire to be. They don't have to be the president of the Optimist Club, but who is going to argue if they are?

SUNSEEKING

Dad *was* a sunseeker. I see it now. But his days at the beach were merely the most literal manifestation of a much deeper mode of being, that of the resilient, magical optimist, the laughing Buddha, always drawn back from dark places to the sun—whoever and whatever kept him vital and present; always rebuilding when earlier foundations cracked or fell apart; always winking at Fate, and even opening the door to let her come in and sit awhile. When that happened, like a plant that has found itself stuck in a shady corner, he just turned his face to the light and continued to reach and grow. By the time I came around, I only knew him as cheerful, generous, sometimes bawdy, and warmly reminiscent.

Dad sought and found the sun in his life again and again, and it started at Savannah Beach. Knowing how to drop everything to sit and play in the sun both reflected and perpetuated an uncanny ability to wear the circumstances of his life, whatever they were, as a loose garment, one that he could shift around in and not be too defined or constrained by. After all, loose garments can be taken in or taken off, thrown away, or replaced with new ones. This ability led to a lifetime of resilience, nimbleness, and optimism in hard times.

He had also stumbled onto the Tao early on. The fact that beyond all the doing (which was legion with him), there is a being, which underlies, predates, and will outlast everything else. It is unassailable, unbreakable, eternal. He was not his suffering. He was not his doing. He was simply his being. Sunseeking was one very effective way to shed the outer trappings and sink into that being where there is no crowding ego, no time, no good or bad, only presence and flow. This is where a person can reboot in the face of every hurt. But if you are too busy doing, you will never be able to find that being, and the healing, growth, and renewal the Pig offers will elude you.

OPPOSITE: *Only four months after Mom died, Dad, at 98, turned his face to the sun once more and picked up a little boxing again. We got him set up in my sister's old room.*

HAVING, DOING, BEING—THE ANATOMY OF AN AWAKENING

The day Dad died, I learned something I think he had known all along. There comes a time in everyone's life when one's doing has been exhausted. For all my lifelong devotion to hustle, and the frenzy of doing that went along with easing his transition out of the world, the fact was that no pursuit, no notch in my belt, no *plan* was going to stop my worst fear from coming to pass. When they finally wheeled Dad's body out the front door, I was so emptied of every impulse, every feeling, every ability, that I was a bit surprised to find myself still there. The doing had ceased, but somehow I had not.

Here I was, sitting in Dad's overstuffed lift chair, almost nonresponsive. It was as if I had defined myself so completely by deeds, and had never learned to just be, that now finding myself incapable of even the barest of intentions, I would suddenly go *poof* and disappear.

But I didn't.

I read somewhere that there are three levels of consciousness: having, doing, and being. The child and adolescent is preoccupied with having, in order to feel safe (things, toys, a home, clothes, family, friends). The young adult is obsessed with doing (establishing careers, differentiating and proving themselves, exploring and achieving). But the wiser, older person is content with just being, because the simplicity of one's presence is the only thing that is real. All else is an illusion or an egoic projection.

With Dad's death, I found for the first time that I couldn't do anything anymore. I didn't prepare a single meal for my family for weeks. I cried all night, got up late, washed myself rarely, trudged around in smelly pajamas, and lost my composure in every room, at every time of day, and in every kind of company. And yet while nothing that had ever defined me until this point was operational, my *being* persisted. Absolutely nothing could eradicate or diminish it. It just went on. I realized, perhaps for the first time, that I was not anything I did, but something I was. I simply *am.*

I existed and persisted in that formless, flexible state for many weeks, and it made me fearless. Doing nothing began to make me feel like maybe I could do anything. My battery was recharging; I could feel the energy rising. Grief also proved a gateway to something invaluable in me that had nothing to do with being seen or heard. I had never spent a day, let alone weeks or months, completely unconcerned with being seen or heard. After a lifetime of relentless pursuit and growth, I was learning the value of stasis and surrender. The fact that I had no choice in the matter did not blunt the impact of that lesson.

I kept pictures of Dad at the beach everywhere, to remind me of the beauty of simply being. On my desk, by my bed, in my sock drawer. I studied every detail. What can we learn from a day at the beach? In my imagination I merged with the pictures before me. I heard the water and smelled the salt air, felt the grit of the sand on my skin, and saw the gulls and scudding clouds above. If I closed my eyes, I found I could almost conjure the memories and daydreams of these people from nearly a hundred years ago. As a human *doing*, I had lived most of my life in my head. But a human *being* enjoys a more embodied, sensory experience, and takes fuel from it, which can then be converted to intentional and empowered action.

WHERE DO YOU WANT TO GO?

I had thought that to live life to the hilt, as Dad had done, I had to go nonstop. I was wrong by half. The most creative and fulfilling period of my life has come only since grief stopped me in my tracks. A supernova of creativity burst forth out of the nothingness that followed Dad's death. A creativity I had been pursuing all my life was now gushing forth, as unsought as it was unstoppable. There was a connection between the being and the doing. I could feel it.

I try not to fear stasis now. Indeed, I am unapologetic about building idleness into daily life. If I am having trouble with something, I do what I can and then let it go. I alternate purposefully between intention and surrender. I am also trying to have more fun.

There is a time for waiting, resting, restoring, which I am still learning how to do, but then also a time for boldly stepping forth to pursue and meet our destiny. Neither one is to be discounted. We can do it alone, or—and this was Dad's wish for me—in the company of like-minded souls. He knew that the right kind of company accelerates everything and makes it more potent.

And if you ever get tired, as you will, his pictures seem to say to me, *go and seek out the sun.*

One late spring afternoon after news of another mass shooting broke, the weight of it all oppressed me. So I took a chance, dropped everything, and went for a walk in search of sun. About a mile into it, I still had found no relief. In fact, I felt worse. *I'm seeking sun, goddammit. That's what I'm supposed to be doing, right?* I sat down, in need of still and quiet. My own walking was driving me to distraction. *Breathe. Wait for gratitude.* I made a quick inventory of my blessings—my children, the animals, my health, the beautiful day, and the lovely town I was stomping through. But today it all sounded like nothing. Lost, I started to cry.

An elderly woman snagged my attention as she struggled to get her car into the parking spot in front of me. She pulled in and out, peered back over her shoulder, forward over the steering wheel, and out the side window. I watched with vague interest, wiped my eyes, and muttered, "I can't find the sun anywhere. I'm surrounded by darkness. Help me."

The woman got out of the car and wandered directly over to me as if it were her mission to do so, maybe even her whole reason for coming to town. She came right up to me and said, "Hello! I just want to tell you that you are sitting in the most beautiful sunbeam right now. It is shining through the brim of your hat, casting marvelous sparkles of light over your face. It's beautiful. I wish you could see it. Say, can you tell me where State Street is?"

I was stunned. I had stomped around for an hour demanding to be shown the light, and when it became apparent that I couldn't see it unassisted, a woman went out of her way to tell me I was awash in it and sparkling.

OPPOSITE: Gongshi. *Gongshi means "scholar's rock." A small scholar's rock might be put on a custom rosewood stand for your table or desk, while large ones might have an entire garden built around them. Their purpose is to inspire contemplation of their subtleties and nuance: their thinness, their perforations, their wrinkles and ridges, their color gradations. Chinese scholars—like my grandfather, T'ai Peng, and his father before him—knew that not all wisdom comes from books, and there is a difference between knowledge and understanding. This piece is paired with calligraphy that reads "Tranquility yields transcendence."*

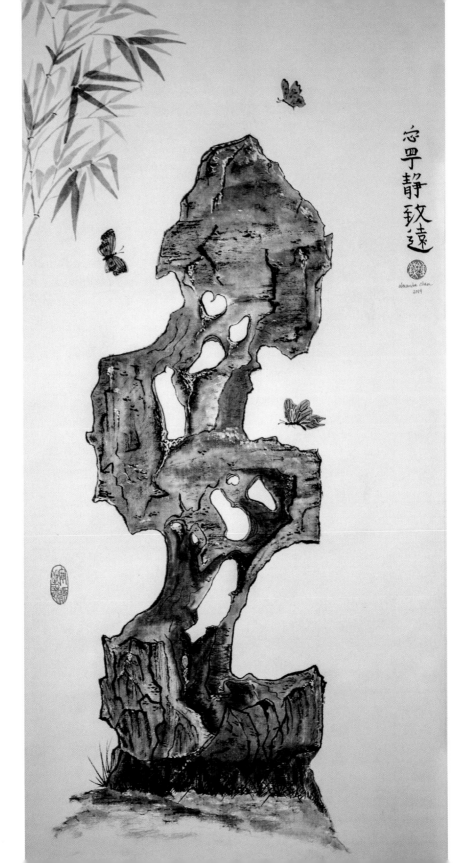

CHAPTER 22

THE EARTH KEEPER

Since the Great Gardening Rampage of 2015, I have been much more keen about the stewardship of my small patch of earth and its creatures. Gardening turns out to be a perfect activity on the spectrum from being to doing. Your hands are busy, there is some purpose involved, but mostly it's just an excuse to be alone with Nature and your own thoughts, which glide easily from subject to subject and offer sparkling flashes of insight.

In 2019, the image of the laughing Buddha, symbolizing the energy for Year of the Pig, really captured my imagination, and I wanted to embody it as much as possible. To me that meant tend the garden and feed the birds, and the squirrels and chipmunks too. Rescue the mice and spiders. Pull the weeds, but only if necessary, and never ever use a chemical to do it. I rid the patio of poison ivy using boiling water alone. That spring I dabbed peppermint essential oil in the crevices of my kitchen, and for the first time in my life, despite a dire forecast of an exploding pest season for New England, I saw neither hide nor hair of the no-see-um ants that normally swarm the house every May.

I have been an attentive gardener in the years since Nam Duck first came to my campfire. It seems our little corner on the way to downtown has begun contributing to the neighbors' sense that our town is a special place to live, and that one should be on the lookout for delight-ful vignettes, which the eye may fall upon at any moment.

A VISITOR

One night in June, upon returning from our weekly pilgrimage to what I believe is the best Mexican food north of the border, we discovered a baby bird cheeping in the potted snapdragons by the stoop. We heard it first and then saw the leaves tremble and heave this way and that, alerting us to the fact that there was something alive in there other than flowers.

A quick survey located the nest in a vent far up the side wall of the house, too high to reach, even with a ladder. So, after much dith-ering and sending the kids upstairs while we figured something out, I tried to make the bird—a sparrow—comfortable in the pot with tufts of grass and clover. Then I got my hand spade and dug up grubs and worms from the garden.

Of course, I had read that one is not supposed to attempt to feed a baby bird because you might feed them too much or the wrong thing, but his plaintive calls could not be left unattended. I wondered out loud to Brent, though, if we should just give up, hope he lived through the night, and get him to an animal rescue in the morning. As I did so, however, we both looked up at the same time to see a red car driving by with a vanity plate that said DONTQT.

We gave each other a humorous look, as if to say, *You heard the man,* and then shrugged in agreement. We knew what to do. I read up quickly on feeding baby birds by hand, noting some caveats along the way. One was to stop feeding while the food is still bulging in the craw, which is the small pouch on the side of the bird's throat. Once the bulge has gone, you know the bird has finished swallowing and you can continue.

I cut the worms into small sections and used tweezers to pick up a piece at a time. Just coming into the bird's peripheral vision caused him to launch his head out in frantic, wobbly expectation, his calls taking on a hysterical note that made my uterus clench. As wide as his mouth was, though, it bobbed and trembled so violently it was a bit like trying to pin the tail on the donkey while galloping on horseback. I began to fear I would not be able to feed him at all, despite my best intentions.

In time, much as with my human children, I got the rhythm of his movements and was able to match them to my own, and he ate eagerly. I relied on instinct and observation to determine when enough was enough. With this little guy, it was clear. He settled down from his panic, got full of worms, and then fell into a wee food coma, letting out occasional contented little cheeps and exhalations even as he slept.

I decided grass and clover were not enough to keep the evening chill out, and I brought the whole pot inside for the night. I dug up extra worms for a nighttime snack and kept them in an empty tomato container whose bottom I had lined with soil. Fledglings do not have to eat every half hour around the clock, I learned, as newly hatched babies do. That was a relief. In fact, birds of this age can usually sleep through the night, and that's just what this little one did.

The following day I was outside in the dark light of morning, in flip-flops and a nightgown, getting his next meal ready. As the day dawned sunny and warm, I brought the pot back outside and set it in the sun. I fed and played with the bird all morning. How feisty and strong he was. How curious! The contrast with the panic of the night before was stark, and knowing that it was because he was well rested and fed gave me a surge of joy. I also delighted in his frequent naps, how easily he slept.

When he was awake, however, I found he couldn't be left alone, which is probably how he had gotten himself into this mess in the first place. He trampled all over the snapdragons, charging hither, thither, and yon, exploring the boundaries of his world. When he reached the rim of the pot, he rested his chin there for a moment, looking out beyond his bubble in a hilarious reverie. Then he lifted his head with a jerk and was off in another direction. At one point, having overestimated his abilities again, he charged right over the edge, the way a toddler bumbles into a street without any apparent instinct for self-preservation. He would have fallen to the sidewalk, wriggling helplessly there until he was picked off by some predator or crushed underfoot by a distracted pedestrian. But I was watching him, and I shot my hand out to catch him.

The warm squirminess of him, the rubbery plumpness, was surprising and felt wonderful in my palm, and I guess he liked it well enough too, because he snuggled down almost immediately to take a quick nap there, pressing himself against the soft warmth of my fingers.

"Such a little sweetheart," I said under my breath. "Look at him go."

The kids named him Lucky. And indeed he was a lucky little fellow, wasn't he? To have fallen from such heights into the soft bed of a flowerpot below, and one that happened to belong to a woman who had been recently thinking of herself as the Earth Keeper on her small plot of land. Lucky.

STATE OF BECOMING

As with all good fortune, the real value of things often lies in their impermanence. I knew we couldn't keep Lucky. We took him to the animal rescue in Cape Neddick, Maine, where they put him in an incubator, and I guess eventually set him free.

It felt good to do this from beginning to end, both as an individual and as a family who pooled resources and ideas to make it happen and were able to bond over the outcome. So, who was really the lucky one here?

When I got home from dropping him off, I looked up the symbolism of the sparrow and found that they traditionally represent self-love and feelings of worthiness, as well as hard work and creativity. The back of my neck prickled as I thought about the agonies of self-doubt I had endured around my writing since Dad's death, how hard I'd been on myself because I didn't know exactly where I wanted to go, let alone how to get there. I began to reflect on seeing and treating myself as the tender being I had held in my palm just hours before. Was this the message for me? Yes indeed, the world is bright with meaning, as the Pig had admonished me to start noticing.

When I saw that baby bird, so feisty and strong, tramping boldly from one side of his pot to the other through the underbrush of obstacles, trying to find the boundaries of his world, before turning around and stomping back, it was not only hilarious but precious. It touched a deep part of me. Just look at him, trying so hard, starting to take risks. He can feel he's got feathers coming in, but he can't fly yet. From my vantage point, of course, I could see that he was full of a potential for flight that would surely be realized, and so I had not a worry in the world for him.

Might not this description and these feelings as easily be applied to myself? *Look at me,* I thought, *so curious and insistent, full of the sound and the fury, feeling called to soar.* It wasn't that I was constitutionally unable to fly; I just didn't have my wings yet. Feeling my feathers come in was making me impatient and demanding.

DEEPER TRUTHS

One morning not long after the encounter with Lucky, I woke up to a phrase lingering behind my closed lids, hovering in the air like balloon letters. It said, *It's okay to be in a state of becoming.* I have taken heart and gained a softer, more loving view of myself since we found and saved Lucky, and I made the connection between his state of becoming and my own. *Here I am,* I thought, *tramping through snapdragons and exploring my flowerpot.* This is me resting my chin on the edge and looking out into the world, wondering what's in store and wanting to get there. And when my feathers are in, I'll not even necessarily know it. I will simply jump from the pot's rim and find that I have taken flight. To where remains to be seen, and I can hardly wait.

CHAPTER 23

EGYPT

For all my work on seeking sun, and embodying the contented Pig, I was still an unnatural sun worshipper on vacation. But it was my last day in the land of the sun god, Ra, and so I flagged down the waiter in a pink polo shirt and ordered a virgin Bloody Mary by the pool. It was well-salted, peppered, and lemony. I wanted to savor it, but the paper straw gave up the ghost partway through, and I was forced to gulp down the second half without it. So much for elegant leisure.

It was April 2019 and we were on the family trip of a lifetime—and for an archaeologist like me, a real bucket-list item. Egypt. We did it all and back again—Cairo, Giza, Aswan, a three-day boat trip up the Nile, and Luxor.

I set my glass aside and gazed up at the Great Pyramid of Khufu, which loomed over us. Thoughts began to crystallize out of the mists that had been swirling in my head the past week, and I put down my book to concentrate.

Something was coming.

THE LUCKY NUT

Travel, to me, is more than vacation. Every time I travel, I find what I call a "lucky nut," some big discovery or moment of clarity that I can take wisdom or healing from, and which aligns me better on my path. All my recent trips reveal themselves in retrospect to have been touchstones in my life, helping me to course-correct in important ways. There was my life before Iceland and after Iceland (and boy, was that a big one), before Spain and after Spain, before Austria and after Austria. I deferred my college enrollment to live with a family in Austria for a year in 1991 and made friends for a lifetime there. In 2018, I had a chance to take my whole family back with me. I sat outside one evening with my old host-mom, Christine, under the plum and apricot trees, and in front of a traditional "Swedish torch" she had set up—a vertically set tree trunk, incised on the sides and burning in the middle. It's a great source of heat and light, and delightfully pagan-feeling. She had brought out her own homemade hazelnut schnapps, and as we sipped, we talked and laughed about love, life, and loss. She was bereaved too, as she had lost her husband and my old host-dad, Herwig, who had died suddenly in his sleep.

"And with a smile on his face!" she exclaimed.

I couldn't keep my new enthusiasm for all things synchronistic, intuitive, and magic out of the conversation, and at some point during that part of it she said, "Talking like this makes me feel less alone." I checked in with myself and found that, yes, I was less alone too, and in fact *not* really "without home or family," as I had been telling myself for years.

Vacation brings reprieve from responsibility and obligation so that deeper truths can come through. Vacation grants permission to stare into the ether, motionless, for long stretches of time. Have you ever tried to find the back of a bottomless blue sky? It's mind-bending and liable to fill your head with all kinds of things you never thought of before. Vacation also lets you make relationships the central part of every moment, so you get clear about those as well.

Perhaps if you are into grittier kinds of travel and adventure, as we are, it is also the unexpected juxtapositions you encounter—the new sights, sounds, tastes, and yes, smells—that jolt your awareness into another dimension, the lurch of your emotions and point of view when confronted with uneasy realities. Street cats, dogs, and children come to mind here. Whatever it is, when I travel, the plug is pulled on my everyday mind, which empties like dirty dishwater. New experience flows in. And somewhere in the process I get flashes of insight on all manner of things that plague and overwhelm me. That is what I call the lucky nut.

The only trick to lucky-nut-finding is that you mustn't go looking for it, because then it will elude you. You must wait and let it come to you. How ironic that my long-awaited lucky nut was coming to me now, just as I was sitting poolside on the Giza Plateau. *What's this?* a laughing Universe seemed to be saying to me. *Traveling the world to sit by the pool, are we?*

TRUST LIFE

When we arrived at our hotel in Giza at 3:00 a.m. after twenty-two hours of travel, we discovered that the connected rooms we had reserved to keep the kids close were unavailable. Brent and I would have to split up to each stay with one child. Once settled, we also discovered that the electric adapters we had brought did not fit in the wall sockets, leaving us without phone or communication, including with the tour company that would be driving us around, and without even an alarm to wake us up in time, about four hours hence. As a photographer, my greatest concern was that I had no way to charge my camera for more than a day's worth of pictures. Imagine being in Egypt for eleven days and not taking pictures for ten of them.

What should have sent me into a fit of panic and outrage . . . didn't. I felt removed from the whole thing and heard the words *trust life* in my head. Somehow I knew that while these were small setbacks, everything would come out all right, and probably sooner than I thought.

The kids, however, started to spiral. While they love to travel, at twelve and nine they were relatively new to the game. Every setback made them think we were definitely going to die. I heard myself telling them, though, with complete calmness and a deep inner knowing, that everything was fine and they just needed to trust life.

Trusting life is the practical thing to do when you are traveling. You are without many of your usual resources, and so what other choice is there really but to take things as they come? But on this, our first night in Egypt, the admonition to trust life felt like something more than just a practical travel tip.

For a start, I normally locate the origin of my conscious thought stream to a thick band above my eyes, like a bandanna around my forehead. These thoughts usually come in picture form—I see them. But I experience my inner voice as purely auditory and originating from behind my right ear. So when I hear a thought rather than see it, and it comes from the back of my head rather than the front, I know it's time to listen up.

This simple-sounding mantra to trust life was meant to represent, or open a door to, something much bigger and deeper than wall chargers and a connected suite. I made a mental note of it and went to bed.

As our trip progressed, I found more and more occasion to reflect on the importance of trusting life and what that means. Let's just talk about Egyptian traffic for a minute. Getting behind the wheel on the streets of Cairo requires a level of trust that I may never reach. There are often no lanes marked on Egyptian streets, nor any stoplights, stop signs, or speed limits. There is also no law about what kind of so-called vehicles are allowed on the road—or if there is, it is not enforced.

Congestion, bottleneck, traffic jam, gridlock—the traditional words and phrases we associate with traffic simply don't do the situation in Egypt justice. Cars and commercial trucks barrel down roadways laced with jitney buses, vans, tuk-tuks, motorcycles (often carrying four or more people, including infants), horses, mules, camels, carts mounded with garlic or heaps of tomatoes, and contraptions that must surely have been built by the drivers themselves out of scraps found in alleyways and the garbage heaps that clog the canals. I missed a picture of an orange seller's cart on the highway, which was a bicycle modified to have a gas motor, and a steam-punk-looking cart twice as tall as it was wide teetering off the back. The cart consisted of four posts, a metal roof, and a platform beneath holding an upholstered dining room chair—presumably for the man to sell oranges from when he came to a stop. A bevy of nylon net bags carrying bunches of oranges hung from nails and hooks up and down all four posts and across the metal roof.

They swung wildly to and fro with every bump in the street, threatening to upset the cart at any moment. Or maybe it only appeared that way.

In Egypt, dogs and pedestrians—including unaccompanied small children—regularly pitch into the streets from both sides and all angles, seemingly unafraid of not making it across the street alive. When our vehicle stopped, it was swarmed by small children making halfhearted attempts to clean the car with a dirty rag, holding out their hands for *baksheesh*—coins that might buy them their next meal. Neighboring cars streaked by, leaving only inches between themselves and these small, soft bodies.

And yet we never saw a single accident, or even a close call by Egyptian standards. There was no incident of road rage. Gradually, although how it really all works continued to elude us, we had to concede that there was a kind of order to the chaos. And doesn't that mean, by definition, that it wasn't really chaos? It only appeared that way because we had not the eyes nor the skill to see and navigate it in its proper context. When it comes to driving in Egypt, we decided the drivers are either complete maniacs or Ascended Masters. We arrived thinking the former and left thinking something closer to the latter.

I was surrounded in all directions by examples of people trusting life and going with the flow as a matter of course. Indeed, I came to see the streets of Cairo as a kind of land-based counterpoint to the great river Nile itself, flowing always onward, with people dipping in and out of the current at will, allowing themselves to be carried along but still getting where they wanted to go. *What an enviable combination of intention and surrender,* I thought. *Imagine what would be possible in life if I could balance my focused intention with complete surrender.*

While Egypt offers a diverse menu of opportunities to trust life in direct, physical ways, I began to extrapolate from this place something much broader and more metaphorical. Trusting life in this sense meant to me not needing to have all the solutions, not even to acute setbacks, in order to have a peaceful, contented life. Like slipping into one of the long, loose *galabiya* that many Egyptian men wear, a garment that is separate from you and allows you to feel it as separate. There, I found myself not only experiencing life but also observing it in real time. In doing so, by being observer as well as participant, I stopped confusing my circumstances, my thoughts, my emotions, my fears, with . . . myself.

Anthropology is all about stepping outside of a situation to objectively observe it from a distance, even as you are experiencing it directly. That said, this kind of participant observation, as it is called, is easier to do on someone else's life than on your own. But there is great freedom in it if you can do it, and I found this state of being coming to me with ease in Egypt. I walked around feeling like I was wearing life loosely, and suddenly it didn't matter what happened or didn't happen because I experienced it all as going smoothly regardless. There was a distinct sense of gliding through the days that I hoped I could carry back with me.

THE ANKH

The Egyptian hieroglyph for Life is the fabled symbol of the ankh. I remember Mom wearing her gold-foil-plated ankh necklace throughout the 1970s, '80s, and '90s, although she never really put it away for long. It was her signature piece. I have Mom to thank in large part, by the way, for my becoming an archaeologist. She had wanted to be one herself, but she entered college at NYU in the late 1950s, when archaeology wasn't considered a suitable or viable career for a woman. What's more, she wanted to combine an archaeology major with a geology minor and was scoffed at. *What does geology have to do with archaeology?* The answer, as we now know, is *a lot*. Her geology professor, she told me, was considered by most academics at the time to be a part of the lunatic fringe. He taught a theory he had about something called "plate tectonics." *Preposterous,* they chorused. *Continents don't move!*

But indeed they do, as we all know today. Everything moves. Nothing stays the same.

Mom was ahead of her time in this, as in many ways, but rather than push on, she tucked away her dreams of becoming an archaeologist and decided to study classics. Afterward, she became a librarian for a while, and then somehow ended up at Kodak as a computer systems analyst, one of the first women coders. It was another trailblazing

TOP TO BOTTOM: *Sitting on the Great Pyramid of Khufu; The boys glide through a Cairo bazaar. Child tuk-tuk driver; The Pyramids of Giza*

field for a woman, but not one that brought her much joy. Satisfaction through challenges met, perhaps, but joy? No.

And so Mom had a gold ankh necklace that she wore everywhere. Our house was filled to the rafters with books about the ancient world, lost civilizations, and ancient human ancestors, with maps, atlases, dictionaries, textbooks, obscure publications, historical novels, and coffee-table books. We'd flip through these together and she'd talk about the wonders of the ancient world, famous sites, and current theories. Her excitement and interest ignited my own. By second grade, I knew the australopithecines as well as I did *T. rex* and *Brontosaurus.*

When I grew up, *I* became the archaeologist. And when Brent and I decided to finally go to Egypt, I knew to pack two things for sure: Dad's college ring, which had seen the world through WWII and later travel, and Mom's ankh, the symbol of Life. I slipped the ring on my finger and the ankh around my neck and didn't take them off for the next twelve days.

Visiting the pyramids, exploring the Giza Plateau, tiptoeing inside the tombs, and touring the Egyptian museum, I thought not just about life but *Life.* One has only to see the teeming streets of Cairo and Giza—the street children hustling, the feral cats and kittens galore, curs by the score, or a passel of plump, sleepy little pups discovered in the shadow of the citadel (which Seu dearly wanted to take home)—to know that while individuals come and go, Life itself blooms eternal.

Amid these musings, I also gained a more nuanced understanding of the ankh, which symbolizes more than just life. It is the symbol of *continuing* life, eternal life; it is also the symbol of family (mother at the top, father at the bottom, children to either side), and Egypt itself (Lower Egypt at the top, Upper Egypt at the bottom, and the Nile crossing and uniting the middle). The absence of any one element disrupts the whole, and no one component is more important than the others, but together they carry on forever. Mom and Dad may be gone, but the family is still intact because I am still here, and the boys carry it into the future.

The pyramids, giant edifices that plant themselves in your psyche, never far from conscious thought, are also all about rebirth and resurrection, continuing life. I looked up into the night sky on the second day of our arrival and saw a full moon—the end of one cycle, the beginning of another. The following day was Easter. So the early part of our trip was awash in symbolism about not only life but resurrection. Not resurrection of the body, as the ancient Egyptians were trying to effect, but reanimation, say, of a tired spirit. A recommitment to, and trust in, Life. New days and good mornings. Couldn't these be possible for me again? Isn't it time?

I had been adrift for three years now, and in some ways it had felt more acute than ever in the early months of 2019. In Egypt, though, I again felt plugged into the Great Life Current. I began to feel a part of something vast. After so many years of isolation and disconnection, I sank into the feeling. Maybe the admonition to trust life on that first night of our arrival was really trying to tell me to plug back in, reconnect, and trust that Life has everything you need.

GREAT RIVER

From the air, it is apparent that the Nile is the giver of all life in Egypt. It wends through the desert like a ribbon. Close to its banks is a sharply defined green zone of fields, canals, banana trees, and date palms. Outside this area . . . nothing. No hint of life or reprieve. Only sand and stone and unforgiving skies.

In a country of one hundred million, more than 90 percent of Egyptians live within three kilometers of the Nile—just 6 percent of the entire landmass of the country. And so even when we were not in actual view of the water—wandering the Cairo bazaars, for example— there was still always the underlying sense, or at least the knowledge, that it was all an extension of the Great River Nile.

It wasn't long before the Nile seemed like a real-world manifestation of the Great River of Life itself. This was an easy jump to make, as everything in Egypt seems to be on the move—flowing, streaming, sometimes whirling and swirling, but never still.

Brent and I wandered with the kids through the bazaars in a dreamlike state, carried on currents of sight, scent, and sound from the hawkers and street traffic, colorful spices, pungent teas, hookahs, incense, alleyways awash with humanity, street cats, lamps, textiles, and souvenirs.

We motorboated up the Nile on day trips, chugging through tall stands of bulrushes, enjoying the breeze, and watching egrets, while the boys took turns arm wrestling our guide, Saber, who was himself a new father (as in, his daughter was born the previous night, he told us blearily that morning). I sat with my camera and alternated between beatifically watching the scenery go by and looking through the viewfinder to frame the next picture. *Dad,* I said in my head, *you were just like this, always one foot in the action, one foot out, never knowing whether to jump in or capture it on film instead.* I grinned, put the camera up to my face again, and scanned the river. There was a small island ahead with a rock outcropping that looked like it would make a pretty picture. I framed the shot, zoomed in a bit for a better crop, and then felt the breath hitch in my throat. There on the rock, sitting *in the middle of the Nile*, was the name "Bob" spray-painted in white. "Hi,

Dad!" I said under my breath and snapped the picture.

Motorboating was for day tripping, but our real journey up the Nile took place on a riverboat cruise. For three days and nights I sank further into the feeling of being carried, cradled, cherished.

The air on the river is sublime. Soft and billowing, never harsh, it is the last thing I expected in a desert nation. The sensation on your skin and in your hair is like that of a caress. How can one doubt that one is being looked after in the presence of such a feeling?

I photographed the bulrushes and flocks of snowy egret; the palms of all shapes, colors, and statures; the little wooden barks hidden in the reeds, evidence of human life and industry. I saw the

children come out to the banks at sundown and shout merry greetings to the passing ship, running barefoot with their comrades along the shore, climbing trees for better vantage points, and shouting in jubilation at any greeting in reply. I saw motorcycles and mopeds, donkeys and carts, tuk-tuks by the score, fishermen mending sails at day's end, and vendors of cheap towels and scarves in rowboats hanging out in the middle of the river to throw a rope and hitch a ride with any passing ship, even entering the locks with us, to try to sell their wares.

The sales hustle was not just for grown-ups. Small boys with no wares to sell floated in the river on old paddleboards, using scraps of wood as hand paddles. Apparently unconcerned by the crocodiles and hippos, they jumped to their knees and bicycled their arms when a motorboat passed nearby. After grabbing some element of the boat and hitching a ride, with their little legs dangling in the water all too near the motor blades, they broke into raucous and cheerful song, including one gratuitous rendition of "Happy Birthday" in English, serenading the tourists in hopes of a baksheesh of Egyptian pounds.

From the sundeck, which I was loath to leave because of the exalted majesty of the air there, I regaled myself on the abundance and flow of life, both on the water and at its edge. I looked up and saw not only the egrets but Egyptian vultures, blue herons, and always a handful of wee birds the size of sparrows and chickadees back home. They sailed and *OPPOSITE, TOP: Languorous days floating down the Nile BOTTOM: Dad winking at me* dipped and circled among each other, silhouetted against the sunset sky, weaving patterns of air in their wake. Every night they ended their dance with a flourish before going their separate ways, each with its own kind, to settle in for the night.

Modern Egypt never felt wholly separate from the ancient sites that dot the landscape. We visited the pyramids of Giza, the Temples of Philae in Aswan, the Temples of Karnak and Luxor in Luxor, and the Valley of the Kings. These places can overwhelm with monumentality not just of the structures themselves, but also of the vision behind them and the collective effort it took to make the vision manifest. Their sheer scale is one of those things "you just had to be there" for. Their antiquity and magnificence put our modern world into perspective, revealing it not at all as a culmination, but as a point on a spectrum that has great variety and depth. They are another reminder of the Great River of Life.

Most of us spend the first few decades of our lives imagining our own selves to *be* the river. We spend all our time finding and marking the banks, staking out our territory, and finding ways to show everyone how deep our waters go, how fast and far they flow. But Egypt shifted my perception on this, and suddenly, amid all this swarming humanity, lush life, and millennia of history, I understood that I am not the river. I am a current, a ripple, an eddy, in a river of such infinite vastness that it is beyond my ability to ever grasp yet encompasses us all. And what does that mean? It means that I don't have to "do it all." I only have to play my part. My ripple helps make the river as big and rich and powerful as it is, but ultimately, ripples, currents, and eddies come and go. They form, sometimes out of nowhere, and dance and gurgle about for a few moments, create pleasing patterns, entertain themselves and others, and then recede back into the whole. And that, in itself, is a worthy thing.

But aren't they delightful to watch, and aren't you glad you got to see them? And didn't that particular one tickle you in a most memorable way? And wasn't part of the delight you felt a result of the fact that you knew it was temporary? It is the nature of ripples and eddies to appear, create patterns, and go. And don't you equally know that just because the ripple is no longer visible doesn't mean that it is no longer there? Indeed, that it has become part of the larger current that buoys you up to the surface to ripple in your own way?

Some might think this comparison is depressing and a rebuke to our sense of importance and self-worth, but I don't. I am comforted by the idea that my life is unique but small, part of a much bigger current that rushes on despite me, but also—*also!*—partly because of me. It makes all my losses less abrasive and cutting. It makes my own eventual end less fearsome. My parents, my aunts and uncles, T'ai Peng, they all rippled and eddied in the most marvelous ways, then faded back into the whole. Just as the people who built the temples and pyramids four thousand years ago did. And the river flows on—forceful, harrowing, beautiful, joyful, but always unabated—to this day. And I am a part of that. That feels good. It is the opposite of isolation, loneliness, or disconnection. It is the opposite of being stuck or left behind.

It is the ultimate contentment and belonging. The ultimate energy of the Pig.

Gazing up that day at the Great Pyramid, the peppery taste of my virgin Bloody Mary lingering on my tongue, I suddenly knew what the lucky nut was. It was an invitation. First, to see myself as a ripple, not the river; second, to step back into that river and know that I am being carried and cradled safely within it; and third, to understand that this is in complete counterpoint to being cast out, alone, homeless, or orphaned. It was an invitation to set my intentions but then to surrender, like the people who day in and day out stepped into the flow of Egyptian traffic. To let me ripple and eddy to my heart's content, knowing I am part of the river and trusting in it to carry me downstream.

Back home in New Hampshire a week later, looking at an assortment of lucky nuts that I had brought back with me from my recent travels, I discerned a pattern. Lucky nuts don't fix things by them-

Grappling with my aspirations and fears at the base of a monument to ancient aspirations and fears. Four thousand years of Sturm und Drang. There is kinship in that.

selves; they are not magic talismans. They are simply a view of how things could be different, and an invitation to try it.

Iceland invited me to rest and be alone with my wounds. It was a chrysalis within which to dissolve my rigid structures and start my nascent healing, and a suggestion to do it through story. Spain invited me to reanimate my frozen heart and slowly start to take breath again. Austria reminded me that family comes in many forms.

And Egypt invited me to step back into the current of life. This time without the fight, and with a new and humbled vision of what my place in it is or even needs to be. Egypt invited me to see myself as part of something vast, and therefore never alone.

Scarab—*"Resurrection"*

BOOK SIX

2020
YEAR OF THE RAT

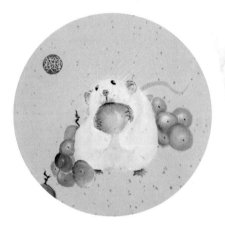

Observant and adaptable, with lightning-quick reflexes, Rat can make a plan for anything and has the unwavering courage to follow it. Like its captive brethren in a lab, Rat sniffs and intuits its way through the maze, even when it can't see around the next corner. It knows that at the end of the maze, reward awaits.

Rat brings healing for 2020, which portends shock, chaos, and new responsibilities in health and economy that will force most zodiac signs to rely on their wits and existing resources like the Rat's food and seed storage. *Winter is coming.* There is good news. The Rat's instincts are perfect for tackling uncertainty, and success is possible if you can be flexible in how you define it. Rat is relentless and resourceful and will never become discouraged by failure. It is also kind and asks you to receive its medicine and be a conduit of it for others. Don't let your mind be clouded by fear. The path out of the maze is there; you just haven't found it yet. Trust the intuition and the healing Buddha heart of the Rat. It knows the way.

CHAPTER 24

MUCHMORE

In the reading I have done for this book, in the poems and writings of both ancient and more recent poets, scholars, and mystics, from Homer and Callimachus to Whitman and Gibran, I have found a tender, new, and subtle kind of belonging. Many times I stumbled on quotations and passages I had seen before, scribbled in Dad's commonplace book from his youth that was filled with quotes, anecdotes, witty and clever observations, things that made him go *hmm*. It was exciting because it meant that I was, as if by accident, treading the very ground he trod before me. It was like finding breadcrumbs that led out of the dark wood. *Ah,* I wanted to say each time anew, *and so you have passed this way too, Dad.* I was becoming an accomplished tracker, the Rat sniffing its way out of the maze, and Dad the jungle scout ahead, always around the bend, motioning with his hand and dropping clues. *This way.*

What a subtle communion and sense of companionship it brought. I am twice as old now as he was when he was making these discoveries and scribbling them in his pocket notebook, but I have always been a late bloomer. It felt significant one day in my reading to stumble upon a passage about fond reminiscence, intellectual camaraderie, and companionship—as if Dad, too, remembered our late-night bull sessions. It was an excerpt from the poet Callimachus's elegy for his friend Heraclitus, in the third century BC (movingly translated by William Johnson Cory in the nineteenth century).

> They told me, Heraclitus,
> They told me you were dead.
> They brought me bitter news to hear
> And bitter tears to shed.
> I wept as I remembered,
> How often you and I
> Had tired the sun with talking
> And sent him down the sky.
>
> And now that thou art lying, my dear old Carian
>   guest,
> A handful of grey ashes, long, long ago at rest,
> Still are they pleasant voices, thy nightingales,
>   awake;
> For Death, he taketh all away, but them he cannot
>   take.

Speaking of becoming an accomplished tracker, have you ever gone on an "intuitive walk"? This is where you empty your mind and let your feet lead the way. I started doing them in the week leading up to Dad's death, when I felt stripped of agency and power. I walked . . . and let the gods have their way with me. And the gods guided me in powerful ways, day by day, right down to the morning I knew *today is the day*, down to the moment I closed the computer, put my dishes in the sink, and got in bed with him to whisper him to the other side.

My brother was still talking about Dad having six months at that point, but my walks had told me *six days*. On the sixth day it did come to pass, as I had known it would. For at this point I was a wide-open portal and I knew everything. Though I have not been so open since, it is the reason I keep doing these walks. They don't tell me everything anymore, but they always leave me with something.

I went on one such intuitive walk in a local cemetery, sniffing my way through the rows like the resourceful and intuitive Rat. It was the early days of the Covid-19 pandemic, when walking was one of the few pleasures still allowed us. I washed my mind clean and gave myself over to whatever wanted to come, but my intent, I can't lie, was to reassure myself that I am never alone. I tried to have no expectations. It was just a beautiful place on a beautiful day. I strolled through the cemetery with an empty mind, only following a tiny tug I felt to go this way or that.

Within the first sixty seconds, I found myself standing by the gravestones of Robert and Annie, the names of my paternal grandparents. I smiled but swatted it away. Further down the row came Mary and Russell, the names of my maternal grandparents. My smile widened.

"But why not you first, Mom and Dad?" I asked aloud, deciding to play along. I turned the corner and met Mother. And Father. I continued to walk. I started hoping to hear from some aunts and uncles, but with names like ours I knew it would be tricky. Was it likely that I would find an Archie here? Well, then came Eunice and Her Husband—no name on the stone. Just "Her Husband." *How odd.* But Uncle Archie's wife was named Eunice, so there was my Archie, standing proud. Did I detect some amusement? *Are we playing a game?*

I felt a buzz and kept going. *All right,* I thought, *let's have some fun,* but my hope soon fizzled. How is there going to be a Bernice, Sandor, Sin Fah, or Gerald here?

I said in my head, *I can feel you all crowding closer; thank you for coming. I am grateful for the signs you were able to send. I'll bet there are more of you here than can be reasonably found on these stones, though, eh?*

At this, and without intending to, I came to a sudden stop and looked up. I was standing directly in front of a family tombstone that said MUCHMORE.

I threw my head back and laughed at the sky.

CHAPTER 25

ORPHEUS

An ordinary late-summer afternoon. My phone vibrated on the couch cushion beside me, letting me know a message had come in. It was from Michael, my nephew who is four years older than I, and Dad and Gretchen's grandson.

What was the name of your dad's favorite tobacco? Captain Black? I can't remember the name.

Getting a message like that in the middle of my day, apropos of nothing, makes me feel less alone. Like a sonar ping sent out from a submarine, it roves the murky depths, listening for echoes of itself. Someone else is out there thinking of our shared past, in meaningful ways and just because. He wants to know if I am too, or if he is alone at sea.

I echoed the pulse back to him, typing with my thumbs.

Walnut. Just Walnut.

Then I retrieved an empty canister from the bottom of the hall closet, where it had been sitting full of pennies for the last two and a half years. I set it on the arm of the couch and took a picture of it to accompany the message.

THE ORIGINAL 19TH-CENTURY PREMIUM ENGLISH BLEND OF THE WORLD'S SEVEN FINEST TOBACCOS says the label, in a wobbly and irregular font evocative of the Artful Dodger scuttling waist-high between greatcoats, an orphaned, wily, good-natured cutpurse on the loose in London's foggy streets. I think that in a Dickensian world, Dad would have been the Artful Dodger rather than the sweet and hapless Oliver Twist. The image behind the lettering shows a pipe and tobacco shop on a gaslit, cobbled street that leads down to a harbor where merchant ships with sails rolled up on their masts bob on the horizon, hinting at more pungent and exotic shores.

Thanks. That tobacco is so ingrained in my experience with him.

A simple statement. But the subtext, I knew, was that Michael missed his grandpa Earl as much as I missed my dad. For a moment, we were in commune.

Me too. I was hoping the canister would retain some of that rich, sweet scent, but, alas, it doesn't.

Michael responded:

I think the tobacco has to be smoked near to when it is placed in the canister to get that succulent, almost opioid presence. I do miss that smell so much. Words cannot describe it.

And then, after another moment:

I'm grateful that I don't crave tobacco anymore, but holy shit-balls, that pipe could put a spell on me.

Was it the pipe or the man that cast spells on mortal men? Dad started smoking a pipe when he was fourteen. Whether out of curiosity, enjoyment, or youthful rebellion, I don't know, but he cut a striking figure with one, a fact which he was not insensitive to, for he had a streak of vanity that he was wholly unembarrassed about.

"Well, it ain't braggin' if it's true," he used to say. He wrote to Gretchen, having a laugh at the expense of some acquaintance in his rooming house.

> *P.S. B___ bought himself a 50c pipe. He's heard the girls saying how peaceful and relaxed I look smoking mine, and how much they like to smell the smoke, and how much they like a man "who smokes a pipe," so he rushed out to make arrangements to "look peaceful and relaxed" and to let them "smell the smoke from his pipe"*

*and to have them fall over him. . . . Right now he looks
like a self-conscious frog with a stick stuck in his mouth,
and he keeps asking, "Don't you think I'm remarkable?
I've started smoking a pipe! Don't you like to smell the
smoke?" Ha! Ha! Ha! Ha!* 12-9-1941

Dad would rarely be seen without a pipe in mouth, hand, or pocket until he was eighty-five.

That was the day the doctor slipped the X-ray onto the light box hanging on the wall and pointed out the small white flecks in the bottom of Dad's lungs. "Early-stage emphysema," he said.

Seventy years a smoker, Dad quit the pipe cold turkey that day, mostly lost the cough, and lived another twenty years unintubated.

That was after I had left the house, though, and so the memory of Dad sitting by the fire with legs crossed, a book on his lap, and a pipe between his teeth is the very image of home. The smell was warm, mellow, and sweet. Walnut smoke is smooth. It pours into your nostrils like a potion and travels to the back of your throat, hanging there heavy and redolent before faint wisps curl forward over your tongue. When it reaches the tip, where the sweet taste buds are, your brain receives the message of candied confection nearby. Oxytocin fires in the brain.

An unbent paper clip made tinny scraping sounds as he cleared the bowl of the dottle—the unburned tobacco remnants left after a smoke—and then came the fleshy thumping of the empty bowl against his palm as he readied and stored the pipe for next usage.

In conversation, Dad puffed away, alternating between amused and serious eye contact with whoever was speaking. He grunted, chuckled, nodded, blew smoke, pipe jutting from his teeth. When it was his turn to speak, he eased the pipe from his mouth and cupped the bowl in an upturned palm. It was an open pose, indicating receptivity, a relaxed demeanor, and thoughtful, honest engagement with the topic and the person at hand.

If you had touched on a hot-button topic, though, he could grab the pipe from his mouth and turn the bowl in his fingers in one deft move, so the stem was now facing outward and could be jabbed in the vicinity of your chest as an apparent (and Michael thinks intentional) extension of his middle finger.

As an archaeologist, I can tell you that artifacts are not just inanimate objects. They speak to you if you know how to listen. Artifacts are exciting because they offer a window into the mindset of the people who used and discarded them—their dreams, aspirations, and daily taken-for-granteds.

OPPOSITE: *Dad in his dorm room at Georgia Tech, ca. 1936, "peaceful and relaxed"* BELOW: *Dad spots an obliging sundial and imagines himself the Winged Mercury, fleet-footed messenger of the gods and good-natured trickster.*

Dad's pipes are collectors' items today—Kaywoodies, Savinelli Long Johns, Stanwell Danish Stars, Craigmoors, Peterson's Kapmeers. As he never had much money, this is a perfect example of how rich with meaning an artifact can be. It goes way beyond simple purchasing power. He preferred the flame grains for their swirls of red wood leaping and gleaming on the bowls, giving the appearance of flickering firelight. He took pride in smoking Walnut, which he called the aristocrat of tobacco, in his Kaywoodie, which he called the aristocrat of pipes.

He also anthropomorphized his favorite pipes, giving them names and attributing character traits to them that were thinly veiled reflections of his own most prominent qualities. There was Orpheus, demigod of music; Morpheus, shape-shifter and master of dreams; Ulysses, legendary wanderer, cunning warrior, and culture hero; and Chiquita, the little girl, but perhaps closer to a hot little number.

I doubt Dad consciously named his pipes after the most salient aspects of his own personality, but it cannot be disputed. Dad *was* a divinely gifted musician. He *was* a shape-shifter. Not in the sense of hiding who he really was, but insofar as honoring and giving expression to all facets of his being. He *was* a legendary wanderer, a cunning warrior, and maybe the most famous culture hero you never heard of. And he was nothing if not a sassy little spitfire, flirtatious and bold, hard to pin down, and the life of every party.

HALF-DIVINE

I learned about Orpheus, Morpheus, Ulysses, and Chiquita from Dad's war letters, and I confess to having had to look up who Orpheus was.

No mere mortal, Orpheus was the son of a Muse and a Thracian prince, a Greek demigod whose divine gift was that of music. There was no limit to his power when he played and sang, and he had no earthly rival. The gods alone were his equal. No maiden could resist the allure of his song; no love he desired could be denied him. Even the stones on the hillside pulled themselves free, and rivers reversed course in sweet surrender, wanting to be nearer to the man with the enchanting voice and silvery melodies.

When Orpheus's new bride, Eurydice, died of snakebite, Orpheus wandered the wild solitudes of the earth alone, forsaking the company of men and finding comfort only in his music. He roamed the world playing music until, one day, he met a band of people who could not hear his song, and who tore him limb from limb.

One thing Michael likes to send since Dad died is music. Often I will open my email or texts and find a link to a jazz piano virtuoso like Jesús Molina. No explanation. None needed. Dad was a great pianist, and he passed his love, if not his immense skill and dedicated practice, to both of us. Neither of us plays as well as Dad did, but we get by. Michael plays better than I do. He also plays in the improvisational style. I have recently rededicated myself to lessons, but I sometimes joke that anyone can read the notes.

But you see, Dad didn't need notes. True, he was classically trained, despite T'ai Peng's wishes. The Chinese boy refugee had grown into the patriarch and had, despite his generally democratic principles and open-mindedness, a few of what Dad called "unsound Chinese ideas." One of those was that piano was for girls. G.G., who was enthusiastic enough, had a wooden ear. She could play anything you put in front of her but sounded like a player piano doing it. Meanwhile, Sinnie, Dad's second-oldest sister, sighed and moaned through lessons. When Sinnie finally announced imperiously that she was through with piano, Dad turned hopeful, pleading eyes to his parents, who—miracle of miracles!—gave in to their son's emasculating impulses.

Dad must have been not only a brilliant but a determined student, because he had learned Liszt's *Liebestraum No. 3* by the time he was a teenager. It starts off simply enough, but don't be fooled. The piece requires virtuosic ability that few can aspire to. And what do you think he did with that raw natural talent for classical music? He turned his back on it. I never heard him play a classical piece in my life. Imagine being able to play Franz Liszt and never doing so!

Dad's soul required something altogether saucier and more invigorating. He sought out Harlem stride, ragtime, old standards, and improvisational jazz.

From there on out, he didn't need notes. Heck, he didn't even need a piano! Any flat surface before him would do as he riffed with elegant fingers on the dining room table, on the steering wheel at a stoplight, or waiting for food at the diner. He hummed along in a low, gravelly voice that welled up from somewhere deep, so you could follow along with the melody, but he wasn't doing it for you. It was spontaneous self-expression, and it was part of who he was. Music was like a bodily function for him; it coursed through his veins like lifeblood.

He lost his virginity under a piano when he was fourteen, which isn't exactly material to the story, but a fitting little piece of trivia. And I'm going to go out on a limb here and say that in the end, music saved his life.

EARL CHAN, COLLEGE MAN, 1933-1940

Dad entered college as a freshman in 1933 at the age of twenty. Before long, he had formed a band, Robbie Chan and the Georgia Five. They played private parties, school dances, and community socials, and though he was on piano there was little doubt, from his look to his talent to his overflowing charisma, who the star on stage was. He made frequent appearances in the gossip column of the *Technique*, the school newspaper, "harmonizing" with girls, "casting amorous eyes at" girls, "dancing" with girls.

> With the idea of becoming God's gift to the fairer sex, Earl Chan, that intrepid scholar, danced hither and yon at the Anak dance last Saturday night, breaking here, capering about there, and really celebrating in a big way.
> —*Technique*, "Co-Op Chatter," October 16, 1936

In 1939 he met Gretchen Best, who was also a college student in Atlanta. They were married on Christmas Eve, 1941.

> *She's due to fall in love with me this winter, because she said, "It'll be a cold day when I fall in love with Earl."*

—Commonplace book of Robert Earl Chan, ca. late 1930s

THE WAR

While he was fighting overseas, Dad's opportunities to either play or listen to music were drastically reduced. But music, or the lack of it, was a frequent topic in his letters back home. He seemed to soak it up whenever and wherever he could, like a moth to a flame, and to shrivel a little at the shadow of the musical life he had led back home. Instruments were hard but not impossible to come by, and he

OPPOSITE: *"Robbie Chan and the Georgia Five" gigged campus dances and parties regularly.* ABOVE, LEFT: *Orpheus if he lived in 1930s America* RIGHT: *Race was no barrier to dating for Orpheus.*

once obtained a foot organ for a few weeks before having to give it up to go back in the field. He showed ingenuity in building a make-shift radio from a downed Japanese airplane. His only complaint was that he had to share musical tastes with everyone around, which he did not.

PAYING IT FORWARD

Dad's piano playing was the soundtrack to my life. I brought my dolls with me under the piano while he played. While I constructed elabo-rate scenarios and used books and other objects to create houses and rooms, the soft mechanical workings of the pedals sounded behind me, the wooden thumping of the hammers above me, and above it all, clear sweet melodies that surrounded and inured me, temporarily, from all stress, strain, or cynicism, all disappointment, fear, or worry. Looking at Dad from the knees down, I knew I was safe.

He was often playing when I went to sleep at night. Many nights I awoke hours later to the sound of music flowing through the house again. Dad never seemed to know what time it was. He played as heartily at 1:30 a.m. as he did at 4:00 p.m., sleeping people be damned.

Dad sent me to lessons when I was nine. He wasn't much into *things*. I can count on one hand the number of things Dad gave me over the years—a beautiful pen, a wall mirror that he made in his woodshop because I asked him to, an exquisite Victorian dollhouse built from scratch, a bookcase with adjustable shelves for my college dorm room, and a well-stocked toolbox. Even at Christmas and birthdays, when the tags read "Love, Mom and Dad," I knew from the way he leaned sideways to get a good look and was as curious and interested as I to see what it was, that Mom was the one doing the shopping.

Dad's gifts were more likely an opportunity to experience something that had been important to him, not just something that was fun or that he had enjoyed. Looking back, I see just how abundantly he gave. There were lessons in piano and horseback riding, but also in photography, skiing, swimming, diving, fishing (although I wasn't a very gratifying student on that count), storytelling, and world literature. There was always travel, and of course higher education. He made sure we all—my brother, my sister, and me, and his grandchildren—had an opportunity to fold these things into our lives too if we wanted to. He wasn't just trying to schedule us; this was reverent gift giving in its purest form. Each of these things had been transformative in his life, and so he was eager to give us the tools to transform our own.

LOVE LANGUAGE

In early July 2015, the cursed Year of the Ram, we were driving home to see Dad in rehab after he'd had a serious fall in the bathroom. He had a hematoma on his temple and several cracked ribs. We had also conspired with Michael to fly in from Oregon with his son, Dad's great-grandson, Owen, as a surprise at the end of the week. I was looking forward to the reunion and the surprise, even if the catalyst was less than ideal.

My phone lit up with Dad on the screen and began to buzz.

"Hi, Dad!" I said brightly. "We're on our way to see you. Only about six more hours. Maybe we can have dinner together tonight."

"Honey?" he screamed. *"Alexka!"*

My stomach fell to my feet. "Dad, what's the matter? What's going on?"

"Honey, you've got to help me! They've locked me up!"

There were loud scuffling noises as he fumbled with the phone. Over the course of the last several years he had lost the use of most of his fingers, including his thumbs, as the tendons in his hands had seized up due to a condition called Dupuytren's contracture. He made adjustments with each new loss in dexterity, but earlier that year he had found he could no longer play piano with his little "T. rex claws," and it was a devastating blow.

"I'm in prison!" he cried, hysteria tinging his voice and making it shrill.

Cold prickles ran down my spine and sweat appeared under my arms. "No, Dad." My mind reeled trying to figure out what was happening. Dad had a little forgetfulness at this point—he was nearly 102—but he was an entirely lucid man.

"You're not in prison," I told him. "You're in rehab right now. You fell. We're coming to see you; we'll be there today."

"I'm telling you, call the police!" his voice rose to a frenzied pitch. "They've got me chained to the toilet, honey! *I'm in chains! Help me! I need you!*"

"No, Dad. It's not true. Let me talk to the doctor. Where is the doctor? Can you see him?"

"For the love of god, you've got to come get me!" If you won't do it, nobody will!"

Then more scuffling, a muffled thud, and the line went dead.

"Dad! *Dad!*" I called him back, but the phone went to voicemail. I looked at Brent and fought the urge to scream, *"Fly, you fool!"* But what good would that do? We had six hours of highway ahead of us. I clasped my hands in my lap and pressed my head to the window glass, squeezing my eyes shut, stifling sobs, and pleading for strength *and speed.*

When at last we burst through the front doors of the Hurlbut nursing home and rehab facility, me speed-walking in front, we found that the episode had passed and Dad was quiet in his bed. But he looked like hell.

The brutal black bruise that covered most of the side of his head did not frighten me as much as his hair. This man had not had a hair out of place in literally a hundred years, and right now he looked like a kitten whose fur had been licked forward by its mother.

The nursing staff told me about hospital delirium, and that it was common for elderly patients to become unmoored when their physical surroundings were suddenly changed. He was calm but not thrilled to see us, mostly because I was the only person he recognized at the moment, and I had left him to the wolves that day. He slid his eyes sideways to meet mine in a grim look of grievance. No one in the room but I knew the volcanic rage that smoldered under such a look. The boys, however, understood immediately that the grandpa they knew was not there. They pulled back and pain blossomed in my chest.

Perhaps drawn to the cluster of new people, Dad's roommate, a dapper, accented, well-coiffed gentleman, shuffled over to Dad's side of the room. He had been a Russian university professor, and was dressed in round spectacles, a tweed jacket, a vest, a plaid bow tie, and a white dress shirt hanging halfway down his thighs. He asked Dad why he had stolen his pants again.

Chaos ensued.

Dad leapt back to life, yelling, "Now, you listen to me, you son of a bitch! I didn't take your goddamn pants! I've never stolen a thing in my life!"

The addled professor shook his head and tsk-tsked at Dad's potty mouth, then went to Dad's closet himself and rummaged through his clothes, looking for the missing pants. Dad sputtered on his bed like a kid telling the principal he hadn't done anything. In his drifting mind these were serious allegations, and his reputation was on the line. The colonel and the professor, both half-naked and arguing over missing pants. It sounds funny, perhaps, but I clenched my jaw tight—tighter— to keep my composure.

The good news was that by the time we left that night, Dad knew his two grandsons again. Every day after that, Jin and Seu went with him to his stationary bike session, cheering him on to hit the numbers he needed to be allowed to go home. They drew a picture of his boxing gloves, writing "Knock 'em out, Grandpa!" in big crayon lettering, so he could hang it on the wall above his bed for inspiration.

We spent a week there, coaxing him back to us. On Friday I came in at lunchtime with his favorite treat, a bag of cherries. I put a handful in a Styrofoam cup and brought them over to where he was sitting in the common room.

"Well, life isn't always a bowl of cherries, Dad," I said, "but that doesn't mean you can't *have* a bowl of cherries!"

This was the clever little banter that Dad loved, that defined him in a way, and I saw his body perk up to the familiar rhythm of our witty repartee. Then he laughed. *Hallelujah!*

While he slurped on his cherries—everything is harder with T. rex claws—I looked up to see Michael tiptoe around the corner behind him, nervous anticipation on his face. He didn't know what to expect either. Tears of happiness sprang to my eyes.

Dad struggled to turn in his seat to see what I was looking at, stared for a moment, confused, and then shouted, "Oh, you son of a gun. Michael! Come here, my boy! Come over here! Sit by me."

"Hi, Grandpa Earl. I heard you got in a fight with the floor."

Dad howled. Owen stepped forward and showed his great-grandpa the new camera he got, and then all three boys, Owen, Jin, and Seu, got to know each other again. Each meal, each day, each conversation, Dad's psychosis faded further into the background. Soon he was singing "Yes, We Have No Bananas" over FaceTime with his great-granddaughter, Owen's sister, who had been too little to make the trip. She showed him her muscles and he told her she was *his* girl. Like days of old.

On Michael's last night in town, we went to the home's dining room, where there was an old upright piano in the corner. Owen wheeled Dad over while Michael took a seat on the bench. A Georgia boy needed some Georgia music to make him feel better. Stumbling a little without sheet music, and breaking off repeatedly to say, "It's been a while since I practiced," Dad still managed to get out some skilled and lively renditions of "Georgia on My Mind" and "Sweet Georgia Brown," among other songs.

The love was palpable, and I knew that night that while Dad still had a journey ahead of him, everything was going to be all right. And it was. Dad loved music his whole life and made it one of his main gifts to others. It was so fitting that in the end, when he had lost his music and, temporarily, his own song, we were still able to hear it and sing and play it back to him.

Dad never lost his taste for singing bawdy little tunes from his days in the college glee club—the cleverer and more off-color, the better. Get him a kazoo and you'd really have something to write home about. I know from the stories that when he was a young man, his music was seductive. It beckoned, promised, and lured his listeners with whispers of their own daydreams and, perhaps, illusions. No wonder he was so popular.

But when I knew him, his piano music had more sorrowful strains that seemed to contain a lifetime of yearning and mystery. He became stoic in his demeanor, a transition that pictures suggest was tied to the war. Although always a conversationalist, he did not often share deep sorrow or pain, and I saw him cry only three or four times in my life.

The first time was when Sandor died. An earthen clod hit the coffin lid, and a hollow thud rang out. Dad took in a sharp, ragged breath. "Oh boy," he said, looking down into laced fingers. "I never really felt it till now."

The second time was on my wedding day. He looked like the Godfather, never taking his sunglasses off. Mom later whispered conspiratorially that partway through the ceremony she'd had to remove a damp piece of Kleenex stuck to his cheek.

When Mom died he was beyond tears, and they never did come. And then the last time I saw him cry was at the end of his life, when he tortured himself over whether he had really needed to kill that Japanese soldier he picked off hiding behind a log one day, floating in retreat down the Irrawaddy River.

"He was just a kid!" he sobbed. "What if he was just trying to get away, and I killed him?"

Victor Hugo wrote, "Music expresses that which cannot be put into words and that which cannot remain silent." Dad's music spoke when words failed him. He played with an emotion that could be heard only with the heart, and if it caught you unawares, the sweet melancholy could make you weep.

When we were planning Dad's memorial, I saw a person I didn't know on the list of speakers. The woman was the daughter of a man who had grown up on Dad's street in Scottsville, New York, the same street where I grew up a generation later. The boy had lost his own father—to an accident or illness or maybe even to the war, I don't remember her saying—and Dad had befriended him. He taught him how to ride a bike and take pictures and fish, to do a little boxing and mechanical work on the car. The boy—now a man—was, ironically, in Savannah on business at the time of the memorial. He had heard of Dad's passing and called his daughter, telling her she must go and speak on his behalf.

She read his prepared statement, and although she had never met Dad in person, seeing what he had meant to her father made her voice crack with emotion. My memory is hazy on the wording, but I remember the feeling. He wanted people to know that Dad had saved his childhood, that Dad was like a father to him, but one who also taught him how to remember his own dad in healthy and healing ways. He didn't know what would have become of him if Dad hadn't seen that lonely boy and known he needed a friend. He ended with a memory of what it was like to live on that street. I am paraphrasing:

> Bob's lights were always on—always. And on summer nights, when he had the doors and windows flung wide, the crickets were chirping and the night was warm, and people were settling into their beds, his beautiful piano music drifted on the breeze, over the rooftops of the neighborhood, and made everybody feel like the world was still a good and decent place, that there was still beauty here, and love. And that everything, in the end, would be all right.

Only in the wake of his death, as I have turned to the piano in my own darkest hours—and more tentatively, playfully, the guitar—have I understood what those ivories did for Dad, and what that nostalgic yearning was all about. Music is like that. The ineffability of it allows your soul fuller expression, even, perhaps especially, when words fail. Hearing and playing it makes a person feel seen, wholly seen, even the broken, crumbling, and dusty bits, and loved anyway. To be seen, and loved anyway . . . isn't that the foundation for building anything your mind can conjure?

Dad didn't just love music. He needed it. It took his pain and sorrow and cleaned it, handing it back to him as something beautiful. He healed himself every time he played, and healed everyone he played for in the process. As if in answer to the kindly and empathic Rat, who asks us to not only receive its medicine but be a conduit of it for others. I think that counts as at least semidivine, don't you?

My own losses and disappointments pale when stacked against Dad's. And yet I knew him as a joyful son of a gun. I never understood until I started writing about him just how much of that was simply a decision to be so. Happiness, it turns out, is an inside job. It takes optimism, grit, and discipline to not let yesterday's failures, fears, grief, or disappointments dictate today's actions. It takes no discipline at all to lie down in defeat or to wallow. No imagination whatsoever to think the world well lost. Music lets a person imagine . . . differently. It can inject mythos straight into the veins. Therein lies its beauty and its power.

I can see Dad sitting at the piano, and I think I hear him saying, *Be disciplined enough to choose a good life, whenever and wherever possible. Remember, it is always possible. Be resourceful, intuit your way, define success broadly. And if you will let it, music can be your guide. Follow the Rat. And keep listening and imagining!*

Orpheus indeed.

CHAPTER 26

WHY WE TELL STORIES

When it comes down to it, every story is ultimately about the search for human connection, and the cost it extracted from you. Every story is about whether you got what you wanted most, or didn't, and who you became in the process of trying.

I can sit here now and tell myself any number of things. *I used to see no way forward, but now I walk a lighted path. I used to be afraid, but now I know I can be brave. I used to think family was everything, but now I stand on my own two feet. I used to think I needed saving, but now I save myself.*

There is a story, and a cost, to linking the first half of those sentences with the second. Am I willing to tell it? The dream of writing this book eluded me for long years, its siren call torturously distant and indistinct. The question became *why*, and I knew if I couldn't say why, my book would never be.

In 2021, the Year of the Ox, I would begin to see telling my stories as akin to me, also an Ox, tilling ravaged and exhausted fields—preparing new ground for growth and renewal.

AN UNEXPECTED JOURNEY

Rewind thirty years. I was twenty years old, had never even been on a proper hike, and was packing for seven weeks on a deserted island off the coast of Alaska.

I'd been instructed to pack light but had also been told to expect a year's worth of weather on any given day. I looked for layers that could be mixed, matched, added, and tossed aside at will. There would also be no laundry or showers, and we would be digging large excavation units by hand, every day, all day, to find clues to the ancient past. I couldn't pack for five days and recycle my outfits. I sorted and re-sorted, looking for the winning combination.

I also packed batteries to power my Walkman, several mixtapes, an optimistic little carry-on bottle of shampoo just in case, and J. R. R. Tolkien's *Hobbit* and *Lord of the Rings* series bound together in one immense tome with the dragon, Smaug, in gold filigree on the cover.

Around this same time, doctors found proteins in Mom's blood that would eventually turn into cancer and carry her away. Because there was only a 2 percent chance of that happening, however, my parents chose to keep the news to themselves. And so, although I didn't know it yet, in retrospect it was fitting to have packed the most famous hero's journey ever written. For I was a Hobbit far from the Shire, and the wheels of my own fate had begun to turn. Little did I know that before it was through, like Frodo and Bilbo before him, I would be a lot farther off the map than a deserted island in Alaska.

At the end of the summer, I sat on the plane heading back home and watched, as if through a periscope, my neighbors putting in drink orders and wrestling with their Cheez-Its and pretzel bags. I had just spent a summer living in a tent in the wilderness, digging a latrine by hand, sleeping to the sound of barking seals, and watching a cadre of bald eagles swoop overhead every day. We lugged supplies and a rescue beacon to the highest peak—which was not actually high enough—in case of tsunami, for we were dead in the middle of the Ring of Fire. This is a hot spot in the Pacific Basin for earthquakes and volcanic eruptions, but the name sounded like a dragon's lair to me. Days were spent filling buckets with dirt, adding water, and then sifting it all through fine-mesh screens, which caught treasures in the form of seeds, charcoal and bone, stone flakes, and other oddments telling tales of daily life from thousands of years ago.

The world there had been soft—sand, mud, tundra, waves, mounded landscapes dotted with domed tents, sleeping bags, and soft bodies sitting shoulder to shoulder at mealtimes, sunrises, and sunsets. Even the clouds were softer than anywhere else, behaving more like liquid than vapor. One day I watched clouds pour over the top of our short-statured mountain and glide down the slope like molasses. The only boundary in our whole small world was the curve of the island's spit, which extended like a dancer's arm into the sea.

On the plane, the surfaces and edges of the civilized world seemed hard, sterile, and obtuse in comparison—tray tables, overhead bins, door latches, seat belts, floors, ceilings, windows, ninety-degree angles everywhere. I felt enclosed, jostled, and overcome with a feeling that I wasn't like these people anymore.

Something profound had happened to me, and nobody could see it. I looked the same, but I wasn't, and I never would be again. Alaska had given me the Bug. I came home thirsty for Life in a way I had never been before. Ever after, I only wanted to see, experience, learn, and do *more*. It awakened the Seeker in me. It was the most important discovery I have ever made, and as an archaeologist, I've made a few. Without the Seeker, I'd have been long-lost.

I found the Seeker in me on Unga Island, Alaska, 1994. Midsummer on Chernabura Island, Alaska, with dig-mate Emily. My first archaeological field school run by Dr. Lucy Johnson of Vassar College.

"You've got to stay curious," Dad used to say. "Never stop learning and you'll always be okay." Dad was a Seeker too. *That's lucky,* I thought. *I love seeing new places and learning new things.*

Between the ages of twenty and forty-two, I took the advice

literally. I did see a lot more adventure at home and abroad, searching for the edge of my comfort zone, and thrilling when I bumped up against it. But have you figured out yet the real pearl in Dad's advice?

It's easy to stay curious when you're having fun.

What happens when you are suffering? Suffering strips us bare of all the old knowing and the old certainties, all the old illusions we have used to console ourselves and build a reality that is comforting more than real. Those illusions can make us feel safe, but they keep us small, and when they are stripped away, it can feel like dying. And indeed, a part of you is dying, and it is difficult to remain curious when it feels like all is lost.

When this happens to you, and it assuredly will, try to remember that it is not really *you* who is dying, but the parts of you that can carry you no further. This is where curiosity comes in. What parts of you are dying? What misbeliefs or limitations have you been suffering under? Why were they a part of you to begin with? And what new kinds of knowledge and new ways of knowing can there be for you, now that the old ways are dead? Suffering breaks apart the rigid, confining, strangling structures of ego and washes them out to sea, so that even if you never learn to let them go—which you really must—you'll never be able to reach them again in the old ways, and you'll be stuck between two territories of spirit, the wasteland. Only curiosity can lead you out of the wasteland. Curiosity is the bridge.

OFF THE MAP

Twenty-two years later, I landed in a wild and unknown wilderness for the second time, but it was of a dark, different, and most unwelcome sort.

Dad had just died, Mom had been gone for almost five years, and I stood at the edge of a world that I did not recognize or know how to navigate. The forbidding landscape of a life without parents felt every bit as harrowing as the goblin tunnels of Mordor. The last thing I felt was curious.

In those early, grief-addled days, I was saturated with memories. I reviewed my parents' lives, especially Dad's, which played across the screen in my mind like a summer blockbuster. Just thinking about their lives, who they were, made me feel a little more invincible, more destined for greatness.

I wasn't aware at the time, but the way I rummaged through stories and memories was not unlike the way I had rummaged through shirts, socks, and hiking gear before a big trip. The first thing I did before embarking on a journey was to lay out my supplies and check my pack, making certain that I would have the four essential components—protection from the elements, sustenance, entertainment, and a good map and compass.

But there were no roads to where I was going. I had no clothes for these howling winds, and my hunger for belonging, connection, purpose, love, was killing. What sustenance could ever satiate that? If memories and stories were all I had left, were they enough for the biggest trip I would ever take, which—no pressure—was only going to be the rest of my life? I felt orphaned and homeless. How would I ever get back to the Shire?

Worse, I didn't even have a Shire anymore, or so I told myself. This journey would be an inward one, an imaginary one, and would require me to find that sense of home, contentment, safety, and belonging somewhere inside myself . . . where the landscape was currently ravaged. There would be no shelter there.

But could there be?

I had an idea that my map and compass might be found in stories, memories. And I knew that if I had a map and compass, they would inevitably lead me Somewhere. Because that's what maps and compasses do, isn't it? They lead somewhere. So I, the grieving archaeologist, continued to sift.

PICKING UP THE PIECES

When I was a teenager banging out the front door to meet up with friends, Dad always called after me, "I'll leave the light on for you, honey. If you need anything, call. We'll come and get you."

I imagine him now, walking just ahead of me, holding high a lantern that casts a circle of light at my feet, the guiding light of his own life and example. I could feel Mom further up the path, a place I desired to get to. I needed only to follow their lead. I searched my mind for any crumb, any clue. Who knew which rock when overturned might reveal the way out?

And so it was, lost in a jungle of grief, that I remembered the time when Dad had been lost in a jungle in Burma, when he also did not know what to do or how to get out. And just like that, the scout who had gone ahead several days earlier had appeared at the bend, beckoning with his hand. *This way, follow me.* Maybe it wasn't so foolish to think there is otherworldly help to be had when life has brought you to your knees or put you in grave danger. I sent a hopeful plea to my parents not to leave me alone and unaided in this dark forest of grief and uncertainty.

But it wasn't just Dad's stories that had gripped my imagination; I also had his hundreds of war letters and negatives from a storied life. I had his commonplace book containing scribbled musings, literary, witty, clever, and deep. I knew that in these sources there was a template for living a better life, and I was struck with the notion that this man, Dad, was not meant only for me. Soon after his death, I became obsessed with the idea of writing a book that would bring to the world his wit, wisdom, clarity of purpose, and let's not forget bold, brash, swashbuckling badassery.

The problem was I couldn't find the signal within the noise. What would the story be that I was trying to tell with all these hundreds of letters, pictures, and parables? The obsession burned like fire.

I grabbed my writer's notebook, turned to a new page, and scribbled, *What do you want out of this? And why?*

I wrote, in part, this:

> *I want catharsis and connection (catharsis in me will connect and elicit catharsis in you). I want Dad to be a magnificent, inimitable, and inspiring figure, but through strange alchemy, abstracted enough to the idea of "Father" that in the minds of my readers, he could be their father, their colossus.*

This gave me courage to start writing. But I was soon spinning my wheels, and I can see why. Reading it now, I see only a young woman in existential crisis grasping at something that is slipping through her fingers like sand and using the idea of the book to shore it up. That something, whatever it was, would be the deepest *why* of all. And I was beginning to suspect that it wasn't even the *right* why. This was a problem, because if you try to write from any place but the right one, you'll never get where you need to go.

My book was going nowhere because I had been trying to tell the wrong story, which itself was the result of my having only partially un-packed my need to tell it. Did I even have a story, beyond *Look at me! I'm the daughter of a great man?*

No one wants to read that story, I thought. *And what does it say about me if I need to tell it?* In effect, I realized, I was Telemachus being asked to step out from the shadow of the Hero Father.

How did I come to so identify with my family, and Dad in partic-ular, that when he died and the family fell apart, it constituted total existential crisis? Where along the way did I lose so much faith in my-self that the only way to exist, let alone be worthy, seemed to be to write a book, spinning mythic tales of a legendary past belonging to a golden family that only half-existed, and therefore could never wholly be written? I have a couple of ideas, and one of them started . . .

UP A TREE

We were visiting G.G.'s house in Savannah, as we did every summer, and I was having a sleepover. *Joy!* My cousin Chan's girlfriend at the time had two kids, Tammy and Eric, whom she would bring around to play whenever we were in town, and tonight we were having a sleepover. Tammy was a year or two older than I, with strawberry-blond waves, a freckled nose, and a bright, sassy temperament I found irresistible.

Tammy was a free spirit. The precocious child of a single mom, she more or less did what she wanted, and when I think of her, she is always running around in circles, laughing, conspiring, thumbing her nose. I considered her to be one of my best friends.

So when Tammy shook me awake in the dead of night and

beckoned me from my sleeping bag on the floor, I rubbed my eyes and followed. It was dark, the house was sleeping, and I could just make out the glow of her white nightgown slipping down the stairs in front of me. She stopped at the squeaky stair and turned to look at me, with a finger to her lips. Carefully skipping that step, she led me to the front door and started fiddling with the lock, causing alarm bells to go off in my head.

"Um, I don't think we're supposed to go out there," I said louder than I had intended.

"Shhh!" she said. "Don't be a party pooper. You said yourself you like to climb trees!"

"Not in the middle of the night!" I whisper-shouted. The lock clicked and she turned the doorknob, pulling the door open a crack. The humid air of the Georgia summer seeped in and hit my bare toes, which curled into the wood floor as if to anchor me there. "You can't do that," I cried, more desperate. "I'm . . . I'm telling!"

"You better not," she said, closing the door and giving me a look.

Out we went, down another set of stairs to the street, and over to the tree that shaded G.G.'s second-floor porch. Tiny pebbles stuck to my feet, which I brushed off against one calf and then the other. I looked up and down the dark cobbled street. All was quiet. I gave Tammy a leg up to the first branch. From there she scrabbled right to the top and leaned way out, her bare feet against the trunk to steady herself, and peered through the windows, which were now at eye level. She called down, "I can see everything from up here!"

She scrambled down and then gave me a leg up. I did like to climb trees. This was the biggest tree I had climbed, and since there was no point in doing it unless I got to peek in the windows, that's what I did. It didn't seem as scary as I had imagined, until I turned to go back down and found that I couldn't.

Tammy stamped her feet on the earth below and whisper-shouted at me to come on, cut it out, and just climb down. The mortification of disappointing her forced me down a branch or two, but I soon realized that I was well and truly stuck. The next branch was too far, and I wasn't strong enough. I was terrified, shaking, dizzy, and deeply embarrassed. *What a party pooper!* And then came the tears, which made it worse.

"Go get help," I wailed.

Tammy was beside herself. *"No way!"* she said. "You're going to get us in so much trouble. Just climb down!"

"I *can't*! I can't do it. I don't know how. I'm going to fall! Help! *Help meee!"*

"Oh my god. *Shhh! Be quiet!"*

She turned in a huff and stomped up the stairs to G.G.'s front door. She shook her head at me and flounced through the doorway to wake the adults.

Within a minute or two the lights started coming on and I could hear the adults tripping over each other in a great commotion. The door yanked open and a blessed yellow glow fell on my face from the hall light, dispersing the dark. There was Dad, first looking this way and that in confusion and alarm. Then, catching sight of me, he relaxed and broke into a silent chuckle. He walked to the banister at the front edge of the second-floor porch and found himself eye to eye with his six-year-old daughter perched in a tree like a possum.

"Oh. There you are. What's the matter—you can't get down?" he said.

Relief flooded my veins. I shook my head. I don't remember much about the rescue. There was some noisy rummaging in the street-level basement, and a ladder involved, possibly some mild shouting among adults over best practices. Tammy defended herself in the background, "O-*kay*!! I'm sorry! How was I supposed to know she can't climb trees?"

Our friendship was never really the same again after that.

Don't trust yourself to take risks, I learned that day. *You'll only get yourself and others into trouble, and if you screw up, they might not like you anymore.*

THE FAT ALASKAN INDIAN AND SPECIAL ED

I was born with a rich fantasy life and vivid imagination that frequently carried me right out of this world. It is one of the treasured gifts I received from my childhood self. To my peers, however, especially in the early years, it might have made me seem a little dreamy and inscrutable, and therefore an object of curiosity and/or derision.

Up until I was nine or ten, I was pure and innocent about it. I steeped myself in small pleasures all day without questioning whether I was worthy of them. I was already keenly aware of being a Chan, feeling as if that was all a person ever had to be. I felt that it set us apart somehow, made us a little bit special. And you can't really blame me. Old Chan Magic is a real thing, and nobody is immune. I was still very connected to this inner bigness, because as a last-minute second

chance for both my parents, I was regarded as delightful, precious, and extraordinary.

Mom and Dad let me know in many ways that I was important to them, bestowing upon me their attention and presence, meaningful compliments, encouragement, and, importantly, ethnically ambiguous dolls, faces I could see myself in. I never cut my hair because I thought beautiful girls had long hair like my dolls. So my hair hung around my hips in disheveled strands because, while I loved to play with dolls, I also spent a good portion of my time crawling up trees—ones I knew how to get down from—and building forts in the underbrush.

I hated baths but loved worms and mud pies. Eating was for burritos and plenty of ice cream. I had favorite clothes, whether they fit or were in style or not. It was the red or purple color I loved, the flouncy ruffle, or because Mom had put butterfly or rainbow patches on the knees to cover the holes. I was a sucker for pearlescent buttons and all things satin and velour. These little details, seen only for themselves, sparked such joy in me when I wore them that I pulled up sharply the first time I overheard myself described at school as a "walking garage sale."

And then there was Karl Hauser*—the boy I'd had a secret crush on since first grade because he was the class clown. He was bombastic and in-your-face, which made me feel lame, but I was drawn to him regardless. I hated my shyness and hovered in proximity to those I perceived to be more socially adept than I.

I came upon Karl and a group of our classmates at the school library one day. His back was to me, and I thought about slipping out the door unnoticed, but instead, with my innards churning, I stopped and said hello.

Two years earlier, in fourth grade, a group of advanced students had been separated out from our classes for an extended studies program, or ESP as it was called. Those kids joked that the acronym stood for Especially Smart People, and as a serious pupil with excellent grades, I'd expected to be part of this group. But I wasn't, and it felt like . . . how shall I say this? The *end of everything.* I was inconsolable at home, which convinced my parents, not normally ones to intervene, to go to the school for feedback on why I wasn't selected and whether there was anything I could do to be selected next time. They came back with a message that my grades weren't the problem, my social skills were. And so Dad embarked on a yearlong coaching regimen with me. He knew that while you can't change a person's character, you can do a lot to change behavior. A shy person can learn to pretend she is not as shy as she really is. I am pretending to this day.

OPPOSITE: *Savannah Beach. Still in tune with an "inner bigness" tied closely to being part of the "Chan Clan." It was the ultimate belonging.*

"The first thing you've got to do is learn to say hello," he said. "And make sure you look them in the eye when you say it." He demonstrated a friendly, level-eyed gaze, which was the default look on his face anyway. He made it look so easy. "And if you really want to make an impression, use their name. Don't just say hi, say, 'Hi, Jack! Hi, Sally!' People will remember and like you better if you use their names. It's just human nature."

I spent the whole of fourth grade walking to school staring at my feet and talking to myself.

"Good *morning*, Mrs. Edgar! How are *you* today? Good morning, Mrs. Edgar!" Then I forced myself to lift my face and smile to the air in front of me. "I'm fine, thank you, and how are *you*? Good *morning*, Mrs. Edgar!"

And do you know what happened next? A miracle! At the end of fourth grade, based on my "remarkable progress" that year in interacting with my teachers and classmates, I was admitted to the extended studies program. It had worked!

And so I overrode my flight response in the library and said hello to Karl Hauser and his friends, who were not, by the way, part of ESP.

But my confidence was new and fragile, and the seconds dripped like centuries while my words hung in the air. Karl turned around, his face lit up as if he were glad to see me, and for a second I thought it had worked.

But then just like that, and without missing a beat, he said, "Oh look! It's the fat Alaskan Indian! Here for more *books?*"

I am neither Alaskan nor Native; this was a coarse play on the sound of my name—a-LESH-ka, Alaska—and a nod to my waist-length black hair and olive skin that was nut-brown in the summer. It also took my proudest accomplishment of getting into ESP and made it feel shameful.

Don't shine too bright, I learned. *It's unbecoming.*

My stomach flipped and the blood turned to ice in my veins. For a moment I couldn't hear through the rushing in my ears, but I could see the other kids laughing. My mind scanned the too-small turtleneck I had on. I was suddenly ashamed of the pretty little strawberries all over it and my lavender suede Nikes. And then I did what the only instinct I had left told me to do, I laughed right along with them as I was dying inside. *Fat Alaskan Indian. More books. Good one.*

To my memory, it was the very same day that I was later sitting on the bus about to take us to the high school for swim class. I stared

out the window in a reverie, tracing movements of leaves in the trees, watching a cat on a clear mission slink under a hedge, and probably thinking about Halloween and how much I'd like to be able to fly, as these were strong preoccupations for me at the time. Suddenly, however, I became aware of two girls across the aisle talking about me.

"I don't know. I've never seen her before," I heard one girl whisper to her seatmate.

"Yeah," said the other, giggling. "Me neither. She must be in special ed."

I snapped back to myself. Special ed? *Special ed? I was in ESP!* I pulled back to observe myself. Odd clothing was a given, but I was also sitting hunched over my arms, which hugged my body laxly, palms up and fingers curled in my lap, forehead against the glass, and, horror of horrors, *mouth hanging wide open* for no reason other than I was completely relaxed and not used to thinking about how I might look to others. I closed my mouth, slowly so as not to alert the girls that I had heard them, and eased myself casually into a more upright and dignified position.

Dad was magic. My aunts and uncles were magic. My grandparents were storied. I had just begun to think that I too might be able to control my own destiny. I'd won myself a place in ESP! But in fourth and fifth grade, a rift began to open between how I saw myself and how I realized, for the first time, I was being perceived by others—*not* brilliant, *not* precious or extraordinary, and *definitely not* magic. Just a fat Alaskan Indian and book nerd. In funny clothes. Or maybe in special ed.

OPPOSITE: *Inner bigness faltering. But purple, yes. To all of it.*

These were challenging years as I first became aware of myself outside the safe and protected womb of my home life, and, with some astonishment, greeted the idea that I had an identity separate from my family. Before this, I *was* the Chan Clan. The Chan Clan *was me.*

Not so, I learned.

An accident of genetics. I am chubby, strange, and ridiculous. It's natural that only my family would really love me. What right do I have to take up space or attention out there in the world?

I think the final nail in the coffin for me, though, just as I was beginning to founder in this way, was likely . . .

THE FIRST AND LAST TIME I
HEARD DAD SAY "FUCK"

It was high summer. The greenery sped past the window behind his head in a dense, lush blur that contrasted with the steeliness of his face in profile. Dad and I were heading out of town on what I imagined was supposed to be a "scenic drive."

"That fucking son of a bitch," he said through his teeth. "I'm going to crucify him by his nuts."

I was ten years old and speechless. My eyes widened, and I stared down at my legs, pulling my hands closer into my lap. *Fuck* and *nuts*? For a moment I forgot to breathe. I glanced sideways at him from the passenger seat and could see his hands on the steering wheel in a vise-like grip, his teeth bared and clenched around the stem of his pipe, his lips moving as he continued to spit and hiss. Dad didn't swear. Oh, you might hear the occasional *goddammit* or *SOB*, but nothing like this. This level of rage would have scared me in and of itself, but today it made my blood run cold because it meant I had been in real danger, maybe even worse than I imagined. And then there was the implication of his words.

"Y-you know who it w-was?" I stammered, scanning through mental images of all our neighbors, up and down the street. All the UNICEF collections, the trick-or-treating, the hellos and smiles . . .

"Yeah, I know."

"How do you know?"

"I just do." The thought of which seemed to unleash a new wave of fury. "That goddamn pervert," he said, starting to laugh in a maniacal falsetto. "I'm going to string him up *by his dick*."

Dick? I looked at my dangling feet and noticed that they were dirty, and still bare. There had been no time for shoes. The man on the other end of the line had asked if I would talk to him while he masturbated. And then he'd suggested he come over so we could play doctor.

"Um, my dad is here," I stuttered. Lame. Desperate.

"Oh, I don't think so," the voice said, amused and breathy. Excited. "I just saw him leave a few minutes ago. He won't be back for a while, I guess. You know how he likes to kill time at the diner. I've been watching you for a long time now. You and your mother and sister too. Karen and Mee Ra. Yes, I know you all. Such beautiful girls, I see you at church and around town." And then with desperate, almost strangled conviction, "I'm coming over right now."

I dropped the phone, my scalp prickling hotly, while drops of sweat beaded at the hairline around the back of my neck. I raced out the back door, scanning the yard and street, up and down. All was quiet. I grabbed my bike, which was a new big-kid ten-speed. Built as it was for more serious cyclists than me, it had sharp pedal spikes to prevent slippage. Now those spikes stabbed painfully into the bottoms of my bare feet as I pumped my legs. I stood up to get more leverage, tried to stay upright while checking over my shoulder to see if I was being followed, and winced as my ankles lost stability on the greased pedals that were made to spin with ease, jerking forward and backward without warning. My toes scraped the pavement each time, picking up bloody lacerations. I knew where Dad was, so I ignored the pain in my feet for four blocks, my ears thundering, until I reached his favorite hangout, the Calico Kitchen, the local diner on our sleepy little small-town Main Street.

He'd be eating chicken noodle soup and a Belgian waffle, or donuts and coffee. He would certainly be mid-laugh when I found him, because that was his way. I held that image in front of me like a talisman. When I reached the corner where the diner was, I jumped off the bike before it had even come to a stop, sending it in a cacophonous clatter to the pavement. I stumbled through the door sobbing, emitting strangled screams, and causing, I imagine, considerable consternation. But I had tunnel vision, scanning over the tables and booths for him. And just as I knew he would be, there he was having lunch and laughing with the waitress. I felt all my fears fall away and collapsed onto him in a heap.

The next thing I knew, we were speeding down a secluded road and I was getting a lesson on the proximity of rage to fear. I didn't know it at the time, but Dad was scared. Maybe as scared as he had ever been. An undefeated boxer in his youth, 33–0; a colonel in the US Army who had taught guerilla-warfare training; a man who had survived capture, snipers' bullets, malaria, typhus, and mortal hand-to-hand combat, who had hijacked a plane to fly himself to freedom, and then, in Manhattan, relieved three other men of a knife, which he kept on his desk. But he couldn't protect his own daughter from the man across the street. And it shook him.

That afternoon he took me to Letchworth State Park, the Grand Canyon of the East. Magnificently scenic, it was a good thirty-five miles south of Rochester. I don't recall that we did much talking. Just driving in silence, and sometimes getting out and looking around. There were gorges and canyons, waterfalls, and roaring streams. Water, wind, and birdsong competed for center stage. I knew that Dad liked to go there and take pictures. He had one on his desk of Mom from their dating days. She looked elegant with a bun low on her neck, gazing out over the canyon, legs crossed, perched on a stone wall. Letchworth meant good things to him—new love, second chances, and a limitless future.

I think he didn't know what else to do other than to take us to a beautiful place, *his* beautiful place. A place that reminded him somehow of what it is we're all doing here.

Some words can't be healed with more words. Sometimes silence and togetherness are not only enough, they are all that remain. I thought that myself years later when I sat by his bedside, holding his hand before he died. I remembered the drive to Letchworth Park that day and took comfort in the feeling that I was doing all that was needed.

We never spoke again about what happened. I never found out who it was that called me that day, although I have an idea. But I do know a few things. While no one on my street was ever strung up by the dick, I never got another obscene phone call. And I know a menace doesn't stop menacing unless somebody makes them. And I know you definitely don't want Bob Chan *making* you do anything.

Dad saved me. *The world is a big and scary place,* I learned. *You'll never make it on your own. Find the saviors and champions, never let them go.* It took me four decades to start unraveling that knot. Writing and telling stories is a big part of that.

REPARENTING

Things happen, you know? A series of events in a particular sequence. Various actors are often involved. I pulled together the three little stories above because together that group of random and otherwise-unrelated events felt like it held the key to a lot of what I am afraid of to this day, maybe some of what was holding me back from carrying my grief more lightly, and even from writing this book.

I experienced some things, and maybe I took the wrong lessons from them. I didn't know they were the wrong lessons. I was just a little kid. As a child, I gathered them up and stashed them away as a road map to survival and success. *Misbeliefs.*

Interestingly, if I look at my life's greatest challenges through the lens of early lessons, they start to look a whole lot different. Disappointments and betrayals I've suffered at the hands of others are suddenly no more than indications of unhealed wounds that set me up for feelings of disappointment and betrayal. And as for what I deserve . . . it is everything good, and to shine on. Same as you. What a difference this slight change in perspective makes.

Now, what to do with this newfound knowledge? Did these little stories hold the keys to why I was stuck in my writing and in my grief—those keys being that I doubted myself; that I was afraid I'd be punished or rejected if I shone too brightly; that I feared success as somehow undeserved, accidental, or selfish; and that I thought the most interesting thing about me was my perfectly inspirational family, which could therefore have no flaws? If so, how could I heal from these misbeliefs, integrate them, and let them go?

I fell asleep one night with these questions on my mind. As I drifted back and forth over the threshold of sleep, I found myself standing at the base of the mighty Skógafoss, my favorite waterfall in Iceland. I was close enough to feel the billowing vapor and cold spray on my cheeks. The thundering waters created a low vibration in my chest. I had one hand stuffed tightly into the pocket of my silver puffer coat. The other was holding the hand of a child. I looked down and saw . . . myself, about age nine. *Hmm, that's curious.* Her hair was in two messy braids, and she wasn't wearing a coat. She stood tense and trembling by my side, pressing her knees together and clenching her other arm to her chest, bouncing lightly up and down, teeth chattering. She looked up at me and I could see excitement, eagerness, and uncertainty playing all at once over her face. *Is it okay for me to be here?* And it struck me just how intolerable it was to imagine a child such as this *ever* needing to ask that question. In truth, I had never seen a brighter, more earnest, imaginative, kind, and, yes, *beautiful* child in all my life, and I was overcome with emotion. I fell to one knee, wrapped her in my arms, and held her tight, as if I could save her, and as if only she could really save me.

"My darling," I said to her. "You are precious to me beyond measure, and I will love you forever." And I meant it as much as I've ever meant anything in my life.

I felt her trembling cease as she relaxed into my embrace. The moment felt so good because I was the one giving the hug, as well as the one receiving it. I felt the love, was infused with it, from both sides. Then I fell asleep.

I think I was called to dredge up these old stories to tell them, first and foremost, to myself. In doing so I uncovered a part of me who, despite wonderful parents and a solid upbringing, did not get all her needs met. For decades, there had been a wounded and fearful child hiding in the wings of my subconscious, yearning to be seen and, more important, *cherished*, and acting out in ways that I was not even aware of because she did not feel either of those things. And now that I've rediscovered her and shone a light on her, I don't have parents anymore who can hug that hurt away. But *I* can hug the hurt away.

It reminded me of a quote from *The Faerie Queene*.

For whatsoever from one place doth fall,
Is with the tide unto another brought:
For there is nothing lost,
that may be found, if sought.

—Edmund Spenser

It means that whatever you have lost, no matter how precious, can be found in other forms elsewhere. It won't be the same, but *if you stay curious* and are willing to look and receive, you will find it is enough.

So here, then, is another reason why we tell stories. Stories, if told right, can show us where our wounds are. And stories, if told right, can help us stanch the bleeding. On the other hand, it turns out those wrong lessons I learned were telling me other kinds of stories, which had been threatening to hide and perpetuate the old wounds that no longer serve me.

My vision showed that my destroyed sense of home, belonging, and feeling safe in my own worth could be found again inside myself, and not just as airy metaphor. In that moment, I had literally become a parent to myself, or at least to the wounded part of me who still needs one. And now I know that all I have to do is close my eyes to conjure that experience again and I don't feel lost or alone anymore. And doesn't that mean that I have effectively found my way back to the Shire?

Stories brought me home. Just as I thought they might. Now I save myself. Just as I hoped I would. At long last, I am neither orphaned nor homeless. That's the best story ending I have ever told, and the Rat sniffs on.

Legacies never die.

CHAPTER 27

A LAUNDRYMAN'S SON LEARNS TO FLY

Sometimes I like to think about the butterfly effect, the idea that small changes in one place can have significant impact elsewhere. For example, Orville and Wilbur Wright piloted the world's first human flight, traveling 120 feet in twelve seconds on December 17, 1903, and here I sit writing about it 120 years later, and the latter could not have happened without the former. How can that be? What's the connection, you ask?

Well, let's light a match together, right now.

Strike!

Now watch it flower.

Hands in prayer.

Dad spent his childhood and adolescent days at Savannah Beach, gazing up at clouds and dreaming. He had heard of the Wright brothers' amazing exploits. By the time he was in his early twenties, he had a pilot's license himself. How? Where? With what means, as the son of an immigrant laundryman trying to pay his way through college?

I don't know. But on December 16, 1941, nine days after Pearl Harbor, Dad had his license renewed. He figured this must have been what it was all about in the first place. He had been in ROTC at

Georgia Tech and had now been called into active duty. At a recruitment office, renewed pilot's license in hand, he attempted to sign up for the air force. But as he took a form, the head recruiting officer approached him, put his hand on his shoulder, and with what Dad always described as kind eyes that belied what he was about to say, said, "Son, you don't have to bother with that form."

"Why not?" said Dad, taken aback, "I already know how to fly," gesturing to his pilot's license.

The officer glanced at the license and raised his eyebrows, but shook his head. "You're not the kind we're looking for," he said.

"And what kind is that?" said Dad, still not following.

"We're looking for . . . boys with blond hair and blue eyes, if you see what I mean."

Dad tucked his lips. "Mm-hmm. Oh, I do see."

He left the air force recruiting office and joined the army, where he rose right to the top.

Fast-forward a few years to the CBI theater, and Dad was now a captain on one of his long-range penetration missions ahead of the Ledo Road construction. The objective was to blow up a train track, thereby disrupting Japanese supply lines, which they did successfully. But in the ensuing chaos, Japanese soldiers poured from the jungle in all directions, blocking the Americans' escape and capturing Dad and a few others. He never saw the others again, but he was taken into the jungle and ultimately to the Japanese headquarters there, where he was put to work around the camp.

Recalling the period seventy years later, Dad shook his head and said, "My mind was going ninety to nothing. *How am I going to get out of this?*" With the quick wit and resourcefulness of the Rat, of course.

One of his jobs was to meet the mail plane that came daily and to help unload the cargo and carry it back to headquarters. It was the same pilot every day, and he flew a biplane much like the ones Dad had learned in. The pilot would turn off the engine, jump out of the plane, unload the mail with Dad, and carry it back to camp with him.

"These were propeller planes that were a pain in the butt to get started," said Dad. "So one day I got an idea. I showed the pilot, you know, with hand signals and everything, how you could turn the engine down low, so the propeller slows down but doesn't stop. Then you throw some chocks in front of the wheels to keep the craft from rolling away. And what do you know, the pilot saw the good sense in that and started doing it."

Perhaps a week or ten days into his captivity, Dad motioned to the pilot. "Don't worry about it. I got this load. I can do it by myself. Why don't you just relax?"

The pilot let him unload the mail on his own and strode into the jungle to relieve himself.

The moment the pilot was out of sight, Dad heaved the sack of mail off his shoulder, ripped the chocks out from in front of the wheels, jumped in the cockpit, and took off, the doomed pilot running with arms in the air, shrinking to a dot behind him. Dad flew until the fuel ran out, whereupon he found a clearing to land in, and not a moment too soon. The plane sputtered and bucked through the air, alerting everyone for miles that someone was going down, but he brought that little plane to heel and crash-landed without incident, sliding to a shuddering halt in a field.

As he clambered out of the cockpit, however, American soldiers who had heard the coughing engine swarmed out of the jungle with weapons raised. And here you must think for a moment what they saw—Dad, looking as he did, in Allied territory he knew not where, climbing out of a plane with the Japanese rising sun on its side and wings. He was a dead man walking.

Except that he had a thick southern accent.

"Don't shoot!!" he yelled. "I'm an American! My name is Captain Robert Earl Chan. I was taken prisoner and I've just escaped. Don't shoot!"

The Americans radioed their confusion back to field headquarters to see if what he said was true. It took some time, but eventually it was confirmed.

I asked, "But Dad, didn't you have any papers or ID on you?"

"No. I didn't," he said. "And it's a good thing I didn't, because if the Japanese had known who I was when they captured me, a high-ranking officer, they would have killed me on the spot."

In fact, the Japanese already did know him, by name at least. The infamous propagandist, Tokyo Rose, had called him out one night as they huddled around the radio listening to the news and music show *Zero Hour.*

"Captain Chan," she purred, "don't you know you're fighting on the wrong side? Why are you loyal to a country that isn't loyal to you?"

Dad, who had no illusions about American society, was unruffled. He was profoundly American in temperament and outlook, and knew true patriots fight for an ideal, even, and perhaps especially, when it hasn't been met yet. If anyone ever asked him what he was, curious about his exotic look, he'd say, "I'm an American," eyes snapping and daring the person to ask twice.

Was this the only time in history that a southern drawl saved a Chinese American boy from certain death? And is this the only time in history that a Chinese American pilot was refused entry into the air force on racial grounds, but then flew himself to freedom in the army? The answer to both questions, I think, must certainly be yes.

One Christmas morning fifty years later, I opened a little box from my parents that contained a small, hand-carved wooden snowman-angel with painted hat, scarf, and mittens, and copper-wire wings. My name, Alexandra, was painted in red across the base. That Thanksgiving, coming home from Vassar College, I had taken an Amtrak train and it had come to a halt on the tracks for several hours. I made small talk with the passenger across the aisle, a dapper, academic-looking man in dreadlocks, black turtleneck, and blazer. I napped some, stared out the window across the dark, snow-dusted fields of western New York, tapped my foot, and worked through hours of impatience and boredom. When the train eventually lurched forward and started lumbering into the night again, we were none of us any the wiser about what had happened. I was supposed to be home for dinner but didn't make it until well after midnight, and it was not until the morning news that we learned a dangerous miscommunication had occurred on the tracks. Our passenger train had very nearly had a head-on collision with another train carrying nitroglycerin—a narrowly averted tragedy that would have brought stunning loss of life.

I let the little snowman-angel dangle from my finger and looked at my parents.

"Sometimes it just isn't your time," said Dad.

"Someone was looking out for you," said Mom. "They knew we weren't ready to lose you yet."

"It also means your mission is not complete," said Dad.

In 2020, that mantra came back to me on endless looping repeat: *Your mission is not complete.* It meant that, even as the world descended into ever-greater chaos and confusion, I (we all) must have been here for a reason. We were rats in a maze, being asked to take stock of our resources and to remember our intuitive gifts for finding our way out. The mantra also seemed to promise reward and a great sense of accomplishment at the end of this trial, and that was something I could have faith in and strive toward. It gave purpose to my walks and my music, my endless paintings of rats . . . and a determination to bring others along with me. By then, I was actively writing this book.

BOOK SEVEN

2021
YEAR OF THE OX

My year, and a hopeful bookend to tumultuous times. The Ox brings us auspicious energy for the problems we face as a society. In any normal year, the Ox's altruism, intuition, and discipline make its hard work effective and rewarding. In a Metal Ox year, however, the intuitive Yin of the Ox is extra potent. After the chaotic elements of 2020, the world needs some spiritual open-heart surgery. Look to the Ox. It knows how to till ravaged fields and prepare new ground that is better for all.

The Chinese believe that the egret, as part of the crane family, symbolizes purity, intuition, and connection to the Spirit World. With the Ox, it is paired here with calligraphy that says wu wei, or right action. Put down the anxiety and negative thinking that have burdened you. Learn to trust again. Life was not meant to be minimal or mundane, survived but never enjoyed. The Ox is capable, honest, and trustworthy; a healthy Ox makes one of the best friends, parents, and leaders because its stolid nature nurtures safety, allowing you to return to your natural state of joy, creativity, hope, and miracles, if you let yourself.

CHAPTER 28

THE CHINESE CHRISTMAS BOX

In March 2021, a White man opened fire in three Asian-owned Atlanta-area spas, saying afterward that he wasn't racist, he just had a "sex addiction." Police infamously concurred that race was not the motivation because the shooter had said so, and suggested the man was just having a bad day. Eight people died, six of whom were women of Asian descent. The incident terrorized the Asian American and Pacific Islanders community, which was already enduring a wave of racial scapegoating and violence in relation to the spread of Covid-19. This tone was set at the top by Donald Trump, who liked to refer to the deadly virus as the "China Virus" or the "Kung Flu," language that has metastasized into everyday aggression and violence against members of the AAPI community. What's more, the fact that the gunman blamed the incident on a sex addiction recalled all the old racist tropes about Asian women being prostitutes. Indeed, this stereotype was one of the explicit underpinnings of the Chinese Exclusion Act of 1882–1943.

The Atlanta shootings felt personal. As the first Chinese American children born in the state of Georgia, the Chan kids were such a novelty that the state, having only two racial categories at the time—White or Black—labeled them as White on their birth certificates. But don't let that fool you. So troubled were they about what to do with these category-defying non-White children, that government agents came to the house on a regular basis for many years to check in and make sure there was nothing to worry about with this growing family. *How much are they proliferating? With whom do they associate? Are they up to no good?*

"Just keeping tabs, Mr. Chan, you understand."

There were six adult Chinese men in Savannah at that time, T'ai Peng the only one with a family. But as the community began to grow, T'ai Peng made sure newcomers who wanted to settle close to other Chinese people did not do so. He urged them to separate and scatter themselves across the city. To his children he said, "So the people of Savannah won't fear us."

Only adults would understand what a frightened White population was liable to do, as newspapers and political cartoonists of the day had dedicated themselves to making the Yellow Peril as frightening as possible. They depicted the Chinese as sneaky and sly, with buck teeth like fangs and fingers like dragon claws. The prime selling point of the new steam washers was that they would rid the land of Chinese, many of whom were, like T'ai Peng, laundrymen. "The Chinese Must Go," cried the ads and cartoons. Two of the most recognizable images from that era show Chinese running from an anthropomorphized steam washer and getting kicked in the rear to the land's edge by Uncle Sam himself. Other cartoons depicted Chinese as monstrous and cannibalistic, devouring Uncle Sam whole, sitting atop a hoard of labeled "monopolies," and engaging in immoral behavior, like washing sheets from a brothel and sprouting dragon wings to scale a fence meant to keep them out. The Chinese, in the American popular imagination of T'ai Peng's day, were the stuff of nightmares.

Dispersing the population, he reasoned, dissolved the target. He knew of the Chinatown massacres of California and the West. He understood the violence the political cartoons threatened, and the way language metastasizes.

Dispersed settlement in Savannah meant the Chinese wouldn't have to compete for business, T'ai Peng argued. Nor would there be as much reason to fear or resent a lone Chinese businessman in the neighborhood. To this day, Savannah is one of the only major American cities with a significant Chinese population not to have a Chinatown. T'ai Peng's handprint is on the very map of the city.

The Willie Chin & Co. Laundry supported T'ai Peng and Annie, their six kids, T'ai Peng's parents back home, and about a dozen employees. Then the Great Depression hit. But T'ai Peng was always dressed to the nines in double-breasted linen suits, straw boater hats, and nice shoes. He traded in the horse and wagon and bought a car for deliveries. A cigar often in hand, he liked to play dominoes and poker, as much for the relationships forged as for the entertainment.

"I like good clothes," he said. "I not like store suit. I spend plenty money for man dressmaker make my clothes. They look better, wear more better. Chinese friends used say, 'Look at T'ai Peng, dress up in foreign country. Fool, what it matter how you look here except in Sunday school?'"

He always had a good answer.

"I got to look decent. I represent my country it no matter where I go." He winked. "If I not be dress decent, I not catch good wife. Maybe catch country girl ain' got no sense, thick skull. But my wife very pretty, very smart."

Dad characterized talk like this as vanity, but the Atlanta shootings offered a different lens. While it is true T'ai Peng was an educated man, never a laundryman in his heart, he was also the family's contact point with White society. But more than that, T'ai Peng was the acknowledged leader of the city's Chinese. As their unofficial goodwill ambassador, he dressed impeccably, in the most up-to-date and modern fashions, and went out of his way to make friendly connections with the city's luminaries and civilian and business leaders. He had to present himself not as a "heathen Chinee," but as an elegant man of business, exotic but nonthreatening. He had children to protect. If there was any money to spare, it was going to a haircut and a tailored suit, and maybe a round of poker with local business owners.

And so it was that every year he also ordered a large "Christmas box" from China.

GREAT PHOENIX, GOODWILL

More of a crate, the Chinese Christmas box was usually about three feet wide by four feet tall and was made of rough wood sealed with oiled paper. After a journey of months, and covered in large Chinese brush characters, it would arrive at the Willie Chin & Co. Laundry looking well traveled and, in the eyes of the children, like a magical dispatch from a bright other world.

To open it, Papa (as the children called him) would drag it to the laundry room behind the store and pry the lid off with a crowbar and hammer. The children would jockey for position as the top lifted, whereupon all six would dive in and tear the packing to shreds, sending tufts of straw and Chinese newspapers flying, littering the concrete floor between the washtubs at their feet.

Inside the box would be silk handkerchiefs for the ladies in jewel tones of turquoise, jade, rose, and purple, exquisitely embroidered at the edges. Then would come oversized white ones—sturdier, and with wide hems—appropriate and stylish for businessmen. There were often delicate, ladle-like soup spoons, chopsticks housed in individual silk bags, tea bowls, saucers, and vases. None of these treasures was for the family, but tokens of appreciation that T'ai Peng distributed to loyal patrons, personal friends, and prominent Americans—judges, lawyers, and government officials who had shown kindness, support, or aid to Savannah's Chinese.

Underneath the goodwill gifts were things for the family: colorful and fragrant tins of oolong and jasmine tea, and wonderful items to cook with—water chestnuts, bamboo shoots, dried mushrooms, and always at the bottom, a large, coarse earthenware jug of soy sauce, corked on top and sealed with red wax at the spout. Other things, which Papa held up with especial appreciation, made the children wrinkle their noses, like salt fish and months-old duck eggs. But there were treats in there too. Sweet bean cakes, candied strips of coconut, and the thin-shelled lychee nuts, which are not nuts at all, but dried fruit. There was nothing like these in American stores, and the children made them last as long as possible, which was not very long because Papa kept a stash of them in the storefront and stuffed handfuls into the pockets of children who came to pick up their fathers' starch-stiffened collars.

"Here, put some in your pocket!" he urged. "Good! Eat!"

Earl's favorite thing from the Christmas box was the red firecrackers, in singles or in long connected strings, which the siblings set off, cracking and popping at their feet, in the walled garden after dark. He also looked forward to the strange wooden rings and metal puzzle boxes that challenged you to take them apart and put them back together again. He found them both mystifying and irresistible.

One year, at the bottom, was Papa's own treat—a stack of phonograph records engraved with the music of his homeland. If he had restrained himself thus far, the emergence of those black discs sent Papa up the stairs two at a time to the parlor, where he fumbled with a new Victrola needle and, by the time they had all filed in behind him, had put the first disc on and turned the volume to full blast. The cacophonous clanging of Chinese cymbals and falsetto screeching of male opera singers made the children plug their ears and giggle and the cat streak from the room. There sat the Great Phoenix, however, flopped in the sagging velvet wing chair with his hands behind his head, eyes closed, and face turned to the ceiling in a look of pure transcendence.

Mama walked lightly to the Victrola and dialed the volume down. "You can hear that all the way down to Bull Street, my darling. What will the neighbors say?"

The Christmas box and the relationships T'ai Peng cultivated with its contents, and his own powers of charm and persuasion, were transformative for the family. Many people are unaware that some of America's Jim Crow laws applied to Chinese Americans as well. The six Chan children, for example, were not initially allowed to enter the White public school system. They had to be home-tutored until Dad, the fifth of six children, entered fourth grade. It was that year, around 1923, that T'ai Peng made a trip to Atlanta and somehow secured an exception from authorities there to allow his children entry into the public school system. How many rounds of poker, porcelain vases, silk kerchiefs, and jade jewelry did it take to desegregate Savannah's school district decades before *Brown v. Board of Education*? Most Chinese Americans of the time were never admitted to public schools.

A hundred years later as the news of the Atlanta shootings unfolded, my mind kept traveling to the past. A new and dreadful light shone on stories I had heard all my life. Suddenly they were not about Grandpa's gambling and joyful vanity, or his being a spendthrift, but about all that he'd had to do to manage White society's perception of him and to create personal connections for his family to be safe and to prosper. The Chinese Exclusion Act barred him from citizenship and the protections it affords. In its absence he was vulnerable—on the surface of things, powerless. "The Chinese Must Go" was the prevailing attitude of the day. Navigating the intricacies and pitfalls of a violently racist society had come down to Grandpa's personal charisma and ingenuity. It had come down to magic. It made my own position feel . . . flimsy or ephemeral, not at all something promised, but something planted a hundred years ago with little more than a prayer that it would take root.

The nation was shocked when eight people died that day in Atlanta. But T'ai Peng had already seen a hundred years prior the dangers that awaited Asian business owners who clustered together. I grieved how little progress had been made in America when it comes to things like racial scapegoating. And yet I was reverent before the image of my grandfather tilling ravaged fields, in the spirit of the Ox, and with no promise of reward, preparing ground that would, hopefully, one day, prove better for all.

I never heard the story of the Chinese Christmas box in anything but joyful, nostalgic tones, something meant to embody the wonderful spirit of Christmas. Dad, G.G., Sandor, and Archie remembered it so fondly that it came up at least once every time we visited Savannah, even in the dog days of summer.

One Christmas morning, as G.G. recalled in a little chapbook she published about it called *The Chinese Christmas Box*, T'ai Peng read to the children from Confucius.[12]

> The ancients who wished to illustrate virtue throughout the Empire first ordered well their own States. Wishing to order well their own States, they first regulated their families. Wishing to regulate their families, they first cultivated their persons. Wishing to cultivate their

persons, they first made their hearts right. Wishing to regulate their hearts, they first sought to be sincere in their thoughts. Wishing to be sincere in their thoughts, they first sought to extend their knowledge.

T'ai Peng dropped the book to his lap and gazed at each of his six children, sitting cross-legged in a half circle around his feet.

"This means," he said, "if a man is good, his family will be good. If the family is good, the country will be good. If the country is good, the world will be good."

In painting this piece, I tapped into feelings of vastness, searching, and T'ai Peng's own Christmas homily that to be sincere in thought, right in heart, and cultivated in person, one must commit to extending one's knowledge. Ideally, life is a pilgrimage of ever-deepening and widening discovery. Discovery is the soul's natural state and "transfigures what is forsaken," says Irish poet John O'Donohue.[13] Or, as Dad always said, "Stay curious and you'll always be all right." I paired the painting with a Chinese proverb that is the calling card of all seekers: "The Sea of Knowledge has no horizon." Ah, to be lissome and nimble in attitude toward things we don't know, to receive difficult changes with a grateful, or at least willing, heart. For these too have their lessons to share. These too belong to the Sea of Knowledge.

Tao of the Waves—*"The Sea of Knowledge has no horizon."*

CHAPTER 29

MAGICAL MAP SHIFTERS

The stories we are told, and which we eventually tell ourselves, influence the way we show up in the world. Stories become everything we think we know about our universe, others, and ourselves. Personal mythology is our horizon, where the sun rises and lights the world, where it sets and creates shadows and dark corners. It reflects us back to ourselves, shows us where we have been, where we fear to tread, and all the places we could yet go.

And as such it came as a surprise to Dad when he learned in his nineties that he had been homeschooled through the third grade because of Jim Crow segregation. The story, as he had always known it, was what his father had told him one day.

"Public school not ver' good," T'ai Peng had said. "Too many cracker. My children mus' go to private school."

Private school simply meant tutors. First came the handsome but dour young man who visited the home above the laundry to tutor the children and nearly bored Dad to death.

"The less said of him the better," Dad would reply when I asked.

But then came the cheerful and ebullient Mrs. Chaplin, who lived on the other side of Forsyth Park. She hosted the children in her doily-bedecked dining room, and opened Dad's eyes to a love of learning and a sense of wonderment that would last a lifetime.

Eventually, as he had understood it, private schooling could take them no further and they had to go to the public school. In fact, there was no "had to" about it. T'ai Peng had made his auspicious trip to Atlanta. Dad and his siblings were enrolled in the White school as a kind of social experiment, hailed in the local newspaper as a successful one, each of the children being top of their class.

A STORY BASED ON TRUE EVENTS

Miss Van Doehren* was scribbling numbers on the chalkboard at the front of the classroom in 3B when there came a rattling knock on the frosted-glass portion of the door. Principal Tipton* eased it open a crack, grabbing the edge with one hand and slipping just his upper torso through.

"Miss Van Doehren?" he said in a hushed tone. "May we borrow Robert Earl for a moment? The cameraman is here."

Earl had been copying the figures from Miss Van Doehren's chalkboard but froze at the sound of his name. He looked side to side, to see if anyone else had heard.

Miss Van Doehren, a scrawny, plain, but pleasant teacher, turned to Earl and nodded toward the door. "Robert Earl, you may be excused. You can finish up when you get back."

Earl stood up and laid his pencil in the groove at the top of his desk. A rushing sound rose in his ears as his classmates rustled and some of the boys started oohing, but he clenched his jaw and stared them all down.

Miss Van Doehren slammed her yardstick on the desk. "That's enough, children," he heard her say as he exited the classroom. "The newspaper is doing a story on Earl and his siblings," she continued as he closed the door behind him. "Let's all be supportive and curious when he comes back."

Newspaper? Earl followed Principal Tipton down the green-and-white-linoleum-tiled corridor. The squeak and shuffle of rubber soles reverberated off the white plaster walls, and safe from view of his classmates, Earl trotted to keep up. They exited a side door into a bilious cloud of bright and humid shade that after the school's inner gloom made Earl squint and duck his head. His sisters, Sin Fah and Gerald, were there, two and three years older than he and enrolled in the Savannah-Chatham Junior High School, as was his brother, Sandor, who was enrolled in high school. Archie had finished schooling and was helping to run the laundry. Earl did not at first perceive anyone else there except for a cat with matted fur and a weeping eye, huddled by the brick wall in the lee of a trash receptacle, squinting at them.

Then he noticed a man in a straw skimmer hat holding a press camera askew by the large flashbulb. A damp, wrinkled suit and crooked tie with a dab of mustard that had been inexpertly wiped away gave him the appearance of a vagrant. Only the camera suggested he was there by design. Earl, a laundryman's son, couldn't help but think, *No self-respect.*

Principal Tipton shook the press man's hand, wiping his own afterward on the front flap of his blazer, and set about arranging the siblings in a row. He took them by the shoulders and marched them this way and that, standing back to take in the effect before settling on the most obvious composition—oldest/tallest to the left and youngest/shortest to the right. Sandor, Gerald, Sin Fah, and Earl.

The press man took out a notebook from his inside breast pocket and drew a pencil from behind his ear. "Okay," he said, licking the lead tip, "so tell me one at a time your name and grade level." He scribbled something across the top of the page and looked up when he was ready. Sandor said his name first. The press man started to write but stalled, staring at the space beneath his pencil. "What was that now?" he asked, frowning. "San . . . do?"

G.G. said, "I'm Gerald," and got another look, at which point she conceded that her legal name was Gladys Geraldine. This is what the man wrote down, to her disgust and Earl's delight. At Sin Fah, the man gave up all pretenses and dropped the notebook and pencil to his thigh. Earl almost felt sorry for him. *Almost.* The man seemed relieved when Earl told him his own name.

"Okay. E-a-r-l C-h-a-n. Smartest kids in the whole school, eh?" he said, underlining something heavily twice and jabbing a period onto the page. Earl unconsciously squeezed his right hand into a fist at his side.

The man looked up, shaking his head. "Ain't that somethin'. That's a real feel-good story. Our readers are going to love it." He slipped the notebook into his pocket and rolled the pencil behind his ear. "Okay, you ready?"

Principal Tipton ran behind the children to take his place just to the side of Sandor. As an afterthought, he reached his hand out and placed it, hesitantly at first but then more firmly, on Sandor's shoulder. "Smile everybody," he said, peering around Sandor to make sure they all complied.

The press man raised the camera to his face and said, "Okay, everybody, one, two, three . . ."

Earl lifted his chin defiantly. The flashbulb gave a burst of light and then exploded with a percussive crack and a thin cloud of smoke.

BEFORE

The Chan children's first tutor had been the floppy-haired and reticent Mr. Gregory,* a man in riding pants and boots, who, as far as Earl

could tell, always arrived on foot. Mr. Gregory also liked to brandish a riding crop against his thigh or on tabletops as they droned through spelling and conjugation drills. Earl was a quick study. He spent lots of time swinging his feet or jiggling his leg under the table during lessons. He felt the hot prickle of the Georgia heat under his collar and turned his head to Mama's kitchen window, which she almost always left open, hoping to catch a breeze.

According to Sin Fah, though, Mr. Gregory was ever so handsome, and so it was with great histrionics on her part that they graduated from Mr. Gregory and started trekking through Forsyth Park, Sinnie openly sulking, to reach the mahogany dining room of old, chubby, and musty-smelling Mrs. Chaplin. Earl rather liked her.

OPPOSITE: The Chan kids with their home tutor, Mr. Gregory. L–R: Sandor with Tricky, Gerald, Bernice (in front), Sin Fah, Archie, and Robert Earl, ca. 1918*

Mrs. Chaplin dressed in tailored one-piece wool or canton crepe frocks with frilled, pleated, scalloped, or otherwise-ornamented collars. She had an affinity for checks and paisley patterns that seemed very fresh and young, and stood in intriguing contrast to her silver floss hair and thickening waist. Likewise, while she was always coiffed in finger waves, her hair all gathered at the nape of her neck, Earl noticed there was often a nimbus of stragglers about her head that made her look harried, excited, and/or out of breath. This effect was heightened by the natural bloom still in her cheeks, giving her the overall gestalt of a much younger woman. She looked old but felt young.

Mrs. Chaplin smiled down her nose at Earl through her half-moon spectacles and gave him a look that said she had a funny secret and was pretty sure Earl was in on it too. He wasn't, but he always thought he'd like to be.

Their new tutor, Earl was delighted to discover, cared almost nothing for drills. Her dining room, with the lace-curtained windows flung high, felt airy and expansive, as did the way she wandered around the room with great billowing arm movements while she talked. While Mr. Gregory had a dour voice for such a young man, Mrs. Chaplin, easily forty years his senior, seemed almost girlish when she spoke. Her voice never droned, but tripped and tumbled, increasing in speed and intensity whenever she found something extra-interesting, which it seemed was most things.

Mrs. Chaplin breezed through their lessons in reading, writing, and arithmetic, at each child's own level and pace. And then it was on to geography and history, which really got her arms billowing. She had a chalkboard on wheels with which she would shuffle in backward each morning and set up diagonally in the corner in front of her china cabinet, which was filled, Earl noticed, with rather plain-looking white dishes. While they learned geography and ancient history, she drew whimsical depictions in chalk of the Pyramids of Giza, the Nile delta, the Sphinx, the Parthenon, the Colosseum, and one day with extra care, the Great Wall of China, already drawn when they filed into her dining room that morning.

Earl's heart swelled at the sight of it. Archie and Sandor took a seat and seemed to be sitting a little taller, while Gerald and Sin Fah were openly grinning from ear to ear. They were six American-born children held spellbound by the romance of Papa's homeland. The five sitting in Mrs. Chaplin's dining room felt kinged and queened for a day.

T'ai Peng was ever the reluctant exile. He spoke of the Cathay of his childhood as you would a beautiful dream.

Although he made a living laundering other people's clothes and starching and curling their collars, it meant something to the children that Papa was "not really" a laundryman. He wasn't a very good businessman either, according to Archie, who, as firstborn, helped run the laundry. Too willing to extend credit to people who can't pay, he said. But what did Papa know about business? His head was in the clouds. He studied the philosophy of Confucius, Lao-tzu, and Zhuangzi, and wrote poetry. The tale of the murderous roundup of his university co-conspirators and his own violent escape in a rowboat was hard to reconcile with the quiet grace of his slender frame, or the delicate way his hands held the brush when he painted poetry or laundry tickets.

And now here he was, half a world away, starching and ironing shirt collars for people and helpfully forgetting to collect the fee. But he sang when he worked, and the laundry workers, all of whom were Black and mostly lifelong employees, chuckled at him, shook their heads, and called him Boss with affection. Earl reckoned no one in the place ever set out *wanting* to clean and iron their lives away, and maybe there was a kind of kinship about that, maybe they understood each other. Papa knew that dignity lay not in *what* you did but always in *how* you did it.

"Roosevelt is a wonderful man, just like Dr. Sun," he used to say. "He like see people eat, not lie down like dog in gutter and look at big limousine pass by." And if he was in the right kind of company, he might also lean forward and say what he really meant. "You know I be a true democrat. I like all be equal, but long time come before that happen. Maybe good thing mix up all races, make a better world. I believe in equal."

Whenever the children found themselves in a morally ambiguous situation, he had but one admonishment. "Remember your name is Chan." Said as if that were the only guidance they'd ever need.

Papa held the children in thrall with his tales when they were at home, but it was thrilling to find themselves talking openly about China here with Mrs. Chaplin. Her effort and excitability hinted, Earl thought, at exotic longings a lot like his own. From what Mama said, Mrs. Chaplin had been born and raised in Savannah and never been farther than Charleston after suffering an early widowhood, but this seemed to have had no bearing on her sense of wonder about the wider world. Indeed, if anything, it seemed to stir the fires of her imagina-tion. Earl pondered whether Mrs. Chaplin might not see their five little black heads bent over her dining room table and think that she was on an adventure of her own making. Anyone could see she enjoyed raising eyebrows. Tutoring the "heathen Chinee," as Chinese Americans of that time were often called, would certainly have raised a few.

Earl pursed his lips in repressed glee. An image had come vividly and unbidden to his mind of his ebullient teacher riding on a camel, tossing the end of a headscarf over one shoulder like one of the Three Wise Men. Although she didn't look the part in any way, there was a feeling about her that if, by some magic, she suddenly did find herself riding a camel or sipping strong coffee in a Turkish bazaar, she'd star-tle for only a moment and then sink down with a conspiratorial smile and avoid detection for as long as possible while she steeped herself in the guilty pleasure of doing what everyone least expected her to do. Earl liked that about her. A lot.

In Mrs. Chaplin's dining room he learned to love school. He began to grasp just how wide and wondrous a place the world was, and he wanted to see it all. He imagined sending Mrs. Chaplin picture post-cards from each of his ports of call.

> *Dear Mrs. Chaplin,*
> *Agra is the bees' knees. I am lunching on fresh man-gos at the Taj Mahal. Do you know what a pangolin is?*
> *Sincerely,*
> *Your pupil Earl*

Earl had never eaten a mango and never seen a pangolin, but at this point he was sure he could identify either one if it ever crossed his path. Mrs. Chaplin also introduced the children to great literature. Reading opened a window onto the world for Earl. Gerald had been reading Grimm to the three littlest, Sin Fah, Earl, and baby Bernice, for years. But Mrs. Chaplin guided Earl toward *The Merry Adventures of Robin Hood, The Life and Strange Surprising Adventures of Robinson Crusoe,* and *Twenty Thousand Leagues Under the Sea.* He had heard that reading was supposed to help one sleep, but when he had to put these books down at night because he shared a room with Mama and Bernice, he often lay awake for hours. He couldn't sleep for all the fierce and savage color, all the magic and swashbuckling magnificence, the mountain peaks, ocean trenches, improbable beasts, enchanted forests, stunning feats of derring-do, cunning villains, clever heroes, and friends of the heart. He tossed and turned, humming with expec-tation for all the world had to offer. Mama would turn over and pull him to her to calm his squirming, but his mind galloped on.

Gerald read all the books Earl did and did it about twice as fast. She soon called for a daily game of Robin Hood and his Merry Men in Forsyth Park during their walk home from Mrs. Chaplin's.

"I want to be Robin Hood!" yelled Earl. His mind had just leapt about ten adventures into the future. Planning was well underway when Gerald pulled him sharply back to the present.

"You can't be Robin Hood," she said. "I'm Robin Hood."

Earl frowned. "But you're a girl."

"Listen, Oil Can, it's *my game,*" she said, snorting at her own joke.

If it weren't his own name, he might have laughed too. He had once thought of a clever retort by calling her Glad-Ass—a double whammy because it played on her most hated name to begin with—but he quickly learned that while she might be a girl, there was still a pecking order, and he was at the bottom of it.

"Don't call me that!" he fumed. "Oh!" he cried, his spirits rising again. "I'll be Little John."

He threw his chest out and surveyed the landscape for footpads and cutpurses. He could knock a man out with a mighty backhand blow! He jumped onto a park bench. What would it be like to see the world from Little John's heights? How long would his stride be? He stuck one leg out and stretched it as far as it would go and took a giant leap. He turned back and was going to do it again in the other direction when Gerald laughed.

"You can't be Little John, silly!" she said.

"Why not?" Earl asked, his chest deflating again, this time real anger starting to prickle his ears.

"Because Little John is huge and you're *little*," she said.

Again he found it hard to argue with her. And so he contented himself with being first one, then another of the lesser Merry Men: Will Scarlet (a great swordsman) and David of Doncaster (a loyal friend). These weren't bad characters, really—quite respectable. But then one night he discovered Gilbert Whitehand, who was a skilled archer. Together with Robin Hood, they were reputed to be the best archers in all of England. At last, Earl had his man!

That night he lay awake again, imagining himself not only hitting the bull's-eye but also the arrow *in* the bull's-eye! Shooting the Sheriff of Nottingham's arrows right out of the sky! He heard Mama's slow and even breaths beside him and he closed one eye, held a thumb up in the air, and focused on a small water stain on the ceiling above his head. *"Pewww!"* he whispered to himself.

One thing was clear. He needed a bow. He mentally sorted through the materials he would need. It couldn't be one of the fallen branches they saw lying around the park; those were brittle and would snap. He needed something supple.

The next day, Saturday, Gerald fashioned herself a newspaper hat with a paper feather, and Earl made himself a bow with a spring branch he cut from the *Althaea* tree in their walled garden and some twine

from the laundry. It took some trial and error, but he figured out that if he notched the ends of the bow, it was much easier to secure the twine by tucking one end into the notch and wrapping it several times around the top and bottom, slathering it with glue to hold. He also put notches in his arrows, whittled from scrap wood taken from out back, so that he could fit them onto the bowstring. His first test shot traveled several feet. He was pleased as punch. Gerald borrowed the Kodak to take his picture.

Gerald and Earl, Robin Hood and Gilbert Whitehand, prowled the park and took cover behind light posts, commando-crawled through azalea bushes, and crouched behind park benches. Gentle Mr. Reilly, the police-man who patrolled the park, was appointed High Sheriff of Nottingham. By Gerald, of course, even though no one could have been more out of character than this kindly Irishman in the role of the hated king's sheriff.

Gerald wore her hair in a pageboy cut that didn't catch in the branches, and she often put on Sandor's old short pants like Earl's. Sure, she drew looks, but she didn't care.

"I knew from the start that boys were considered better than girls," she said to Earl one day, breathing heavily on the ground next to him. "And if I can't be a boy"—she ran in a stooped trot across the path to crouch behind the bench across from him—"at least I can wear pants, and don't have to go by Gladys. I'm going to be a writer. No one is going to publish the works of Gladys Geraldine!" She had no patience for skirts and curtsies, or for that matter sewing, cooking, or dolls. The 1920s had come not a moment too soon for Gerald. She and Earl rolled their eyes at Sin Fah's prissy antics, so moody and boring. Gerald was a bookworm and an adventurer like Earl, and it is no surprise that even though she was three years his senior, she was his favorite playmate.

OPPOSITE, TOP: Gilbert Whitehand, master archer, with homemade bow and arrow, ca. 1923 BOTTOM: Sandor (left), Bernice (front), Gerald (in short pants and tie), and Archie with a friend from across town, ca. 1923

On these walks home, Archie, the oldest brother and almost done with schooling, would run ahead to get back to the laundry, now on Whitaker Street, where he was expected to work until suppertime and beyond. He didn't like the stories as much as the others did anyway. His big passion was the circus. Any time off from the laundry would find him out at the carnival grounds by the big tent if the circus was in town, or otherwise painting and cutting figures for his home-designed flea circus. A budding businessman, he charged neighborhood kids a penny to come and see it, which they gladly paid, and stood in line to do so.

Sandor, second oldest, would soon have to follow Archie into the family business, but sometimes he still took a turn as the Sheriff of Nottingham. He did so only on occasion, though, and only if it might foil and annoy Gerald. He was the trickster in the family, but always gentle, never mean.

Meanwhile, Sin Fah might ordinarily have liked to play Maid Marian, if her older sister weren't always Robin Hood. "What's romantic about that?" she had railed. So she walked at a distance from the others, far enough away that she didn't really have to play, but close enough that she could follow along and snipe criticisms about what they were doing wrong. Bernice, the littlest, was still at home with Mama.

Two years on, they learned that they were going to go to school with other children—White children—and it was time to leave Mrs. Chaplin. Mama and Papa came to collect the children on their last day, a bright and balmy May afternoon. They brought with them two tea bowls with saucers, made of thin, cool porcelain that lightened to translucence at the rim and were painted in the long-life and rose-medallion pattern. They were a gift for her kindness and the great skill and care she had taken with the children.

T'ai Peng presented the tea bowls to her with a little bow. Mrs. Chaplin's face was bright with emotion, and she fussed over the delicate things sitting like eggshells in her palm, priceless treasures. T'ai Peng helped her give them pride of place in her china cabinet, the central spot on the middle shelf, where they popped beautifully against her plain whitewares. She stood back with hands to her face, shaking her head in delighted disbelief. She looked gratefully at Papa, reached a hand to Mama's arm, and then cast her gaze over each of the children's dark heads, blinking her eyes as the color rose in her cheeks.

She cleared her throat before speaking. "Mr. and Mrs. Chan, what an adventure it has all been. You have no id—" She took a deep breath and finished, "You have curious and delightful children. I know that more regular schooling will take them far, and I can only imagine what they will bring to the classroom and their new classmates. I will miss them all dearly. You hear that, children?" She turned to them, stroking Earl's hair with her palm. "Don't forget poor old Mrs. Chaplin. Come back again for tea and cookies and tell me everything that's new."

Earl was sad to go, but he never did go back for tea and cookies. One day he would indeed see a pangolin and know just what it was, and he would remember his days under the tutelage of Mrs. Chaplin as some of the happiest of his life.

THE POWER OF STORY

Nothing in Chinese mythology had led T'ai Peng to imagine that the Great Phoenix would live and die in obscurity in a foreign land, stripped of citizenship, social standing, and many basic rights enjoyed by the majority. He had grown up believing that when he spoke people would listen. In the end he wasn't wrong, but his influence didn't extend to society at large, and it didn't work the way he had imagined it would. His influence would be profound, but less quantifiable. He was still a change agent, though, affecting Savannah's development as well as the course of lives and lineages.

There were no high schools for non-White adolescents in Savannah at that time, not even segregated ones. By gaining entry to the public school in the elementary years, Dad was able to get a high school education as well. Having a high school diploma then made it possible for him to be the first in his family to go to college, and from there his trajectory was straight to the top. Chemical engineer, optical engineer, colonel in the US Army, top secret work for the CIA's first spy satellite program, developing the first lens to take pictures of Earth from space, and thirteen patents in photographic processing, aerospace engineering, and optics. He also flew planes and jumped off cliffs, circling in his hang glider on thermal updrafts like the mighty T'ai Peng itself, surveying horizons and returning only reluctantly to earth. He scuba dived, rode horses, learned to ski at forty-five, drove fast cars, traveled the world, married twice, had three children, never stopped trying new things, and lived and loved hard. And when he died, he was remembered as being magic.

Would it all have happened that way if Dad had known, had grown up believing, that he was considered unworthy of public schooling? I don't want to put the weight of a century of powerful living on a single shift in fate, but the discrepancy between what had happened and what Dad had lived a life *believing* had happened got me to thinking in yet another way about the essential power of story. *In this case, the power of a lie,* I thought when I learned the true history of desegregation in Savannah. *Grandpa lied and redrew the map for all his descendants.*

But was it a lie to say public school wasn't very good? Is a segregated school system good? Wasn't the reason it was segregated because there were, in fact, "too many crackers"? Perhaps it did not come down to truth versus lie here so much as to the power of one truth to imprison and another to liberate. Here we have the same fact—the Chan kids couldn't go to public school—but entirely different lenses for making sense of that fact. He could have told his children that they were homeschooled because our society thought they weren't worthy of an education, or he could have told them, as he did, that they were homeschooled because they were so smart nothing publicly available was good enough. And indeed, Mrs. Chaplin proved herself to be much better than what was publicly available. She left her mark on Dad's life. How else would I be able to tell the tale today, a hundred years on? So

T'ai Peng didn't lie. He told the more empowering truth. As a result, the Chan kids grew up not knowing everything they weren't supposed to want or be able to do.

A good storyteller can do that. Their unique magic shifts the map. They have the power to end harmful inherited patterns and curses (traumas handed down generation to generation until someone is ready to exorcise them); to intercept and transmute unexpected obstacles; and to transmit the seeds of growth and self-actualization that have taken root in them to their children and descendants. Good storytellers respect themselves, live well, love well, and teach others to do the same. They establish new lineages and better ways of being in the world. They can, and often do, break with the past, lead the way with the light of their own example, and invite others to join them.

Good storytellers also implicitly let the world know there are no unprecedented times. You are not alone. Nor are you lost. You are simply in the labyrinth, and the labyrinth, the whole of it, is known. For good storytellers and map shifters before you have walked it and shaped it in their wake. Listen to their stories, for they tell you what is possible and leave crumbs to lead you out.

In January 1939, T'ai Peng sat in the apartment above the laundry, hosting G.G. and a colleague, who had both been employed by Roosevelt's Federal Writers' Project to interview Americans from all walks of life. Her interviews with some of the last surviving people held as slaves were collected in a coauthored volume called *Drums and Shadows*. On this day she was interviewing a Chinese laundryman, who happened to also be her father.

OPPOSITE: The Three Questions.

Is it not pleasant to learn with perseverance?
Is it not delightful for friends to come from distant quarters?
Is he not a man of virtue, who feels no discomposure though men may take no note of him?
—*Confucius*

Herons are second only to the Phoenix in bird symbols for the Chinese. Thought to bear the souls of the departed to the heavens and to tether us to spirit realms where the deepest wisdom resides, herons also remind us of our own strength. Their graceful legs may look brittle, but they are sturdy, and a heron is one of the most sure-footed creatures on the earth. Put your foot down undaunted and unafraid and ask yourself the Three Questions. Remember that people who lead bold and compassionate lives are never truly alone and never, ever without consequence.

學而時習之　不亦說乎？
有朋自遠方來　不亦樂乎？
人不知而不慍　不亦君子乎？

Her submission was noted by her superiors on the last page as "excellent" and was tagged with key phrases for categorization and future research. Among them were the following:

Laundry owner and employer

Raised in China

Revolutionary temper

Ardent American friend Rooseveltian [sic]

Man loves independence

Features—A good citizen.

At the end of the interview, T'ai Peng grew quiet. He smiled and said, "I have long, happy life, more better than many man got. Good wife, good children all living, plenty grandchildren, good health, good name in foreign country, enough money for suit me. What more I want? Old-time poet Po Chü-i say, 'Drink from gourd and not ask more.'"

Only a phoenix, a sunseeker, a mythmaker, could tell it so. Only a map shifter and remarkably good storyteller. That's some of that Old Chan Magic.

CHAPTER 30

THE THIRD RAIL

For all of Dad's pipe smoke and magic, there was an intensity about him that I have learned to recognize since his death as symptoms of a "third rail." The third rail on an electric train is the (usually concealed) source of electricity. In writing, it is the hidden impetus that drives a story forward and controls a protagonist's worldview and actions without their knowing it. It is almost always based on a fundamental misbelief, or inner conflict, that the protagonist has about themselves or how the world works and used to be, more ominously called the "fatal flaw." That's unfortunate because it is not fatal, or at least it doesn't have to be. If you are compassionate enough in looking at it, it's nothing more frightening than a helpful signpost pointing to these misbeliefs and telling us where there is healing to be done. We all have these misbeliefs, and most of us spend our lives overcoming them. That's what human life, growth, and development are about.

Misbeliefs almost always develop during early childhood and can result from a single event or a set of circumstances that may repeat and accumulate into adolescence. But they are discrete and bounded, and soon they step into the driver's seat of a person's life, staying there until and unless the person can come to rights with them. If you excavate your character (or yourself) carefully and truthfully, you can

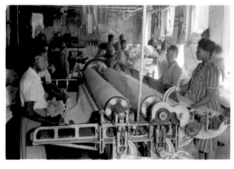

figure out what your main misbelief is, where it sprang into being and took root, and how it promoted either growth or failure at key points throughout your life.

I knew that for Dad—who never talked about race and who remained disinterested in questions about his own—race and the intricate, sometimes harrowing navigation of the color line in American society was his third rail and the elephant in every room. It went a little something like this: A mixed-race boy in the Jim Crow South thinks he must be twice as good as anyone else to get half the love. Navigating the color line in American society is an ambiguous endeavor but one that holds high stakes. There are consequences for getting it wrong. This creates unconscious anxiety in the boy, and a compulsion to control the world around him and, through it, his own destiny.

In Dad this led, on the one hand, to a magical life. On the other hand, control proved elusive, and attempts to maintain it made him rigid. Ultimately, on his deathbed, he discovered that control is an illusion, that he must let go of grudges and disappointments and accept that he has been worthy all along. He reconciled with the youngest child, let sleeping dogs lie with the oldest, and deepened his connection

OPPOSITE, TOP: *Cousin Wing (?), left, and Dad, right, at the car dealership for the family's first car. Tricky is at their feet.* BOTTOM: *The Willie Chin & Co. Laundry in action* ABOVE, CLOCKWISE FROM TOP LEFT: *Collar work; Folded shirts; Waiting for packaging; Wrapped and ready for delivery.*

with the middle. He crossed the threshold from control into command, and soon thereafter released himself to death.

After his death, I became interested in unpacking Dad's third rail—where he got it and what the struggle with it cost him. I sensed, in retrospect, a struggle somewhat like my own, to find a lasting sense of belonging, worthiness, and home. If I could unpack some of his life in this way, I could learn to unpack mine. I had begun to suspect strongly that I had more than one misbelief and that if I didn't find it and fix it, I would remain an outsider in my own life forever.

Come, let's light a match together, right now.

Strike!

Now watch it flower.

Hands in prayer.

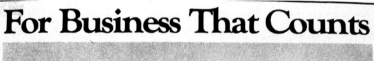

For Business That Counts

Count On ABACUS!

Don't toy around with computers. We'll consult with you; help decide if your business needs a computer; show how software, training, installation assistance and service can give you a total solution.

SIMPLE, RELIABLE SOLUTIONS

ABACUS SYSTEMS, INC.

7805 Waters Ave. Savannah, GA   (912)354-4606

G.G. modeling for Abacus Systems, Inc. in 1982. This would not have been a pose invented by the art director. A hand in the air, a little jig, or clicking heels were G.G.'s signature modes of self-expression. She and all the Chan kids had, of course, been using a real abacus since childhood.

"Mama was a little half-Chinese girl," said G.G., whenever I asked her about our family, which was often. "She was only four feet eleven inches tall! Papa met her at a fair in Atlanta, and used to say, 'She walk like little grass.'" At this, G.G. would herself tiptoe and sway across the room to demonstrate, as T'ai Peng before her had done. I was only nine years old but thought I knew *exactly* what a blade of grass would look like if it ever got up and went for a walk.

Though G.G. did not go to college, you wouldn't have known it. She and Dad both valued erudition, imaginative play, and curiosity. They were both seekers and poets—she quite literally, as a founding member of the Poetry Society of Georgia and a celebrated poet published in such diverse publications as the *Atlantic*, the *New York Times*, the *Washington Post*, and *Weird Tales*, and he more figuratively, in his poetic view of the world. They shared in gaiety and intellectualism; loved music, gossip, and a good joke; and were both particularly adept at helping children to bloom.

When Dad got on his high horse about something, G.G. could take him down a peg by looking around the room and deadpanning, "That's my baby budder, Oil Can."

There was no one else he'd take it from. I can't think of a closer or more loving relationship. They talked on the phone like middle-school girls at a sleepover. Perhaps once a week they talked, Dad sitting in his basement office, leaning back in his swivel chair, his face lit from below by a tiny banker's light on his desk. Frequently hours would pass as he alternately laughed, talked, and bellowed with his favorite sister about all manner of things. They also maintained a magnificent written correspondence.

When Archie died, G.G., a longtime diabetic, collapsed at the funeral from a dangerous plunge in blood sugar. I watched Dad at age seventy-four scoop her from the floor and carry her in his arms like a small child out toward the double doors of the church, the brilliant white light of day silhouetting them as, silently and with haste, they made for the car and the hospital. There was some family kerfuffle later in the aftermath over whether Dad really needed to leave with her, before the service was even over, no less. Was it proper? Necessary? For not one, but two siblings to be absent? With two others, Bernice and Sandor, already dead?

"It was necessary," he answered, eyes snapping.

To me, G.G. was the font of all family history and wisdom. I stored my questions to subject her to a fusillade of them every summer when we made the trip south. I found Dad's apparent ignorance of all family things insufferable. It was not just that he didn't seem to know much; it was as if he had never cared to ask. *How can you come from a family like this and not wonder about anything?*

"Hmm, I don't know. Why don't you ask Gerald?" he'd say. He let me know, though, that his sister was a poet who took poetic license as a divine right and a sacred calling, so I should take anything she said with a grain of salt because she was determined to see only the best in people and the beauty of any situation. *And this was a bad thing?*

"No," he said, "it's just something to know."

"Tell me more about Grandma Annie, G.G.," I would say. "Dad says I look like her."

"You do have the same little bump on your nose," she said, "and your eyes turn down at the corners like hers. The shape of your face is like hers, not like mine, a round mooncake." At this she laughed and put palms to her cheeks and pushed them up and back, willing them to stay lifted. "She would have spoiled you rotten! Papa too. Mama's father was a Chinese laborer named Sing Li." She enunciated her grandfather's name, letting it roll off her tongue. "And her mother was Spanish."

"Spanish?" I asked. "You mean, like Mexican?"

"No! Not Mexican." G.G. drew back in annoyance. "She was *Spanish*, from Argentina. Your great-grandmother was *pure*."

There was a note of pride in this purity that is funny for a family like ours, but I found myself feeling proud of it too at the time. Pure Spanish from South America. It sounded exotic and vaguely aristocratic. How and why did that happen? What kind of Spanish woman from Argentina had found herself in San Francisco having a child with a Chinese laborer? I did not think to ask at the time. But families tell themselves all sorts of stories to fill in gaps, to feel important, to find an identity that helps make sense of current circumstances. And to dream.

When I was in grad school in Boston, I told this story to a new Chinese friend of mine. Her response was swift and surprising, and I never quite stopped rolling it around in the back of my mind after that.

"Sing Li is not a name," she said. In fact, it isn't anything at all. Just gibberish.

————ꙮ————

In September 2007, my book on the archaeology of slavery in the North, *Slavery in the Age of Reason*, was published. I unboxed my author copies at the dining room table and thrilled at the thought-provoking cover art when I pulled the box flaps back to reveal the stacks of satin-finish hardcovers within.

That month there was another surprise in the mail when Dad got his DNA results back. I had bought him one of the first-available genetic tests for his ninety-fourth birthday. And since there was no doubt where T'ai Peng had come from, he chose to test his mother's line. Grandma Annie was supposed to have been an orphan, and while there were stories told about her, they did little to dispel the sense of mystery. A few weeks later, Mom wrote an email asking me to go over the results with them because something wasn't adding up.

"We figured you are kind of the expert here. What do you think they mean?" she asked.

I clicked through to his results page, scanned the screen for a moment, and felt a giggle burbling in my chest. *Oh my god.* Haplogroup L. I looked at the stack of my newly published books still sitting on the table beside me, and the giggle died as tears sprang to my eyes. Suddenly I was a very little girl again in the historic local library of my all-White town, sitting cross-legged on the floor in front of the shelves of Civil War books. The air was musty and sweet with the smell of old wood and paper. Dust motes floated through sunbeams on syrupy-thick currents of air. I liked to find a sunny spot in the history section and pull books from the shelf into my lap. I flipped through the pages, looking for pictures of the enslaved, whereupon I would bring the book right up to my nose. I gazed at their faces, their hands, their wounds, and tried to imagine them in life—moving, working, praying, laughing, grieving, comforting. I couldn't look away. I pulled more books from the shelves, the pile growing haphazardly around me. There were occasions, though not often, when I would see elderly Black men in real life, in a doctor's waiting room, at a bus stop, or on our trips to Georgia. I noticed, with curiosity, an urge to approach them and slide my hand into theirs and hold it there, for no good reason that I could give except that their hands looked comforting and familiar to me.

From those early days with my nose pressed into picture books about early African American life, I made almost a straight trajectory to my career and reputation in the archaeology of early African American life. It's an unusual path for a little half-Chinese girl in an all-White town, don't you think? I could never account for it. It was simply the way it had always been for me.

Now, sitting in front of Dad's DNA results and trying to compose a letter to Mom, I wondered, *Ancestors, was it you? Have you been with me all this time, leading me to things you wanted me to see?* A tear spilled down my cheek. *Have I told your story well?*

"Mom," I wrote, "Dad is haplogroup L, and there is no two ways about it. Haplogroup L means African. There is only one major way for an African blood group to get to this part of the world before 1881 when Grandma Annie was born, and that was in the hold of a ship. As for what it means, it means that Grandma Annie wasn't Chinese . . . *or* Spanish. None of the story we thought we knew is true. If we take away the Chinese, which we know came from Grandpa, that leaves Grandma to have been mixed-race—Black and White, a tiny bit Native, pure and simple. And from the looks of it, both her parents were too. Based on Dad's results, and regardless of how she presented, Grandma was probably about a third African. What does Dad say about it?"

"It's like I already knew," said Dad with furrowed brow. "It feels like the final piece to a puzzle that has dogged me my entire life."

"You know, Dad," I said, "Annie always said she was an orphan. It's possible she wasn't lying to you, but that she really didn't kn—"

"No, she knew," said Dad. "There isn't one little doubt about that. Mm-hmm. *She knew.* Mama never wanted to talk about her past. I figured she'd had an unhappy life before she met Papa. And then when I grew up, I tried to get some information from her more urgently—when I went into the army, you know—and she got mad and clammed up. That's the last I ever talked to her about it."

"It's sad, Dad. I'm so sorry she had to live a life of secrets and go to her grave thinking that there was something about her that was so unacceptable that no one must know, not even her own family."

"Well, it wouldn't have been shame that kept her quiet," said Dad. "She did it for us kids." We both went through a mental checklist of everything that wouldn't have happened or been possible had the Chan kids been seen as Black rather than merely Chinese. All the terrible things that *might* have happened instead.

"I can't stop thinking about what it means to cross the color line," I said. "One way or another, there's emotional violence implicit in the move. And it means inviting fear to steer the rest of your life, lest you be exposed. I mean, maybe she didn't have a happy life, like you said, and maybe there wasn't much for her to lose by crossing that line, but there must have been *someone* she was forced to leave behind."

"Well, if you were Black and in Georgia, there was going to be fear any way you cut it. Fear of being found out, or just fear of being. Take your pick. Golly," said Dad, sucking in his breath. "I wish Gerald were alive to talk to about this."

"I know, Dad." I switched gears. "I guess we know where you got that pomade-defying curl at your temple," I joked. It would never behave and always sprang loose—hinting, I liked to think, at a host of barely contained energies within him. Think Cab Calloway. I loved that curl.

"Yep, I guess we sho' 'nuff do." He smiled and nodded, brightening, "Yeah, how 'bout that?"

"Do you think Grandpa knew?"

"Probably. He's probably the one who gave her the idea to be half-Chinese in the first place. You know, since she couldn't pass for White."

This is true, I thought. My experience with Chinese people is that they don't even believe that *I* have Chinese ancestry. I meet them from time to time through my art business and they always want to know how I can paint in the Chinese way so well, and why I even do it. When I tell them about my grandfather, the most common reaction is "No. You are not part Chinese. *Are you?*" My Chinese friend from grad school went so far as to assume I was German! So that was settled. Grandpa wasn't talking in hypotheticals in his Federal Writers' Project interview. *Maybe good thing mix up all races, make a better world. I believe in equal.* Grandpa walked the talk and talked out loud, almost daring people to look behind his words more closely, maybe endlessly amused when they didn't.

In search of more clues, I looked where no one else in the family had ever thought to—the US census. And there it was for all the world to see. Unbelievable. The 1900 census recorded that Annie Chung Chang [*sic*], laundress, and wife of Robert Chan, was Black, from Georgia. In the 1910 census, now with two young children and an infant to protect, she was Chinese and Spanish, from California. By the time she died in 1959, the death certificate simply listed her as Chinese.

OUR GANG—ANOTHER STORY
BASED ON TRUE EVENTS

In August 1923, the Chan kids started at the public school. Earl took his seat in the front row on the first day and could feel the stares from the other kids boring into him from all sides. He wasn't nervous. Papa had told him that morning to walk tall. If Earl caught someone staring at him, he looked them straight in the eye until the other kid broke the gaze and smiled into their desk. Making friends was easy after that.

Earl recognized more than one student in the corridors as being among those kids who stopped by the laundry to drop off or pick up shirts and collars for their fathers who were bankers, lawyers, judges, dry-goods kings, and automobile dealers. He soon found out that several of his classmates also lived only a few blocks from him. This made it easy to fall into a little impromptu group of friends that they soon started referring to as Our Gang. Will, Frank,* and George* were in his grade. Ned* was older but had been held back at least a year and looked comically large in the schoolyard. Will's and Frank's fathers were a dockworker and a bricklayer, respectively, and Ned's father worked at the forge at Kehoe Iron Works. George's father was a small cotton farmer who'd been hit hard by the boll weevil outbreak that would soon sink the state economy.

Will was Earl's first friend at public school. Some of the kids called him Wee Willie Winkie to get his goat, but they learned soon enough that they put their own hides at risk to do so because, although he was small, he was built like a bull. He was square-jawed and pugnacious, but overall an outgoing and good-natured kid who was never really wicked, but just wanted to have a good time.

While Earl went to lengths to control his rooster tail and make sure his hair was always well-parted and combed down, Will had a shock of wild curls he rarely took a comb to and chose to control mostly by wearing a baseball cap, always turned to one side. His clothes were often dirty, and Earl's were never so. They couldn't have been more opposite on the surface, but they got on like gangbusters. They played jacks and marbles, and stickball in alleyways. They went to the five-and-dime for penny candy and loitered on the front stoop to eat their butterscotches, Peanut Chews, caramel creams, and Bit-O-Honeys.

One day when they reached the store, there was an old Black man sitting on the bottom step, leaning against the post. His clothes were clean but old and they hung on him, Earl thought, like maybe he used to be a much bigger man. But then Earl saw the way his ankles showed, and he figured maybe they were hand-me-downs. He fingered his own waistband, bunched up under his belt, and wondered what an old grandpa was doing in hand-me-downs like a kid.

The old man needed a shave, but when they approached, Earl could see by the way he lifted his head as if to catch a breeze, looking out in the middle distance, that the man was blind. Earl reckoned you could forgive a man for not shaving every day if he couldn't see what he was doing. He held a little tin cup on one knee, and Earl stopped in front of him. He knew what the cup was for, but the man didn't ask for anything, he just looked almost at him and smiled.

"Hey, Mister," Earl said, smiling back.

"Hello, child," the man said, waiting. And because Earl didn't say anything, "It's a mighty fine day today." He turned his head to catch another breeze and closed his eyes. "Yes, sir, a fiiine day. You goin' in to get yourself a cold drink?" he asked, leaning in with an eager look cast just over Earl's shoulder. "A Coca-Cola?"

Earl stared at his nickel, rubbing it between thumb and forefinger. "Nah, I was just here with my friend. Gonna get us some candy," Earl said, although this was a much less delicious-sounding proposition than it had been.

"Candy! Oh, now . . . let me see. I remember I always wanted to get the licorice . . . and them Cracker Jacks! Those were the berries! They came with a toy surprise inside." He chuckled.

"I like the butterscotches," said Earl. "And the Peanut Chews. The dark ones!"

Will was standing in the doorway, waving at Earl to *come on*. Earl dropped the nickel in the man's cup and followed Will inside.

"What'd you do that for?" asked Will, put out, as if it had been his nickel Earl had dropped in the cup.

"Bless you, honey," called the man through the screen door that slammed behind the boys. "Bless that child," he said again to himself.

"I don't know," Earl said to Will. "I just felt like it. I'm not hungry anyway."

"Who said anything about being hungry?" said Will, indignantly.

Will and Earl played hide-and-seek in the park and ran races on stilts made of tin cans and twine. Will was Earl's first playmate in the outside world. Earl never laughed so hard or had so much fun in his life as he did with him. Will made him feel like he belonged to something more than just his family.

On Friday nights, Earl took to going to bed fully clothed so that on Saturday mornings Will could swing by the laundry early and tug on a piece of string Earl had tied to his big toe and dangled out the second-floor bedroom window before going to sleep. He felt that tug and his eyes flew open as if he had been waiting up all night. He unhooked the loop from his toe, jumped out of bed, grabbed an apple or a slice of bread from the kitchen, and ran downstairs ready to embark on their next adventure.

Will had a lot of friends. Some of them Earl liked and some of them he didn't as much. It was all the same to Will, though. You know the sort. If he could have a good time with you, you were in. Ned was one of the ones Earl didn't like as much. He was older by at least a year, maybe two, big, blunt-nosed, and sometimes surly. Earl, who was beginning to play with language at that time, thought Ned's hair and body bristled like a baboon with a toothache. Earl giggled at the image. Ned liked to pound a fist into his palm whenever he got to talking about someone or something he didn't like, which occurred pretty much daily. He wasn't aggressive toward Earl, not really, but Earl knew he confounded him. Ned often addressed himself to everyone in the gang and pretended Earl wasn't there. Earl supposed they tolerated each other because they both wanted to remain friends with Will. Earl had never had playmates his own age before, and he didn't want to ruin it.

George was another of Will's friends. He was tall and lanky, and Earl liked him a good deal. But even at age ten, he walked with an old-man stoop to his shoulders, like he was trying to shield something precious and delicate against his chest. This gave him the initial impression of being chicken-chested, but he wasn't. To tell the truth, Earl kind of felt sorry for him. George's father sometimes turned up at the schoolyard in the middle of the day, disheveled and belligerent, alternately trying to coax or command George to come speak to him through the fence. George would see him coming and spin his back to the road and make as if he couldn't hear, but his father would kick up such a fuss, pacing and calling out and sometimes rattling the fence, that George would have no choice but to go over to him. Earl could still see him standing there, hands in his pockets, looking at his feet, while his father's voice, indistinct and wheedling, sometimes angry, carried on the breeze. George nodded or shook his head in response before trudging back to the schoolyard, shoulders hunched and in a foul mood, liable to lash out. Earl could see why. Try as he might, it was impossible to imagine being ashamed of Papa.

When George spoke, which was not all that often, he tended to fidget and look down and away, or he rolled his eyes up to the ceiling, as if eye contact were painful for him. One-on-one, though, he was a pretty good egg. Earl also saw that George couldn't stand Ned, and since Earl had himself pegged Ned as a big, dumb bloviator, that tacit understanding became part of George and Earl's budding friendship.

Finally, there was Frank. Frank was small like Will, but without the big personality. He went along with whatever the gang was up to, but fed off the momentum they had going and was likely to go too far with it, ruining the fun. After that he'd fall into a despondent funk of self-excoriation, which was tiresome in its own way. For instance, if they were playing tag he'd tackle one of the others and knock his teeth in the dirt, and suddenly the game would be over. Or if they were swimming in the river and splashing each other, he'd try to dunk one and hold him under. They'd all march back up the riverbank, coughing and spluttering in sodden disgust, with him scrambling behind.

"I'm sorry, y'all! I didn't mean it! I was just trying to have fun! Come on, don't go, don't leave! I won't do it again, I swear, scout's honor!"

Everything was copacetic except that Earl did make the mistake one day of telling them that Gerald called him Oil Can . . . and the name stuck. Ned found it extra funny, and it was one of the only times he spoke directly to Earl.

"Yeah, 'cause you look like you fell in a vat of oil!" Ned taunted. "Hey, Chinymun, you're *oily*. You better wash that off!"

"No, dummy," said Will. "It's his name. *Earl? Oil?* You get it? *Chan? Can?* Gee, Ned, are you stupid?"

Ned drew himself up and started punching his palm, but Will was untroubled. Earl looked down at his hands and saw them, maybe for the first time, through someone else's eyes. Then he looked at Ned and thought (if anyone had asked, and they hadn't) that Ned looked like something that just crawled out from under a rock, bloated and pale. Earl put his hands in his pockets and wandered off to gather chestnuts for his slingshot. After he husked one from its spiky shell, revealing the deep swirls of brown and amber and a smooth, mesmerizing gloss, he couldn't help but notice it was the same color as his hand.

JIMMY AND THE DEAD GIRL

One day a boy named Jimmy* turned up at the river. He came upon the gang sitting on the bank, trying to make fishing poles. Earl had his whittling knife out and was demonstrating to the other boys, who were seated around him, how he had smoothed a branch for his bow and arrow, and how to tell the best kind of branch for a fishing pole, not too stiff and not too soft. He was getting ready to demonstrate the pièce de résistance, how to notch the end to facilitate the attachment of the line, when Jimmy sidled up to the group.

He said, "You don't have to do all that, you know."

Earl's annoyance at being publicly contradicted soon turned to curiosity when he saw the boy's face was open, helpful, and matter-of-fact. His hackles smoothed. "How so?" he asked.

"See?" the boy said, pulling something out of his pocket and holding it out. "Look at this." It was just a wooden dowel about the width of his palm, with string knotted around the center and wrapped in a thick coil around. He had a hook tied to one end, with a little lead sinker, and he was also carrying a tin can of earth for worms.

"It's called handline fishing. My daddy taught me. We get catfish around here, largemouth bass, and bluegill, on the regular. My grandmama fries 'em up on Sundays."

Jimmy had red hair cropped close under a ball cap. He was the first redhead Earl had ever seen up close, and he couldn't help but be curious and stare at Jimmy the way Earl's own classmates had stared at him. Jimmy's eyelashes grew in deep auburn at the root and lightened to yellow at the tips. They rimmed dark and earnest eyes the size, it seemed to Earl, of Mama's cookies. It was an arresting combination that made eye contact hard to avoid and easy to hold, even for George. Jimmy was quiet but not shy, and Earl liked him immediately.

Jimmy didn't go to school with Earl and the rest, but he started turning up for their after-school capers on a regular basis, eventually almost daily. He was calm and easygoing, what they called copacetic, and balanced out the group well, Earl thought. He didn't go in for all Ned's and Frank's hokum and was untroubled by Will's direct nature but not beguiled by it. Earl started to think Jimmy might mainly be hanging around for *him*, which made him feel pretty good.

The gang often met at the river, but you could catch them pretty much anywhere, sometimes even taking the streetcar to the edge of town and wandering around in the sticks where the insects grew louder and the vegetation closer, Spanish moss hanging in great sheets over their heads.

There were old plantation homes out there, some falling to ruin. Gerald said they had probably been burned by General Sherman during his storied march to the sea. The gang traipsed into the surrounding overgrown lands, tiptoed across rotting verandas, peered into broken windows. They gaped at the rain-soaked, dismal, crumbling remnants of impossible luxury—dusty chandeliers, cracked mirrors, shattered glassware strewn across the floors, splintered balusters, soot and mold licking up the walls. A thick layer of grime lay over everything, and piles of leaves were banked in the corners. Everywhere they looked, animal droppings evidenced the new inhabitants. It gave them the heebie-jeebies, and they loved it. They also played hide-and-seek in the row of slave cabins and among the once-elegant gardens that had gone to seed, creating all sorts of secret spots.

One day Will's voice called out from a distance, "Y'all quit hiding! You gotta come see this! You hear me? Come out! Come see! I'm over here!"

Earl crawled out from under a thick curtain of rhododendron and followed the sound of Will's voice to a back corner of the land, where he was standing under an enormous magnolia next to a rectangular structure that, upon closer inspection, revealed itself to be a family tomb. The stone was covered in lichen and algae. Masses of ivy grew at its base. Decades of rain and weather had worn the carved details down to indistinct lumps, but Earl could still make out two fat cherubs floating on either side of a central crest with the family's name in distinct lettering—MANIGAULT.*

Yet what Will was pointing to was not the tomb itself but something next to it. The boys drew closer and peered around the side to where he was looking. The door to the crypt had been broken, and a smallish cast-iron casket was protruding from it, the bottom still resting on the crypt floor and the head down on the earth at their feet as if someone had tried to drag it out but given up midway and just dropped it. Hot, spidery prickles shot up and down Earl's spine and crawled over his scalp. He heard his own heartbeat in his ears, and his breath came quick and hard.

This was no ordinary coffin that Earl had seen, but cast into the shape of a shroud, the folds wrapped and draped in an awful, ghostly manner. He thought of the mummies in Egypt he had learned about in Mrs. Chaplin's dining room and felt his knees wanting to buckle. More astonishing still was the oval plate glass affixed over the head, where the face would be. They leaned in and, with great cries of fear and loathing, leapt back as one.

"I'm gonna upchuck!" yelled Ned, wheeling out of control and trotting to a halt well outside the circle of shade cast by the magnolia. He broke into laughter and bent at the waist, gripping his belly and pretend-retching. Will, George, and Ned ran around in circles trying to wrangle each other and force first one, then another to come in close for another look.

"No! You think you're the big cheese around here, *you* go!" said Ned to Will, dodging his grasp and spinning away with surprising agility.

Meanwhile, Jimmy and Earl were rooted to the spot. Earl was in no mood for tomfoolery. He and Jimmy glanced at each other over the coffin, then both slid their eyes back down to see. Earl fell to his knees and leaned over to get a good look through the window. He could feel the warm moisture of his own breath reflecting off the glass onto his face.

The girl inside looked like she was sleeping, her head resting to one side. There didn't seem to be anything dead about her. Earl raised his hand to the glass as if to tap on it and see if she would wake, but let it hover there motionless instead. He guessed she was about his sister Bernice's age—six, maybe seven. He turned his head sideways to get a better look at her. Her cheeks were still chubby and pink, her eyes lightly closed. Her blond hair was parted in the middle and done in tight ringlets, with a pink bow fastened above the curls on each side.

"How long do you think she's been here?" asked Jimmy in a half whisper.

"I have no idea," Earl said, "but I've never seen hair like that." He looked up at Jimmy. "You?"

Jimmy shook his head, eyes wide. "She could have died fifty years ago. Seventy-five!" he said.

Earl looked down at her. The little Manigault girl was maybe old enough to be someone's grandma, had she lived. He could see her kneeling by her bedside, hands clasped fervently beneath her chin. *Now I lay me down to sleep, I pray the Lord my soul to keep. If I should die before I wake, I pray the Lord my soul to take.*

Earl didn't tell his parents or anybody else about what they had seen that day. It was their secret, and it seemed to bring the gang closer together. Dead bodies can do that, he supposed.

It took them some time to build up the courage to return to the Manigault house, and when they finally did, they discovered that someone else had found her too, but they were vandals. Someone had cracked the faceplate with a rock. The little girl's flesh, which had been so pink and plump at first discovery, had now, in a matter of weeks, grayed and caved in on itself. Her eyes were withered in sunken pits, and her mouth pulled back in a rictus grin showing her milk teeth, white and widely spaced like a picket fence. It was foolish to think such magic could last. Some people see a good thing and just want to wreck it.

AN INITIATION

By the following October, when Earl had started fifth grade, the boys had settled into a well-worn routine. Riverbank meetups, fishing, swimming, rambling, roving, ice cream treats, games of tag. They knew how to get each other's goat, and mostly enjoyed doing so. George's mood had darkened since the summer, though. His father had lost the cotton crop and, it was looking more likely, the family farm as well, to the boll weevil. When George came humping along with his shoulders around his ears and a deep frown, they all knew to give him space for a little while.

It was on one such day that they were kicking pebbles on a country road outside of town and had fallen into a natural game of tag. George had arrived last, looking disheveled and surly, but they could feel him relax a little more with each hundred yards they left the town behind. It started to feel safe to drum up a little fun. Jimmy was "it," and it was all a good time until he tagged George in what George felt was an unfair manner because he had been blocked from dodging the tag by a tree that, according to George, "got in the way."

Obviously, a tree can't *get* in anyone's way, Jimmy reasoned. "A tree has roots and doesn't move. You just *ran into* a tree!" he said, snickering. "That's a whole other ball of wax! I tagged you, you're it!"

"I'm not it!" said George.

"Yes, you are," said Jimmy. "Cheater!"

"I'm not a cheater!" said George, seething. "Take it back."

Earl had never seen George be the aggressor. But something inside George must have snapped, because without warning he lunged at Jimmy with bared teeth and a growl that was pure animal. Jimmy was quick and light on his feet, but George was tall and his reach was long. It wasn't but a few seconds before he grabbed Jimmy by the back of his shirt, ripping it from his waistband, and swung him around like a rag doll. The fight was on. They grappled with arms locked around each other's shoulders, peeling at each other's fingers and each trying to reach down and grab the other by the knee or ankle. George finally got hold of Jimmy by the belt and swung him hard in an arc, out and away, grabbing the ball cap off his head as Jimmy skidded into the dirt.

Jimmy landed resting backward on his elbows, knees up, and stuck there like a statue. His stillness was preternatural, almost like he was summoning protective coloration like a chameleon, like he was trying to pass for a rock or something. Only his chest heaved up and down, and Earl thought of the mouse he once cornered in Mama's kitchen with broom and bag in hand—tiny, still, and gasping.

George had staggered backward a few steps and had Jimmy's ball cap in hand. He continued to scowl, open-mouthed, but the spell was broken. They were all frozen in their respective places.

Jimmy's hair, normally hidden under the ball cap, now stood up in unmistakably textured curls. His eyes, dark and vulnerable, scanned the group and found Earl's, whose insides had turned to liquid. Was he waiting for Earl to say something? He could hear Jimmy's voice in his head, with just a hint of a question, *Earl?* Earl opened his mouth and closed it, like a fish hauled up on the riverbank and left to gape. He tried to lick his lips, but his mouth had run dry. At last, he couldn't bear it and broke the gaze. He looked at his feet and shuffled backward, heat rising in his chest.

He looked to the side and saw Will squinting with cocked head, like he was considering a bug in a jar. Frank giggled nervously.

It was Ned who broke the silence.

"Well, well, well. Lookee what we got here, boys," he cried in glee. His voice, which was in the middle stages of puberty, sounded more abrasive than usual, serrated even. "Looks like Jimmy here's a *nigger!*" He laughed in disbelief and said it again. "Jimmy, how come you never said nothin' about you bein' no *nigger?*"

Earl flinched and shoved his hands deeper into his pockets.

George looked down at the cap in his hand and frowned, confused almost, and tossed it at Jimmy's feet. He turned and ambled away, rolling his eyes to the sky and shaking his head almost imperceptibly. He hadn't meant for things to get out of hand like this. Earl could see that. Earl also knew that a rock set in motion stays in motion, until and unless somebody stops it. Who was going to stop it?

Jimmy reached for his cap, never taking his eyes from the others, and gave Earl a last, lingering look. Earl managed to gaze back at him but found he could say nothing. He ducked his head and took another step backward. At that, with hat in hand, Jimmy scrambled to his feet, turned tail, and ran as fast and as hard as Earl ever saw a boy run, all elbows and knees, shirttail flapping, never looking back.

"Run, nigger, *run!*" yelled Ned, throwing a pebble after him.

"Yeah, *scram*, nigger," shouted Frank, who seemed now finally to have found his part to play. Earl looked over at that little pip-squeak and saw him for the sorry sidekick he was.

And what does that make you, Oil Can?

WILLIE CHIN & CO.

Earl hung his head and scuffed his Converse shoes in the Georgia dirt, turning them a deep dusty yellow at the toe. He kept his eyes on his toes, mind empty, ears ringing. He clicked his teeth together in absentminded patterns, sliding them side to side, listening to the light scraping sound of enamel on enamel. Nobody said anything much after that, and Earl walked well away from the group.

The boundary between dirt road and cobblestone was abrupt. When you could see yellow sand in among the cobbles, you knew you were back in town. The boys got to the turnoff where Will, Ned, and Frank had to go in one direction and Earl in the other. George had peeled off some time earlier. The atmosphere was subdued. Even Ned seemed, if not contrite, at least sorry that all the fun had been ruined, and annoyed that everyone seemed to be blaming him.

"Bye, Earl," the boys muttered not quite in unison. "See you tomorrow?"

Earl gave a half-hearted flap of the hand over his shoulder and turned toward home. In fact, he didn't see them tomorrow, or the next day. The magic was gone. *Some people see a good thing and just want to wreck it.*

Papa kept the sidewalk in front of the laundry swept clean, but Earl came in the back way, along a dirt alley bursting with weeds. Shards of glass, rotten bits of wood, rusty nails, and old roof flashing accumulated at the base of the buildings and crunched underfoot if he left the center of the path, which he did, for it was mucky with poor drainage. He kicked out of the way a sodden shoe that lay on its side. Pushing open the weathered wooden gate, he entered the walled, dirt-swept courtyard behind the laundry. On the left there was a dilapidated lean-to filled with old buckets, scrap wood, barrel hoops, crates, broken furniture, and broken broomsticks. A mildewed brown blanket was thrown in a heap on top. The door to the laundry room was open to circulate air. It was hot as blazes inside, even in October.

Earl looked to his right and saw Charlie, the laundry foreman, on his break, sitting on one of the lower steps that led to the second-floor residence. He had one knee up and was resting an elbow on it, a hand-rolled cigarette smoldering between two fingers. Charlie's hair was sprinkled with gray, but his arms were smooth and muscular like those of a man twenty years his junior. His once-white shirt, now a dingy, sodden brown, was open halfway down his chest, with sleeves rolled to the mid-upper arm. It was a comparatively cool day for October, but his dark skin was slick with sweat right down to the backs of his hands.

Earl shuffled toward the stairs to head up to the kitchen. Charlie had been eyeing him since he walked through the gate. Earl didn't feel like saying hi. He put his hand on the rail and made to squeak past Charlie.

"Hey, boy," Charlie said with a chuckle in his voice. "What you lookin' so glum for?"

Earl slid his eyes up to Charlie's and pursed his lips in a tight smile, then looked down again. "Aw, I ain't glum," he said and went up the stairs.

Charlie turned to watch him, and Earl felt his eyes on the back of his head, which prickled, but he didn't turn around.

Earl had known most of the people who worked in Papa's laundry his whole life, but Charlie was a special friend of his. He had helped Earl make his own handline fishing dowel like Jimmy's, and even upped the ante by showing him how to tie a fly to the hook and telling him the best holes to go to.

Charlie was friendly with all the Chan kids, but there was a special twinkle in his eye for Earl. He called Earl a little scrapper and burst out laughing at a lot of the stuff Earl said and did. Mama might be exasperated and Papa mad, but Charlie was amused.

His favorite story to tell, and he told it often, was how when Earl was a little boy of maybe three years and he got tired of the church ladies, as he called them, coming over and taking up Mama's time, he would take that wooden chair—"That one *right there*," Charlie would say, pointing to a chair whose seat was shin high, still sitting in the corner of the courtyard—"and *throw it down the stairs!* And then what you think? That boy start *cryin'* like it was *him* that went tumblin' down, and Miss Annie'd come *runnin'.*"

When he recovered himself, if Earl was in striking distance, Charlie would grab him and ruffle his head or give his bottom a friendly smack and sum it all up for everybody, the same way every time: "Look at Robert Earl. This boy knows what he wants. And knows sho' 'nuff how to get it too!"

However, there was one time when Earl opened Papa's large black umbrella and jumped from the second-floor balcony roof, imagining he would float down like he'd seen in the moving pictures at the Savannah Theatre. Mama saw him fly past the kitchen window like an anvil. She came running all right, but it was Charlie who got there first. He found Earl bruised and winded in an azalea bush, and his eyes weren't laughing then.

He said Earl reminded him of his own boy.

"Where is he?" Earl asked one time.

"I don't know," said Charlie, straightforward, simple.

Sometimes Earl had to sit in the laundry all day on a stool next to the water gauge, checking the temperature and making sure it was always where it needed to be. It was the worst. All the kids had to work in the laundry in some way or another, except Bernice, who was still too little. Archie, as the oldest, had to do almost everything Papa did, and some stuff he didn't do anymore, like mucking out the stables for the horses and hooking up the wagon for deliveries. Sandor apprenticed with Archie, so they were gone for much of the day. Gerald and Sin Fah were in the front welcoming customers, taking orders, and writing out tickets.

It was Gerald who ground the ink and used Papa's calligraphy brushes to swipe bold numbers on the ticket papers for customers. She worked the cash register too because she was responsible and good at math. Sometimes she even used Papa's abacus, just for show, to the delight of customers. Papa had gained some local renown when a story spread about a traveling adding-machine salesman who tried to make a buck at the Willie Chin & Co. Laundry. Papa had challenged him to a duel, abacus versus machine. Papa and the abacus had won, of course, and customers took vicarious pride in that. *Our Mr. Chan is a good one. Have you heard the story about the adding machine and the abacus? And the children use it too!*

Sin Fah, on the other hand, was the family actress. She flitted around the store pirouetting and practicing her small talk, making eyes at the young men, and falling into a morose pout when the store was empty again. If she ever had to actually do the work out there, the aggrieved sighs made it so miserable for everyone that she'd be relieved of her duties so she could return to her pliés and glissades, and her well-I-nevers and I-do-declares. Earl had a good view of these antics from his stool in the back laundry room because it was near the doorway that connected the front to the back.

As dull as Earl's job was, Charlie would talk to him like a man when he was back there, and he'd let Earl hand him the wrench while he was fixing laundry tubs.

One day, Charlie heard Earl yammering about his cousin Wing, who was not really a cousin—their fathers had just come from the same village—getting a BB gun. Not too long after, Charlie took Earl out to the courtyard. He squatted down and brought out from behind him a long object rolled in newspaper, checking over his shoulder to make sure no one was looking out the back door. Then he turned to Earl with an eagerness Earl hadn't seen before and handed it to him.

"What is it?" Earl asked.

"Why don't you take the paper off and see," said Charlie.

Earl unrolled the thing and felt the breath hitch in his throat. He looked up at Charlie with eyes wide. "You got me a BB gun?" he said, dumbfounded.

"Yeah," said Charlie, ducking his head in a nod, his eyes searching Earl's face for something. "What you think?"

"I love it," said Earl. He ran his fingers over the rich red grain of the wooden stock. He turned the gun up and looked more closely at the oiled black metal, then closed one eye and peered into the barrel.

Charlie ripped the thing out of Earl's hands, startling him. "Never point a gun in your own face," he said sharply.

"It's not loaded, is it?" said Earl.

"You don't know that," Charlie said. "Never point a gun at anything you don't intend to hit." He hesitated for a minute to satisfy himself that Earl had heard, and maybe to consider if he hadn't just made a terrible mistake. Earl squirmed under the intensity of his gaze.

Charlie handed it back to Earl. "You gonna go hit some targets with Wing now?" he asked.

"No," said Earl.

If Charlie was surprised, he quickly hid it. "Why is that?" he asked.

Earl told him, "Well, Wing's daddy broke his BB gun over his knee a couple days ago and then stomped on it and kicked it down the stairs because Wing shot his sister in the butt."

Charlie, who was still squatting at eye level with Earl, broke into such a laugh that it made the boy jump. Earl started laughing too, and soon enough couldn't stop.

Charlie eventually stood up, leaned on his knees, and gave Earl's bottom another smack and told him to go on and git. "Go set up some cans, then, and get shootin'."

Earl ran out the back gate into the alleyway and could still hear Charlie laughing as he went back into the laundry to work.

Earl kept that BB gun for many years. Turns out, he was a crack shot. One day he would be a sharpshooter in the US Army, and he never aimed at anything he didn't intend to hit.

So, it was Charlie who was on Earl's mind when he went through the door at the top of the stairs and entered the kitchen. He was feeling mighty low. Mama was bending over to get some cold ham out of the icebox for lunch, and Earl slid sideways and slumped into a chair at the table. Mama dropped the ham on the cutting board on the counter and reached for a carving knife, glancing over her shoulder to make sure nothing had happened.

"Mama, are we niggers?" he asked. The word felt coarse and unpleasant on his tongue, but then, he was feeling coarse and unpleasant.

The sound of the knife clattering in the enamel sink jolted Earl out of his churlish reverie and snapped him back to the present, and it wasn't one he recognized. Mama spun around and steadied herself on the counter behind her. He had never seen her like this and knew immediately he had made a mistake. He leaned back in consternation and moved his mouth a bit, but nothing came out. Speechless for the second time that day. Her mouth was pursed and her chest heaved. What scared Earl the most, though, was that her cheeks flushed a violent, blotchy red that went right up to the rims of her eyes, which were blazing.

Mama was not a screamer or a hitter. Papa, despite his generally good nature, could hit, and hard, but Mama was gentle, and hardly taller than Earl himself. Even so, Earl was in uncharted territory and didn't know what to expect, and the waiting was agony.

After a moment, Mama had reached someplace either high above or deep within, for she restrained herself to a simple, quiet admonishment. "All people are children of god, Robert Earl."

In the silence that followed, by way of explanation, Earl told her what he had seen, and what he had been unable to do, his shame and sadness bleeding out onto the kitchen table before him. But if he thought Mama was going to stitch him up, console him, or help him make sense of what had happened or how to feel about it, he was mistaken. She listened without interruption. And when he was done, she didn't say anything. She moved rigidly back to the ham on the counter, picked up the knife, hesitated for a second, put it back down, and then hissed over her shoulder, "We are *not* Negroes. Go on back outside now."

After he died, I concluded what Dad had seemed to labor under most was the idea that his value out there in the world was nebulous, precarious, and might be revoked at any moment. Moreover, both of his parents were refugees, after a fashion—T'ai Peng in the usual sense, and Annie in the sense of being a race refugee, for she had lost everything and everyone when she crossed the color line. Part of what she gained in return was a lifetime of fear of being outed like Jimmy. Dysfunction can, and often does, arise in immigrant and refugee families, as they cope, often imperfectly, with the pain of their losses. That trauma can, and often does, become intergenerational. I believe Dad's need for self-perfection was based partially on racial anxiety accrued through his own experiences, but partially too on refugee anxiety inherited from his parents. If things aren't perfect, was the whole ordeal of escape, loss, and rebuilding even worth it? The parents in such situations, who experienced the immediate trauma, may spend the rest of their lives consciously or unconsciously looking for evidence that it *was* worth it. Meanwhile, many children of those immigrants and refugees find themselves condemned to a life of proving that yes, it was worth it, or indeed proving that *they themselves* were worth it. How much more complicated is it when the children feel compelled to shine in a society committed to hating and fearing them?

Dad was quite popular on the surface of things: a gadfly, exotic, mysterious, and alluring, the more so for his time, when people who looked like him were likelier to be found in kitchens and laundries, not holding court. He seemed quite aware of this, however, and so underneath that easy grace, his posture was almost defiant. He intimidated some people, triggered demons in others. There was no neutral feeling about Bob Chan. He had built a charisma around that core wound, which made him impossible to look away from, either in envy, admiration, or fear disguised as dislike. At the end of the day, a part of him always still felt, or believed, that his presence in any room, no matter how earned or deserved, relied on the will, whim, curiosity, tolerance, or patronage of White people whose positions were secure. That reality was not unique to him. But his reaction to it was to become driven, perfectionistic, intense, defiant, and sometimes unbending to the point of creating tumult around him. Sometimes he was the eye of the storm; other times he was the storm itself.

Where did the ethos and pathos begin? I argue that they were seeded in 1889 on a dinghy in the South China Sea and watered into bloom by a social experiment on the banks of the Savannah River in 1923.

Ninety-two years later, and with the help of DNA cousins who had intact genealogical knowledge of their family lines and could triangulate with me, I was happy to be able to share with Dad the name of one of his grandfathers. Even T'ai Peng's parents remained aloof, name-less, and afar as "grandparents in China." This, then, would be the only grandparent whose name Dad would ever know: Cudger Williams, or, more likely, Cudjoe, an early transliteration of Kojo, the West African Akan name for a boy born on a Monday. The name has roots in what today is the southern region of Ghana. Grandma Annie was not part of his legitimate line. He may not even have known of our family, which was also his biological family. But there it was, and now it was I, not G.G., who let the delicious-sounding name of an ancestor roll off my tongue. *Cudjoe. Williams.*

He was not a Chinese laborer, but according to the US census, a free mulatto from North Carolina. A farmhand and sharecropper. He was married to a woman named Dinah, and father to a son also named Cudger. Much more about his life, the records do not tell. But his younger brother, Shade, made quite a stir. *Shade Williams. What a name!*

So it is my grandma Annie's uncle Shade who must stand for that part of the family and shine a light on how it might have been for ev-eryone. He too was a farmhand and sharecropper. One of the Civil War colored troops in the Union Army. Illiterate. And in the scant details of his life, it seemed to me, uncannily familiar, with personal charisma and potential at odds with what society wanted to grant him, and a knack for living to tell the tale.

CHAPTER 31

OLD ISSH'Y

Free Blacks held a peculiar and precarious place in the antebellum South. Neither enslaved nor completely free, they were at the whim and mercy of White society. Their rights and freedoms fluctuated, even in a single location, and then waned precipitously with the nineteenth century as poor White men gained power in the zero-sum game of White supremacy.

There were not many free Blacks in the colonial and early post-colonial period of American history—about 7 percent of the Black population in 1790 was free, around 13.5 percent between 1820 and 1840, and 11 percent on the eve of the Civil War. Most freepeople, as they were sometimes called, had gained their status by having rendered military service in the Revolutionary War; by having a White mother (by law, children inherited the legal status of their mothers); or by obtaining the occasional manumission by conscience-stricken White fathers or slaveholders. Running away was another, but less common, means of obtaining one's freedom. There is no record that I have found to indicate which of these methods resulted in the Williams brothers being born free in 1835 and 1839, respectively. Their parents, Jacob and Matilda, are shadowy figures who do not turn up in any records of their own. They are only known because they were named on Shade's death certificate.

As part of the Upper South, North Carolina had traditionally been more accepting and lackadaisical than its immediate neighbors about having free Blacks in their midst during the eighteenth and early nineteenth centuries, which encouraged some freepeople to flow in from Virginia and South Carolina. But all that was about to change.

The Williams boys were born at an increasingly unfortunate time for North Carolina's freepeople. Nat Turner's bloody rebellion in a border county of Virginia in 1831 had put the fear of god, or at least the fear of "chickens coming home to roost," into North Carolina's White population. Free Blacks had heretofore enjoyed certain limited freedoms there that might surprise modern readers. Between the end of the American Revolution and 1835, for example, free Blacks in North Carolina could testify in court (although not against Whites); preach and organize churches; own and carry a gun; hunt with a dog; and sell food, liquor, or other goods to anyone who wanted to buy them. Most improbably of all, they could legally vote in the early nineteenth century. The boys' own father, Jacob, might well have been to the ballot box.

But by the mid-1830s, fearful Whites had begun to see keeping free Blacks around in a slave society as akin to keeping matches in the tinderbox. In the face of anticipated insurrection, as well as increasingly aggressive abolitionist feeling and campaigning in the North—perhaps one of our nation's first culture wars—North Carolina's early acceptance of free Blacks evaporated, to the detriment of all free persons of color living in the state. In 1835, state lawmakers clamped down. They struck from the state constitution the right of free persons of color to vote. Suddenly, even Black veterans of the Revolutionary War, who had been proudly casting their votes for decades, found their ballots denied with no recourse. It was a bitter turn. Life became immeasurably harder for Black people after that. The state began to enact, county by county, regulations designed to curb or eliminate the remaining rights of the freepeople in their midst. These "codes" stripped them of the right to travel freely, preach, carry firearms, marry either White or enslaved people, or even transact business with the enslaved. No longer could free Blacks travel into the state without incurring a $500 duty and an order to leave within twenty days on pain of being sold into slavery for ten years.

Manumission, previously almost unrestricted for "good and orderly slaves" and "honest and faithful service," also now came with a tax, and the responsibility for permanently transporting said person out of state. This proved prohibitive even to enslavers who had grown a conscience. No one under the age of fifty could be manumitted at all anymore. There were no legal southern counterparts to the northern Black churches, schools, newspapers, and fraternal societies, which gave cohesion, aid, and a sense of community and common cause to the Black population there.

By the early mid-nineteenth century, the plight of free Blacks in North Carolina was dire; opportunities to thrive, or even strive, were almost nil. Shantytowns cropped up on the outskirts of larger population centers, and for those who weren't tradesmen or artisans, scraping out a living proved nearly impossible. In 1886, David Dodge, an observer for the *Atlantic*, wrote that as a class they were reduced to "piddling," which meant surviving by hawking watermelons and other fruits and nuts that could be grown or gathered from poor soils, or fashioning any baskets, doormats, stools, or chairs as could be cobbled together or woven from reeds at the riverbank.

By midcentury, free Blacks in North Carolina were perceived on a level with vermin, even by those who were themselves enslaved. After the war, Dodge writes, newly freed Blacks, known as new issue, or colloquially, new issh'y, and existing free Blacks, known as old issue or old issh'y, did not intermingle, for association of any kind with old issh'y would have been detrimental to a new issh'y's fragile reputation and standing.

Cudger and Shade were old issh'y.

And yet . . .

THE ROBESON COUNTY MURDER

The boy named Shade must have had a shine about him. If his later kin are any indication, he was handsome and possessed an ease of movement that, if he weren't old issh'y, would be called grace. We might imagine, too, that he had a certain verbal dexterity that belied his lack of letters and cut through the blunt, mute fog of indigence and exclusion that sought to keep others of his class in silent, amorphous anonymity.

I have a hunch that Shade, my great-great uncle, like other elders of mine I have known, was the type that couldn't be anonymous if he tried.

Court records from 1860 indicate that, at twenty-one, he had certainly caught the eye of Mrs. Abi Rhodes, who was twice his age, married, a mother of six . . . and White. Who knows how the wife of a tailor named Benjamin Council Rhodes, eleven years her own senior, came to cross paths with the tantalizing Shade. He had no trade, was likely what David Dodge referred to as a piddler. He never did rise above the status of sharecropper. But in 1860, it may be that he was a hired hand at a neighbor's farm. Perhaps she spotted him digging postholes in front of her husband's business. Or perchance she bought a melon off his meager pile on a hot day as she exited the post office, and they got to talking.

Abi Rhodes, born Grimsley, had been married off to a grown man when she was thirteen. She hadn't grown up in the normal way. Census records suggest her husband had had the decency to leave her alone in the early years, fearful and distraught as she must have been. But starting at seventeen, it was baby after baby. By the time she was thirty-one, she was a mother of four boys and two girls. And at forty-two, when she felt the bloom of her wasted youth all but shriveled, and never once used well, she met a shining young man, younger than her own firstborn, who carried none of the stodgy, patriarchal condescension of Benjamin or her sons, who seemed to be taking after their father. Shade was attentive, curious, and affable, not to mention startlingly good-looking. He was also forbidden, which must have appealed greatly to Abi, who had never done anything in her life except for others and as she had been told.

Shade offered her an alternative vision. He was young enough to still carry the world and its absurdities lightly . . . or maybe age had nothing to do with it. Abi liked the way he poked sticks at the sanctimony and pretensions of White society, but without ever going so far as to cause dangerous offense. Decrepit ideologies about race, intelligence, or potential crumbled to dust in his presence. He thumbed his nose at *should*, and paid no never mind to the *shoulds* and *oughts* that ruled Abi's world. He was fun. He made her laugh. At first, there was just the frisson at running gratuitous errands in the hope of encountering him somewhere and striking up another conversation with the young, bright-eyed old issh'y freeman.

But then, when she was alone at night, something also thrummed in her at the thought of those eyes that sparkled so good-naturedly, warm and black as coffee. Not the piercing, cold eyes of her husband, the pleading or truculent ones of her children, or the judging, disapproving stares of neighbors.

Abi made him her paramour, and the whole affair hit her like a storm. Shade awakened desire in her she had never experienced, shook her foundations, and exposed, in his being, illusions upon illusions of the world. His name was Shade, but his gaze shone like the sun, and warmed her in ways that negated rigidity and duality, separation, Black and White. Even the idea of Shade asked her to transcend everything she had ever known, take the third path, and embrace what is true.

In her mind it was a great romance, no less than any she had read in the novels and plays of history, and a chance to live a life she had never yet imagined—her own. She longed to live openly and freely with him at her side. No more rude encounters in goat sheds and behind chicken coops, but languorous mornings rolling around in clean white linens. Merry banter over morning toast. There would be others like them up north, she wagered. They could find their set. They could make a life together, couldn't they?

As for Shade, he was only really surprised at her ardency, and her childlike but unshakable insistence that theirs was a love story for the ages. *Crazy White lady* came to mind. No harm in carrying on and letting her think what she would. He liked her, she was good-looking, and the chemistry was real enough. He felt sorry for her. Rhodes was a hard man. A cheat, too. Shade harbored no regrets on Rhodes's behalf. Abi's oldest son had already set up his own household, but when she brought up the notion of leaving the other five children and running away north to live as man and wife, Shade felt a deep sense of unease. And it only grew. He teased to deflect her, but to no avail.

In time he did begin to see the possibility of an escape. A ticket north—to freedom, and maybe, with enough gumption, a little opportunity. Abi had money, and there was no doubt she loved him, cherished him even. *There are worse things to be,* he thought, *than loved and moneyed.*

Abi said Benjamin sometimes used counterfeit currency in the day-to-day but kept $2,500 in real money, paper and silver, stashed throughout the house. She could grab it all, sneak out in the dead of night, meet up with Shade at the station, and they could catch a train north.

"Now, how a White lady like you and a colored fella like me going to ride in a train together?" said Shade one day in another attempt to tamp down her ardor. Her lack of caution unnerved him. She was going to get them both killed . . . *or more likely, just me.*

"I've already thought of that," said Abi. "We'll be like William and Ellen Craft."

"Who?"

"The Crafts!" said Abi. "I read about them in the newspaper some years ago. A slave couple down there in Macon, the woman nearly White. They set out for Pennsylvania, she dressed like a White man and he as her slave to evade suspicion, until they crossed the Mason-Dixon. Don't look at me like that; it worked! They're free! That could be you and me, Shade. Think of it!" And more softly into the silence that followed, "I want it to be you and me."

Abi said the Barnes brothers, farmers Hardy and Kennedy, were men she could trust. She was sure that Hardy would transport her to the cars for a small fee, if Shade could find his own way and meet her there. Hardy knew something of her agony being married to Benjamin.

"Hardy will be a friend to me," she said.

Shade thought it sounded crazy. *So crazy it just might work.*

Except it didn't.

First, Shade landed in jail for a debt and the plan was put on hold indefinitely, as there was no telling how long it would take for him to get out. Abi told Hardy to hold off.

But one Friday night, Kennedy Barnes went to a neighbor's place around sunset and let it be known that Shade was at last out of jail. Hardy got word to Abi, and a new plan was hatched for that very night.

In the wee hours of Saturday, June 9, Abi Rhodes donned one of her husband's traveling suits, tucked her hair beneath a top hat, grabbed a pillowcase, and scurried and stumbled from room to room, filling it with silver and paper money. Finding a stash of counterfeit bills in her husband's desk drawer, she grabbed that stack too, just for spite, and turned to go. Seized with a thought, she turned back, crumpled one counterfeit dollar bill in her hand, and threw it on his desk with a giggle, where it unfurled in the moonlight.

Outside, she could hear the *clip-clop* and rattle of a horse and buggy as it came to a stop. Happiness coursed through her. To think that in perhaps as little as an hour she would be in Shade's arms again— Shade, whom she hadn't seen in weeks. And then off they would go, chugging all the way north, where they could live the way a man and wife should. She would write to the children, and in due time they would visit her. She slipped out the kitchen door and ran silently along the side of the house to the front where Hardy Barnes was waiting. She threw two carpetbags in ahead of her—one for her and one filled with her husband's and older sons' clothes for Shade—then hoisted herself up into the seat next to Hardy. They smiled at each other, and she nodded to him. "I'm ready," she said. "Let's go."

Hardy Barnes clicked at the horse, slapped the reins, and rolled the buggy into the night.

On Monday morning, Abi Rhodes's beaten and mutilated body was fished from the Lumber River, and word spread like wildfire that she had eloped with an old issh'y freeman just days before. It was enough to make the papers all over the state. By later that week, Shade had been arrested for murder.

From the *Weekly Courier* in Fayetteville, North Carolina:

> Saturday, June 16, 1860
>   Mrs. Abi Rhodes, wife of Benj. C. Rhodes of
> Sterling Mills, Robeson Co., was found dead in
> Lumber River on Monday last with her throat cut,
> head mashed, and other marks of violence. She
> had a few days previous eloped with a free
> Mulatto by the name of Shade Williams, taking
> with them about $2500 in money. Williams has

been arrested and lodged in Lumberton Jail to
await his trial for the murder.

And that, under ordinary circumstances, would have been the end
of the story. But things are not always as they seem. Powerful trickster
energy had been unleashed on the citizens of Robeson County. Hardy
Barnes was seen Saturday morning soaking wet, saying he'd had to get
in the water when some of his buggy gear had got loose. Other wit-
nesses came forward over the next few days with things they had seen
or heard. One noticed Hardy's buggy in the high woods near a sort of
pond "back of the oat patch, where [they had] never seen a buggy before." It was covered in mud and had a top hat and a metal rod on the
floor. Another noted that he had heard Hardy talking in recent weeks
about the fact that he was looking to come into $2,000 or $3,000 soon
and boasting he could probably make $1,500 in fifteen minutes when
he had it fixed. And then, too, came the revelation that Kennedy Barnes
had lied when he spread word that Shade had been released from jail—a
ruse, perhaps, to get Abi and her $2,500 out after dark and alone. And,
of course, to lay the groundwork for letting Shade take the fall.

From the *Carolina Observer*:

> Monday, June 18, 1860
> The Robeson Murder—We learn verbally that
> the murder of Mrs. Rhodes is ascertained to have
> been perpetrated after her paramour Shade
> Williams had been committed to jail for debt. Two
> men named Barnes are now accused, and have
> been arrested.

And from the Raleigh *Weekly Standard*, the following spring:

> Wednesday, May 29, 1861
> Superior Court—In Cumberland special term,
> Judge Saunders presiding, Hardy Barnes of
> Robeson was convicted of the murder of Abby
> [sic] Rhodes, and sentenced to be hung on the 21st
> June.

SACRED TRICKSTER

What was, sadly, the end of the road for Abi and threatened to be another one for Shade turned out, in his case, to be but a sharp detour. Sacred Trickster, one of the world's oldest mythological figures, had come calling. In African folklore it may take the form of the spider, Anansi. In African American lore it is Brer Rabbit, and in Native American cultures it is often Coyote. In Asia it is Kitsune the fox; for the Norse, it's Loki; and in ancient Greece it could be the god Prometheus, or the messenger of the gods, Hermes. It is an archetypal energy recognized the world over, for what could be more fundamentally human than one's best-laid plans and most earnest desires going to rack and ruin?

Trickster characters operate outside traditional frameworks of right and wrong. They do not recognize or adhere to the rules of society, nor to what you think is *supposed* to be. They are also far from simple, as they can be alternately deceitful and helpful, childish and wise, generous and greedy, clownish and clever. But any way you dice it, tricksters have amazing powers of survival and, in rare cases where they do come to a sorry end, regeneration. Trickster energy just keeps on keeping on. It is the disowned shadow side of the world, society, and ourselves, and thus can never be fully outrun. Not that we should try. Trickster energy is also a gift, a sacred mirror held up to show us what we do not want to see—and more, to encourage us to accept it, get curious about it, and eventually heal from and integrate it. Only then can we meet ourselves honestly, if painfully. Only then can we grow. As such, Sacred Trickster is a wise teacher, and ultimately a kind one, even if it feels like the end of the road in the moment.

Shade both carried trickster energy and found himself at the mercy of it. How fitting that this sacred mirror showing society its own shadow would be named Shade.

When Sacred Trickster arrives, mayhem ensues. It destroys even the best-laid plans; it breaks dreams if those dreams aren't meant for you. But is it not in the breaking of the known that we find wisdom, truth, growth, and deep understanding of ourselves and the world? The understanding, for example, that running away with a naive and desperate White woman was never going to save you. No one can rescue another, for the only real rescue comes from inside and knowing that you are worthy and sovereign, with or without another's patronage or love. Or the understanding that the color line is an ill-conceived, lying, illusory thing of violence, a live wire snaking at our feet, never still. We embrace the illusion at our own risk, and dance with it, often, to our mutual detriment and destruction.

Perhaps chastened by his rodeo ride on the color line, Shade settled back into the life of an old issh'y freeman, piddling, odd-jobbing, and farming. Who knows if he ever gave up his dreams of escape, or what he eventually might have made of his brush with fate? There is no evidence that he attempted to leave again, but there might also never have been another opportunity. He lived his life out as a farmhand and a sharecropper. In early 1865, he threw his lot in with the Union Army when he enlisted as a private in the Fourteenth Regiment of the US Colored Heavy Artillery, which organized in North Carolina. There must have been some restored dignity and self-empowerment in that, an opportunity to exert some control in a life long controlled by others. I dare say it was a defiant act of hope, imagination, and faith that tomorrow was a brighter day. And perhaps Sacred Trickster had revealed to him a sounder, more grounded and authentic way to try to effect change for himself. Trickster encouraged my great-great-uncle Shade to discover his own dream, not Abi's.

In 1866 he married Leah, and they went on to have nine children together. He died in 1915 at age seventy-five, never knowing about his six Chinese grand-nieces and grand-nephews Archie, Sandor, Gerald, Sin Fah, Robert Earl, and Bernice, nor they about him. When I think about what he reached for in his life, I can't help but imagine that if he'd known them and seen their special brand of magic, he would have embraced them as his own. He would also have undoubtedly recognized Dad as another like himself, most favored by Sacred Trickster, which is no comfortable or easy path, but always a powerful one.

May we all be granted the gifts of Sacred Trickster in broken times, and may broken times alert us to Trickster's proximity and invitation, so that we may choose to answer it. The Ox brings all the staid, intuitive, hardworking energy you need to mend the brokenness.

CHAPTER 32

THE BLACK WOLF

What's madness but nobility of soul
At odds with circumstance?

—Theodore Roethke

The black wolf came for me from a den opening onto a riverbank that was well known to me. She poked her head out just far enough for the moonlight to cast silver threads across her ears and snout before she slid noiselessly back into the dark. The burrow led north, and I followed the sound of her breath ahead of me, which was muted at first, swallowed by the warm, moist soil surrounding us. Root tendrils tickled my face and arms and pulled at my hair. Soon enough I felt fresh cold air wafting in on my face, and her breath began to echo back from walls that had frozen solid. I noticed that the tunnel was leading us back aboveground, where we ran, she and I, through a snowy wood of giant sequoias under a spray of stars that twinkled sharply like shattered ice. The air seared my nasal passages and my fingertips burned, but the companionship of a wolf, and the exhilaration of snow, stars, and running among giants held me rapt. We came to a rocky promontory overlooking a lake, quiet and glassy in the light of a full moon overhead.

There the black wolf let out a mournful howl, whereupon we were joined by the rest of the pack, who began to jostle each other, paw the earth, and howl in unison. The black wolf led me to the lakeshore below and sat with me by silver waters.

"You can't do it alone, you know," she seemed to say to me. "And you don't have to." She looked up at the pack that was still gathered on the promontory behind us. "Speak truly and the ones you belong with will come."

She trotted away and came back a moment later with an enormous pine cone, a gift for me. Then we returned to the promontory and ran the pack, leading from behind, through the snowy wood to a cave where I joined a sleep pile of wolves nestled on a bed of juniper boughs near a fire that crackled merrily, sending off sparks of green. My heart softened, my trust in the pack fluttered wanly to pale life. I did not rise, did not move; I lay with the wolves, willing the feeling of safety, trust, and belonging to persist.

When the drumbeats changed rhythm—the callback—I made my way mentally back to my Chinese teahouse, where all my meditative journeys begin and end, and then opened my eyes to the ordinary reality of my own bedroom, knowing that I had experienced something powerful.

WILD GODS

As 2020 bled into 2021—is that the right word? Yes, I think it is—I had an unsettling sense of coming unmoored and undone once more. The Covid-19 pandemic, the murder of George Floyd and others, the new civil rights movement that ensued, and the final year of the Trump administration, which culminated in Trump's deadly coup attempt on January 6, 2021, left me feeling flayed and close to madness.

Some of us had thought, perhaps, in the beginning of the pandemic, that we would at least all have a bit of forced rest and a chance to reset some things. But proper rest eluded me, as it did many, because it was not accompanied by the mental and spiritual ease required to benefit from not doing very much. It was less rest, more paralysis. I wasn't relaxing, I was in a defensive crouch, bracing for impact under a relentless rain of blows.

I had thrashing, sweaty nightmares about white supremacy, lynchings, fascism, abuse, and dead-eyed indifference. Dread infused my waking hours, and my sleep-tracking graphs showed a disturbed and restless spirit. Fear and fatigue begat a long holding pattern of not knowing who I was anymore, or what was next. I was thunderstruck by a thought that maybe everything I had ever done, all of it—the good stuff too, the achievements, awards, and honors—had merely been done in service to a wound, one that might not even have been entirely my own but handed faithfully down from generation to generation, an admonition from long-dead refugees to prove that *I too am America*.

Therefore, continuing to do any of it amounted to feeding the wound. If I intended to heal, I was going to have to dump all of it, everything I had defined myself by, because none of it was real. I was foggy and in flight mode, running on fumes and accomplishing nothing. I had no plan. I wanted to write but wrote nothing. My music and creativity dried up. *Do we need to move to Canada? When? How would we know? Is Canada safer than here?* I doomscrolled through the night, looking for evidence that I could relax. I found none.

This was a winter of the spirit, as described by Katherine May in her book *Wintering*, that had nothing to do with the changing seasons. Its presence felt like a towering, hollow-cheeked specter yawning its great void at me, threatening to blot me from existence. This, I recognized from my previous bout in the wasteland, was ego death. Maybe not the Big One of 2015–2016, but a formidable aftershock nevertheless.

Over time I began to feel an unnerving sense of dislocation, as if I were but a desultory dirigible, tethered and drifting behind my meat suit below, which I had begun to feel was not me at all but something separate, alien, squishy, absurd. *Meat suit.* Trudging down the hall, I let out a brittle cackle, the sound of which made me laugh harder.

I didn't care about social media likes. I didn't care about maintaining social connections. I was unbothered by the idea of several friends fading into the ether. I hated the very idea of hustle. *I am not here to sell myself to you,* I kept thinking. *If you don't know my worth from the get-go, it won't be I who convinces you of it.* I also lost my words. A writer who doesn't care for words! I hadn't written so much as a journal entry in a year. Grunting would have sufficed for me.

In June 2021 we entered the brief respite of what people began calling a post-pandemic summer . . . although it wasn't. What I felt was not relief so much as reentry anxiety. This manifested as irritability and even flashes of anger at the thought of having to see and interact with other people and my old life. It seemed to me that in the past year we had put on one mask and ended up taking off one or more others. I was not the same person now that I had been going into the pandemic. Or perhaps *I* am always the same, but the layers of illusion and projection that we all carry around with us had changed or been dropped. Under duress, ever more layers of artifice got peeled back, revealing more and more of the true self beneath. And the true self has zero tolerance for inauthenticity.

The hustling extrovert, the people pleaser, the self-betrayer for belonging, the tap dancer for love . . . all gone. I was now uncertain of how many connections—attachments?—made pre-pandemic were with the most authentic parts of me, or instead might have been made with layers, facets, or masks I had since shed. Meeting up with any of the usual people and finding the mutual resonance dissipated or gone would be an unpleasant discovery that I didn't feel like dealing with. So I wrapped myself in an irritable shell, walled off my heart, and continued to avoid social interaction.

There had been such a superabundance of disappointment, fear, and betrayal since the Year of the Ram. Six years in, it felt as though I had numbed myself completely from it. My intention to rebuild only those aspects of my old life and friendships that felt real, and to invite the new in mindfully, almost certainly meant that not everyone or everything would make the cut. I lived in dread of finding out—one person, place, or circumstance at a time—who and what would not be crossing the threshold into new territory with me.

At some point I began to get the unshakable feeling that I was becoming feral, the tendril roots and vines of an old mythic wildness beginning to coil around me, threatening to consume me whole. The more I struggled, the faster they wove about my limbs, up my neck, and down my throat, immobilizing me. I lost my creative spark and enjoyment. I felt brittle and hysterical, unsafe, betrayed, powerless. I had simply lost my will to make sense of it all anymore. Which means that I had begun to fall back out of *story*, and the larger perspective that story reminds us of: that no growth comes without pain, no progress without setback. By seeing through only one lens, we miss seeing through the larger, more epic one, the one that asks us to look beyond the newspaper headlines and petty posturing of people who are as stuck in the wasteland as anyone. As I faltered in this way, the howling winds of the wasteland began once again ripping at my heels. I could hear their hollow screams at the edges of my mind like a tangible thing. Familiar. Present. Looming.

It was during this time that there emerged from the fog and gloom of my inner wilding, as I had begun calling it, a deer with branches instead of antlers, and a sound of clinking metal cones when it tossed its head. It was quite pagan, and—clear as day in my mind's eye—both expectant and insistent.

Soon I was drawn to shadows and forest creatures of all kinds. Foxes, rabbits, squirrels, owls, and yes, the black wolf. These animal energies came to me from out of the darkness behind closed lids, unbidden and often intrusive to my ordinary daily activities. I slid a shirt over my head and in the momentary darkness of my eyes being covered, *bam!* There stood the deer, shaking its head, pawing the earth, sharply exhaling a cloud of steam in impatience. I added items to a grocery list and *kapow!* There crouched the wolf, making eye contact with me from the opening of its den, then retreating into the shadows of the black countertop. *Come with me.* I helped the kids with their homework, and the flap of feathers distracted me as a great snowy owl extended its furry talons and landed with a *thud* on some driftwood in the dunes at the edge of my mental vision. *Thunk. New territory. Arrival.*

There was something in the dark that each of these animals wanted me to see. They were all unmistakably beckoning, and I found them to be both eerie and thrilling. I began to paint some of them—calling them in, as I say. The results felt less like art than like missives from a bright other world. It was unnerving in one sense—I felt half-mad—but seemed inevitable and irreversible in another.

Shortly thereafter, I stumbled on, or perhaps was led to, the poem by Tom Hirons, "Sometimes a Wild God." My discomfort eased. *Aha. So that is what has been happening. I am not mad; my own wild gods have come calling.* The poem starts evocatively.

> Sometimes a wild god comes to the table.
> He is awkward and does not know the ways
> Of porcelain, of fork and mustard and silver.
> His voice makes vinegar from wine.
> When the wild god arrives at the door,
>
> You will probably fear him.
> He reminds you of something dark
> That you might have dreamt,
> Or the secret you do not wish to be shared.

It is a poem to be read many times, a crescendo of imagery and sensory feeling that engulfs the reader in our own wild depths. In stanza after stanza it builds in tension and intensity, until we reach the final one, which precipitously falls quiet again. Picking up the low, incantatory rhythm of the first, it also adds one crucial extra line that lands sonorously, and for me, worked to pry me open.

> Sometimes a wild god comes to the table.
> He is awkward and does not know the ways
> Of porcelain, of fork and mustard and silver.
> His voice makes vinegar from wine
> And brings the dead to life.

Boom. The wild god may feel like death or madness, but in time it reveals itself to be the resurrection of one already dead. I had been dead once. Stuck in the wasteland. The poem also put my undoing of recent months in another light entirely, as if wild gods had seen me losing ground once again to the wasteland and come, as great disruptors, to the rescue. They began to surgically undo all the things that threatened to pull me under, helping me to shed yet more layers of ego that had kept me caught. It hadn't been a madness during the pandemic but a necessary deconstruction, a gift, a wild and divine intervention. I was moved. My own wild gods had seen me teetering and arrived just in time, urgently, insistently, intrusively, to break the spell the wasteland was set to cast again, and to lead me to safety. *Come with me,* they said. *This way.* My own jungle scouts.

It worked. The wilding is nothing like the wasteland. It is a deep, healing, gestational dark. You are isolated there, but not alone. It contains the seeds of rebirth, renewal, invention, creation, and growth. For me it became a siren call to deeper authenticity. It peeled back the layers of being until it seemed there was nothing left but what was real . . . although this too was illusion. There will always be more layers to reveal.

The wilding starts when you are no longer okay with living life by others' expectations. It is a refusal to play the game anymore, or at least no longer as you did before. Even if you're still mired in it, that old game feels less like air or water, less ordained, less inevitable or decreed, more open and available to deconstruction and reimagining. The wilding is an inner heaving against our patriarchal, warmongering, growth-and-domination-based culture that bleeds us all dry, causes runaway climate change, the mass extinction of species, and zero-sum-game calculations about life.

The wilding is about asking yourself what you really want, and then listening to the answer. It also manifests in being less of a consumer; becoming unplugged from the driving need for new, better, more; and understanding the utter meaninglessness of celebrity. It means beginning to emotionally detach from impossible expectations of beauty. One finds an acceptance of silver hairs framing one's face, a noticing without gut-clenching panic of loosening skin under the eyes or along the jawline. Perhaps I am not *free* of these things, but the wilding feels like a new awareness of the illusion and the absurdity of it all, and of the fact that your previous ways of being in the world were often arbitrary and sometimes artificial.

The wilding also invites clarity about relationships. How many are born of real connection versus sheer habit? How many were cultivated simply because you had a higher tolerance for not standing in your authenticity? This is false belonging, which is killing. An inner wilding requires belonging of an altogether more authentic and fundamental sort. An earth belonging. A soul belonging. Can you learn to belong to yourself? The wilding is an invitation to try.

I summoned the wolves to a hanging wall scroll to make them manifest. Wolves spoke to two aspects of the wilding for me. On the one hand, freedom and more authentic, instinctual living, represented in the painting as the black wolf, and on the other, a healing for my damaged trust in the pack, meaning society and community, represented by the blond wolf.

The black wolf had brought me a pine cone, and we had slept on a bed of juniper boughs. The sacred geometry of the pine cone has made it a universal symbol of enlightenment, expanding consciousness and regeneration, since ancient times. A beautiful gift to encourage me on my seeker's path. Meanwhile, juniper is a tenacious tree that can live for centuries. It claims the land it is on with a shallow but wide root system that allows it to cling to anything. No place is inhospitable to a juniper. It can grow on solid rock and withstand every onslaught of wind, sand, snow, or erosion. It is therefore a balm for feelings of disconnection from place. People have also often used junipers as boundary markers, and, symbolically, the juniper is associated with the idea of healthy boundaries. What better medicine for a person who is feeling violated or defenseless?

Thus the wolves brought me messages of healthy boundaries, embracing the seeker, and belonging that is sovereign and independent of location. I sold the scroll within hours of finishing it, but the healing message left tracks on my soul.

CHAPTER 33

MONADNOCK

If I were a place, I would be an island, rooted between land and sea, belonging to neither. Not a sunny, peaceful, sand-covered little thing with a palm tree just so. My island is huge and dark with mystery. It awes as much as it beckons. You may be afraid to approach, floating in your little dinghy, tossed about on roughening seas as you move this way and that to weigh the risk of coming nearer.

Wouldn't it be safer to return to the mainland, to certainty and the well-known, as broken as it may be? Yes, you worry, but you haven't turned your boat around. There is something here for you, and the call to discover it is siren. I know because I took a dinghy here myself when I, too, was trapped on the mainland, and dead without knowing.

Now I am craggy coastlines of cliff, stone, and sea stack. I call forth storms to shape my own topography, scouring here, tumbling there, flooding caverns, draining bogs. My winds howl, cut through clothes, tie hair in knots, and suck breath right out of the lungs. But do not be afraid. I mean only to awaken and exhilarate.

So, stand on my spit of stone and sound your exhilaration into my storm. Let it strip you bare of all illusions and disillusions, let it break all your tired stories, your self-doubt and worry, your need to be other than what you are. Let it break them into bits and draw them back out to sea, far away from you, where you will never be seduced or bamboozled into picking them up again.

When you've recovered your breath and shaken yourself free of what weighs you down, look around and see how I have allowed the pounding surf to scoop cavernous hollows at my rocky boundaries. If you are brave enough to swim the tunnels, you will find they lead directly to my interior. I have no interest in keeping my gifts a secret, you see, or hoarding them away from all but those deemed worthy. I offer them freely to any who venture to my edgelands, which are really their own edgelands, and then further, to find the gifts where they are. I have interior caverns and pools that will restore your equilibrium from the storm. The pools reflect whatever you most need to know and invite you to get more comfortable with shadow and dark.

But take heed. The pools do not reflect, nor the caverns shelter, those who come too heavily laden with illusion.

My peaks offer higher perspectives and are a favorite sit spot for visitors. There is not much billowing or soft about me, no artifice. I am blasted raw and jagged at my peaks and edges. Low meadow and tundra, a few trees here or there, and braided riverbeds blanket my heartlands. I am the layers beneath the layers. I am a distillation of essences, unhidden, laid bare, seen as I really am. Whatever festive or soft thing you find, know that I have mindfully put it there. Or found that it belonged there and mindfully let it stay.

It is only in the stripping bare that you can find what is real and what is truly yours. And to my delight I have discovered that my island only looks frightening from afar. It has everything I need, everything I have ever needed. I am the safest I have ever been. And you are safe here too when you come as you are, and not as you have pretended to be.

The places we end up connecting to geographically in our physical world are sometimes how we see, or want to see, our own interior geography—do you agree? There is internal resonance that can feel very powerful, especially in times of heightened emotion, good or bad.

Consider my soul-level response to Iceland's bare, windswept, and ensorcelled landscapes in 2015.

I seemed to land "randomly" in New Hampshire. I took a job and moved up from Boston with little thought, and for various reasons spent long years feeling like I didn't belong here. The Trump years made me suspect I wouldn't feel like I belonged anywhere, so there was no point in leaving. Come 2021, I became interested in New Hampshire's geology, as a whimsical outgrowth of my writing. *This is who I am,* I said, addressing my home state, and after writing about my dark island of mystery. *Who are you?* When the kids were young, they looked small, chubby, and cute, but they felt like boulders. I joked I had two blocks of New Hampshire granite on my hands. We were, after all, living in the Granite State. But that, I discovered, is a bit of a misnomer. New Hampshire is less than half underlain by granite. In my reading, I learned that much of the ground beneath our feet is schist or gneiss, which are metamorphic, igneous, or sedimentary rocks that have been changed through heat, pressure, and shear. They are squeezed, scraped, and heated into completely different structures and forms, resulting in something that is stronger than the original.

Feeling a spark of recognition, I read on.

I was a principal investigator at Monadnock Archaeological Consulting, named for the landform known as Mount Monadnock, located in the southwest corner of the state, where our company's headquarters were. Although I was there for a decade, I hadn't investigated the meaning of the name, and assumed that *monadnock* was likely an old Abenaki word for "mountain," which, in fact, it is. But my budding interest in local geology led me to learn that this landform has also been made into an archetype for geologists who now define a monadnock as an isolated resistant peak rising from a less-resistant eroding plain.

In other words, I thought, dropping my pen to the desk where I was taking notes, *it is what's left when everything else has been stripped away.*

I, who never felt I belonged here, was perhaps exactly where I was meant to be.

I too am a monadnock.

A more pagan version of the deer was my first visitor during my wilding period. The deer in this painting, while influenced by the original, is gentler and more delicate, as I had begun to experiment with ideas of nimbleness and agility in hard times over straight resilience, which can be hardening. I paired the deer with the characters for *intuition* and included a snail to remind myself that home is part of us, always with us, no matter where we go. If my art follows the arc of my descent into the dark wood, then this piece correlates with the early part of my return—tentative, light-footed, listening.

OPPOSITE: Deer—*"Intuition"*

CHAPTER 34

WILD THINGS

THE PEACE OF WILD THINGS

When despair for the world grows in me
and I wake in the night at the least sound
in fear of what my life and my children's lives may be,
I go and lie down where the wood drake
rests in his beauty on the water, and the great
heron feeds.
I come into the peace of wild things
who do not tax their lives with forethought
of grief. I come into the presence of still water.
And I feel above me the day-blind stars
waiting with their light. For a time
I rest in the grace of the world, and am free.

—Wendell Berry

As I tried to characterize the feelings of dread, dislocation, and despair I had been experiencing since the Year of the Ram, I came up with a shorthand that seemed to encapsulate it all. I was having a crisis of belonging. *Where was my home? Who were my people?* I felt bereft of both place and community. I knew the importance of having the right people around, and how rare and precious the right ones are. I had learned, too, the importance of turning inward through meditation, breath work, both philosophical and analytical thought, journaling, art, and mindfulness to heal the wounds that made me think safety, love, and belonging could be found only outside myself. Some of the writings in this book are a direct outcome of that process. But as much progress as I made with these endeavors, and as much inner healing continued to occur, a deep sense of rootedness eluded me, the sense that *this is home, and I am okay.*

It is hard to feel connected to, or to care about, what we don't know. Most of our ancestors had, by default, deep knowledge of their places and communities and the very land beneath their feet, so there was never any question of where they belonged. But modern society has lost much of that. And I was just emerging from the wasteland, where there simply *are* no roots.

With time and intention, I learned that grounding looks like getting out of our own heads, with their constant tortures and ruminations, and returning to the world. Trade scouring hurt for a bracing wind, circular thought for the bilateral rhythm of walking on solid earth, and you will find that you have begun the process of grounding. Remember how to walk barefoot again. Get your hands dirty. Inhale the mineral brine of a tidal creek or the clean, fresh petrichor of a wooded trail. Then you must get to know the other life-forms, plant and animal, that share the land with you. Do you know their names? Their ways of being in the world? How they weather the seasons? What do you know of the origins and history of your community? Or the ecology and geology of your land?

If you want to learn to belong, says mythologist Sharon Blackie, get to know your place. Anchor there. Anchors, she says, make so many of our problems fade away. I became enchanted with the idea that one could *learn* to belong wherever one's feet may have landed.

In 2020 and 2021, when we were bound to our places because of the pandemic, I got a chance to test the proposition. I started looking for a sit spot or a wander route that I could visit at all times of day and all seasons of the year. The local cemetery where I found beloved company and Muchmore was one place I was beginning to think of as mine.

Another was the rocky shore at Odiorne Point State Park. One morning, close to a year into lockdown, I drove the few minutes there. It was a glorious winter day with bottomless bluebird skies, dazzling sun, a fresh fifteen inches of snow, and frothy seas. I had been feeling homesick for travel. Not just traveling, but the easy invitation to growth that travel brings.

Sighing over my pictures of Iceland, I realized that we have some stunning North Atlantic scenery on the New Hampshire seacoast as well. Indeed, geologically, we are likely part of the same system. New England has the volcanic substrate that has beguiled me from Nova Scotia to Iceland to Scotland. Isn't it just a mindset, then? Do I need to be traveling the world to bring a traveler's heart to my home area and my every day? I got to the snow-covered rocky beach and was gladdened by a parent and child, bundled to the eyes, flying a kite of many colors. I watched it wave and snap in the wind as if I, too, were shaking off negative energy with a flick.

I climbed the boulder levy and approached the beach. The tide was out farther than I had ever seen it. But the sea was foamy and powerful, and it beckoned. So, just as I would have done if I had come upon this spot in a foreign land, I stumbled over the kelp-strewn rocky beach. It was treacherous. *But if I were on vacation,* I thought, *I would not just drive by a view such as this.* I would not just pull over and take a quick picture. I would make my halting way down to the waves whose thunder vibrated my chest cavity and loosened all that was frozen there. I would sit on a rock and watch a parent and child fly a kite. I would inspect the tide pools for crabs and periwinkles. I would take time to remember that the tide always comes back in, but wasn't it good and beneficial, and fun too, to search for the treasures while it was out?

The kelp laid in humps, like hair strewn on a pillow, as if Earth herself were sleeping, luxuriating, and . . . a funny thought came to mind . . . perhaps even *dreaming me* into existence? For a fleeting moment I felt a singular truth vibrating in my bones. I belonged to Mother Earth; I was one of her beloved creatures. The feeling slipped through my fingers like the sands that pulled away from beneath my feet. But flashes of that recognition do return, more often now, as I continue to awaken to the vitality and magic of open spaces; to allow Nature, in effect, to reclaim me; and, therefore, to explore a more ancient and universal source of belonging than hometown, nationality, or lineage.

LEARNING TO BELONG

One warm June evening, I discovered a third spot to practice this outdoor sort of spirituality, when we wandered into a pocket nature conservancy nestled almost secretly within our own community, minutes from my front door. The Loughlin Family Open Space Preserve was created by Peter and Nancy Loughlin, who bought seven acres to protect them as open space and wildlife habitat. A sign at the entrance invites the public to enjoy the trails and views from sunrise to sunset.

It was around six o'clock in the evening and the sun was full and low in the sky, pouring liquid gold over everything. It was sixty-eight degrees with a fresh breeze that made you want to go on a jaunt and let it all wash over you—the air, the wind, the juicy golden light. This is my favorite kind of summer's eve. My favorite time of day. The sun shines from the side like stage lighting, giving everything a deep, dramatic beauty.

The first thing you notice when you step off the neighborhood street and into the conservation area is the burbling, twittering birdsong. The birds are not hidden here, as in the main part of town, but are joyously out swooping and diving, often in pairs, chasing each other from tree to bush to tall stands of reeds. My heart softened, sang in harmony with the birds, and I felt a transcendent kind of ease and contentment, pure enchantment seeping into my heart space, which had become warm and melty.

My attention was drawn toward movement on the ground where I saw a pair of cottontail rabbits, shoulder-deep in grass and clover. And then a young one over there, and oh, look! Two more down the mown path. Had I fallen into a Beatrix Potter book? Six rabbits, all told. I caught my breath as if to catch and hold the moment, but the rabbits were joyful and free and soon scampered from sight.

A mass of bulrushes, perhaps two hundred yards in all directions, bounds one side of the preserve. The way they sway and rustle in the late-day sun, while red-winged blackbirds *chak-chak*, trill, dip, and dive just over the golden-hued tips, is nothing short of magical. Two whimsically built birdhouses have been set up right in front of the bulrushes, and it makes such a very pretty picture that I almost started looking for fairies.

On this evening, we walked on a wide path. White clover blossoms crowded the edges, as profuse as a fresh dusting of snow. The sun, low in the sky, sent beams streaking through small stands of birch, maple, and wild raspberry, casting stripes of gold across our way. It was so lovely I couldn't speak. A couple of male red-winged blackbirds waddled through the grass ahead of us, signaling they had nothing to fear here, not even on the ground.

We followed the path past a break in a stone wall where the land unfurls around a beautifully kept red barn. A gentle hillside covered in meadow grass that was already turning fluffy in shades of lavender, green, silver, red, and gold seemed made to show off the evening light. The feathery ends of the grasses glowed.

I felt my heart opening. *I love this place.* What a relief from the angry, alienated numbness of recent months, and even years. What a privilege to encounter so much wildlife simply going about its day, unafraid to be observed and even approached.

Over the following weeks, I returned to the preserve morning, noon, and evening, on cloudy days, sunny days, rainy days. I checked my bird guidebook to help me identify the species I encountered there, and tried to memorize their calls so I would always know who was talking. I downloaded a plant identification app on my phone. Soon I wasn't wandering through generic beauty anymore, but among my beloved purple loosestrife—which I was chagrined to learn is invasive—horseweed, common jewelweed, and purple grasses. I discovered elderflower in among the cattails, watched the dragonflies and the bees, and learned to greet the gray birch and the white, the rowan tree, the ginkgo, the Italian cypress, and the cedar. I also have a rowan tree in my back garden, I realized, whose bright clusters of red-orange berries I had been in a habit for years of gazing at and casually appreciating, as it bobbed in the breeze outside my dining room window. I had not once thought to find out what it was. The rowan is sometimes called the traveler's tree, believed to guide people lost on their journey and to help reunite self and soul. Its fine hardwood also makes excellent walking sticks for pilgrims as they follow their calling. My rowan tree had been waving to me, trying to catch my attention through the window for a decade. I just didn't have the eyes yet to see it.

One day, I felt called to visit beeches all over town. And I do mean called, for it was as if a person I knew had said my name from another room. I felt the expectant pause, and the inner tug of being about to answer that call. I had never experienced one coming from Nature before, but I was far enough along in my journey that I took it as it came, without too much analysis. I devised, through trial and discovery, a loop through town that took me to several beeches along the way. I was not above hugging one, if accessible, letting the nurturing, dignified, stolidity of its tree presence wash over me, head to toe. A tree doesn't need to learn how to anchor. To anchor is its nature. It doesn't just grow up and out, it grows deep, pulling nutrients from within the earth, feeding itself, integrating seasons of growth with seasons of damage and loss into one enormous embodiment of weathering, expansion, impermanence, and the beauty of imperfections. Who wouldn't want to hug such an impressive thing? But if hugs were not available, I would greet it like an old friend, compliment it on its beauty, its shade-giving abilities on a hot day, its copper-colored, ridged foliage or the artistic lines of its bare branches. One beech I know has an enormous burl, big enough for one slice in cross-section to make a round table befitting King Arthur's court. It must have grown over a considerable wound. How enlightening to learn that furniture makers favor burl wood because it is stronger than other wood and has fascinating patterns in the grain that increase its beauty and value. Mom had a burl-wood pendant the size of my palm that she liked to wear. I wear it now too, sliding it prayerfully over my head and feeling the elegant heft of it against my heart, where it reminds me that your wound can become your strength and your beauty.

Visiting my tree friends became a part of my daily rounds. I did wonder why, especially, the beech tree called, and I was interested one day to find that the German word for "beech"—which is *Buche*—is the likely origin of the word *book*. It was one of those serendipities I had ceased to be surprised by but still took delight and comfort in. Mother

Nature was cheering me on, like Mom and Dad in days of yore, as if to say, *Why don't you write that book you've been wanting to write, honey?*

I learned to pick out the feather mosses, ferns in extreme miniature that curled wildly in and among the true mosses that carpeted New England's ubiquitous stone walls. I learned to notice and love the ruffled shield lichens clinging to spring-wet tree trunks, looking for all the world like a leprechaun's dress shirt hung up at night's end after an evening of ribaldry. I learned that privets are poisonous, and that Japanese barberry, whose brilliant red berries I loved to see dangling in winter-bare branches, are, like the loosestrife, exotic and invasive. At some point it also occurred to me that when we visit or commune with nature, we see only the animals that have survived, only the plants and trees that have weathered seasons and storms. When we go into nature, we are—all of us, everything as far as the eye can see, from the grass at our feet to the midges at sunset to the hawk flying above—the ones who survived. You almost want to tip your hat to everything. *Ah, hello, you've made it. Aren't you lovely? Isn't it amazing? I'm making it too.*

One evening after a day of torrential downpours from the northern tail end of a tropical storm, the sun came out just at sundown and I headed to the preserve, where I found the tufts of purple meadow grass bejeweled and glinting like a field of diamonds. It was there I ran into Mr. Loughlin himself, wandering about the wet grounds in red Wellington boots, surveying his land. He had planted three hundred conifer saplings, he told me, and was glad for the soaking rain after such a long dry spell. He pointed toward all the mowed pathways he kept, and commented with great and quiet satisfaction, "It feels like a different world back here." It reminded him of a poem his mother used to love, by James Russell Lowell. He closed his eyes and knit his brow to recall a portion of the verse.

"It starts with 'And what is so rare as a day in June?'" he said, opening his eyes and smiling, watching for my comprehension. "'Then, if ever, come perfect days / Then Heaven tries the earth if it be in tune, / And over it softly her warm ear lays: / Whether we look, or whether we listen, / We hear life murmur, or see it glisten . . .'"

By this time, it was I who was glistening.

"But the best line, for me," he said, "comes in the second stanza.

'Now is the high tide of the year, / And whatever of life hath ebbed away / Comes flooding back, with a ripply cheer . . .' I can't stop thinking about it being the high tide of the year. I come back here on a day like this and look around and it's just . . . it's like . . ."

"A poem?" I asked.

"Yes!" He chuckled. "Well, there you go. It's a poem. It is, indeed, a poem."

Maybe it wasn't just the world that was different back here, but us. More open, more surrendered, more willing to see beauty around us, in each other, in ourselves. Who are you, and where would you have to be to trade lines of poetry with a stranger in passing? Surely you'd have to be your best self and in a special place.

My special place might be different from yours, but can you see the urgency of finding one? Everyone needs a place where they are allowed to be their best selves, spontaneously, unabashedly.

Think of the unwitting, positive ripple effects that people can have when they act from their heart space. The Loughlins, moved by true generosity of spirit, had turned acres of their own land into a secret garden for anyone to stumble into, a pocket of wilderness. Mr. Loughlin, now widowed, maintains and shares it with the world, asking nothing but the visitor's own enjoyment and succor, and perhaps a cheerful exchange, in return.

I could see his satisfaction in that, but does he know how wide and deep it goes? Look how this humble offering from a retired landowner has become an important piece in my own journey of belonging after long years of desperation. How wondrous! And I am but one person, decades into the Loughlins' project. They can't have known or imagined all the deep ways their gift might trigger good things for others, how the gears of people's lives turn and sometimes interlock in surprising, profound, and perhaps never-anticipated ways. I was gripped with a sense of quiet grandeur and beauty and made teary-eyed. A man started tending some land in 1982, the very year that my own sense of safety and belonging began to unravel, with the threatening phone calls from our neighbor, and the bullying and exclusion at school. And here I was, forty years later, using that same land to restore a sense of safety and belonging for myself.

Sharon Blackie wrote in *The Enchanted Life* that "in losing our respect for other life forms, we have also lost a sense of who we are. We can only be fully human in context." *Is this what I have been doing, rediscovering my own context?*

I thought of the Great Gardening Rampage, our adventure with Lucky, and the ways I have tried to become a better steward of my little plot of land. I looked around at the endless embrace of my daily walks and explorations of the past year, my tree friends, bringing a traveler's heart and intention to every day, learning the names of plants and animals. I felt the solid foundation of metamorphic rock beneath my feet and saw the great Mount Monadnock in my mental periphery. Have I not felt I was coming haltingly back to life and becoming more fully human with each passing day? Has the feeling of my own futility and ephemerality, my virtual nothingness, not receded steadily in the face of grounding myself in the physical world around me? Have I not felt less and less separate and alone, the more I see myself as part of it all? Do I not, at the very last, and barring all other things, still belong to Mother Earth and Father Sky?

CHAPTER 35

FOUR SEASONS

SPRING PEONIES

In the spring of 2021, I began to paint peonies. This was new. I normally preferred the animals whose stalking, writhing, coiling, galloping, swinging, roaring, and soaring have worked to loosen and exorcise my stuck energies. In my grief-maddened state, I chased the powerful yang of the animal kingdom—hot, active, moving—to feel that I was *doing something,* for the love of god, *going somewhere.* Plants offer the gentler, softer, intuitive, and healing energy of Yin—how to live quietly and beautifully in the world. They are powerful, but less bombastic, and when grief has made you deaf and insensitive to subtler energies, they can feel bland, almost impotent, and may even rub you the wrong way. Yang brings the storm and blasts away the debris. Yin caresses your spirit with a gentle breeze and playfully ruffles your hair. For long years, I had been conjuring storms and screaming into the gale-force winds, *Come and take it all, you bastards!* Painting flowers, by contrast, made me feel sullen and irritable.

I had continued to grow and find comfort in my real-life garden, however. Peonies were Mom's favorite flower, and I have several bushes of them now in different varieties and colors of pale blush, magenta, and coral. It was one bright spring morning after watering the peonies that I was seized with a whimsy to paint some. I didn't have a composition in mind, but I took out one of my largest wall scrolls and started painting on it as if nothing could go wrong. I don't normally paint a large scroll without a plan. It's expensive and wasteful if you make a mistake. As I didn't have any ideas beyond just the peonies, I simply painted three of them and a bud hanging in blank space, and let the scroll sit for a few days. What else might come to me from that bright other world? I felt neither sullen nor irritable. On the contrary, I felt rather like a bud myself, growing plump from within. A soft, insistent energy was rising in my body, like water flowing up a stem. I was being pushed from the inside, while a gentle tug from the outside encouraged me to open, as I imagine the warmth of the sun does to the flower about to bloom. And what had Dad taught me about turning toward the sun? I returned to the studio and let myself go. Utter extravagance poured forth, flowing through me like an enlivening spring freshet. It was a current not of my own making. I was just along for the ride.

I stood back and let my gaze rest on all the symbols before me, reflecting on the parts of my inner life that had given rise to each. So disparate, and yet . . . all here together in such harmony. I couldn't question it. There were the peonies, yes. In Chinese culture, these are thought of as the King of Flowers, and represent honor, beauty, reputation, and good standing. A bouquet from the ancestors. *Infinite blessings be upon you.* I bowed inwardly. *You have been my crucible and my guides,* I told them. And I knew that in their estimation I have walked honorably and with dignity, *like a Chan,* through this, my most challenging chapter thus far. I have not bowed my head. What's more, I am returning with gifts to share.

I was feeling so abundant and lucky that I just kept loading the painting with symbols of good fortune—persimmons, the cat, and the cricket. Persimmons, for example, represent luck, longevity, and kindness. When found in twos, they indicate that things will go smoothly for you now, and I felt this to be true. Cats conjure the peace and domesticity of a happy home. Their purr is scientifically proven to lower our blood pressure and help us to live longer, happier lives. And the Chinese have revered the beautiful song and warrior spirit of the cricket for thousands of years. Considered lucky charms, live crickets were sometimes kept in wooden boxes like pets and given as gifts to people moving into a new home. They symbolize longevity, wealth, and abundance, and are thought to attract happiness to a household.

Then I added the toad, which is a lucky animal, a folk symbol of wealth and prosperity that often comes bearing gold coins. As a lunar Yin creature, however, it also brings the gift of deep insight—for others as well as for ourselves. And that is worth more than gold. *Self-knowledge has indeed brought happiness,* I reflected, *just as my little monk promised it would years ago.*

In the Buddhist tradition, pomegranates reflect fertility. Lots of seeds, lots of kids. But I included it broadly, representing fertility of the body, mind, and spirit. With these in alignment, how can life be anything but fruitful?

At the heart of it all was the dragon on the vase, symbolizing harmony and good rain. *Story is good rain,* I said to myself again. A worthy container for this new energy that was filling my life to the brim.

Still, something was missing. In a final flourish, I painted cherry blossoms in an arc over it all. They symbolize springtime, renewal, and love, yes, but they also remind us of the fleeting nature of life. This too shall pass—winter, hard times, but also spring—as all things must. It is the very fleetingness of it all that gives it such exquisite, almost unbearable sweetness.

And knowing that, would you have it any other way?

Be honest. Would you?

SUMMER LOTUS

With high summer, the garden grew boisterous and flower energies continued to burst into my studio. I became preoccupied with the concept of flourishing. Flourishing is a complicated notion for me. I have nearly always been high-achieving, flourishing since birth. But I am also nearly always beset by internal struggles that belie the surface well-being. As a young professional, I was a serious up-and-comer, and had no personal strife to speak of. I was popular, impressive, included, admired. Lots of possibilities were open to me, so I had high expectations for the future. But this also ushered in the beginnings of a yearslong depression. More recently, in the years since Mom and Dad died, I've grown two businesses, raised kids, followed my heart, and written a book. This too is me flourishing, but born of, and simultaneously marred by, catastrophic grief. I have never had a period of flourishing that wasn't compromised on some other level. Perhaps I have misunderstood the concept of flourishing to mean untroubled. But what if trouble is part of the deal, even required, for a true flourishing to occur?

As the Chinese say, no mud, no lotus. The lotus is revered in the Taoist tradition because, as the lotus rises untainted from bulbs lodged in the mud, so too can our spiritual growth and integration become the beauty born from hardship. But the true symbolic power of the lotus lies in that it cannot grow or flower *without* the mud. Can a human life become beautiful without sorrow or pain? Have our hardships mired us . . . or merely planted us?

I love the way that Nigerian essayist Báyò Akómoláfé refuses to pathologize brokenness, for he sees it as the condition for transformation. Brokenness is not secondary to wholeness. *When you fall apart,* he admonished in a public Facebook post, serendipitously on the sixth anniversary of Dad's death, *don't forget to love the pieces.*

I pulled a summer-green scroll from its cubby and started painting lotus. In the open lotus flower, I saw wisdom gained and openness to all experience without attachment to ideas of good or bad, desired or undesired, whole or broken, but a willing *presence* to the whole kit

OPPOSITE: Spring Peonies—*"Double Happiness"*

and caboodle of it. Overlooking the divine drama unfurling below, I painted two parrots. The Chinese consider parrots celestial animals, bearers of good news and signaling opportunity. As vocal and communicative creatures, they also symbolize the power of our words, spoken and unspoken, the stories we tell others and ourselves about the world and what has happened to us. Stories make us who we are. Only a good story—a healthy story rooted in love, for self, for other, for luck, for pain—can make the lotus grow.

Rejoice, the painting seemed to say to me. *You are free of old patterns that have kept you caught, now free to grow and flower— extravagantly. New consciousness unfurls. You have* chanted *your lotus into bloom and are hereby and henceforth declared . . .* enchanted.

AUTUMN MOON

There is a story the Chinese tell about the Jade Emperor who long ago, in trying to ascertain the character of his people, descended from his palace in the sky. Disguised on Earth as a palsied old man dressed in rags, he shuffled from subject to subject to beg for food. First he encountered Monkey, who, being a gregarious and helpful animal, gathered fruit from the trees to share with him. Second he met Otter, who, being playful and altruistic, slid down a little waterfall in the river and returned with fish to share. Third he approached Jackal, who was not noted for his generosity, but who loved to show off his stealth and trickery. So Jackal too obliged the old man by stealing his own favorite treats—a lizard and a pot of milk curds—from a neighboring village. At last the emperor came upon Rabbit, who, knowing grass and clover are no fare for a human being, hung his head in shame and sorrow. With hardly a thought, he offered his own body, leaping straight into the old man's pot simmering on the fire.

The Jade Emperor was so moved by Rabbit's selflessness that he reached into the fire and flung the animal up to the moon, where it

OPPOSITE: Enchantment—*"Spirit, Color, Graceful, Abundant"*

神采奕奕

became the immortal Jade Rabbit and spent each night in the Moon Palace pounding herbal medicines into elixirs of healing and immortality. Some say when you look up at the full moon you can still see Jade Rabbit holding his magic pestle and pounding his healing elixirs for beloved mortals below. In this way, the Jade Rabbit embodies the spirit of the ancestors—our own, as well as the ones we hope to become.

For more than two thousand years, the Moon Festival has been one of the most important celebrations in the Chinese cultural calendar. Families will gather in the light of the harvest moon to eat mooncakes, snacks, and fruits, play games, and light colorful lanterns—some with good wishes written on them to be released into the sky or onto the water like prayers, that the ancestors might receive them and know they are loved.

———— ⊗‖⊗ ————

T'ai Peng, still in a reflective mood, settled further into his seat cushions and pulled on his cigar. No, things had not turned out the way he had thought they would. How the world turns, how things just carry on.

"I come to America," he said, gesturing with his elegant but now work-worn hands. "Make money for revolution. Revolution need money, you know, not need no cut-off-head corpse. I think I stay little while, then go back, but I not see China yet to this day. You know, I be seventy year old this past April." He paused in amusement to let the news sink in as he knew it would. "Yes," he said and laughed, dropping cigar ashes on the rug, "I look young. Always work hard, not eat too muchee, not worry too muchee. If you worry about trouble, you better go die."

He sighed, looked at his cigar, and rolled it between his thumb and two fingers. "I used be very pretty when I boy in China, my face very smooth, my clothes very nice. All my sisters love me because I was baby boy, and all makee silk coats and embroidery my pants. I ought to

OPPOSITE: The Moon Road—*"Good Fortune, Ties That Bind, Bountiful"*

be spoiled but I was good. They all cry hard when I come to America. Then I only nineteen year old. My fodder, my mudder, die with we far off here." He moved his jaw left and right, then locked it to one side, seeming to come to some silent conclusion for himself. "Someday I go home to burn incense on their grave," he said. "Close the circle."

In doing some due diligence for writing certain parts of this book, I was reading up on what intergenerational trauma looks like in Asian refugee families. I wanted to ensure I was writing with awareness and integrity for my book's characters, who were, after all, also real people. I knew facts and events of their lives, but in trying to re-create the interiority of those experiences, I wanted some subjective understanding about the refugee experience. What I was not expecting to find was a description of my own life, and it rocked me.

Just what did I think intergenerational trauma was supposed to mean? I am the granddaughter of a refugee who faced a calamitous initiation. Did I really think there would be no legacy of it in my own life, just two generations later? I had never given it any thought, I suppose. I had readily accepted all my fears and foibles, my chronic overachieving, my persistent feelings of unbelonging, my debilitating anxieties around performance, rejection, and failure, as exactly that—my own.

But I learned that refugee trauma can create those same patterns in the later generations, with an endless cycle of parents feeling like something is missing for the rest of their days and children internalizing their parents' pain. Hence T'ai Peng, in his Federal Writers' Project interview, pining for the chance to burn incense on his parents' graves more than fifty years after his ordeal—or, as a younger man, standing wistfully on the banks of the Savannah River, watching egrets, while his daughter Gerald watched him.

In this kind of dynamic, the children learn, subconsciously and wrongly (those troublesome misbeliefs again), that they have not been *enough*. They can feel their parents' longing and conclude it must be for a better, more accomplished and successful version of themselves.

The feeling of having lost *home*, never finding a sense of rootedness, belonging, and community, can also plague refugee families in exile for generations. I thought of my own crisis of belonging and my recent attempts to get to know the land, root down, and find home, and raised an eyebrow. Was this crisis entirely my own, then?

The cycle continues when the children grow up and, feeling they are not enough, begin to look to their own children, the grandchildren, to help make up for it. Having good children—accomplished, impressive, successful, and admired—can be part of how the child of a refugee tries once again to find a way to feel enough themselves. When those children disappoint, as grandchildren of the refugee, they become a further painful indication of the parent's own not-enough-ness. Strife and further wounding of the next generation can ensue. This will carry on forever unless and until a disruptor comes along who is willing and able to feel the pain, and who is curious enough to find out where it comes from and why. Only then can the pain, made conscious, felt honestly, and in the revelatory light of Truth, be unmasked, revealed, released, and integrated into a new and higher consciousness. Only then can it cease to wreak havoc in a person's life; only then does it cease to be passed down to the next generation.

I had always accepted Dad's magic, and Old Chan Magic in general, as uncomplicated and real. But my dawning understanding of intergenerational trauma cast that magic in a different light, that of a little boy trying to show his parents that he was worth their pain. From this perspective, his magic was not passive but something he was driven to conjure. He was only fortunate that his inborn talents and abilities were equal to what his demons demanded of them. Stay thirsty, my friends? Imagine gulping down water for a century and never slaking your thirst. That sounds less amazing than I thought it did when I started the Bob Chan Dos Equis social media campaign in the Year of the Ram. My heart softened for this man, my colossus, whose vulnerabilities I had barely guessed at while he was alive.

I turned this new lens to myself. Is it my abilities and honest desires that have gotten me this far in life? Or has intergenerational pain simply chased me this far? Am I still sprinting from failure, tap dancing with hat in hand, to show that I too am worth it?

It was a tough day of writing, of unpacking all the spectral suitcases I've been dragging around that have been asking to be put down for decades because they are not mine. They belong on a dinghy in the

South China Sea 140 years ago. I couldn't stop crying at the thought of Dad being hounded to make magic, or of the boy, Grandpa, who barely survived a life-changing event and never intentionally made anyone responsible for his pain. And yet here I was almost a century and a half later . . . apparently still carrying elements of his pain.

I cried for the butterfly effects of all pain whose origins never get excavated and healed in the light of day, and which continues to tear the fabric of families and society. Generations of it. A world full of it.

I have been donning the mantle of the Jade Rabbit recently, thinking of myself more as ancestor than descendant. Understanding how both pain and healing get passed down through the generations, inevitably leading to the question *What will my role in that be?* Am I living in such a way that my descendants will one day, in pain, sorrow, or trouble, be able to look back to me for a way forward, just as I have looked to my own ancestors? It is endlessly important.

Your healing may echo down the centuries. And so could your failure to heal. The evidence is all around us. Racists, abusers, and mass shooters galore. Fragile, authoritarian, or incompetent parents. Corrupt officials, megalomaniacal leaders, domestic terrorists, and dead-eyed corporatists. Emotionally disturbed children. All rooted in unhealed, often unconscious, intergenerational pain. My pain became a keyhole view to the pain of the world. And what I saw was a world not simply ugly or evil, but crying out for relief, for us all to heal ourselves, to hear the call, and to take the matter of our own physical, emotional, and spiritual wellness in hand. Each of us, individually, must do this, for it is not only ourselves at stake, but our descendants and all the world.

My kids were born shortly before my healing journey began. They've had a better mother for it. And all along the way, they have been happy to show me where the wounds still are, where I become reactive. Recently I was gratified to see evidence of their having taken one of the spectral suitcases I had been trying to make them carry and thrown it unceremoniously back into the South China Sea. Jin had decided he was done with piano, and it felt like a knife to the heart. Piano lessons had been one of the most important components of my determination to keep Dad "alive" and present in the kids' lives. Jin moving on from piano felt, in the moment, like he was moving on from Dad, and I was devastated. Then both boys declared they were quitting tae kwon do. Jin had his black belt, at least, but Seu hadn't quite gotten that far. He was so close, and the word *quit* was practically a cussword in my house when I was growing up. Again I went into a spiritual tailspin of devastation, feeling like I had failed somehow to pass on the Chan family secret sauce.

Looking back, of course, it was nonsense and I'd blown it all out of proportion. In time I came to know that I had tried, quite inadvertently, to pass to my two boys a suitcase that Dad had handed me, and that his father had handed him, and the boys both said, "No thanks. That's not ours." It was devastating in the moment because the pain was still unconscious, and their rejection of the suitcase felt like a rejection of me, of Dad, of our family legacy. But dragging the suitcase into the light that way finally let me see it for what it was—deadweight. And importantly, as my children had known before me, not mine. The idea of "quitting" is so fraught, so rooted in refugee trauma. Whatever happened to just feeling safe and empowered enough to give your attention to the things that light you up, and to leave off things that don't anymore? Whoever said that stopping an activity somehow magically erases all the benefit it ever gave you, as though you had never done it at all? No one wise, that's for sure. What punitive, self-loathing blather.

One day, shortly after the incident, I stood at the sink, brushed my teeth, and stared in the mirror. If my pain around performance, perseverance (i.e., never quitting), achievement, and never quite belonging—something I have defined myself by and understood to be my very personality—is not my own and never has been . . . can I learn to exist without it?

Who would I be if I put it down?

Who could I be?

I felt a spiritual shackle unlock. A feeling of lightness. A wave of energy rippling from my core out to my extremities. *Boom.* If life were a video game, I had just gotten a bunch of XP and leveled up. What at first felt like failure had revealed itself to be success in its truest sense. I have disrupted an old pattern and shifted the map for future generations, because while I may continue to struggle with it in some way or another for the rest of my life, my kids don't carry that pattern. The buck stopped with me. It is the first step toward becoming Elder.

Not everyone becomes an elder. Some only become older. But the world and our families need elders. Rumi said that the cure for pain is in the pain. I like remembering that it was Dad who first gave me a book of Rumi. Thus, while there may have been things that he and his mother and father before him were unable to fully resolve in their own lifetimes, and some things I have been left to unpack for myself as a result, all have still joined the Jade Rabbit on the moon, pounding healing elixirs and giving the only gift that lasts or matters—themselves, freely and authentically. Some pain came through, yes, but so too did the means to unpack and heal it.

Could this book have been written without them? What good elders they became, despite it all, and what good ancestors they continue to be. I want to join the Jade Rabbit too. And in healing myself of this particular pattern, I not only change the map for my descendants but also close the circle for my ancestors. Grandpa was ever the reluctant exile and died with unfinished business. So I have been finding a more ancient and universal kind of belonging for us both. Dad grew weary from certain suitcases he never figured out how to put down, so I have put them down for us both. With this book I burn incense on the graves of my ancestors, I release a lantern painted with prayers in the light of the full moon. I close the circle.

WINTER OWL

Every exit from one place is an entrance to somewhere else. Have you ever shuddered at changes that were beyond your control? Been knocked off course so badly that you were left in an arid wasteland somewhere half beyond the veil? And have you ever traversed that wasteland on hands and knees, unable to stand, let alone fly, but found yourself one day (one day!) airborne again, ready to return to the world? Where you return to won't be the same old place, no. That place is gone. As is the self that inhabited it. This is a new place full of wide vistas and open possibilities; it is the place you are now ready to make your own. Doesn't it feel good to find a place to land in your new realm? Don't you feel relief knowing that this is where you be-long . . . for now? The truth is, our lives will be full of departures. And things may be comfortable for a period, but it can't last . . . because nothing lasts. No physical place, nor specific constellations of people or circumstances.

Perhaps our best option is to make our unique dance with dark-ness and change the home we seek. Can the dance itself be home, the snail's shell that travels with us everywhere we go? Can home be not a place, but a practice? A practice of *beholding* the circumstances of our lives during times of seismic shifts or brokenness, as opposed to merely seeing them. To see is to be removed, analytical, sterile, ob-servational, and seeing goes only as deep as the surface of things. To behold is to inhabit in a state of wonder and curiosity. Beholding sinks you deep beneath the surface. Seeing—logos—can tell you where you are, but only beholding—mythos—can tell you why, where to go from here, and how.

Owls can both see and behold. They carry the gift of sight beyond illusion; they see what others cannot, which is at the heart of wisdom. They also navigate the darkness without difficulty or fear. Many cul-tures believe the owl carries messages from guides and ancestors that help each of us on our path. And so the owl is like a Sherpa through hard times. It flies ahead and scouts the land. When you are lost, it brings you insight and occasional nourishment on your journey, and ultimately it can also lead you back to the world. When I painted the snowy owl, I was thinking about the difference between seeing and beholding. It also spoke to me of crossing a threshold and landing in new territory, a new territory of spirit, confident that you are about to make it your own, and knowing that you belong there.

In learning to belong for myself, I learn to belong for my ancestors, whose exile and exclusion I carry in my veins. In doing so, I think I find something of what they died still searching for. And so, in this way I have become an owl for the ancestors, the scout, the Sherpa, traveling ahead to find new territory of spirit for all the lineage, and communicating the lay of the land back to them across the veil. *Here is how we learn to belong. This way. Follow me.*

I close the circle and prepare fresh ground for my descendants, who are also my ancestors' descendants, to root down in. I shift the map and bring healing to us all, three generations forward, three generations back.

OPPOSITE: Behold

CHAPTER 36

IN THE GARDEN
BEHIND THE MOON

When I was in college, G.G. and I kept up a robust correspondence. One time she sent me the manuscript of a short story she was working on, called "The Moon Dragon."

It concerns a little boy whose mother is deathly ill. But she had always told him, "Ping-lo, when you are sad or in trouble, sing. Music always helps." As she lies dying, however, Ping-lo finds he cannot sing. And when he wants to call for the doctor, his father tells him there are no earthly remedies for what ails his mother, and only a piece of ginger from the Garden Behind the Moon could make her well. The boy determines to go to the moon that very night, but his father cautions him the road to the moon is enchanted and only visible to those who were born to see it.

"And you cannot see it, Papa?" asks the boy.

"No," says the father, "though I have hunted for it."

The Garden Behind the Moon, where the healing ginger grows, is jealously guarded by a fearsome dragon who loves ginger more than gold, emeralds, or pearls.

The boy waits until his father is asleep, slips his pillbox hat with the round button on top from the shelf, tiptoes to his mother's bedside, and kisses her pale cheeks. "I am going to find the Moon Road," the boy whispers. "Mother, I shall bring the ginger to make you well."

When he stands up and turns to go, he sees that a shaft of moonlight shining through the window has become a road of silver dust that slants from the window up to the sky. There is the Moon Road—the boy can see it!

Ping-lo dips his toe in the ethereal silver sand, and the enchanted path catches hold of him and carries him, swift as moonlight, into the sky. When he reaches the moon, he finds that a silvery door bars his way. He cannot simply stroll into the garden; he will have to find hidden ways and secret routes. Perhaps he will have to carve his own path. But he is a clever boy, and his motive for obtaining the ginger is pure, so when he does find his way in, he sees the garden whose flowers are made of stars, a fountain spouting rainbows, and the ginger tree in the courtyard, just as legend foretold.

The Moon Dragon soon discovers the trespasser and chases the boy into hiding beneath a giant mulberry leaf, taunting him to come out and take his ginger. It is then, when he is most afraid, that the boy remembers what his mother told him long ago. *When you are sad or in trouble, sing.* And suddenly the boy does remember how to sing, and the dragon, beguiled, closes his eyes in ecstasy, dancing this way and that, and forgets all about the ginger.

While the dragon sways through the garden, the boy runs to the courtyard and breaks off a piece of the ginger from the tree . . . but in his stealth and concentration, he forgets to sing for a moment. The spell is broken, and the dragon stops dancing, opens its eyes, sees the missing ginger, and rages through the garden, looking for the boy. But the boy has, by this time, run back around the curve of the moon and found the shining road that whizzes him past the stars to his family's grass-roofed hut below. He can hear the dragon bellowing in the garden, but he is unconcerned. *How glad I am,* he thinks, *that I was born to see the Moon Road!*

Ping-lo enters the hut through the same window he left by and puts the ginger next to his mother's wooden pillow. And then he falls fast asleep, still in his clothes and little pillbox hat with the button on top, safe in the knowledge that he has brought back the magic ginger, and his family will be well.

THE MOON ROAD

G.G.'s story is kept in a repurposed junk-mail envelope postmarked March 1995 and reading PHIL GRAHAM FOR PRESIDENT, which she had scratched out with black Sharpie. I would have been a junior at Vassar College at that time, and although the envelope is addressed to me, I do not remember ever seeing or reading this story before. I rediscovered it a few days ago while searching for something else. I pulled a book of poems from the shelf, and the envelope came with it. I was writing the section *Autumn Moon* and had stalled on how to bring together the Chinese ideas of circle and family, the full moon, ancestors, and healing. I read the story of the Moon Dragon and thought, *Hmm, it may be that I have two ghostwriters.*

G.G. had given me a new myth with which to behold the healing of intergenerational, as well as collective, pain. Ping-lo's mother suffered from a mysterious illness for which there were no earthly remedies. What is this but a description of someone cut off from mythos and stuck in the wasteland? There are remedies for such illness, though, like the magic ginger from the Garden Behind the Moon. But the road to get there is invisible. Only a healthy embrace of a mythopoeic lens will make it appear.

Did G.G. send me the story thinking that I, like Ping-lo, was the type to see a shaft of moonlight and imagine the Moon Road? Maybe. Perhaps she wanted to issue the invitation regardless and plant a seed. G.G., like Mom, was a gentle gardener, and like Thoreau, had great faith in a seed.

It took nearly thirty years, but it seems I have finally become Ping-lo. When I was sad and in trouble, I started to sing, for what are the stories here but my song? I picked up a strand of renewal in the black sands of Iceland. I followed it to the Moon Road and let the enchanted path carry me to the Garden Behind the Moon, a bright other world where healing grows on trees. My way was barred at first by the silver door, as it has been for others before me. And my grief and anguish were a formidable dragon to be outwitted and kept at bay by song. But I was a clever girl, and my motives were pure, and so with time and intention, I found my way in. There I sang my way to the ginger tree. I broke off a piece of the magic root and planted it in my new garden, which the Ox had tilled for me with story, and where it grew into this book.

The magic continues if you find some piece of ginger here for yourself and plant it in your own garden. The best gardens, after all, are friendship gardens—seeded in part with bulbs and cuttings from friends and neighbors, where they will hopefully take root and remind you for long years of the gift of friendship and neighborliness that put them there.

BOOK EIGHT

2022
YEAR OF THE TIGER

Dawn breaks on Year of the Yang Water Tiger. The Tiger is full of vigor and valor, a fierce and generous protector, who is less interested in glory than in what brings the greatest good to the highest number. General He E surveys his dominion with relish. As another of the sixty Tai Sui of Chinese mythology, the happiness, health, and good fortune of all mortals will be his alone to rule for the year. He steps onto the dais from which he will rule all earthly affairs, and first scans the horizon for the Ox, which is beloved to him. So determined and reliable, the Ox, so honest and earnest, a powerful and benevolent force when turned to good.

For sixty years he has planned it. At long last, the Ox is his. What should he start with? An abundant and joyful garden? Fresh opportunities for travel and discovery? New friendships? Personal milestones? *A puppy?* It matters not. The Ox will be showered with love and bounty. And if it doesn't think itself worthy, it will be showered some more. *It is more than time,* thinks the Tai Sui.

So say the Chinese.

Is it good fortune or destiny that I was born in the Year of the Ox, same as Dad? I never meant to be the beloved protégée of a celestial being, but here I am, riding the crest of a sublime wave set in motion by 2022's Tai Sui. And I feel certain Dad is still around, somewhere by my side, riding it with me.

Under the wise, honest, and benevolent rule of General He E, the Ox will find that its already prodigious powers of strength, determination, and resolve will carry it further than they ever have before. Its inborn altruistic tendencies will spill out and color all its endeavors and successes, to the benefit of many. The year 2022 is the Ox's most fortunate year, and no matter what luck it may encounter, the Ox will be able to turn it into good fortune with friends and helpmates old and new, and in high places, auspicious places, serendipitous places, and the day-to-day.

I knew a little something of the Tai Sui in 2022, and once again I seemed to feel the light whisper of a mustache as it brushed past my ear. This time it sent a thrill through me rather than a shudder, and I could have sworn I heard a voice whisper, *You have forged yourself anew and are standing firmly in the light. Hold it and cast it wide.*

The Ox will reach its highest potential and be showered with love in 2022, the Year of the Yang Water Tiger. It is written.

CHAPTER 37

INTEGRATION

I am standing at the edge of the canyon, one hand on the trunk of my cherry tree, and looking out over the misty blue peaks and sandstone pillars that surround my teahouse in the Wulingyuan District of my mind. I am only half-surprised to look down and see pink feathers erupting from the skin that covers my arms, shoulders, and back. Before long I am a fully fledged flamingo and I leap from the precipice. Flamingos, I will later learn, symbolize love, grace, and personal authenticity to the Chinese, and are considered a good sign that you are in your dharma and about to reach a major milestone in the myth of your life. They are also thought to have been the original inspiration for the legends of the T'ai Peng. Right now I know none of that. But aren't you glad that I soon will, and the Universe will demonstrate its magic to us all, once again, and just because? The world is indeed bright with meaning.

My flight is effortless. I am filled with a sense of ease and knowing. I can see far ahead of me and far behind. I can fly up to the clouds, cool vapors buffeting my face, and dip down to the ground where I drag my feet through shallow waters. Though it was a cold and foggy day on my cliff ledge, I soon find myself in more humid, subtropical climes, with the sun beating down on my back, on the crown of my head, and in my heart. I smile insomuch as a flamingo can smile, and revel in the warmth, flight, and the sensation of well-being. I expend no effort. I can feel the internal tug of natural homing abilities that simply draw me along as if I'm tethered to an invisible, unbreakable thread. *I know the way.*

In time, I look down and recognize the blue, green, and gold scenery of the Georgia low country spreading out before me, the salt marsh and winding tidal creeks of the sea islands, as inviting and beautiful a place as I have ever seen. As a flamingo, I think I must be meant to land here, but no. The thread draws me on. I fly inland and soon see signs of urban development. It is the city of Savannah below me—not the Savannah of today, but of another age. The roads are only half-paved, I notice, and electric streetcars share the road with carriages powered with and without horses. I also see a good old-fashioned oxcart, with an ox standing patiently in the shade. *Hello, old friend,* I telegraph to him, *don't worry, this is our year.* Ahead, I steer toward a growing fleck of green, and soon recognize it as the fountain where I used to feed the pigeons with Dad. Forsyth Park, where Dad and G.G. played Robin Hood on the way home from Mrs. Chaplin's. The homing sensation grows, and I begin my descent on the far side of the park, landing, once again in human form, on what I soon surmise to be Whitaker Street, which directly abuts the park's west side.

It is a humid summer morning, but the heat is not yet unbearable, and the air is thick with the lemony sweet scent of magnolias and four o'clocks. Known as the Forest City, Savannah boasts a chorus of songbirds, whose twittering is now all the louder so close to Forsyth Park. I make out the distinct calls of mourning dove, Carolina wren, blue jay, and mockingbird, while spring peepers fill the silence between. The bark of an excitable small dog echoes in the distance, and I smile at the effusive soundscape of a quiet morning.

When I reach the 300 block of Whitaker Street, I pass a couple of bicycles leaning against the row of buildings, the J. H. Washington Shoe Repair, and see ahead of me the Food Palace Meat Market advertising groceries and quality meats. I stop, turn to my right, and see the large, curlicue saloon letters on the store window of the Willie Chin & Co. Laundry. My heart swells to see it in person like this, the old family business having been razed long before my birth to build a multistory parking garage, and I grin with eyes that prick and glisten. I cup my face against the window to see inside and take it all in. I can almost see G.G. sitting on the high stool behind the counter, flicking abacus beads up and down and painting ticket numbers with Papa's paintbrush. Straight on back, I can just make out the stool where later today, Dad, still in short pants, will sit and monitor the water gauge while handing tools to Charlie.

T'ai Peng has hung signs advertising ONE-DAY RETURNS! and prices for different garments and services—shirts, collars, flatwork. But the business is closed and quiet, for it is still early morning. I check the door anyway, just in case. It is locked. So I wander around the corner, down the little alley, to reach the back side of the building. And there I see it—a length of string hanging out one of the second-floor residence windows. The chorus of peepers grows. I give a gasp of recognition, a giggle, a half sob. I reach out and rub the string between my fingers, then let it drag across my palm and fall back down, where it dangles and quivers in place, as if it's electric, sentient. I look up at the window with an expectant smile and see a lace curtain flutter to life in the breeze—an invitation. I grab the string and give it a tug.

The whole blue world sings with meaning.

—Henry Glassie,
Passing the Time in Ballymenone

ACKNOWLEDGMENTS

In some ways, this book might be my own "inner genius," as understood by the Greeks, the inner purpose hidden within each life. I might almost have been born with the blueprint to write it embedded in my soul, as if it were somehow written in the stars as an important waypoint on my earthly journey. It would have been invisible, though, and inaccessible, until I had undergone what needed undergoing. At which point I imagine it appearing on the wall in front of me, behind glass, and with a sign next to it that reads "BREAK GLASS IN CASE OF EMERGENCY."

Yes, there is a certain feeling of "destiny" around this project, but "making it so" has been anything but a solo endeavor. When I look back over the decades, particularly over the last several years, I see a brilliant symphony of circumstances and people, entering (and exiting), helping hands, encouraging words, sparks of recognition and inspiration, and no shortage of serendipities. And so, in what might be best organized in more-or-less chronological order, my deepest thanks go out to each of the following, who have all had their part to play in helping me on my long, meandering journey to greater authenticity:

To my parents, who planted so many seeds, and took such care sheltering them, watering them, and exposing them to sun. What choice did my eventual garden have but to become abundant and joyful?

To my nearest and dearest: Brent, who faithfully supports my every creative instinct, urge, and endeavor, and further, invariably believes I can do it before I do; and to my two sons, Jin and Seu, who have grown into interesting, witty, curious, and wise young men since the stories in this book unfolded. Boys, you have brought grounding, happiness, and a lasting sense of purpose to my every day. Little did you know what life buoys you were and continue to be. Don't tell me, "It's not that deep, Mom." It is that deep.

To everyone who ever told me I "should write a book" about my dad. Your calls have kept me true. Even if, in the long run, the book didn't turn out to be "about" him in the way you imagined, the journey of discovery around this project was exactly what my soul needed, and I guess he's in it well enough, eh?

To Jill Gormley, who followed a nudge and mentioned her own practice of shamanic journeying over soup and sandwiches one day and thereby set me on a course to permanently change my life and worldview for the better. Looks like I had a lunch date with Destiny. Thank you.

To Bruce Iverson, my brush-painting teacher, who gave me all the new tools with which to tell my stories, and in a way that would connect me inadvertently but directly with the healing, bright other world of mythos. Learning to paint awakened my mythic imagination and gave it a vehicle for manifestation. They say, "When the student is ready, the teacher will come." Thank you for being that teacher.

To Amy Robinson and Joanna Potenza, the fearless other two of our Writers' Accountability Club of three. I will treasure the memories of our WAC (or "wack"? as we joked) meetings forever as a golden example of supportive friendship and of the magical potency and positive outcomes you can expect when good folks get together in converging purpose. Ladies, it has been an honor.

To my first editor and *very* first reader, Nina Bruhns, whose enthusiasm let me know I had done something good, and whose thoroughness let me go forth with confidence into the world, knowing this was meant to be.

To my wonderful team at Flashpoint Books, many thanks for your warm welcome into the world of commercial publishing and your enthusiastic and dedicated work in making my book this beautiful reality. More particularly, to Ingrid Emerick, president and cofounder, and my incredibly clear-sighted, talented, and generous developmental editor, for understanding so deeply what I was trying to do with this book. Thank you for helping me to bring it into its clearest focus, and for making my mission part of your own: to see this thing out, free and in the wild. To Sara Addicott, my publishing manager, and Adria Batt, my marketing strategist, for the steady, sound direction and advice throughout the day-to-day of this process, and for making our regular meetings something to look forward to. To Paul Barrett, my art director, what can I say? You gave me the cover of my dreams, and the ancestors are dancing with me. Thank you. To Katherine Richards, my production editor, and Allison Gorman and Carrie Wicks, my co-pyeditor and proofreader, many thanks for making sure nothing like typos or awkward turns of phrase would get in the way of this book's message landing the way it was meant to.

I am indebted to you all as I ponder the threads of fate that connect us to each other and the world.

NOTES

1. O'Donohue, *Eternal Echoes*, 19.
2. Meade, *Living Myth*, episode 1.
3. Rose, *The Art of Immersion*, 14.
4. Larsen, *Mythic Imagination*, 42.
5. Ibid., 3.
6. Campbell, *Hero*, 18.
7. Larsen, *Mythic Imagination*, 19.
8. Jones, "Story Writing."
9. Chan, *Slavery*, 227.
10. Sieg, "Laundryman."
11. O'Donohue, *Eternal Echoes*, 76.
12. Chan, *The Chinese Christmas Box*.
13. O'Donohue, *Eternal Echoes*, 20.

BIBLIOGRAPHY

Blackie, Sharon. *Courting the World Soul.* "Module 4: The Hero/Heroine's Journey." Online webinar and workshop, 2019.
———. *The Enchanted Life: Unlocking the Magic of Everyday.* Toronto: House of Anansi, 2018.
———. *If Women Rose Rooted.* Tewkesbury, England: September Publishing, 2019.
Campbell, Joseph. *The Hero with a Thousand Faces.* Princeton, NJ: Princeton University Press, 1968.
Chan, Alexandra. *Slavery in the Age of Reason: Archaeology at a New England Farm.* Knoxville: University of Tennessee Press, 2007.
Cron, Lisa. *Wired for Story.* Berkeley: Ten Speed Press, 2012.
Ghosh, Amitav. "Brutes: Meditation on the Myth of the Voiceless." *Orion*, Autumn 2021.

Gilbert, Elizabeth. *Big Magic: Creative Living Beyond Fear.* New York: Riverhead Books, 2015.

Glassie, Henry. *Passing the Time in Ballymenone.* Bloomington: Indiana University Press, 1982.

Hirons, Tom. *Sometimes a Wild God.* Devon, UK: Hedgespoken Press, 2017.

Jones, Catherine Anne. *Way of Story Writing Course.* Daily Om, 2018. https://www .dailyom.com/courses/way-of-story-writing-course/.

Larsen, Stephen. *The Mythic Imagination: The Quest for Meaning Through Personal Mythmaking.* Rochester, VT: Inner Traditions International, 1996.

May, Katherine. *Wintering: The Power of Rest and Retreat in Difficult Times.* New York: Riverhead Books, 2020.

Meade, Michael. *Living Myth.* Podcast, 2017–2021.

O'Donohue, John. *Beauty: The Invisible Embrace.* New York: Harper Perennial, 2003.

———. *Eternal Echoes: Celtic Reflections on Our Yearning to Belong.* New York: Perennial, 1999.

Oliver, Mary. *Upstream: Selected Essays.* New York: Penguin Press, 2016.

———. *Winter Hours.* New York: Ecco, 2000.

Phillpotts, Eden. *A Shadow Passes.* London: Cecil, Palmer & Hayward, 1918.

Rose, Frank. *The Art of Immersion: How the Digital Generation Is Changing Hollywood, Madison Avenue, and the Way We Tell Stories.* New York: W. W. Norton & Co., 2011.

Sieg, Gerald Chan. *The Chinese Christmas Box.* Beaufort, SC: Peacock Press Ltd., 1970.

———. *The Far Journey.* Savannah, GA: Poetry Society of Georgia, 2002.

———. "Laundryman." US Federal Writers' Project. Interview with Chung Tai-Pan [T'ai Peng], January 20, 1939.

———. "The Moon Dragon." Unpublished typescript, 1995.

Stephens, Greg J., Lauren J. Silbert, Uri Hasson. "Speaker-Listener Neural Coupling Underlie Successful Communication." *Proceedings of the National Academy of Sciences of the United States of America*, July 26, 2010. doi: 10.1073/pnas .1008662107.

ABOUT THE AUTHOR

Alexandra Chan is also the author of *Slavery in the Age of Reason: Archaeology at a New England Farm*, as well as numerous journal articles and book chapters about the archaeology of northern slavery, early African America, and questions of race, place, identity, and becoming.

As a mom, an archaeologist—lover of soil and history—a photographer, a painter, and a writer, it is natural to wonder, "What ties it all together?" Why, story, of course. At the end of the day, she is only ever doing what she has always done—watching people, searching for beauty and meaning in unusual places, and telling stories.

Alexandra continues to be an avid traveler and collector of "lucky nuts," and to walk, garden, paint, write, stitch, build, and dream herself into ever gentler and more creative ways of being alive and human. She lives with her husband, two sons, and their menagerie of animals in New Hampshire.